The Arab Shi'a

The Arab Shi'a

The Forgotten Muslims

Graham E. Fuller
and
Rend Rahim Francke

St. Martin's Press
New York

ISBN 0-312-22178-9 (cloth)

Library of Congress Cataloging-in-Publication Data
Fuller, Graham E., 1937-
    The Arab Shi'a : the forgotten Muslims / by Graham E. Fuller and
Rend Rahim Francke.
        p.   cm.
    Includes bibliographical references and index.
    ISBN 0-312-22178-9 (cloth)
    1. Shi'ah—Arab countries.   2. Middle East—Politics and
government—1976-   I. Francke, Rend Rahim, 1949- .   II. Title.
BP192.7.A65F65   1999
297.8'21'09174927—dc21   99–24292
                                                             CIP

Design by Letra Libre, Inc.

First edition: December, 1999
10 9 8 7 6 5 4 3 2 1

*Written under a grant from the
United States Institute of Peace*

Contents

Acknowledgements

This book is based on nearly two hundred interviews conducted in Lebanon, Kuwait, Bahrain, the United Kingdom, and the United States. We spoke to Arab Shi'a, Sunnis, and Christians; government officials, parliamentarians, scholars, activists, businessmen, clerics, lawyers, and other professionals; and to western diplomats, scholars, and other students of the Middle East. We are grateful to all for generously giving us their time, knowledge, and experience.

Many individuals inside and outside the region placed themselves at risk in talking to us about a subject still perceived as dangerous and threatening in the Arab world. We are especially indebted to the generosity and courage of these people and only regret that they must remain anonymous. We would also like to thank personal friends in the region, in the United States, and in the United Kingdom who privately assisted this project by providing support, contacts, and valuable insights.

Parliamentarians and senior personalities in Lebanon were kind enough to speak to us extensively and candidly. Mr. Nabih Birri, Speaker of Lebanon's Parliament, and Sayed Hussein Fadhlallah were most generous with their time and insights, as were Mr. Mohammad Baydhoun, MP, Mrs. Nayla Moawadh, MP, Mohammad Fneish, MP and Mr. Mohammad al-Sammak, advisor to former Prime Minister Hariri. Mr. Jamil Mroue, publisher of the *Daily Star* newspaper, gave us indispensable assistance in Lebanon. We were privileged to speak to members of the Shura Council in Bahrain and to the Ambassadors of Bahrain in Washington and London, Dr. Muhammad Abdul Ghaffar and Shaykh Abdul Aziz bin Mubarak al-Khailifa, respectively. Professors at the faculties of Political Science and Sociology at the University of Kuwait provided a wealth of analysis and data not only on Kuwait but for the region as a whole. Parliamentarians in Kuwait were also kind enough to talk to us, and we especially thank Mr. Ahmad Al-Sa'doon, Speaker of the Kuwaiti National Assembly at the time of our visit to Kuwait, for providing a valuable historical perspective on Kuwait.

We must give special thanks to people who provided us with a broad context for our research through documentary sources and contacts. Members of the Khoei Foundation in London, foremost among them Sayed Majid al-Khoei and Sayed Yousef al-Khoei, shared with us their incomparable experience in Muslim and Shi'a affairs throughout the Middle East. Mr. Ghanim Jawad, now also with the Khoei Foundation, was helpful with sources and contacts with Arab Shi'a in several countries. Mohammad Abdul Jabbar and Mowaffak Al-Rubaei arranged meetings in London and helped with source material on Shi'ism.

We are grateful to the United States Institute of Peace for providing the grant that made work on the book possible.

Graham E. Fuller
Rend Rahim Francke

Introduction

Thirty years ago a book about the Shi'a would have attracted the attention of no one in the West except a handful of regional specialists on the Middle East. But starting in 1979 the Iranian revolution placed its Shi'ite brand of Islamic radicalism on the ideological map of the Middle East, sparking a series of guerrilla and terrorist actions across the region by Arab Shi'ite organizations that challenged the West militarily in ways never seen before in the region. As a result, Shi'ite populations of the Middle East have unfortunately become known in the West primarily for the politics of violence, fanaticism, and the deadly suicide bomber. What has brought the Shi'a—even if only a minority of their population—into this kind of uniquely violent politics? What grievances have driven them to engage in some of the most dramatic and effective terrorist and guerrilla operations the world has seen over the past two decades?

Strategically, the Shi'ite population of the Arab world lies at the heart of the largest oil-producing area of the Middle East, athwart the oil arteries out of the Persian Gulf. Together with Iran, the Arab Shi'a could in theory exert dominant control over most of the oil of the Gulf. Yet, this Arab Shi'ite population of some 14 million people scattered across five Arab Gulf states has remained all but unknown to Western policymakers—excluded as they have been from a policy voice everywhere except in Iran. Even today, when Shi'ism is examined, it is primarily Iran—where the Shi'a are in power—that receives Western policy and scholarly attention, not the Shi'a of the Arab world. While Arab states of the region of course are deeply aware of their Shi'ite populations, they have systematically suppressed them over centuries, creating domestic tensions and an ongoing source of instability.

If Islam as a religion suffers from some degree of misunderstanding and prejudice in the West, then Shi'ite Islam lies at the far end of that negative spectrum. The American experience with Iran during the Iranian revolution and the hostage crisis, followed by devastating acts of Shi'ite terrorism in Lebanon through the 1980s, created the image of the Shi'a that is still dominant. This Western stereotype of Arab Shi'a portrays them as a monolithic community, ideologically extremist, loyal to Iran, and fanatically opposed to the West. In reality, all of these generalizations, while containing some grains of truth, are fundamentally misleading.

The problem is not only in the West. Tensions in the region between Sunni and Shi'ite Islam over the past few decades have risen higher than at any point in several centuries. Understanding the reasons behind this reality is central to understanding a great deal of politics in the Arab world in general and the Persian Gulf in particular. Our concerns for these tensions provide the genesis for the present study. We believe that the Shi'a as a community not only suffer from an inaccurate portrayal in the Middle East, but that a solution to the problem will come only in the broader context of political reform in the region.

This book undertakes an analysis of the character and role of Arab Shi'a in contemporary Middle Eastern politics, society, and religion. We have limited ourselves to an examination of the *Ithna-'ashariyya* ("Twelver," also called *Ja'fari*) sect of Shi'a, simply because it is the largest, the most important, and the most politically active in the politics of Shi'ism. We have omitted the Zaydis of Yemen, and the 'Alawis of Syria who represent a heterodox form of Shi'ism. We have also left out those few Isma'ili Shi'a who live in the Arab world (compared to the large numbers of Isma'ilis in Asia). We have also focused on countries in which the Shi'a make up a significant part of the indigenous population and not just part of the expatriate community. We chose not to examine the Shi'a of the United Arab Emirates or Oman as well, mainly due to time and resource constraints and because they figure less importantly in the politics of those states than the "front-line" states we have chosen.

While a study of the Arab Shi'a in their various communities constitutes a voluminous subject, our interest here is practical rather than academic in nature. The issue of the Shi'a comes up repeatedly in policy discussions both in the West and in the Middle East in a variety of contexts. The topic permeates politics in Iraq, Bahrain, Lebanon, and Saudi Arabia. Any discussion of Iran's policies in the region must invariably consider the role of the Arab Shi'a in the Gulf. Policy discussions relating to terrorism and counterterrorism regularly involve discussion of the organization and activities of Shi'ite groups. Discussion of the viability of democracy in a future Iraq frequently founders on anxieties about the Shi'ite majority in Iraq and its implications for Iranian influence in the country in the future.

The question of the Shi'a in the region has implications well beyond mere sectarian politics. The dilemma of the Shi'a—both as an oppressed religious *minority* in a number of states, and as an oppressed religious *majority* in two others—gets to the heart of the dilemma of modern Arab politics. What is the character of the state in the Middle East, and whose interests does it represent—the interests of ruling families, or of ideological-elite minorities, or of majority populations? Whom does the state include and whom does it exclude, by ideology as well as practice? Does the state set preconditions for citizenship and loyalty that exclude sectors of the population? How can minorities be integrated into the political order of the majoritarian state? What are the political and social implications of democratization in Iraq and Bahrain where Shi'ite *majorities*—now excluded—will indeed gain a majoritarian voice when democratic rule is established? Neither Washington nor the regional states can any longer ignore these realities. Indeed, the failure to integrate the Shi'a represents the failure of the Arab state in microcosm.

Specifically, we seek to address the following practical questions:

- Who are the Shi'a and what do they seek?
- What is the nature of their role in Middle Eastern society and politics?
- What is the nature of the "Shi'ite problem" from the point of view of Sunni society and government?
- How will the dynamics of state policies and Shi'ite attitudes influence internal and regional developments?
- What strategies, if any, are likely to be adopted by the Shi'a and the state to address the Shi'ite issue?
- How should Western governments think about the Shi'a in the context of future policies towards the region, particularly as they relate to processes of democratization?

We are aware we are undertaking a very broad task here, requiring complex and necessary judgments about the nature of Shi'ite communities in politics over a range of states. Indeed, better scholars than ourselves have examined many aspects of both Shi'ite and Sunni society over the years in a variety of scholarly studies. Despite the many fine works of scholarship that exist, few have ventured to pose these particular types of policy questions. It is precisely because we are interested in the impact of the Shi'ite issue upon *policy* in both the West and the Middle East that we feel no need to apologize for seeking some kind of broad responses to these grand policy questions, for they are precisely the questions that busy policymakers can and do ask. If we or other scholars do not seek to supply some general answers to these questions in policy terms—how to think about the problem—then others in government will, often with little background and less interest. We have chosen what we believe are the key policy questions central to understanding something of the nature of conflict in the region.

Second, this book is about the Arab world. While there have been many studies written about Shi'ism, most of them are about Iran or Shi'ite theology; there are few if any studies of the Arab Shi'ite communities as a whole. We hope this book will fill something of a gap there. We do not wish to suggest that Sunni-Shi'ite frictions are the core problem of the Muslim world or even of all the countries examined in this book. These frictions are nonetheless symptomatic of a larger complex of problems that afflict many Arab states, problems of political participation, democratization, and the forging of an inclusive national identity. The existence of a "Shi'ite issue" is a manifestation of failures in regional political systems.

For a number of reasons we have actually approached the writing of a book about Arab Shi'a with some trepidation. First, the subject is anathema in the Arab world. Many Arab friends and acquaintances were uncomfortable that we undertook the project at all. In their eyes, the problem is too sensitive, and writing about it will only open old sores or exacerbate the issue by drawing attention to it. Some Sunnis are reluctant to acknowledge that it is an issue at all. Second, many Middle Eastern governments whose domestic and foreign policies toward the Shi'a are short-sighted would also prefer that the reality of these issues not be examined or made public, especially to Western audiences. Third, some people wonder just what "our own agenda" is in writing the book. Some fear that it represents old-fashioned "orientalism" in seeking to create or magnify differences within Muslim society where little or none exist, thereby making Muslim society seem prejudiced, divided, vulnerable, or weak. Or that we are facilitating a "divide and rule" approach to the region that has, for example, been publicly advocated by some Israeli strategists over past decades—a "Middle East of minorities," and so on. Others fear that however "sincerely" we ourselves may approach the work, this study may end up only facilitating the agenda of those who actually do not wish the region well for any number of reasons. In short, why wash dirty laundry in public when it may only serve to exacerbate a delicate issue best left alone?

We are sensitive to these arguments. We feel under some obligation ourselves to be honest in making our own "agenda" quite clear. First, we are interested in the welfare of the region and its peoples themselves. Yes, we are concerned with American interests too, but we believe that real American interests will best be served over the longer run mainly if they coincide with the interests and welfare of the people of the region. And the welfare of these people at present is sadly at a low level.

Through this book we would like to encourage citizens and policymakers—Western and Middle Eastern—to think more deeply about the Shi'ite issue rather than ignore it, and to develop open-minded approaches about how to solve it. We believe that you cannot create strong and stable societies in the Middle East unless all citizens have a sense of belonging to the state and a vested interest in its welfare. This book seeks ultimately to unite rather than divide Arab Shi'a and Arab Sunnis. We do not believe that Shi'a and Sunnis are destined to be hostile, but that the nature of the problem needs to be recognized and treated.

Next, we believe that American policies toward the region can do a much better job of combining American interests—however defined—with the interests of the peoples of the region than those policies have so far done. Graham Fuller, with more than twenty-five years of experience in U.S. government and policy circles, has had more than ample opportunity to witness these policy shortcomings. American policies toward the Middle East have been narrowly conceived, skewed largely toward emphasis primarily on Israel's needs and wants, and upon "oil" in the narrowest sense with little regard for the critically important broader political and social systems that surround the process of bringing oil out of the ground and exporting it. Policies have focused upon "security issues" in the narrowest military sense—largely as military "quick fixes"—while ignoring long-term interests and political evolution of the region. In addition, frequent Western intervention over decades has hindered the political maturation of these societies, as has largely uncritical American support for entrenched authoritarian regimes. In spite of its rhetoric, Washington has had precious little interest in democratization in the region. And the absence of good governance in the region as a result up to this day is the primary source of crisis and instability. Of course oil and Israel are a central part of U.S. interests; the challenge to America is to formulate a more enlightened sense of self-interest that can better combine the interests of both the United States and all the people of the region. U.S. policies have conspicuously failed in this area—at growing cost to all.

If we have any broad philosophical bias in our approach to the region, it is a belief in the essential need to expand the democratic process. Rend Rahim Francke, an Iraqi American of mixed Sunni-Shi'a background who has worked on issues of democratization in Iraq, has been particularly troubled by the obstacles placed in the path of democracy and pluralism in the Arab world—obstacles that are often erected by Arab governments with the unfortunate acquiescence of the United States. We do not advocate imposing American-style institutions upon the Middle East or promoting wholesale regime-change. But we do believe that democracy in one form or another is a universal value; that good governance should serve the interests of all the people, including their moral welfare; that all peoples have a right to exercise a voice over who rules them and with what policies; and that all peoples should be protected from harsh, arbitrary, and despotic rule. We also believe that religion—and of course primarily Islam in the Middle East—can help frame the moral debate over the application of these issues. But clearly there is also major debate over "who speaks for Islam" that greatly complicates the role of Islam in politics. Finally, we see no reason why all these general principles of human rights and representative government are not compatible with Islam—and most *Muslims* would agree.

Lastly, this book is not meant to be an apology for the Shi'a. We do not seek to promote the welfare of the Shi'a over that of the Sunnis, nor the converse. The book represents rather an examination of the conditions, relations, and aspirations of the Shi'ite community in a Sunni world. The issue is how to achieve responsive, responsible, and equitable governance for all communities.

Shi'ite attitudes and self-definitions are obviously heavily influenced by the sociopolitical environment in which they live. We therefore have felt it necessary to devote some of the discussion to the nature of the regimes in the region that shape that environment. While we would prefer to avoid general fixing of blame upon specific regimes, we felt we could not remain silent where we believe a regime does in fact bear major responsibility for the crisis with the Shi'a—particularly in Iraq, Bahrain, and Saudi Arabia. Where we see regimes doing well, especially in the case of Kuwait, we have also said so.

Methodology

While a great number of writings exist about Shi'ism as a theology, and a few excellent books about Shi'ism in Iraq and Lebanon, there have been far fewer works devoted to the Arab Shi'ite communities as a phenomenon in themselves. In the process of writing this book we have consulted a considerable body of literature about Shi'ism and about the Arab countries under study. But we have also felt a strong need to go beyond purely academic studies to examine the actual attitudes and daily experiences of Arab Shi'a themselves. As a result we conducted some two hundred interviews with individual Shi'a from all states in which Shi'a are a significant group. These interviews make up the essential backbone of our work. A large number of the interviews were conducted in the Middle East itself, although in a few cases, such as Iraq, it was not feasible to do so. We also interviewed large numbers of Arab Shi'a living outside the Middle East, many but not all of whom are active in Shi'ite politics. We spoke with a broad spectrum of people including clerics, Islamists, secularists, academics, and public figures, women as well as men, young as well as old. Both authors shared fully and equally in all aspects of interviewing, researching, analyzing, and writing the book.

We are well aware that the position of the Shi'a in the region depends at least as much on Sunni attitudes as it does upon the Shi'a themselves; we therefore discussed the problem with many Sunnis, also of varying backgrounds including religious and nonreligious, to gain their perspectives on the Shi'a as a group, how they perceive "the problem." In Lebanon we also benefited from the views of Christian academics and members of parliament.

While we have focused consistently on a few key questions at the outset, none of our interviews consisted of formal questionnaires but were instead far-ranging and tailored to the individual and the situation in question. As a result we feel we have gained a fair understanding of attitudes among a broad range of Shi'a, and to a considerable extent among Sunnis as well. We have not taken a quantitative approach to these interviews, but rather sought to gain a solid understanding of the attitudes, psychology, situations, problems, anxieties, goals, and interests of the many interviewees. We recognize, too, that some individuals may have been less forthcoming than others or may not have wished to fully share their deeper concerns. Other individuals may have found the interview an occasion to express a lot of pent-up grievances that exceed the perceptions of other Shi'a in the same community. We have taken it upon ourselves to try to find the right balance in assessing the conditions of each country. We have not sought to simply faithfully report what we were told, but to make our own synthesis and analysis of these views and to determine what kind of a broader picture they portray.

In nearly all cases we felt compelled to assure our interviewees that their identities would be protected, an assurance usually requested in any case if they were to speak with relative freedom. In the interests of consistency therefore we have refrained from explicit identification of identity in nearly all cases. We owe a great debt of thanks to all who agreed to interviews with us, helped us locate sources, and provided documentation and literature. We deeply regret that we cannot give them public credit.

The book consists of three sections: (1) four chapters that make up a broader analysis of the generic situation and dilemma of the Shi'a as a whole; (2) five chapters that represent case studies of the key countries of Iraq, Lebanon, Kuwait, Bahrain, and Saudi Arabia, written out of recognition that the Shi'ite community is not monolithic—a key point of the study. There are differences both *within* Shi'ite communities in any given country and *between* Shi'ite communities in different countries. Finally, (3) two chapters discuss the Shi'a vis-à-vis the West and the policy implications of the study, followed by a succinct summation of the key findings of the study.

In a broad study of this type generalizations are inevitable, indeed required, if we are to make any sense of the broader phenomenon. Those generalizations we have made are partially justified by the great similarity from country to country in the basic problems encountered within the Shi'ite community across the region. We hope that the chapters focusing on specific countries will provide the distinctions and the shading that qualify the general observations.

We are also mindful of the danger of thinking of the Shi'a as an ethnic group, or dealing with the issue as if it were an ethnic problem, which it is not. However, the strong cultural identity of the Shi'a, and the way they are perceived by the majority Sunnis, do present similarities with problems experienced by ethnic groups. Furthermore, the solutions to these problems often resemble the kinds of solutions also required by ethnic problems—recognition of identity, nondiscrimination, issues of integration and assimilation, potential external loyalties, and so on.

We apologize in advance for the inevitable errors that creep into any work. We also apologize to any who might be offended or made uncomfortable by this book. That is not our intention. We sincerely hope that Shi'a who read the book will feel that it fairly—and, even more important, usefully—represents their views. We hope that Sunnis who read it will find some insights that will benefit them in cooperating with their Shi'ite countrymen to help bring about a better future for everybody in the region. The problem of minorities in Middle Eastern societies affects both groups, since both Shi'a and Sunnis are minorities in one state or another. And we hope that the book may assist Western policymakers in putting the issue of the Arab Shi'a in a broader and richer political and social context that can facilitate the formulation of more understanding policies.

A note about terminology: we use the word "Shi'i" to refer to individual persons; we use the collective Arabic plural "Shi'a" to refer to all Shi'ites collectively; and we use the English word "Shi'ite" only as an adjective.

Graham E. Fuller
Rend Rahim Francke
Washington, D.C.
October 1999

CHAPTER ONE

The Shi'ite Identity

To speak of the Shi'a of the Arab world is to raise a sensitive issue that most Muslims would rather not discuss.[1] To some it is a nonexistent issue, but to many more it is simply best ignored because it raises disturbing questions about Arab society and politics and challenges deep-rooted assumptions about Arab history and identity. Sunnis by and large prefer to avoid the subject, and even many Shi'a are uncomfortable with it. Yet beneath the superficial denial lies a tacit acknowledgment that the Shi'a present an unresolved problem in the Arab Muslim polity—from the start of Islamic history—that can profoundly influence the traditional ways of ordering society and government in the Arab world.

To be Shi'a in the Muslim world is of course part of an identity issue that cuts to the heart of politics and society in the Arab and Muslim world. The world is replete with identity issues, and their salience has been on the rise over the past decades, especially after the end of the Cold War. The same is true in the Middle East where identity is as often as not linked to religion as much as to ethnicity. Nor is the issue of being Shi'a or Sunni the only identity issue in the Muslim world, or necessarily the determining identity. Other religious identities in the region also come into play: Muslim versus Protestant, Catholic, Orthodox, Zoroastrian, Druze, 'Alawi, or Jew. Nor is religion necessarily the paramount identity. Indeed, all individuals have multiple identities—tribe, clan, region, nationality, religion, gender, profession, class, race, language, culture, and so on. Some identities are marked by international boundaries that separate a Jordanian from an Iraqi, a Saudi from an Iranian. Other identities can cut across national boundaries. But all of these distinctions can be important to one's position and status in society and can affect economic or social well-being or access to power and privilege. (In an informal survey carried out by the authors among Iraqi Shi'a, for instance, they were asked to list the components of their identity in order of importance. Invariably, at the top of the list was the Iraqi identity; this was followed by the Arab identity or the Muslim; Shi'ism was usually the fourth component. Not all Shi'a would adhere to this ranking, however.)

In the end, external circumstances tend to determine the salience of one facet of an individual's identity over another at any given time. Discrimination against a particular feature of one's identity reinforces that feature in relation to others. It is an unfortunate characteristic of much of Muslim world politics that the issue of Shi'ite identity should remain a key element in political and social affairs in most countries. The Shi'ite identity need not be that important an issue, but it does acquire heightened significance when it becomes a factor in the attitudes of non-Shi'a. In other words, the responsibility for the salience of Shi'ite identity in society and politics lies not with the Shi'a alone, but at least as much with the Sunnis who dominate social and political attitudes in all Arab states except Syria and Lebanon.

The "problem of the Shi'a" is not simply the usual issue of a minority in society. In fact the Shi'a are not even numerical minorities in several countries in the region: in Iraq and Bahrain they constitute a clear majority, but nonetheless they still suffer "minority" status. The Shi'a represent a plurality in Lebanon, where only in recent years they have gained a degree of political power commensurate with their numbers. Regardless of their numbers, the dilemma of the Shi'a is in many ways more complicated than a minority issue, because it is far more subtle, unstated and virtually unmentionable. Christians, for instance, are a recognized religious minority while the Kurds in Iraq are a recognized ethnic minority; they both occupy an acknowledged niche in society, however underprivileged and uncomfortable that may sometimes be. Theoretically at least Christians and Kurds can sue for specific protections and rights from the state without rubbing salt in the wound or upsetting the established social order. This is far from the case with the Shi'a.

The sensitivity of the Shi'ite issue runs deep and touches upon the earliest discords in Muslim society. The *umma* of Islam (the totality of the international Muslim community) in theory is homogeneous and united, so that emphasis placed upon differences within it are often quickly condemned as schismatic. The Shi'a, merely by proclaiming their brand of Islam, their difference—even their existence—present a sensitive problem that assails the core of Muslim unity and undermines the traditional historiography of the Muslim state, which seeks to present Muslim history as an unbroken and untarnished continuity. In the past, Arab and other Muslim governments have been loath to address this issue head on, preferring to ignore or disguise it as part of the "unfinished business" of Islam. However, evasiveness does not serve to solve the problem and may no longer even be an option.

At the heart of the "Shi'a problem" is a series of stereotypical beliefs in traditional Sunni thinking, many of which arise from the myth of the unity of the umma. In the framework of unity, Shi'ism is the dreaded "mother split" in Islam, especially destabilizing because it occurred so early in the history of Islam. In the stereotypical depiction, the Shi'a represent a schismatic religious group, whose Islam is unorthodox and suspect, whose attitude toward the state is unreliable, who prefer to maintain a communal life separate from Sunnis, and whose *spiritual* loyalty, at least, lies outside the Arab states toward Shi'ite Iran. None of these stereotypes is accurate, but all have an element of truth in them at certain times and under certain circumstances.

The West also looks at the Shi'a in stereotypical terms, as a homogeneous group marked by religious zeal, violent methods and radical acts, and all of whose members are antagonistic to the United States. This oversimplified picture is based on the most sensational manifestations of Shi'ite self-assertion, which reached their peak in the decade following the Iranian revolution. The tidal wave of the Iranian revolution, as it washed over Lebanon, Iraq, and the Persian Gulf region, has understandably predisposed the West to view Shi'ism as fanatical and aggressive, and to ignore the distinctions that exist between Iranian and Arab Shi'ism, and within Arab Shi'ism itself. Such a broad-brush notion was facilitated by the paucity of substantial scholarship on the Shi'a, and more particularly of Arab Shi'a, prior to the rise of Khomeini's Iran. Thus the approach of the West to Shi'ism was impressionistic rather than analytical, based on snapshots that missed the larger canvas of the Shi'ite world, and was propelled by reaction rather than investigation.

The reality of the Shi'a in the Arab world is far more complex. As this study aims to show, there are common denominators of religious beliefs, cultural lore, and historical memory that create a sense of community among the Shi'a, especially those in the Arab world. We must also recognize, however, that the Shi'a are not an undifferentiated mass: there is diversity of belief and purpose, as well as differences in adherence and commitment to the common denominators. Moreover, even though many of the problems experienced by the Shi'a across the region are similar, they are not identical but rather are modulated by the different histories and circumstances of the communities in individual countries. This has created divergent approaches and responses by the Shi'ite communities toward the broader societies in which they live.

Constituents of Identity

The "Twelver Shi'a" are so named because they recognize twelve Shi'ite Imams (spiritual community leaders) as guiding the Shi'ite community until the last went into occultation late in the ninth century, to reemerge one day according to God's plan.) They are also called Ja'fari, after Imam Ja'far al-Sadiq, the sixth Imam and a great scholar who laid down the principal traditions and doctrine of Shi'ism. The Twelver Shi'a represent about 10 to 15 percent of the Muslim, predominantly Sunni, world. It is difficult to give precise figures for the Arab countries, but it is acknowledged that they form significant minorities in Kuwait, Saudi Arabia, and Oman, a plurality in Lebanon, and a majority in Iraq and Bahrain. The history of *tashayyu'*[2] (Shi'ism) began, according to many interpretations, immediately after the death of the Prophet Muhammad as a political protest over the issue of who was to succeed the Prophet and how succession was to be determined. This proto-Shi'ism evolved into a recognizable and separate doctrine only from the ninth century onward. Shi'ite centers of learning developed in Iraq and Iran during the 'Abbasid period, then more vigorously under the tenth-century Buyid dynasty in Iraq and the Hamdani in Syria, both of which had Shi'ite sympathies. Thus the early spread of Shi'ism in Iraq, Lebanon, and Bahrain, as well as Iran, long predates the official establishment of Shi'ism in Iran, which came only under the Safavids as late as the sixteenth century.[3] Indeed the Safavid Shah Isma'il (and subsequent Persian rulers) invited Shi'ite *'ulama* (religious scholars) from Jabal 'Amil in Lebanon and from Bahrain to Iran to enlist their aid in the formidable task of propagating the creed across the length and breadth of Sunni Iran.[4]

With the long history of Shi'ite communities in the Arab world and their distribution across regions, states, and national identities, it is legitimate to ask whether there is such a thing as an encompassing shared Shi'ite identity. It presupposes a broad common ground that transcends geography, history, politics, and even ethnic origin. While it is accepted that ethnicity does have the power to retain cohesion, it is less clear whether sectarian adherence has a similar force. The evidence suggests that there are both intrinsic and exogenous factors that contribute to Shi'ite identity. Common religious, social, political, and economic factors have characterized the experience of Shi'ite communities, and, notwithstanding local or individual variations in these elements, they create common ties and contribute to the shaping of a Shi'ite identity.

The Shi'a share with Sunnis a belief in the tenets of the Muslim faith as set out in the Qur'an, the Sira (account of the Prophet's life) and Hadith (collected and edited sayings) of the Prophet Muhammad, and adherence to the five "pillars" of Muslim religious observance. However, significant interpretative divergences and devotional additions set Shi'ite practices apart. At its origins the split among the Muslims occurred over the political question of who should succeed the Prophet in leading the umma of Muslims. The partisans (the literal translation of "Shi'a") of 'Ali believed that succession should go to

Muhammad's family via the Prophet's bloodline, represented first by 'Ali (the Prophet's cousin and son-in-law) and subsequently by 'Ali's descendants from his wife Fatima, the daughter of the Prophet. As Twelver Shi'ism took shape and crystallized, twelve descendants in particular were regarded as Imams and by right were owed allegiance as the leaders of the community in their lifetime and veneration after their death. The Shi'a believe in the infallibility of the twelve Imams and in their direct divine inspiration—doctrines that the Sunnis view as contrary to the teachings of Islam, some even as idolatrous or non-Muslim. Further, belief in the temporary occultation of the twelfth and last Imam, in the ninth century, led to the millenarian Shi'ite Doctrine of the Return, when the hidden Imam will reveal himself and lead the faithful against the forces of evil. In the absence of the Twelfth Imam, the affairs of the faithful are referred to surrogates, learned 'ulama, *maraji' al-taqlid* (literally "sources of emulation," singular *marji*), who have mastered Islamic jurisprudence and have the authority of interpreting Islam's texts and dicta in terms of contemporary life.

The central drama of Shi'ism is the tragic slaying of Husayn, the third Imam and grandson of the Prophet, at the hands of the 'Umayyads in a hopelessly uneven battle near Karbala in Iraq in 680. The "martyrdom" of Husayn, which Fuad Ajami calls the "Karbala paradigm,"[5] has become the leitmotif of Shi'ite interpretation of the world, around which much of Shi'ite ritual and iconography revolves. From this drama springs the double helix of martyrdom and dispossession that runs through Shi'ite history, spreading offshoots of belief in *'adl* (God's justice), a millenarian struggle at the end of time, and the deliverance of humanity by the reappeared Twelfth Imam. The tragedy of Husayn's martyrdom is literally revived and reenacted yearly at the anniversary of the massacre, 'Ashura, when full vent is given to grief, remorse, and lamentation in processions, drama, and music. What is ambivalent is whether the lamentation is for Husayn alone or for the burden of all the Shi'a and their accumulated history of rejection and defeat.[6]

Far more than the Sunnis, the Shi'a have transformed their beliefs into an exuberant culture of religion as powerful as the doctrine itself. Thus a reference system of texts, rituals, folk practices, popular legends, and religious observances, many of which are peripheral to the doctrine, has been woven into the fabric of Shi'ite collective consciousness, endowing it with a rich and distinctive iconography. Ahl al-Bayt (People of the Family of the Prophet) are especially venerated and loved by the Shi'a. The graves of members of Ahl al-Bayt, and especially of the twelve Imams, are holy shrines with emotive and spiritual power, giving cities like Najaf, Karbala, Qom, and Mashhad a special sanctity. Visits to the shrines of the Imams in these cities, especially Karbala and Najaf in Iraq, are as important as the pilgrimage to Mecca, more frequent, and far more festive. For Shi'a from Bahrain or

Lebanon who find it too arduous or expensive to travel to Mecca with millions of others at the specified time of year, Karbala and Qom are more accessible and welcoming and provide a locale to meet Shi'a from around the Muslim world. Pious Shi'a visit these shrines frequently, seeking benediction and the intercession of the Imams for personal problems. Burial in the Iraqi city of Najaf, near the first Imam, 'Ali, is the desideratum of every Shi'ite believer, and the city once derived a substantial portion of its revenue from burial of the dead brought from as far away as Pakistan and India.

Like the medieval Christian church, the Shi'ite year is marked by seasons of commemorations, devotions, and observances that are most often performed communally. Study circles, oratory, and charitable distribution also mark such festivals as the Ghadir Khom, when Muhammad, according to Shi'ite belief, designated 'Ali his successor. The Muslim month of Muharram is a period of intensified religious observance and piety and expanded gatherings at *husayniyat,* or Shi'ite community centers. The most important event in the Shi'ite calendar is the yearly 'Ashura procession, commemorating the martyrdom of the third Imam, al-Husayn. Processions of thousands of men present a public display of drama and lamentation, in some places including a passion play depicting the story of Imam Husayn's martyrdom—despite the fact that human representation is forbidden in Islam. Flagellants with bare bloodied backs and chests are common sights in these processions. Public recitations of the writings of the Imams were until recent years the equivalent of Friday prayers for the Sunnis. In Shi'ite eyes, then, the practice of Shi'ite community life and ritual is an exceptionally rich and warm tradition. To many Sunnis, however, it represents unorthodox accretions that defy the injunctions of Islam and border on the heretical.

But some observant Shi'a point out that Shi'ism in and of itself isn't a religion at all, it is simply "a way to think about Islam." In other words, there is full agreement about the nature of the Prophet's revelations, but there is no agreement about what happened after his death. This line of argument maintains that the revelations are by definition sacred, but that the history of Islam itself is not sacred, despite many efforts by subsequent Islamic scholars to equate their collegial interpretation of Islam with the faith itself. One may have differing views about the relative merits of the leadership of the early umma after the Prophet without departing from Islam. What the Shi'a depart from is the interpretation and *implementation* of Islam into the political order; this is not about Islam, but about implementation. Implementation cannot be equated with revelation. This line of thinking further argues that the Shi'a have no political agenda for the future other than to protect the welfare and interests of the Shi'ite community. This goal makes no reference to Sunni Islam and should not be threatening to Sunnis.

An additional major element of the Shi'ite identity is the *marji'iyya,* or institution of juridical referral on matters affecting religious practices, social relations, and theology. It is specific to Twelver Shi'ism, especially the dominant Usuli school, and closely connected to the principle of Imamate, or guidance of the Muslims. The principle of Imamate stems from the belief that God, who had sent the Prophet Muhammad and the Qur'an to Muslims to enlighten, instruct, and lead them in the true path of His worship, would not leave his umma, or nation, without guidance after the Prophet's death. God's love for the umma, and His concern for the welfare of every Muslim in life and in the hereafter, dictates that in every age Muslims must have guides, imams, to continue the essential function of instructing the umma in the path of righteousness. Those given the power to interpret God's law in its contemporary significance and relevance were known as *mujtahid,* or interpreters.

Every practicing Shi'i had to follow the directives of one or more mujtahid in almost every aspect of their life. Mujtahids were also venerated for their justice *('adl),* the purity of their lives and their personal piety, and were exemplars for devout Shi'a. Financially, the highest class of mujtahids, the maraji', commanded considerable resources. A practicing Shi'ite is required to pay a tax, *(khums),* and a charitable contribution *(zakat),* to a marji' for distribution to the needy. Many wealthy Shi'a also make endowments *(awqaf)* usually in the form of income-producing property, that are administered by mujtahids or maraji'. These financial contributions have in fact become a measure of the importance of a marji' and the size of his following. Maraji' could establish seminaries and other schools, support students of theology and lesser clerics, build orphanages, and finance publications, as well as give alms to the poor and needy. The financial resources were not only a measure of the importance of a marji', they also helped to expand the influence of the marji'.

Finally, as the representative or deputy of the Imam, the marji' also carried political weight, although the precise nature of his political role remained somewhat nebulous. The twelve Imams were regarded as the divinely ordained leaders of the umma in both the spiritual and temporal realms. The Muslim rulers who came after 'Ali were illegitimate because they had usurped the leadership of the umma from the Imams and governed in *dhulm* (injustice); these rulers can be tolerated by the Shi'a or challenged, but they cannot become the ultimate authority over the conscience of the Shi'a. Thus the issue of who can have legitimate political authority over the Shi'a after the occultation of the twelfth Imam was left unsettled. The maraji', as representatives of the hidden Imam, and because of their expertise and justice, were most suited to rule the umma in the absence of the Imam. Thus in the early 1970s Ayatollah Khomeini published a landmark book that developed the concept of *wilayat al-faqih* (the governorship of the juristconsult) to resolve the uncertainty, but the concept has not been universally accepted by the senior 'ulama of Shi'ism. Nevertheless, the maraji', as the highest authority over the Shi'ite community, have had considerable political sway even when they did not hold the reigns of power, and they were consulted by practicing Shi'a on political issues, including opposition to the government, jihad, formation of political parties, and other purely political questions. The apogee of clerical political rule of course occurred in Iran after the revolution of 1979.

The maraji' therefore exercise authority over their followers and act as a binding force uniting their emulators and followers, who can be regarded as belonging to the same school and following the same mentor. However, this unity is somewhat diminished by the important fact of the multiplicity of maraji'. In practice, there have always been several mujtahids in any given era, and only rarely was there a supreme marji' to whom all deferred. In part this proliferation was necessitated by the wide geographic spread of Shi'ism and the difficulties of communication when Shi'ite communities needed a local authority to respond to their pressing questions, and the multiplicity of mujtahids presented limited scope for friction. However, the concentration of mujtahids in cities like Qom, Tehran, and Najaf, as well as vastly improved communications, does create occasions for conflict among mujtahids and, by extension, among their *muqallids* (followers).

A practicing Shi'i can choose his or her mentor freely among the maraji' and can even choose a different marji' for different needs, although this rarely happens, for once a personal bond is established with a marji' loyalty usually stays firm. Because the maraji' occasionally disagree both on secondary and even major issues, their divisions are reflected in divisions within the Shi'ite community as a whole. One of the salient examples of such differences was the activist political role adopted by Khomeini in the 1970s and 1980s, contrasted with the apolitical stance of several senior maraji', including Ayatollahs Khoei in Iraq and Rouhani in Qom. These senior clerics, who had a higher religious station and together commanded a far wider religious following than Khomeini, were never sympathetic to his concept of *wilayat al-faqih*. Such major disagreements are an additional factor in the divisions within the worldwide Shi'ite community.

The prominent role of the maraji' has emerged only over the past few centuries but has become a vital part of Shi'ism's ability to apply interpretation to modern conditions, giving Shi'ism, in principle, a more liberal approach to interpretation of Islam than the Sunnis have. Indeed, once a marji' has died, his interpretations and fatwas are no longer binding upon his followers and can be reinterpreted by his successor.

The maraji' provide spiritual leadership to the Shi'a across national boundaries and act as focal points for consensus among their followers as well as guides in times of crisis, especially when other forms of higher authority are absent or suspect. Thus during the 1920 popular revolt against the British in Iraq, the maraji' in Najaf, Karbala, and Kadhimein were consulted, particularly Muhammad Taqi al-Shirazi, on the validity of armed struggle, even though the revolt was not exclusively religious or Shi'ite but was regarded as an Iraqi national movement against British colonialism.[7]

Because this complex reference system has taken root in the tradition, culture, and very social life of Shi'ism, its power to delineate Shi'ite identity extends far beyond mere theological belief or those who are strict observants to include the large numbers of doctrinally faint-hearted Shi'a. Many "cultural Shi'a" participate in the rituals and folklore of the community not necessarily out of theological fervor but because these have become the vernacular of community self-expression—much as Jewish holidays have a strong cultural hold over relatively secular Jews. Thus Shi'ism has created a language, both literal and metaphoric, through which a broad spectrum of Shi'a can communicate with each other and interpret the world.

But the question of who is a Shi'i is a matter of some dispute within the community itself. For most Shi'a, the definition of Shi'ism is a compound of religious, cultural, historical, and social attributes, usually acquired by the circumstance of birth, and it is ultimately a definition determined by the individual. For some the stress may fall on the religious component, for others on the cultural and social components. However, not all Shi'a accept such an elastic definition. For strict religious observants, Shi'ism is a religious faith and a way of life based on that faith. Shi'ism as an identity is inseparable from adherence to the religious faith, and it is the active practice of Shi'ism that expresses identity. In this purist definition, cultural and historical Shi'ism (for example, being Shi'ite by birth) that is not rooted in religious belief does not constitute sufficient ground for being considered Shi'ite. In this view, nonpracticing Shi'a and "cultural Shi'a" are therefore outside the fold and cannot be considered part of the community. This conservative view is usually glossed over in face of the indiscriminate pressures placed on the Shi'ite community by the sociopolitical environment, but it remains nevertheless an incipient source of tension, already visible in countries such as Lebanon where there is now a sufficient margin of maneuver for the Shi'a to allow themselves the luxury of squabbling over appropriating the Shi'ite platform.

In geographic terms, Shi'ism has in one sense remained on the peripheries of the Arab world, but in another sense it lies in the absolute heart of the Persian Gulf with its communities clustered around the oil-rich shores of eastern Saudi Arabia, Bahrain, southern Iraq, Kuwait, and to a lesser extent the UAE, Qatar, and Oman. Only Lebanon is the obvi-ous exception to this regional clustering. In the twentieth century, Shi'ism has been absent from the centers where Arab history was being made: Cairo, Damascus, Baghdad, Riyadh, or Jeddah. But this geographic prox-imity in the Gulf region has facilitated movement among Shi'ite areas, re-sulting in intermarriage and ties of kinship. Indeed, many Shi'a refer to the Gulf coastal region as the Shi'ite heartland, in which they live in a rel-atively consolidated fashion. While from the Sunni perspective the Shi'a seem to live on the periphery, even from the point of view of Islam, this is not so. These regions are intimately linked to the early years of the ex-pansion of Islam into southern Mesopotamia and the Gulf coast. Indeed, this is proximity to the roots of Islam, not distance.[8] Although increas-ingly in the second half of the twentieth century the rise in urbanization and mobility has expanded the range of the Shi'a into major Arab cities, the areas along the Gulf coast remain the home base.

In addition to intrinsic elements of identity that develop naturally from common beliefs and practices, Shi'a also possess an ascriptive identity, that is, elements of identity that are ascribed by others to the Shi'a. As early as the ninth century the Shi'a were labeled Rafidha, or "rejecters," by mainstream Sunni Muslims, referring to their rejection of the line of succession estab-lished after the death of Muhammad, and thus the entire basis of legitimacy that successive Muslim dynasties built on (even though the legitimacy of most of those dynasties were based on the realities of power and not theolog-ical or moral grounds). More than that, the label has unmistakable under-tones of heresy, implying a rejection of mainstream (Sunni) Islamic doctrine and probable religious deviation. And it is only a short step from *al-rafidha,* those who reject, to *al-marfudhun,* those who are rejected, indicating os-tracism of the Shi'a from the main body politic, or umma, of Islam.[9]

Shi'ite identity was thus formed as much by external pressure applied on the community by the surrounding environment as by any intrinsic quali-ties. With only brief intermissions, the Shi'a have endured varying degrees of ostracism, discrimination, or persecution. The stigmatization of the Shi'a was validated on the three issues of theology, politics and, in modern times, state allegiance. Shi'ite veneration of the twelve Imams; their belief in the power of intercession; and their visits, prayers, and sacrifices at the shrines appears to contradict the principle of unitarianism or oneness of God *(tawhid)* that is cardinal in Islam and lends Shi'ism a suspiciously unortho-dox color in the eyes of Sunnis. At the extreme, Shi'ism came to be seen not as a separate school of Islamic thought but as a heretical movement that un-dermines the principles of Islam.

Politically, the Shi'a are perceived as dissenters from the start, unwilling to endorse the system of *khilafa* (succession) and the established order; therefore, Shi'ism is a *fitna* (sedition), designed to tear apart the solidarity of the umma. Lastly, Shi'ism is accused of being a non-Arab movement, an ideology fashioned and promoted by *Mawali* (non-Arab Muslims) to undermine Arab culture and the Arab character of Islam, and indeed to undermine Islam itself, the supreme product of the Arabs. This latter charge has been resurrected in modern history in the term *Shu'ubiyya* (anti-Arabism) used against Shi'ism by writers on Arab nationalism.

The engagement of the Shi'a in public affairs has thus been, and continues to be, constrained by these charges. The political participation of the Shi'a was limited to failed insurgencies under 'Umayyad and 'Abbasid rule and brief periods of tolerance under local sultans in the tenth and eleventh centuries; otherwise political estrangement was the norm for the Shi'a during much of Muslim history. The Shi'a consequently retreated from public life and affairs of state and were in turn marginalized in the affairs of the great Muslim empires, with the significant exception of Iran starting in the sixteenth century.

The implications, ramifications, and consequences of the status of the Shi'a as *rafidha/marfudhun* (those who reject and those who are rejected) form the matrices of any study of Shi'ite identity in the Arab world today. The position of the Shi'a in the states and societies in which they live is the historical legacy of their rejection of the legitimacy of government, the reciprocal rejection by Sunni authority of the Shi'a, and their consequent sense of dispossession and alienation. The concepts of *'adl* and its opposite, *dhulm* (injustice or oppression), figure prominently in Shi'ite theological, social, and political thinking. To the classical understanding of justice in its juridical sense, *'adl* in the Shi'ite lexicon adds the theological dimension of "following the just will of God" and "acting according to God's righteous will." Politically, this is translated into the notion that the only legitimate government is one that follows the righteous will of God; social justice and the equality of Muslims are also manifestations of divine *'adl*. By these standards, most Muslim governments have only practiced dhulm in nearly all respects.[10]

Reinforcing the cultural-religious dimension of Shi'ite identity is their social identification as the poor and uneducated, the underclass of the Arab world stretching from south Lebanon to Bahrain. The Shi'a regard themselves as living under dhulm, reinterpreted into the very modern understanding of authoritarian government that denies their rights and practices discrimination. The Shi'a point to a pattern of neglect and poverty resulting from discriminatory practices of governments from Ottoman times into the modern era. The Shi'a, from Lebanon to Bahrain, formed the peasantry and poor rural sector of their societies.[11] For decades they remained outside the advance of urbanization and modernization that began in the Arab world after World War I and accelerated after World War II. The benefits of modernization manifested in education, health services, communications, job opportunities, and a higher standard of living were very late in reaching Shi'ite areas, and the relative poverty and underdevelopment of the Shi'a in southern Lebanon, southern Iraq, and in the Bahraini villages is still striking today. Until the 1960s, these regions formed a hinterland of quiet and forgotten deprivation, largely dependent on agriculture, which itself was a declining sector of economies increasingly dependent on oil, financial services, and industrialization.

The Shi'ite sense of discrimination and the unfairness of their lot in society is a widespread and powerful feature of Shi'ite self-awareness and solidarity, felt by even those Shi'a who have a minimal attachment to the religious doctrine. One Shi'ite scholar commented ironically that perhaps Shi'a "ought not to complain," that their doctrine has taught them that persecution will be their lot, that they are not destined to rule until the Mahdi comes. This kind of belief, in his view, poses a genuine philosophical dilemma to Shi'a. Should they simply suffer passively in silence? Or should they "help history along" by building the strength of the Shi'ite community and preparing the groundwork for the Mahdi's arrival?

Many Shi'a who would otherwise identify themselves in nonsectarian terms understand that they are classified by others as Shi'a first, regardless of their own self-definition. To the extent that this is a label that is stamped on them by the outside world, they are powerless to change it. Shi'a interviewed for this study complained that there is no escape from the label of Shi'ism, and that even if a Shi'i were to convert to Sunnism, he or she would remain a Shi'i in the eyes of Sunnis. On a popular level, this sense of ingrained discrimination extends into the folklore: in Lebanon, common folklore claims that the Shi'a have tails; in Saudi Arabia, the Shi'a are thought to spit in their food before eating it; devout Wahhabis believe that shaking hands with a Shi'i spoils a Muslim's ablution. Many Wahhabis believe that most Shi'a secretly aspire to smear the Ka'ba (the central shrine of pilgrimage in Mecca) with human excrement during the Hajj (pilgrimage). In Iraq, an article in the official Ba'th newspaper after the Gulf war accused the Shi'a of the south of sexual perversions and depravity, among other moral defects.[12] Although these are extremes of folk prejudice, they indicate the impasse that the Shi'a find themselves in: in the final analysis, it is not how one defines himself but how society around him defines him that determines his identity and his relations. As a result, Shi'ism became a way of seeing the world as dominated by dhulm, with the Shi'a destined to be the permanent outsiders, enclosed upon themselves and fearful of exposure. From this ensued a long tradition of political quietism and withdrawal from public affairs, confining the Shi'a to a physical and social hinterland where they could be forgotten in a dark corner of Arab consciousness.

Divisions Among the Shi'a

Shi'a are divided as a community by a broad number of factors. Some of these factors are imposed by external circumstances, the most obvious of which are the political borders between Arab states in which large Shi'ite communities live. Despite the fact that the Shi'a have little say in shaping public life in their states, their own conditions are inevitably affected by the historical and economic developments taking place in their immediate environment. For example, in the 1920s, while Iraqi Shi'a were opposed to the British mandate and led an uprising against British presence in Iraq, the Shi'a of Bahrain were appealing to the British authorities on the island for protection from the abuses of the ruling family and tribes.[13] This reality, coupled with regimes exercising tight security controls, means that easy and casual travel across borders in the region is not always easy. Communications between the Shi'ite communities have been even more restricted in recent years because of the security concerns of regional governments, while the opportunities for the Shi'a to establish cross-border support and cooperation have become more difficult.

Shi'ite communities are further divided by the tenor of relations between the regimes of the countries in which they live. The nature of relations between Iran and Iraq represent the most vivid example of this problem. With broad tensions existing between the two states actually degenerating into eight years of war between them in the 1980s, the Shi'a were caught in the middle. In the war for Kuwait the Kuwaiti Shi'a were impelled into conflict with an Iraqi army, a majority of whose enlisted troops are Shi'a. While Iran sought to use Iraqi Shi'a as a fifth column in the Iran-Iraq war, and Iraq may have hoped to at least neutralize the Kuwaiti Shi'a, in fact in both cases the Shi'ite communities acquitted themselves well in demonstrating overall loyalty to the state in which they reside. Needless to say, the Shi'a have almost no voice over relations among states with large Shi'ite populations.

But most of the differences among the Shi'a derive from internal community reasons. The many shared components of Shi'ite religious and cultural identity and common suffering indeed serve to bind the community to some degree and may appear to create a close-knit, coherent force, with shared purpose and destiny. In reality, however, shared beliefs and experiences have limited power to overcome inherent differences. The Arab Shi'ite community is diverse and in some cases divided upon itself, limiting its ability to act in concert and making it more difficult to define, let alone achieve, common goals. Several of the factors that bind the Shi'a can also separate them. While religious doctrine is a shared attribute, it can also be a subject of discord; the institution of marji'iyya is both a tie and a source of clash;

class and economic status separate the Shi'a of one community, and political orientation can be a cause for antagonism.

Variations in Religious Commitment

The primary source of difference among the Shi'a is the degree of religious adherence. Not all Shi'a practice Shi'ism equally, or are equally committed to the theology of Shi'ism. Since the 1970s there has been an increase in the number of Shi'a who observe the practical injunctions of Islam such as prayer and fasting, perform acts of piety such as joining the circles of recitations from the Qur'an or the traditions of the Twelve Imams, and commemorate the holy 'Ashura. The Husayniyat, the Shi'ite centers that serve as places of prayer, celebration, and community meetings, have undergone a revival in attendance. However, there are significant qualifications to this trend. First, the increase in religious commitment among the Shi'a is part of an overall Islamic revival, and there is no evidence to suggest that the Shi'a have turned to religion in greater numbers than other Muslims have. Second, as is the case among Sunnis, the increase in Shi'ite religiosity is by no means universal or uniform. Religious belief among the Shi'a lies along a spectrum that ranges from strict observance to indifference, and the disparities cause a serious rift within the Shi'ite community.

The degree of Shi'ite theological adherence raises the issue of identity once more. To what extent can one claim Shi'ism without believing firmly in the tenets of Shi'ism? Does religious laxity lessen the intensity of a Shi'i's identity? These questions are perennially asked and encountered by the Shi'a. In addition, since the beginning of the twentieth century, the Shi'a have been subject to many influences more or less alien to Shi'ism. One is exposure to Western culture, institutions, and education. Another is the powerful influence that socialist ideologies exerted on Shi'ite communities throughout the region from mid-century on. A third is the various forms of Arab nationalism espoused by large numbers of Shi'a: Nasserism, Ba'thism of different varieties, and other smaller movements. These political constructs sidestep religion and at least superficially purport to transcend it. As a consequence of these new intellectual allegiances, religious ties are much looser for many Shi'a today than they were at the beginning of the century.

Overt agnosticism is rare because of the stigma and heavy penalty placed by Islam on apostasy. Within that red line, however, there are infinite gradations of belief in Shi'ite theology. At the most elementary level, most Shi'a proclaim their belief in Islam and in the broad principles specific to Shi'ite doctrine, such as the legitimacy of 'Ali's bid for the Caliphate, the special status of the Twelve Imams, and the just cause of Husayn's martyrdom. But not all would accept the principle of infallibility attributed to the Twelve Imams, and some may regard the adulation of Husayn and the other Imams as unwarranted excess. Shi'ite leftists deemphasize religion as a factor of cohesion and stress instead the importance of political repression in binding the community. Leftists are often skeptical about the religious basis of discrimination, attributing it instead to the need to preserve class interests and political supremacy. This doctrinally "lapsed Shi'ism" is often assailed by devout Shi'a, who, at the extreme, maintain that religious commitment is an indispensable element of identity, and that nonpracticing Shi'a are not Shi'a at all and cannot be included in the community. Strong adherents of Shi'ism tend to portray themselves as the true representatives of the Shi'ite community, the standard-bearers and vanguard of Shi'ite liberation.

Political Differences

Opinions regarding the nature of the state, the prerequisites for the legitimacy of government, and the role of Islam in politics form another matrix for dispute among the Shi'a. Nor are these disputes solely between the hardline Islamists and the secularists, but they arise internally within each camp. Political Islam, at its most fundamental level, believes that Islamic Shari'a (law) should be enshrined as the law of the land and the sole source of legislation. Many Shi'a are opposed to Islamization of the state at such a level. At one pole of the argument stand the maximalists of Islamization, for whom only an Islamist state based on the Shari'a and the Qur'an has legitimacy; at the other end are the staunch secularists who insist on the separation of mosque and state, on keeping Islam a private choice and practice. In between the two extremes lie many gradations of opinion.

On the surface it may appear that the political split overlaps with the divisions over religious adherence, but in fact the two fault lines do not necessarily coincide. While it may be true that Shi'a whose religious sentiment is weak tend to be political secularists, many among them recognize the necessity of establishing Islam as the religion of the state—not necessarily synonymous with an "Islamic state"—and of acknowledging the value of its moral precepts in public life. Similarly, not all ardently religious Shi'a are political Islamists in the sense of insisting on unwavering adherence to the Shari'a in the conduct of public affairs. Some devout Shi'a, in keeping with the quietist tradition, view their Shi'ism as a matter of personal piety that should be segregated from politics.

There is also a purist objection, arising from the theological dilemma of government in Shi'ism. The strict Shi'ite view holds that just—that is, Islamic—government can only be instituted by a designated Imam with divine guidance, and that all other governments are tainted. Therefore, it is futile to call for or proclaim an Islamic government in the absence of the

Imam, and the Shi'a have to make do with defective government until the fullness of time. The most compelling reasons, however, to moderate Shi'ite views on political Islamism are the practical obstacles arising from domestic and regional factors.

Where Shi'a are the minority they cannot hope to impose an Islamic state even if the Shi'ite community wished to do so, and a similar attempt in states where Shi'a are a majority raises the obstacles to Shi'ite accession to dominant political power even higher in the eyes of minoritarian Sunnis. Furthermore, the difference in attitude toward the nature of the state is echoed in the political platforms adopted by secularists and Islamists respectively. The Shi'ite Islamists hold to a specifically Shi'ite platform that emphasizes the grievances of the community and calls for redress and reparations for the Shi'a, although it is often linked to other national issues such as adequate representation, equality under the law, and equal opportunity. The Shi'ite secularists, while not denying Shi'ite grievances, are less prone to adopting a specifically Shi'ite rhetoric and situate the problem in the broader context of overall state failure affecting the entire population. What at first glance looks like subtle nuance is in fact a deep split in the political approaches of the two Shi'ite groups on how to solve Shi'ite problems. However, it is noteworthy that there is an emerging third platform on the Shi'ite political scene, which advances a Shi'ite secularist, or at least non-Islamist, agenda, but that nevertheless is committed to promoting Shi'ite interests and redressing grievances. This remains a pioneering platform trying to break new ground, and it is not clear whether it can acquire legitimacy or following, but it further splits the Shi'ite political position.

The Marji'iyya

Among practicing Shi'a, the marji'iyya—the institution of spiritual (and perhaps political) guidance—represents a further issue for divergence. The status of *marji' al-taqlid* (guide for emulation) in Shi'ism is attained by divines through a fluid process of acquiring high theological eminence and amassing a substantial following among the population. There are no rules for election or designation of a marji', and thus several can emerge concurrently. Because there is no single universally accepted marji', a devout Shi'a can choose any one of several spiritual leaders. This multiplicity of maraji' has been particularly the case since the death of Ayatollah Khomeini in Iran in 1989 and Ayatollah Khoei in Iraq in 1992.

Although the principal areas of guidance provided by maraji' are on issues of theology, religious practice, and private conduct, their influence in reality touches on a wide sphere of activity that affects relations between individuals and the community and with society at large. By extension, a group of Shi'a who follow the same marji' are likely to define their relations to the social and political order similarly in line with the teachings of their marji'. This in turn can create differences among groups of Shi'a not only in theological and personal matters, but also on public issues. For example, in the 1980s, the followers of Khomeini had a pronounced activist, revolutionary outlook toward political life and the engagement of Shi'ism in the public arena. At the same time, the followers of al-Khoei pursued a more quietist tradition that stressed the traits of personal piety and a neutral stand on public affairs. The two ayatollahs also represented rival centers of learning, the one in Iran, the other in Iraq, which also had implications for the geographic orientation of their followers. Centers in Iran, especially Qom, have grown at the expense of the Iraqi centers, attracting an increasing number of Shi'ite religious scholars from the Arab world, and raising problems of allegiance for the Shi'ite communities. Since the death of Khoei and Khomeini, the rivalries among the several maraji' and their emulators has only intensified, even inside Iran itself, while a new contender for the role of marji', Sayid Muhammad Fadhlallah, has emerged in Lebanon. In Saudi Arabia the Shi'a are divided between followers of the "Line of the Imam" or the teachings of Ayatollah Khomeini, which are revolutionary in character, and the teachings of Ayatollah Shirazi, who has preached caution in the political arena.

Social Disparities

Classic forms of social stratification also divide the Shi'ite communities, affecting relations within the community as well as between the community and the prevailing sociopolitical order. Although the Shi'a constitute a very high percentage of the poorer segments of Arab society in the Gulf region and Lebanon and have fewer economic and professional opportunities, there are nonetheless prosperous and educated Shi'a even in societies in which they are most disadvantaged. In Iraq, where until the 1960s wealth derived from land ownership or commerce, Shi'ite landlords in the south and merchants in Baghdad and the southern cities controlled much of the country's wealth. To a lesser extent such a merchant or feudal class existed in most countries of the region. While political power in the early decades of this century was concentrated in the hands of a Sunni oligarchy, economic well-being was accessible for some Shi'ite families in Kuwait, Bahrain, the UAE, Lebanon, and Iraq.

Social class is a powerful element of identity, separating the rich from the poor, the urban from the rural, the educated from the semi-literate. The economic and educational gains of some Shi'a created a rift with the poorer masses of their coreligionists. For one, the richer landowners and merchants in Lebanon, Iraq, and (to some extent) Saudi Arabia moved from the provinces to the big cities, thereby geographically alienating themselves from the rural majority; in addition, the prosperous city dwellers identified with city values and adopted city mores and therefore blended more easily into the common life of the city. For these Shi'a, the predominant culture shifted away from a Shi'ite frame of reference to a city frame of reference, with its cultural diversity and multiplicity. A Shi'ite middle and upper-middle class, living in urban centers, close to other communities and often exposed to foreign cultures, identified far more easily with the state, even if they wielded little power in the political arena.

These class disparities led to different affiliations and self-definitions among the Shi'a, while economic privilege was often reflected in disparities in other areas. Usually only the more affluent and urbanized Shi'a were able to travel to the West for education or work. The financial edge enjoyed by this class created new ways of relating to the world and to modernity that were alien to the more traditional and economically disadvantaged classes. On a visceral level, the urban, affluent Shi'a tend to think of the poor rural classes as rabble, while the latter often accuse the middle classes of "inauthenticity" and having sold out to the system. As a consequence, political reality itself is understood differently by the different social classes, giving rise to clashing interpretations of the problems and conceptualizations of desirable solutions.

Because of these various, sometimes overlapping fault lines, it is impossible to speak of a homogeneous Shi'ite community in any single country in the region. The common religious, cultural, and historical ties are sometimes in themselves sources of frictions and disagreement, and they are influenced by other historical and cultural vectors that have operated at least since the start of the century. The rise in Shi'ite self-awareness has somewhat mitigated these differences, harnessing more energies toward a common cause, but this phase of greater unity may be a symptom of a period of struggle for the Shi'a, which could well dissipate under more politically propitious conditions. Such a trajectory can be seen in the history of the Shi'ite movement in Lebanon, where a communal movement in the 1970s fragmented along class, religious, and geographic grounds once the Shi'a had acquired a greater political share of the political framework.

The existence of these manifold differences among Shi'a are important to remember when outsiders sometime conjure up fear of what "Shi'a in power" might mean, for example, in a future Iraq. Under normal circumstances Shi'a will find themselves forming coalitions with other like-minded non-Shi'a, with whom they have shared interests that far exceed narrowly conceived communitarian interests that are mainly forged under oppression.

The Rise in Shi'ite Political Awareness

The revival of Shi'ism, which began to take active political dimensions in the 1960s, is a variant of the revival of political Islam as a whole, and it shares with Sunni Islamic revival some of the same causes and objectives. Additionally, the Shi'ite revival can also be attributed to the strong sense of injury and disenfranchisement specifically experienced by the Shi'a. Unlike Sunni Islamism, Shi'ite Islamism from the start had a strong component of clerical leadership, a natural consequence of the prominent role played by the 'ulama in guiding the community.

What led to the Shi'ite revival? Several factors, some of which are not unique to the Shi'a. Both Sunni and Shi'a share a disillusion with modernity and Western-style ideologies; the defeats of Arab governments over the issue of Palestine; and the fracturing of society as a result of urbanization and bureaucratization, without corresponding tangible benefits to the mass of the people. All of these helped stimulate the rise in Shi'ite adherence to religion both as personal creed and as political ideology. The Shi'ite revival has additional roots in Shi'ite experience, deriving from age-old political marginalization, government restraints on religious freedom, erosion of the autonomy and financial independence of religious institutions, and overall economic and social discrimination. In the next section we will see how the process of politicization took place across the Arab world.

The Emergence of Politicized Shi'a

The development of a Shi'ite political identity was an inevitable development in response to a long-standing need. Shi'ite political protest broke onto the scene out of a background of more traditional quietism that had dominated Shi'ite life for centuries. Quietism indeed is only one face of Shi'ite response to a world of dhulm. Although Shi'ite spiritual leaders have historically maintained a studied aloofness from political life, there has always existed a strand of activism among the Shi'a as a whole, erupting periodically in the early Islamic era, and thereafter whenever conditions of weak government permitted such expression. The legitimacy of activism is based on verses in the Qur'an and sayings of the Prophet and Imams (Hadith) that exhort Muslims to resist unjust and ungodly rulers.[14] Some Qur'anic verses and Hadith are interpreted as placing a personal duty on the individual Muslim to deny cooperation as well as actively resist unjust government.

The struggle for political recognition embodied Shi'ite frustration at their exclusion and second-class status and provided an alternative to the crosscurrent of political ideologies. The emergence of Shi'ite assertiveness has not

been uniform but has varied from one country to another according to domestic and external conditions. Despite popular Western perception, Shi'ite
social and political activism in the Arab countries is not a by-product of the
Iranian revolution of 1979, and its causes are complex and largely home-
grown. Certainly the revolt in Iraq in 1920, which was spearheaded by
Shi'ite notables and 'ulama, was theologically justified by the maraji' as resistance to non-Muslim (British) governance over a Muslim people. The senior Lebanese cleric, Sayyid Husayn Fadhlallah, spiritual mentor to
Hizballah and a rising marji' to Shi'a throughout the Arab world, wrote a
treatise in 1976—three years before the Islamic Revolution in Iran—on
"Islam and Strength," arguing the necessity of active struggle against iniqui-
tous government and citing the example of Imam Husayn.[15] It is possible to
trace the growth of Shi'ite self-awareness from origins of social discontent to
militant political activism in three broad and interpenetrating phases.

The early phase expressed socioeconomic discontent, when Shi'ite grievances were framed in terms of the disparities in benefits and economic opportunities and the need for "just" government. In mid-century the
socioeconomic grievances were translated into European concepts of a class
system. The Shi'a, from the 1940s on, joined socialist and communist parties and (illegal) labor unions in Iraq, Lebanon, Bahrain, and even Saudi
Arabia. The grievances were no longer viewed in sectarian terms but along
secular European class-struggle lines. The third and current phase has produced a specifically Shi'ite political struggle to assert their presence, and the
issues are no longer limited to economic improvement or social equity but
extend to the more vital question of political power and the share of the
Shi'a in the institutions of the state.

Independence brought to power governments that were nominally national, but in fact rooted in limited Sunni sectors of society (a military or
feudal class, a tribal/clan group, or combinations). Despite their different
shapes and outlooks, all the governments that came to power after independence failed to forge a partnership embracing all sectors of the population.
There was nothing approaching an equal distribution of economic benefits
and social services. Political opportunity was negligible, and nepotism and
profiteering were widely practiced in government bureaucracy. Inevitably,
the Shi'a, regardless of their relative numbers, were among the losers, getting
less than anyone else, and the notion of dhulm (injustice) was revived in a
modern setting.

The Cold War era was reflected in the Arab world in a confrontation between two camps: a conservative camp, comprising the regimes installed at
independence, which maintained its alliance with the West, and another
camp, which gravitated toward leftist politics of all types and claimed the
mantle of nationalism. The rise of communism and socialism in the Arab

world in the 1940s and 1950s was fueled by a large influx of Shi'ite young men who, as they acquired education, became increasingly alienated from their traditional societies but at the same time disenchanted with their prospects in the sociopolitical order. This defection of Shi'ite youth from the social and religious fold to communism and socialism represented a loss to Shi'ism and alarmed the clerical establishment. An effort at "reclamation" of Shi'ite youth was already evident in Iraq in the late fifties; in1963 the chief Iraqi marji', Sayyid Muhsin al-Hakim (perhaps with the encouragement of the new Ba'th regime in Baghdad), issued a *fatwa* condemning memberships in the communist party as anti-Islam. The clerical fear of communism was dual, as it both presented a godless moral threat to society and undermined the prestige, influence, and financial health of the religious establishment itself. The clerics therefore were braced for a fight to win back their defectors and reclaim their status as leaders of the Shi'ite community.

By the 1960s a confluence of factors boosted the momentum for Shi'ite political awareness and self-assertion. The drain on Shi'ite resources by secular ideologies and the decline in the clerical institution triggered a backlash among religious Muslims and prompted the reentry of Shi'ite clerics into public life. The Shi'a found an alternative inspiration in the writings, guidance, and charismatic presence of Shi'ite clerics such as Sayyid Muhammad Baqir al-Sadr and Sayyid Mahdi al-Hakim in Najaf, Iraq; and Sayyid Musa al-Sadr, who arrived in Lebanon from Iran in 1959.

In the early 1960s, Sayyid Muhammad Baqir al-Sadr published his landmark book, *Falsafatuna* (Our Philosophy), that was a rebuttal of both communism and capitalism as foreign ideologies based on materialism that degrade the human being. It held up Islam as a political philosophy based on the benevolent will of God and an Islamic humanist ideal. The book was followed by his *Iqtisaduna* (Our Economy), an elaboration of an Islamic economic system. Although these treatises were not addressed to an exclusively Shi'ite readership, they and their author became magnets for the Shi'a and a springboard for the rise of Shi'ite consciousness. For many, a religious revival was essential to Shi'ite political commitment, although it is difficult to say whether there was a causal relationship between the two: by all evidence, religious faith and political activism were part of a newfound Shi'ite pride, an assertive response to long grievances, and a display of confidence that wished to express itself on all possible levels.

The 1967 Arab-Israeli war shook Arab certainties and left a gaping vacuum of belief that was waiting to be filled by competing ideologies. It strengthened the belief that only an indigenous, "authentic" alternative could "empower" people and yet remain close to the people's culture and beliefs. In Iraq, the Islamic backlash to the failures of Arab regimes, to secularism, socialism, and Arab nationalism (all deemed inauthentic and alien) contributed to the formation of the Islamic Da'wa party in 1967.[16] Though not conceived or presented as a Shi'ite Islamic party, in practice its adherents were Shi'ite young men and women, and although its membership was largely nonclerical, it looked to al-Sadr and Sayyid Muhammad Mahdi al-Hakim, the son of the senior Iraqi marji', as its political and spiritual mentors. At about the same time, Sayyid Musa al-Sadr, the cleric from Iran who claimed Lebanese descent, organized and led Harakat al-Mahrumin (the movement of the deprived) to protest the poverty and deprivation that the Shi'a in southern Lebanon endured. The Haraka was primarily a call for 'adl and a repudiation of dhulm, but its implications went beyond economic redress. The movement became an expression of Shi'ite self-worth and assertiveness in a country where the political system of proportional representation failed to acknowledge their increasing numbers, and the Shi'ite feudal landlords upheld their private interests rather than the interests of the community. Again, as education spread among the Shi'a and emigrants returned with greater wealth, the system was closed to social and political advancement. Harakat al-Mahrumin tapped into a large and deep reservoir of frustration and inferiority felt by the Lebanese Shi'a.

The causes espoused by the two al-Sadr clerics were not identical, and the goals of the movements they inspired differed: in Iraq it was a revolutionary political movement based on the tenets of Islam; in Lebanon it was a movement of social protest that eventually got caught up in the maelstrom of the civil war. But they had similar results: they created a platform for the Shi'a distinct from other opposition movements and produced a hitherto unknown Shi'ite empowerment that raised political aspirations. Furthermore, in both cases Shi'ite clerics returned to the foreground in the political and social leadership of the community, giving them a prominence they had lacked for several decades. The impact of these two indigenous movements had reverberations to the south in the Persian Gulf countries with sizable Shi'ite communities.

Thus the Iranian revolution did not spawn a Shi'ite revival, but it supported and provided a focal point for a Shi'ite political identity that was already in formation. Shi'ite pride, and the ability of the Shi'a to overcome injustice, was manifested in the revolution, which attracted Islamist and secular Shi'a as well as many Sunnis. After the Iranian revolution, it was no longer an embarrassment to declare one's Shi'ism, however the West may view Iran or Shi'ite parties. Iran emboldened the Shi'a in asserting their identity and gave them the tools, for better or worse, to make their presence felt. Ironically, Arab Shi'a are now assiduously proclaiming their Arabness along with their Shi'ism, disengaging from an identification with Iran and emphasizing instead their national identities in all the countries of the region.

Conclusions

The Shi'ite identity is an admixture of religious belief, political experience, social isolation, developed cultural heritage, and communal grievance against marginalization and injustice. But that identity is also thrust upon the Shi'a, even upon the staunchly secularist, by Sunni communities and governments around them. These elements of intrinsic and attributed identity create the common factors that tend to unite the Shi'a on an abstract level. This identity and solidarity are sharpened and radicalized by negative state policies and the social conditions that prevail in each country. But because these components of identity are variable rather than fixed, they are also factors in dividing the community. The degree of religious adherence, differences in political belief, and social status create rifts among the Shi'a and often hinder effective unity. Additionally, geography and local conditions differentiate the experiences of the Shi'a, creating variations within the larger community.

For many Shi'a, religion is indispensable to identity and to the Shi'ite political struggle for recognition and equal rights. This has given clerics a large role in the Shi'ite awakening, but that role is not acceptable to all Shi'a; Shi'ite secularists and even some Islamists are reluctant to grant the religious hierarchy the authority to shape the Shi'ite future. Despite these latent and actual differences, the Shi'ite identity is strongest in the current "period of struggle" as a response to external repression, and it serves to bind the Shi'a in a common pursuit

Indeed, in the contemporary post–Cold War world where issues of identity everywhere have gained far greater salience, the Shi'a may be in the process of "re-inventing themselves"—in the sense of Benedict Anderson's concept that all communities "invent themselves" through conscious self-definition, without which identity does not exist. Does the very concept of Shi'ism have new meaning in today's Middle East where community identity is becoming more assertive? Do the Shi'a have something special to say about democracy, politics, and political culture in the Middle East as minorities who have developed a different perspective on the course of Islamic history and its failings? There is nothing any more "valid" about the Shi'ite view of Islam than the Sunni, but in an age in which authority is being challenged, the Shi'ite view of greater separation of faith from state power may gain greater following. (Indeed, the rule of the clerics in Shi'ite Iran is seen by many Shi'a as a heresy.)

Almost as if receiving inspiration from the historical vision of the Shi'a, Sunni Islamist movements today are moving to distance themselves from the oppressive state and denouncing "suborned clergy" who serve the interests of the state and not of Islam. The debate of course is not simply about theological, legal, and governmental principles, but also about communities and power; thus the purely theological issues are often shrouded by other, more concrete and competing interests of the differing communities. In this sense, Shi'ism once again perhaps should not be thought of as a religion or a political agenda, but as a body of interests with the goal of community welfare and self-preservation.

In the long run, as the Shi'a eventually attain integration into their national societies and gain equal rights of citizenship—religious, economic, and political—the Shi'ite identity may become diluted and the issue less pressing. Although some constants of a common culture and history will always remain, divisions over who is a Shi'a and who has the right to represent the community are apt to intensify as the social and political pressures ease. Under improved conditions, as Shi'a move out of the status of being a beleaguered community, then "normal" competing focuses of loyalty will emerge—professional, regional, class, ideological—that will strongly counter the idea of a homogeneous community united in hardship.

CHAPTER TWO

The Arab Shi'a in the Sunni State

The basic reality is that, whatever their numbers, all Arab Shi'a live in "Sunni states," that is, a state and social order in which dominant power lies with Sunnis and in which Sunni political culture, traditions, and interpretations of the course of Islamic history prevail. This reality poses two distinct problems for the integration of the Shi'a into the state order. In countries where the Sunnis are the majority, the Shi'a's political task is how to liberalize Sunni society toward political and social forms that are not discriminatory against the Shi'ite minority and that will permit Shi'a self-expression and security. But in two Arab states—Iraq and Bahrain—the Shi'a actually represent the majority, yet the Sunnis still dominate the political order and social culture. Under such circumstances an even more serious imbalance exists in the character of the state, and Sunni determination to perpetuate the status quo creates a potentially explosive social and political situation.

Minority Status and National Identity

With the exception of Saudi Arabia, no Arab state has actually institutionalized a specific school or sect of Islam as the sole permitted state religion. Islam is cited as the state religion in the basic law or constitution of most states, but there is no mention of sectarian affiliation. (An exception is Lebanon, whose constitution is based on the multiplicity of religions and sects.) In theory at least, all citizens, regardless of their sectarian allegiance, have equal rights and opportunities. In practice, however, this has not prevented the state from pursuing policies that support Sunni elitism and marginalize the Shi'ite population. Although all citizens are theoretically equal, some are "more equal than others." Even in an avowedly secular state such as Iraq, where the state ideology of Ba'thism is allegedly nonsectarian, discrimination against Shi'ite citizens prevails in both overt and subtle ways as an unstated but tangible policy. Indeed, secularism serves as a cover for perpetuating sectarian practices and a pretext for deflecting discussion of discrimination.

Shi'ite grievances vary considerably from state to state, ranging from mild forms of discrimination to institutionalized or outright persecution. In the states where the Shi'a form a minority, the issue is one of building mutual trust, providing equitable participation of the Shi'a in the larger polity, and actively discouraging discriminatory practices. Where the Shi'a form a majority, the imbalance poses a deep structural problem, since granting the Shi'a rights and powers commensurate with their greater numbers challenges the very basis upon which the Sunni order is built. For this reason, in countries where the Shi'a are a majority, one might turn the question on its head and argue that these states contain a "Sunni problem," that is, an unwillingness of the Sunnis ever to accept democratic rule, which would require ceding substantial power to the Shi'a and accepting a reorientation of the political culture away from centuries-old Sunni dominance.

As we saw in the previous chapter, there is a widespread sense in the Arab world that Arab culture is somehow "inherently" Sunni, that Sunnism is the natural state of the Arabs. From this perspective, the Shi'a are by definition schismatics who have willingly taken themselves out of the Arab fold by espousing Shi'ism, perhaps even with some Persian connivance. While thoughtful Arabs might reject this interpretation, it nonetheless does not lie too far beneath the surface as a common, even if unconscious, attitude among Sunnis.

In some respects the Shi'ite issue can be situated in the broader framework of minorities in the Arab world. The population of Arab countries is no more heterogeneous than other states—in some instances far more homogeneous. However, the discussion of minority issues is carefully avoided or drastically oversimplified by the state. The generally rigid nature of political power in the region sees diversity as a threat and promotes conformity to a single sociopolitical culture, with the terms of reference defined by the ruling elite. Further, blame for the difficulties encountered by Arab states in forging a national identity and a sense of citizenship is partly projected onto minorities, who are seen as part of the state's problem. These problems are not, of course, unique to the Arab world.

The strategy adopted by most countries of the region has aimed at absorption—usually under pressure—of minorities into the dominant culture without regard for preserving any of their distinctive cultural features, which are viewed as problems rather than contributions to the political culture or society. (Thus one has the absurd spectacle in Iraq of Kurds becoming distinguished members of the "Arab Ba'th Party"). Any move to broaden the terms of reference of citizenship, for example by permitting expression of religious or ethnic difference, is seen as a challenge to the state sometimes bordering on the treasonous. But despite efforts to gloss over the problem of minorities, these unresolved issues are a source of serious discontent and social imbalance. Both socially and politically, minorities remain on the margins of Arab polity. Barriers to their full integration in society are evident in the social and political structure of Arab states, and minority participation in the political process is limited to tokenism rather than real representation. (Lebanon, and to a considerable degree Kuwait, have recently made major strides away from this phenomenon.)

But the character of the problem transcends normal majority-minority issues as encountered in most states of the world. The Arab Shi'a in legal and social terms are in fact a strange breed, a special subset on the map of Middle East minorities. They are recognized neither as a majority in Iraq and Bahrain, nor as a minority in other states. Where they are a numerical minority their situation is comparable, but not identical, to that of non-Arabs (such as Kurds) or non-Muslims (such as Christians or Jews). But unlike Kurds in Iraq or Christians and Jews in most Arab states, the Shi'a are not accorded the status of minority, making their situation more complex and emotionally charged. Since most Arab societies are nominally organized within an Arab-Muslim matrix, the Shi'a, as Arab and Muslim, are ostensibly not a minority at all, but part of that matrix of Arab-Muslim culture. What remains unsaid is that political power, with all the benefits that flow from it, is organized specifically around a narrower Sunni Arab matrix (or even a subsection of the Sunni population) to which the Shi'a are outsiders in respect to voice or power. What the Arab Muslim regimes signally failed to deliver was "Muslim sectarian egalitarianism."[1]

The contradictions, spoken and unspoken, of the prevailing system present a deep dilemma for the Shi'a, a catch–22. They are reluctant to claim minority rights, as Christians and Kurds can, since that would formalize and consecrate the distinctions between them and the Sunnis politically and socially. It would intensify the suspicions of the Sunnis and minimize the prospects of true integration. Worse, when the Shi'a express their grievances as a community or call for greater Shi'a participation, they are accused by Sunni governments and communities of actively promoting sectarianism, damaging the unity of society, and seeking to destabilize and disrupt the state. At the same time, acquiescence to the established order and acceptance of the undeclared rules of power has not benefited the Shi'a much or gained them a larger role in the affairs of state during the past decades of Arab independence.

This concealed duality in the system comes into sharp focus in the attitude of Arab governments to the employment of the Shi'a in the bureaucracy, a sector disproportionately large and immensely powerful in all Arab countries. The employment of Shi'a in government jobs is very small in relation to their actual numbers, and they rarely rise above mid-level posts in ministries. This is especially true in the vital sectors of the state affecting national security, such as defense or interior ministries, intelligence and security organizations, and the treasury. On occasion, token Shi'a will be selected for ministerial or other senior posts, but this always comes as a gift from higher authority, bestowed for exceptional loyalty and service, or a concession to deflect possible criticism. The appointment of Shi'a to senior positions remains the exception, a conscious political act rather than a norm or process. It is neither a normal nor customary procedure, nor is it done on a large enough scale to qualify as a deliberate attempt by the elite to include the Shi'a in the system at all levels. Since Arab countries began to gain independence in the 1930s, only in Iraq during the 1940s and 1950s, and in Lebanon after 1989, following a devastating civil war, was a concerted effort made by governments in those countries to give the Shi'a real representation in the political system.

Whether the problem is viewed from the perspective of the Shi'a or of minorities as a whole, it is part of the larger underlying problem of forging a genuine national identity in the Arab world, a project still far from complete and in many respects inadequate in most countries in the region. The creation of a sense of collective citizenship, with binding interests and values, is indispensable to the sense of belonging that creates national identity. So is the conviction of all citizens that they have a vested interest in the state and that the political order represents their interests too. If the state is too closely identified with a select group, the sense of belonging and vested interest is enfeebled.

Under these terms, the Arab Shi'a are left out in the cold and alienated from their own states. They have no confidence that the state serves their interests or reflects their values and aspirations. The contract between citizens and state, in which loyalty is exchanged for service and accountability—weak in most Arab states—is doubly defective as far as the Shi'a are concerned. As a deprived sector of the population, their citizenship is "less equal" than others. With few exceptions, Arab governments have failed to draw the Shi'a into the fold and to persuade them that the state operates in the interests of all of its citizens. While this problem, again, is hardly unique to the Arab world, it has reached crippling dimensions in much of that region.

The Arab world is of course known to present special problems in the area of creating nation-states, due to the existence of a strong pan-Arab identity—stronger than almost any other "pan-" identity in the world. This pan-Arab identity, often mocked for its political weakness and inconsistency, is still real enough that it often saps the "national" legitimacy of existing Arab states that operate within fairly arbitrary international borders drawn across very uncertain "ethnic" lines. Some 60 or 70 years after independence most Arab countries have by now achieved a "national" profile or personality of sorts, based on traditional regionalism, political attitudes, folk culture, historical memory, and even stereotyping—the rich Saudi, the mercantile Syrian, the hot-headed Iraqi. But the nation-building process is incomplete, slanted, and has been achieved at the cost of suppressing diversity in order to strengthen the culture of the ruling authorities. Partly to avoid the pitfalls of attempting to build an unconvincing national identity, some Arab countries opted to reinforce supranationalism, pan-Arabism, at the expense of local character. Arab ideologues looked to the greater Arab nation for terms of self-definition, stressing Arab ethnicity, a shared Arab history and culture. Gamal Abdul Nasser's pan-Arab clarion was one such attempt. Ba'thism, too, was in part another attempt (interestingly, conceived by a Christian, an 'Alawite and a Sunni) to reconcile the elements that made up the nations of the Arab region by proclaiming an all-embracing pan-Arabist ideology, which, while strictly secular, nevertheless recognized Islam as the culture, if not necessarily the religion, of all Arabs, including Christians and those of other smaller faiths. Ba'thism promoted an idealized regionwide identity at the expense of local, state-centered identities, which presented thornier and more threatening challenges to the already weak state. Although pan-Arabism periodically served as a useful platform to legitimize many Arab regimes, it remained abstract and divorced from the realities and problems of heterogeneous populations. It also implicitly endorsed the culture, history, and political power that belonged to the Sunni majority (or a portion thereof), demanding a submergence of differences and an assimilation into the superstructure.

Though ostensibly inclusive, pan-Arab ideology was in fact used by governments to perpetuate the hegemony of different forms of oligarchy. Many among the Shi'a, and Arabs of other religious persuasions, accepted the ideology at face value, also seeing in it a way out of narrow identity politics. However, pan-Arabism left many issues unresolved. Though propounding inclusiveness, it was not able to synthesize the many strands of Arab culture and history into a representative compound. On the most obvious level, it did not take into account the fact that the Arab world contains many ethnic minorities, including Copts, Kurds, Persians, Turks, Circassians, and Berbers. The view of Arab and Muslim history from the Shi'a perspective was problematic and hence ignored, with the result that the dynastic period was extolled as the golden era of Arabism, whereas in the eyes of the Shi'a it is seen as a betrayal and corruption of Islamic polity.

Further, in propounding its abstract generalizations, pan-Arabism ignored the social and historical realities on the ground in each country. In declaring Islam the overriding cultural stamp of Arabs, it implicitly endorsed the Islam of the majority of Arabs, Sunnism. It also endorsed Arab history in the form of the 'Umayyad and 'Abbasid (Sunni) dynasties and ignored the more contentious Shi'a component of Arab history. Sunni history almost by definition *is* the history of vanquishing Shi'ism, among other things. Thus Arab nationalism established an official historical text that deleted much that was valuable to the Shi'a and potentially even to Islam. Most damaging, Ba'thism, for all its revolutionary rhetoric, ultimately failed to change the prevailing political culture to make it more inclusive of minority groups or more representational of the population as a whole.

The claim of nonsectarianism advanced by all Arab governments should theoretically have led to equal economic and professional opportunity for the Shi'a, allowing them to integrate fully into the political and economic structure of the state. In practice, however, equality never materialized, and the political order failed to provide for equitable participation and a fair share of economic benefits. The Shi'a remained at the political margins, with restricted access to senior positions in government posts and "sensitive" areas of the state that held the strings of power and finance. Arab nationalism, as it is practiced, has come to be seen by some Shi'a as a state alibi providing deniability for discrimination in the very name of national unity. More grotesquely, any call by the Shi'a for democratization is viewed by the state, and by many Sunnis, as nothing more than a "Shi'ite agenda" for increased Shi'ite influence and possibly hegemony over the Sunnis. Yet, experience has shown the Shi'a that if they acquiesce and accept the status quo without protest, discrimination at any level that the state believes desirable is certain to continue. The search for effective means of overcoming this impasse shapes much of Shi'ite debate and is the source of much division.

Loyalty

The most basic charge leveled against the Shi'a by modern Arab states is the question of their "loyalty." This issue encapsulates more than any other the question of integration versus alienation of the Shi'a in relation to Sunni Arab society. It also raises a critical question about the nature of the relationship between state and society in the Middle East: just what are we talking about—loyalty to whom or what, and on what grounds?

Distrust between the Shi'a and the state is a perennial problem. As we have seen, from the very start the Shi'a have regarded the state as usurped by power and realpolitik, and as not in conformity with their own emphasis upon moral legitimacy and bloodline descent from the Prophet, while the state saw Shi'ism as a magnet for dissent. Doubts about Shi'ite loyalty have intensified with the formation of modern Arab states—not surprisingly creating a self-fulfilling prophesy. In the eyes of absolutist rulers, loyalty is perceived as a one-way street—something given unconditionally by subjects to the ruler. Yet in modern social orders, loyalty is not an absolute and involves a two-way set of obligations: if citizens are expected to owe allegiance, the ruler has an obligation to respond to people's needs and wishes. In the West these ideas go back to concepts of a "social contract" between people and their government and are further amplified in documents such as the American Declaration of Independence, in which citizens' right to revolt is expressly established.

But the concept of a contract is not alien to Islam either.[2] The principle of *bay'a* is rooted in Islamic thinking about governance and the relationship between ruler and ruled. Although the term is commonly translated as "an oath of allegiance," the root of the Arabic word is *baya*, meaning to trade, barter, buy and sell. Bay'a, as defined by Bernard Lewis, is "a contractual agreement between ruler and ruled by which both sides undertake certain obligations toward one another—or, as we might say, a covenant" that serves to "validate" authority.[3] However, these Muslim concepts are not sufficiently explored and developed in Islamic political theory to a point at which they can embrace the full panoply of modern content. On the contrary, the term bay'a especially has been degraded to mean no more than a public show of endorsement through an oath of allegiance, and it has been thus abused by modern ruler such as Saddam Hussein, who stages periodic bay'a ceremonies in Iraqi cities to validate his rule. But the fact remains that the notion of a "covenant" has a seed and a history in Islam that Muslims are beginning to refer to in questioning the legitimacy of contemporary rulers and their demand for blind loyalty.

In most states where the Shi'a live there is no declared covenant or contract under which the government is answerable to the ruled for a set of recognized obligations. The absence of a contract is hardly restricted to the Shi'ite population—indeed in most countries in the Middle East it is the majority Sunni population that is now questioning the legitimacy of government without a social contract and without answerability. However, for historical and political reasons the Shi'a suffer more under this type of arbitrary rule than do Sunni Muslims. The government assumes that the Shi'a, by doctrinal belief and presumed foreign allegiance, are intrinsically disloyal, and that the state must be protected from them. In response to these charges, the Shi'ite communities contend that the question of loyalty turns in a vicious circle: because they are assumed to be disloyal, the state excludes them and undermines their interests, thereby engendering Shi'ite discontent and possible disloyalty.

The condition of "outsider" that the Shi'a acquired was complicated by the fact that Shi'ism attracted Persians and some Turks early on in Islamic history when Arab conquerors—in the name of political power and not Islam—tended to view non-Arabs as second-class Muslims. While orthodox Islam would emphatically reject any such idea, the ground reality tended to push many non-Arabs into rivalry with the Arabs in a struggle for political and cultural supremacy. In the eighth and ninth centuries Shi'ism received support from the *mawali*,[4] the non-Arab converts to Islam, who hoped to improve their lot in the predominantly Arab order. The sympathy of the mawali toward Shi'ism marked it with an indelible stamp of foreign clientism. In the twentieth century, this stigmatization of Shi'ism as alien to Arabism was revived indirectly by linking it to the concept of *shu'ubiyya* (anti-Arabness) a name from the medieval period attached to non-Arab, especially Persian, scholars and literati.[5] The shu'ubis are accused of being anti-Arab, of denigrating and undermining Arab civilization and achievement and elevating the cultures of rival ethnic groups within Islam, specifically the Persian. Shu'ubiyya in the twentieth century was also associated with communism as a foreign and anti-Arab force. The triangular negative linkage of anti-Arabism, communism, and Shi'ism *(shu'ubiyya, shiyu'iyya, tashayyu')* became a standard political adage in Iraq.

Three factors underpin state worries about Shi'ite disloyalty or divided loyalty. The first is the presence of relatively large numbers of Shi'a of Persian descent, the 'Ajam, in Arab Gulf states, who settled as clerics and students of theology in the holy cities of Iraq, or as traders in Bahrain, Kuwait, and the UAE. These Persian immigrants acquired citizenship in the host countries, prospered, and achieved prominence, whether as members of the theological establishment or as merchant families. Their integration within Shi'ite Arab communities varies from country to country, being highest in the Iraqi shrine cities. Intermingling of Persians and Arabs through marriage, mixed neighborhoods, and business partnerships is common throughout the region and depends principally on economic and social status. The settled 'Ajam maintain family, trade, or religious relations with Iran that have on the whole remained uninterrupted by changes of government or revolution in Iran. Traditionally, the Arabized Persians have stayed out of politics; in Kuwait, Bahrain, and the UAE the evidence suggests that they court the favor and protection of the state, and their trading interests favor a stable status quo.

More worrisome for Arab governments is the gradual decline of the Iraqi holy Shi'ite cities and the consequent rise of the shrine cities in Iran. The political turmoil ushered in by the revolution of 1958 in Iraq, followed by the encroachment of the Ba'thist state after 1968 upon religious institutions, undermined the preeminence of Najaf and Karbala as centers of Shi'ite scholarship and theological training and as magnets for pilgrimage. The nationalization of the *awqaf,* or religious endowments of the Shi'a, impoverished the clergy in Iraq, whose institutions and foundations depended on funds from substantial endowments to subsidize indigent students of theology. The decline of Najaf and Karbala from the late fifties on, directly attributable to oppressiveness of Ba'thi policies, gave an opportunity to Qom and Mashhad in Iran to gather enhanced prestige and influence. Increasingly, the spiritual guides of the Shi'a, the maraji', tended to be either Iranians or Arabs almost compelled by circumstances to take refuge in Iran. Progressively, Shi'ite students of theology from the Arab world therefore went to study with the 'ulama in Iran rather than those remaining in Iraq, expanding and deepening the ties that the Shi'ite communities of the Arab world already had with Iran.

Arab states are also concerned about the spiritual leadership of the Shi'a, represented by the maraji', or religious mentors. In the modern era, most maraji' have been either Iranian, or Arabized Iranians living in Arab countries, usually Iraq, until forced to flee. The decline of the shrine cities and religious institutions in Iraq only intensified this imbalance, and progressively most Arab Shi'a looked to 'ulama in Iranian cities for theological guidance. A notable exception to the Iranian dominance was Grand Ayatollah Abu'l Qasim Al-Khu'i (Khoei), until his death in 1993 the leading marji', who was of Iranian origin but continued to live in Najaf.

The close connections that Arab Shi'a have with Iran, and the fact that Iran, a non-Arab state in the region, is the standard bearer of Shi'ism, causes deep anxiety for Arab governments. For centuries Iran was seen as the traditional political, military, and cultural rival of the Sunni world, first in its relations with the Ottoman empire and later vis-à-vis the newly independent countries on the Gulf coast. Its size, history and nationalist aspirations are seen by Arabs as a permanent latent threat to the Arab world. In strategic terms, the Arab states are painfully conscious of the potential power of Iran to exert its influence or spread its hegemony across the Gulf region (see Chapter 4). The Shi'ite population plays a central role in these fears, warily watched as a possible fifth column for the Iranian state in Arab society. Both historical memory of shu'ubiyya and modern experience of Shi'ite enthusiasm among at least some of the population for the Iranian revolution feed into these fears.

In fact, such fears are not entirely baseless. In Shi'ism, clerics are not only spiritual guides who advise exclusively on matters of doctrine. The role of the 'ulama extends far beyond these classic responsibilities and, in principle, can encompass the whole life of an individual: his private life, personal conduct, public and private relationships, and his entire worldview. It is reasonable to expect the 'ulama to have potentially major influence over students on political and social issues. Under the circumstances, the distrust of the Shi'a in Arab states was only intensified by the actual or perceived sway that Iranian 'ulama have over the Shi'ite population.

Perceptions of Shi'ite loyalty are directly affected in more recent times by external conflicts that impact upon local Shi'a. The nature of relations between Iran and Iraq represent the most forceful case in point. With broad tensions existing between the two that degenerated into eight years of war in the 1980s, the Shi'a were caught in the middle. In the war for Kuwait, the Shi'a of Kuwait were brought directly into conflict with an Iraqi army, a majority of whose enlisted troops are Shi'a. In both cases the regimes in question sought to use the Shi'a as fifth columns in the other country and failed as the Shi'a acquitted themselves well by demonstrating overall loyalty to the state in which they resided. Considerable communitarian tensions were nonetheless present at various times. In short, Shi'ite communities are inevitably domestically affected to some degree by the state of relations between their state and other states, much as a Moroccan Jew is affected by war between Egypt and Israel, or an American Muslim in the eyes of the FBI or even of some Americans during the U.S. war with Iraq.

In a further example, Iran, as the major Shi'ite country of the world, as a matter of policy has shown an interest in Shi'ite communities abroad and has been willing to send representatives to them and to seek to assist and influence them. Arab Shi'ite communities, in the eyes of Iran—even under the Shah, although to a far lesser extent—were viewed by Tehran as "natural instrumentalities" for extension of Iranian influence into the Arab world (see Chapter Four).

Lastly, Shi'ite communities with genuine grievances are often sought out by enemies of the state in which they reside to provide underground opposition. Or, radical leaders of the oppressed Shi'ite communities are tempted to deal with external states or Shi'ite organizations that might be in a position to assist them in their struggle for greater rights within their own state. Thus some elements of the leadership of the Saudi or Bahraini Shi'a, for example, may look to the benefits they might gain from ties with radical Shi'ite organizations in Lebanon such as Hizballah, or for certain kinds of support from Iran. In their struggle to change the regime of Saddam Hussein, a sizeable number of Iraqi Shi'a have been willing to utilize Iranian support such as a base, a place of refuge, and diplomatic support in what is virtually all-out war between the Shi'a and Saddam's regime.

These factors can also spark counterreactions on the part of Shi'a, forcing them into what is almost an unnatural withdrawal from politics. Precisely because the loyalty of the Shi'a to the regimes and societies in which they live is sometimes suspect—especially when regimes seek to marginalize or exclude them—Shi'a often seek to avoid identification with any broader

Shi'ite movements or Shi'ite communities in other states. Shi'a show nervousness about activities or even expression of attitudes that might suggest that they are "internationalist" in outlook, or "Shi'ite-oriented" in their political views. Even in our interviews, numbers of Shi'a insisted they had "no interest" in the Shi'a of other countries. While that may be true to some extent, we also sensed a strong desire on the part of such interviewees to be seen as modern and nonsectarian in outlook, and to say nothing that would even seem to compromise their loyalty, even when concerns for "pan-Shi'ite" issues might manifest themselves in other ways. Even "secular" Shi'a admitted it would be unnatural not to have some interest in the welfare of other Shi'ite communities, even if only on a cultural or humanitarian basis. But because of the penalties often imposed by authoritarian regimes on Shi'ite communities for any signs of potential disloyalty, many Shi'a will studiously avoid involvement in Shi'ite affairs outside their country.

The Shi'ite Concept of Legitimacy

It is revealing to trace the political and psychological outlook of the early history of Shi'ism, particularly as regards the state. A number of political doctrines placed the Shi'a historically in a difficult position vis-à-vis the state. Shi'ism arose as a political movement in support of Imam 'Ali, the Prophet's cousin and son-in-law. The partisans of 'Ali (the literal meaning of *Shi'a*) regarded him as the rightful successor to the Prophet Muhammad in leadership of the umma, the community of believers, and believed that the Prophet had designated him, or at least favored him, for leadership. Indeed there are strong indicators that such was probably the case, based on 'Ali's very early conversion to the Prophet's message, his long and outspoken loyalty and defense of the Prophet, and his personal piety and wisdom.

But 'Ali was opposed by powerful older candidates from the tribe of Quraysh, who were selected through a consensus of community elders, and was thrice denied the caliphate until 24 years after the Prophet's death. As Shi'ite doctrine was codified over time, the Shi'a came to believe that certain descendants of 'Ali (in the Prophet's bloodline) were endowed with divine grace and were the legitimate spiritual and temporal leaders (Imams) of the Muslims, and who alone could rule in righteousness (*'adl*) and thwart injustice (*dhulm*). Unlike the method of consensual succession that followed immediately after the death of the Prophet, the Shi'a believed that the leadership of the umma should pass down to the descendents of the Prophet through specific designation. In the eyes of the Shi'a, then, the 'Umayyad and subsequent caliphs were usurpers with no legitimacy to rule; as a corollary, the loyalty of the Shi'a to the caliphs was questionable.[6]

Indeed, after Imam Husayn, none of the subsequent Imams even sought to claim the caliphate. During the 'Umayyad period and early 'Abbasid rule, the Shi'a mounted a number of weak challenges to the ruling powers with unsuccessful, and at times disastrous, results, most notably in 680 when the third Imam, al-Husayn, and his kinsmen were killed in an uneven battle in Karbala, Iraq. The Shi'a were also severely disappointed in the 'Abbasids, whose successful revolt against the 'Ummayyads they had supported in the expectation that the new caliphate would at last revert to a rightful Imam. Shi'ite rebellions continued intermittently but without much success well into the 'Abbasid period. The label Rafidha (Rejecters)[7] originated in the 'Abbasid era, indicating continued Shi'ite defiance of the legitimacy of government and probably continued persecution. The Shi'a believe that several more Imams after al-Husayn were poisoned by 'Umayyad and 'Abbasid caliphs.

Repeated defeats and disappointments changed the complexion of Shi'ism in the late ninth century. The Imams themselves devoted their lives to the study of theology and jurisprudence and to the spiritual guidance of the community, taking no part in the sporadic and ill-fated revolts carried out by Shi'a groups during the 'Umayyad and 'Abbasid eras. Shi'ite belief in the occultation (the going into hiding, or *ghayba*) of the twelfth Imam, al-Mahdi al-Muntadhar ("the awaited divinely guided one") in 874 without leaving an heir marked a watershed for Shi'ism, both in theological and political terms, closing the canon of recognized Imamate teachings that Shi'ism adopted to supplement the Qur'an and the teachings of the Prophet.

The occultation of the twelfth Imam had political implications as well. The Shi'a believe that the only legitimate leader of the Muslim community was a designated Imam, who combined within his charismatic nature both spiritual and temporal power. Even though most of the Imams had not sought such power, during their lifetime or retrospectively they were regarded as the only true successors to Muhammad. The occultation meant that the Shi'a had no more candidates with whom to contest the caliphate. The twelfth Imam, who had never died, would reveal himself in the fullness of time to rule in righteousness and combat evil. Only when the twelfth Imam revealed himself again to the faithful would there be a lawful, divinely guided leader who could command the loyalty of the faithful. Consequently, the act of revolt was deemed fruitless until the ultimate return of al-Mahdi. In principle at least, the purist Shi'i would find it hard to grant true legitimacy to any government that precedes the reappearance of al-Mahdi. This political resignation bred of defeat induced the Shi'a to withdraw into their own communities and to dedicate themselves to developing their theology and canon and elaborating their history and rituals. With few and brief exceptions, the prevailing political regimes in the Muslim world were "accepted de facto but not de jure"[8] by the Shi'a.

Finally, long-standing Shi'ite debate over what constitutes the legitimacy of the state raises other questions in Shi'ite minds. Because of the dominance of injustice in the world, Shi'a may be more psychologically predisposed in some sense to expect that governance will be unjust and oppressive. Unfortunately, large numbers of regimes in the Middle East often fulfill this expectation. Shi'a are thus theologically more readily equipped to distance themselves from unjust or bad governance, or possibly even to attempt to do something about it. Sunni jurisprudence, having over the centuries developed under the wing of the state, or even as a pillar of the state, is more inclined to the conservative view that in nearly every case *fitna* (chaos) is worse than oppression. Such an interpretation, long encouraged by the state even if by no means fully accepted by all Sunnis, is decidedly useful to existing regimes that wish to maintain the status quo and crush opposition.

Indeed, in a strange kind of role reversal, contemporary Sunni Islamist movements have actually now moved toward a more "Shi'ite" view of the unjust state: acceptance of the principle that unjust governance in Islam not only should not be tolerated as "better than chaos," but in fact positively requires the believer to resist it. The theology of these Sunni Islamist groups is often accused of being "Shi'ite" by authoritarian regimes who feel their legitimacy thus threatened. In short, this instinctive view of Shi'ism on the part of Sunni power helps raise intrinsic doubts in the minds of regimes about the inner loyalty of their Shi'ite subjects to the regime.

Among many Shi'a today a religious commitment to Shi'ism in purely a theological sense—apart from its social and communitarian aspects—is still quite strong. During interviews with us, some Shi'ite scholars spoke of Shi'ism as the "only real Islam"; in this sense they spoke of Shi'ism as one day destined to achieve a global acceptance because of the purity of its message. In their view the Sunnis have corrupted Islam by injecting it into state politics and requiring it to support the state, thus sullying it with power politics. They continue to see Shi'ism, however, as an abiding body of religious ideals and a pure doctrine constantly to be aspired to, as opposed to Sunni Islam that, under pliant Sunni clerics, long ago became a debased state ideology.

Factors of Alienation

The alienation of the Shi'a arises from both Sunni societal attitudes and state policies—not declaratory policies, but from attitudes that are mostly undeclared but nonetheless implemented, operating by tacit consensus of the ruling oligarchies. The acuteness of Shi'ite alienation varies considerably from one country to another, depending on the openness and flexibility of the political structure. But on both counts, the Shi'a as a whole feel discriminated against socially, disenfranchised politically, and they are always made aware of their distinctiveness. The Shi'a tend to see a continuous thread of unjust government beginning at least with the usurpation of the caliphate and extending into twentieth-century colonialism that favored the Sunnis and guaranteed their hegemony in the Arab world (except in Syria, where the French favored the minority 'Alawis, a highly heterodox form of Shi'ism, who rule there until this day).

The dominant position of Sunnis in public life, even in countries in which the Shi'a are a majority, was fortified by the legacy of both Ottoman and Western colonial rule—both of which relied heavily on a local Sunni civil service that tended to perpetuate its own interests—and by the high degree of state centralization practiced by Arab governments after independence. But Sunnis, and many Shi'a as well, blame the Shi'ite community for its insularity and refusal to change their conservative ways. Nonetheless, subsequent Sunni governments had precious little interest in improving the economic and social status of the Shi'a or in improving their opportunities politically and professionally. Most governments were happy to keep the Shi'a marginalized and isolated.

As the countries of the Arab world moved toward independence in the early decades of this century, there had in fact been openings for the Shi'a to play a role in nation building, particularly in Iraq, Bahrain, and Lebanon. The first and most noteworthy of their attempts came in Iraq in 1920 when Shi'ite clerics and lay notables took a leading part alongside Sunnis in a revolt against British rule. The "revolution" of 1920 aborted, and the Iraqi Shi'a fell back into a quiescent backwater, as the British confirmed their reliance on a corps of Sunni ex-officers of the collapsed Ottoman empire. With a few exceptions, those Shi'a who subsequently engaged in political life did so most frequently in the framework of banned leftist or communist organizations, and to a lesser extent in the Ba'th party when it was still an underground organization.

Even as government bureaucracies in the region expanded, they did not encourage the recruitment and promotion of Shi'a into the government sector, and their employment in the civil service and at lower levels of the bureaucracy remained unrepresentative of their numbers aside from scattered instances of tokenism. Conversely, in the early decades of state formation in the Arab world, Shi'ite communities themselves, prompted by a conservative and wary clergy, distrusted government and held back from participation, even in accessible fields. Typically today, in the "sensitive" areas of the military, security, and police organizations, Shi'ite presence is still rudimentary in all countries of the region. It would be hard to point to any specific legislation, decree, or documented decision barring Shi'a from jobs; the consensus operates by implicit understanding and tacit enforcement. Further, the system of patronage, kinship, and social networking that is prevalent in the Middle East means that even where there are no restrictions on the employment of Shi'a, jobs are not available to them because they do not have the social connections necessary to obtain them.

Shi'ite Political Dissent

It is natural to think of Shi'ite political dissent as the product of Shi'ite Islamist movements. Yet this is an oversimplification, as Shi'ite dissent was voiced intermittently for decades before the formation of Shi'ite Islamist parties, through a variety of channels and by multiple means. It is equally customary to think of Shi'ite activism as inspired and prompted by the Iranian revolution, yet this too, is a simplification of reality. The burgeoning of Shi'ism in modern times as a political identity in the Arab world predates the Iranian revolution by at least a decade and can be more accurately pegged to the establishment of the Da'wa party in Iraq in the late 1960s or even as early as the late 1950s.

Modern Shi'ite protests against the policies of ruling authorities date back to the beginning of the century. In Saudi Arabia, for example, when King Ibn Sa'ud occupied al-Qatif, the center of the Shi'ite region, a Saudi cleric, 'Allam Hasan 'Ali al-Badr, called on the people to resist Wahhabi forces. The lay notables, however, deemed resistance impossible. In light of their unhappy experiences with periods of Wahhabi occupation in the nineteenth century, the Shi'a capitulated on the basis of an agreement with King Ibn Sa'ud that preserved their religious and social rights.[9] In the early 1920s, the Shi'a in Bahrain repeatedly appealed to the British for redress from mistreatment by the ruling al-Khalifa family, itself protected by the British. Following two years of Shi'ite protests, clashes with the police, and intercommunal strife in 1953 and 1954, the Bahraini Shi'a signed several petitions calling for reforms, equal legal rights, and a representative assembly.[10] In Iraq both the clerical establishment and the secular Shi'ite leadership were active in championing equality for the Shi'a. In 1935, the Iraqi army had to put down a rebellion by Shi'ite tribal chiefs, and shortly thereafter a charter was signed by Shi'a notables in Najaf decrying the "policy of sectarianism," discrimination, and the absence of Shi'a appointees in the civil service, and asking for justice in taxation and military service.[11]

More direct Shi'ite political protest in Arab countries occurred mid-century within the framework of leftist movements, including the Communist party and unauthorized labor unions. Membership in the leftist organizations during the period was so heavily Shi'ite that one author on the period describes the Communist party in Iraq as the only political party that represented the Shi'a. Labor unrest, spearheaded by the Shi'a, broke out in

Bahrain, Saudi Arabia, and Iraq in the 1950s and extended to demands for representation, equality, and a nationalist agenda in government. Although the 'ulama during this period avoided political controversy, they continued to defend religious freedoms, the independence of religious institutions, and the welfare of the community.

A qualitative change in Shi'ite dissent occurred with the formation of the Hizb al-Da'wa al-Islamiyya (the Islamic Call party of Iraq), which formally declared its existence in 1967 but is said to have existed in an embryonic form since 1958. The Da'wa was materially influenced by the ideas of the Sunni Muslim Brotherhood in Egypt and its principal ideologue, Hasan al-Banna, and advocated Islamic regeneration and just governance.[12] However, the party appealed only to young Iraqi Shi'a and recruited primarily among the Shi'ite middle and lower-middle classes—precisely where the communists had their traditional base of support. The Da'wa made several innovations in Shi'ite activism. It was the first Shi'ite political organization that represented the Shi'a in an explicitly Islamic format, rather than as a nonreligious movement with a broad reformist agenda. Unlike previous loose movements, it was organized along strict party lines that adopted the Marxist-Leninist model. The party functioned in secrecy, with small cells, anonymity, and a strict hierarchy. Furthermore, the party actively sought the support of the senior clergy and obtained the backing of the gifted and charismatic Muhammad Baqir al-Sadr, as well as Mahdi al-Hakim, the son of the Ayatollah Muhsin al-Hakim. It was a revolutionary movement, operating entirely outside the state system and adopting overtly confrontational tactics against the regime. Clashes became inevitable, and following a particularly brutal crackdown by the government during the 'Ashura celebrations of 1977, the party launched armed resistance and acts of sabotage against the Iraqi government.

Da'wa party members and suspected sympathizers were severely persecuted in Iraq throughout the 1970s, and Muhammad Baqir al-Sadr, along with his activist sister, was executed by Saddam Hussein in April 1980, possibly in anticipation of the Iran-Iraq war. But by then the Da'wa had already established roots in Gulf countries, especially Kuwait, in Lebanon, and in revolutionary Iran, through immigration and support from a network of like-minded lay activists and clerics, at least some of whom were tied to Da'wa members by bonds of kinship.[13] In the Arab world Da'wa was instrumental in organizing Shi'ite dissent and assisted in the creation of Hizballah in Lebanon. Certainly acts of Shi'ite terrorism in Kuwait in the 1980s were attributed to the Da'wa and gave rise in turn to a series of airline hijackings by Lebanese Da'wa/Hizballah operatives. In fact, the Da'wa provided the earliest example of a Shi'ite regional network that was later emulated by Hizballah in the late eighties and early nineties.

It was only well after this deep independent rooting in Iraqi politics that the Da'wa began to come under Iranian influence. That the Da'wa party should come under the sway of Iran probably became virtually inevitable after it was heavily repressed and forced to take its major organizational leadership out of Iraq, while Iran had become one of the few safe havens the party could find. It was also inevitable under these conditions that the party would begin to act in the early eighties as an instrument of Iranian policy. However, it is essential to bear in mind that the Da'wa was an entirely home-grown movement, equipped with a formidable and independent intellectual vision of Islam and the state that was quite contrary to the Khomeini vision of clerical rule. It was born out of conditions of repression and alienation in Iraq deemed intolerable and hopeless by many young educated Shi'a. Further, the escalation in violence was a consequence of ruthless persecution by the Iraqi Ba'thist regime, which saw the Da'wa as the single greatest threat to its existence and sought its eradication.

Equally, in Lebanon, the emergence of Harakat Amal (Hope Movement), followed later by the establishment of the more radical Hizballah, was a product of the Lebanese war and the internecine sectarian fault lines that the war rapidly demarcated. The role of Iranian/Lebanese cleric Musa al-Sadr was the driving force behind the galvanizing of Amal, but such organizational activity came under the Shah and not the Islamic Republic. Furthermore, the ingredients for Shi'ite dissent in Lebanon in terms of disenfranchisement and discrimination were amply present prior to the Lebanese civil war and the Iranian revolution, although the persecution that was the hallmark of the Iraqi state was absent in Lebanon. But when Musa al-Sadr mobilized the Shi'a his goals were integration and building the capabilities of the community from within. The Lebanese war rendered such lofty aspirations irrelevant, and a new framework called for more radical and violent methods.

Clearly, the revolution in Iran, as well as its long war with Iraq, was a constant force that influenced the domestically-generated Arab Shi'ite struggle in the 1980s. At an obvious level, it lent momentum to Arab Shi'ite movements by giving them moral, rhetorical, and material support. More profoundly, it raised the banner of Shi'ite pride and signaled to the Shi'a that change is possible, that there can be an end to injustice, and that an oppressed group can elevate and liberate itself. The Iranian revolution did more: it highlighted the religious aspect of revolution and struggle and focused upon the role of the Shi'ite clergy.

But the violent phase had now run its course. The fading of revolutionary zeal in Iran, the end of the Iran-Iraq war, and the entry of Hizballah into mainstream Lebanese politics all served to modify Shi'ite strategies in the direction of greater emphasis on public and international recognition of their predicament. The Shi'ite struggle now focuses as much on the international media and international organizations as it does on the streets of Bahrain or Baghdad. Only in Lebanon has violent Shi'ite engagement led to material political benefit for the Shi'a. In Kuwait, where the Shi'a now enjoy a good level of integration and civil rights, the improvement came about through an increase in democratization and pluralism, spurred by the end of the Gulf war. In Bahrain, Shi'ite dissent has led to increasing government repression and political deadlock. In Saudi Arabia, a delicate truce has been declared between the state and the Shi'a. In Iraq, where the stakes are high not only for Iraqi Shi'a but for the entire region, Shi'ite armed opposition continues. Shi'ite anger is at explosive levels and there is no prospect of any negotiated agreements that might defuse the situation. But when the regime of Saddam Hussein ends, Iraqi Shi'a will assuredly not be content with half-measures and palliatives.

Conclusion

In the final analysis, it is not the Shi'a alone, but the dynamic between the state and the Shi'a that will determine how inevitable change will occur. A basic affliction of the Arab State (and elsewhere in the developing world) is its usurpation of the claim to represent and embody the "people" and the "nation." When the state is the sole vehicle of the "nation," then maintenance of the state and its usurpers becomes the sole measure of loyalty; reform that threatens the state's power and its custodians becomes treasonous. This broader problem lies behind all Arab politics and is a direct source of the problem for the Shi'a, among others.

In assessing future relations between the Shi'a and the state we posit that, first, change will occur since the status quo is neither just, tenable, nor acceptable to the Shi'a (or to most of the population). Second, democratization will inevitably bring major shifts in political and social power in states where the Shi'a represent the marginalized majority, no matter how gradually and sensitively the transition occurs. Third, the Shi'ite goal of liberalization of the state is not necessarily distinct from the goals of Sunni reformers, liberals, and democrats, who also threaten existing established and entrenched Sunni political elites. Thus democratization of any kind will bring major changes in the social order, even among Sunnis. Fourth, the Shi'ite struggle against the state, whether peaceful, democratic, or violent, is not necessarily directed against the broader population of the country itself, since the state cannot be said to represent "the people" or "the country."

Regimes that do not perceive the Shi'a as a vital threat to the established order may opt for a gradual process of integration that coincides with greater pluralism and democratization of the system as a whole, as well as a more inclusive definition of citizenship and loyalty. In states where the Shi'a are the majority (or, as in Saudi Arabia, where out of desperation they harbor secessionist tendencies) the dynamic will be fraught with far greater problems. If the (nonrepresentative) state views its relations with the Shi'a as an existential struggle for its very survival, it will certainly continue aggressive measures to eliminate the perceived threat, raising the level of violence between the state and the Shi'a and guaranteeing a destabilized order. Definitions of citizenship and loyalty will then narrow to the point at which only loyalty to the beleaguered and unrepresentative regime becomes the sole acceptable touchstone of "loyalty" and even real "citizenship." Under such conditions, it is not only the Shi'a who become losers, but the entire population that watches the further narrowing of its already limited freedoms and rights in the name of the preservation of "the state."

How closely will the Sunnis identify with the existing state, however oppressive? How successfully can the state manipulate fear of change among Sunnis, as in Bahrain and Iraq, in order to perpetuate despotic and bad governance? To what extent can the state compel Sunnis to believe that their interests coincide with the state, however unjust and bad? What are the relative trade-offs for the Sunnis in choosing between the repressive state that maintains the status quo, and the inevitable social shifts that will emerge from liberalization? These are the key questions that will determine future relations between the Shi'a and the state.

CHAPTER THREE

Shi'ite Demands
and Strategies

The basic political goals of most of the Arab Shi'ite community include few demands specific only to the Shi'ite community. On the contrary, most of what the political and social gains the Shi'a seek are compatible with what most other citizens of the Arab world want. Some Shi'a may aspire to a Shi'ite Islamic state, but that is not the dominant aspiration, any more than a Sunni Islamic state is the dominant goal among Sunnis. Indeed, despite our earlier discussion of theological differences between Shi'a and Sunnis, religion itself does not really lie at the heart of those differences. Historically, such differences have emerged over differing concepts of the state, and from Shi'ite alienation from the Sunni state, whose leaders have abandoned principle and morality for realpolitik goals. In the contemporary Arab world what matters most to the Shi'a is equality. While equality should seem reasonable to all as a goal, the quest to establish more equal relationships in the presently skewed political order inevitably creates new winners and losers, with politically volatile results.

Furthermore, the conditions the Shi'a encounter vary considerably within the Arab world, thus their political goals, demands, and strategies correspondingly vary. But in every case the Shi'a are fighting against "minority status" and the second-class citizenship that accompanies it—especially where they themselves actually constitute the majority. Certain common goals, therefore, exist among all Shi'a, although common goals do not suggest a common program or common effort for alleviation of these problems. The need for political and social liberalization and democratization are the single most commonly shared goals from which all Shi'a would stand to benefit. Sunnis across Arab society would themselves benefit from increased political liberalization, but the gains would be less dramatic for them than for the Shi'a, and liberalization would involve potential losses for the Sunnis as well, at least for entrenched ruling elites. But recognition of the broad, nonexclusivistic nature of Shi'ite goals is very important to understanding what is sometimes referred to slightingly as the "Shi'ite agenda."

What are the key demands of the Shi'ite community and how are they expressed?

Equal Rights of Citizenship. The attainment of equal civil rights—equality of citizenship on a par with all other citizens of the state—sums up the heart of Shi'ite goals within the state. In principle, the state has the power, and duty, to accord equal civil rights to its citizens, and in fact almost no state in the region withholds such rights from its Shi'a community on an official basis. Nonetheless, freedom of speech, of political or community organization, and equality before the law are more severely curtailed for the Shi'a than they are for the Sunnis. In some states (Iraq, Saudi Arabia, Bahrain) genuine political rights are enjoyed by none; the Shi'a therefore share equally in the absence of rights. But when the state grants few political rights to anyone, the possibilities for discrimination against the Shi'a, both formally and informally, are greatly enhanced. Thus even "equality of deprivation" bears down more heavily on the Shi'a community. Saudi Arabia presents a special case, since there the Shi'a are formally assigned a legal status inferior to that granted to the Sunnis: a Shi'ite may not testify in court against a Sunni, for example.

End to Discrimination. The call for an end to discrimination in one sense is the corollary of the quest for equal rights. Again, no state except for Saudi Arabia discriminates officially in any arena against the Shi'a. But given the hidden nature—nonformal, noncodified nature of discrimination against the Shi'a in most states, the search for an end to discrimination is perhaps a more meaningful formulation than discussion of equal political rights. And on an informal basis nearly all states discriminate against the Shi'a in significant ways. Shi'a are viewed by the security services as "more suspect" or "less loyal" and therefore will be accorded special scrutiny, face a greater likelihood of arrest or abuse by police, and are less likely to be promoted to sensitive positions in government. "Glass ceilings" are the rule, not the exception, and universities favor Sunni student applicants over Shi'ite. Today it is Lebanon that probably enjoys the best record of treatment of Shi'a, followed by Kuwait. It is no accident that these two states are the only ones in this study with a modicum of functioning democracy.

Democratic reforms and protection of human rights. Democratic governance and the protection of human rights should, in theory, be an absolute good in the eyes of most people in the Arab world. Yet the issue is not so simple when problems of majority and minority status are taken into consideration.

In states where the Shi'a constitute a minority, democratic practice would offer them safeguards under a rule of law that is absent in authoritarian systems. There is the danger that if democracy is interpreted narrowly as blunt majority rule, Shi'ite minorities can be endangered in the event of a substantial rise in Sunni fundamentalism hostile to Shi'ism. But while the "tyranny of the majority" represents a potential danger, in practice the institutionalization of democracy and constitutional rights benefits the Shi'a by offering avenues for redress of grievances not otherwise available under authoritarianism and gives assurance of personal security and equal opportunities.

In states where the Shi'a constitute the majority, democracy is an obvious Shi'ite goal directly benefiting their status in ways impossible under Sunni authoritarian orders. However, democracy under the Shi'a would lead to dramatic changes in the prevailing political order that would threaten the end of the Sunni monopoly on power. Democracy then becomes part of the "Shi'ite agenda" rather than an absolute good, perceived as little more than a vehicle for the Shi'a to attain power. Indeed, democracy could turn into a tool for the Shi'a to practice a tyranny of the majority and discriminate against the minority Sunnis, turning the entire process into a zero-sum game whereby the gains of the Shi'a will come only at the expense of the Sunnis. Political liberalization thus will need to be buttressed by a more comprehensive system of safeguards, including national "pacts" or political codes of conduct and constitutionally guaranteed checks and balances. Ultimately, democratic reform is the only sure method to redress long-standing imbalances and to end the dispossession of Shi'ite majorities in several states.

Since the Shi'a are among the main victims of the absence of human rights, they therefore strongly support the strengthening of human rights norms in their societies as of direct benefit to them. But how serious and abiding will the Shi'ite commitment to human rights be? Will they uphold full human rights for Sunni minorities at such time as Shi'ite majorities come to power in Bahrain or Iraq? That is a key concern of the Sunni minority in those states, a fear that is exploited both by Saddam Hussein and the al-Khalifas as a way to bolster their autocratic rule.

Minoritarian rights. While the Shi'a seek absolute equality of treatment on a par with Sunnis, they also seek specific freedoms and protection of their own freedom of cultural expression. Chief among these is religious freedom. Unlike equal voting rights, equality of religion implies freedom to behave differently than Sunnis in the public practice of religion, and the freedom to express publicly, in education, writing, and speech, religious beliefs that differ from those of the Sunni community. Shi'a want the right to propagate their own faith and culture without interference from the state, on whatever grounds. Yet in Saudi Arabia Shi'a are denied the right to teach Shi'ism in the schools and, more important, are usually proscribed from the public practice of their faith, especially religious processions. In Bahrain and Iraq, the practice of Shi'ism in public is limited by the government, which sees these public expressions as synonymous with antigovernment expression—which it often has become. Public expressions of faith such as 'Ashura processions are especially restricted, since they represent cultural and political expression unique to the Shi'a that can be interpreted as a threat to an oppressive state authority.

Some Sunnis are inclined to see these rights as "concessions" to a Shi'ite minority. What is required is a Sunni understanding that at stake is the equal right of all religious groups, minority or majority, to express their religious faith and culture (or ethnicity and language, under other circumstances). Therefore, for minorities to enjoy these same rights should not be viewed as a concession or special privilege at all, but as a mark of equality.

A second goal under minoritarian rights expressed by some Shi'a is regional autonomy. This goal is realistic only in those states large enough to have distinct regions, and in which there is a well-defined Shi'ite region, such as in southern Iraq, eastern Saudi Arabia, or southern Lebanon. Not all Shi'a concur on this goal, because it encourages isolationism and runs counter to the goal of integration at every level within the larger national body. But some Shi'a welcome the gain of additional political and cultural freedom under this kind of arrangement, especially where the centralized state has tended to deny them political and cultural rights in the past. Such regional autonomy could range from confederation or federation to more fluid forms of administrative autonomy to be worked out with the state. In a state such as Iraq, regional autonomy is probably required for all three major groups at a minimum—Kurds, Sunni Arabs, and Shi'ite Arabs—if the state is to survive as a unit.

To date, most Middle Eastern states have been notoriously hostile to concepts of federalism or even regional autonomy. Regimes regard relinquishing direct authority over any aspect of life as undercutting centralized state control and thus as a threat to the state itself. Even in Lebanon, where Shi'ite gains have been a product of decades of evolution and conflict, and where the central state is the weakest, the notion of administrative autonomies has not been considered as a serious option.

Political Sectarianism. A further special goal discussed by some Shi'a is the application of political sectarianism or even affirmative action to make up for past discrimination and inequality of opportunity. Where Shi'a have routinely been denied jobs in government or administration, and have suffered from inferior education or other inadequate investment in the infrastructure of Shi'ite regions, some Shi'a believe that programs of affirmative action should be granted to them to compensate for past shortcomings. The argument is that the state must take specific action to right the wrongs of the past, and to help the Shi'a attain a numerical presence within institutions, especially within the bureaucracy, that is roughly comparable to their demographic weight in the state. This goal is obviously controversial since the Sunnis will correspondingly lose presence as a result of any special privileges accorded to the Shi'a. Yet one hears this argument from Shi'a in Bahrain and Saudi Arabia in particular, especially with the example of Lebanon, where the logic of the Lebanese civil war has effectively forced the state to practice undeclared affirmative action.

Implicit in the concept of affirmative action are ideas of proportional representation, symbolized nowhere in the Muslim world as explicitly as in Lebanon. In Lebanon a system of proportional representation has been present since at least the end of World War II and the establishment of an independent Lebanese state. Known as political sectarianism *(al-ta'ifiyya al-siyasiyya)* the Lebanese system carefully accorded positions in government to the eight main religious groups in the country by prearrangement: the president was always to be Maronite Christian, the prime minister Sunni Muslim, the foreign minister Christian Orthodox, the speaker of the parliament Shi'ite, and so on. Parliamentary seats are divided according to proportional formulas. The system gradually extended into the government bureaucracy where senior positions were to be accorded proportionally by sectarian affiliation. In a state such as Lebanon the system was designed to establish and stabilize peaceful coexistence among the eight religious communities. The system worked fairly well until it came apart in the mid-seventies for two key reasons unrelated to the concept of the system itself, but rather arising from the implementation of the system. First, the demographic realities of Lebanon had shifted dramatically over the decades in favor of the Shi'a but were not officially acknowledged by the system, and the Shi'a remained the greatest object of social discrimination. Second, the system collapsed due to pressures of the Arab–Israeli conflict, which spilled over into Lebanon, especially with the arrival of massive numbers of Palestinian refugees who broke the traditional sectarian balance and stimulated the creation of sectarian militias for community self-defense.

The system of political confessionalism (sometimes referred to as "consociationalism") is regularly criticized by nearly all members of the Lebanese population at some point, often because of its patent absurdities—de facto separate hospitals, schools, even television stations for each sectarian community, for example. Yet when traditional power relationships—both political and economic—have been considerably unequal in the past, the system has served to provide a rough measure of "social justice" in a demonstrable way. While it is the exact antithesis of the American vision of a "color-blind" society, or meritocracy, the Lebanese system of proportional representation based on religious communities may have provided a crude but workable form of equal rights that may now prevent further sectarian clash. (Others might argue that only the Syrian presence in Lebanon has prevented the continuation of violent sectarian conflict and that such conflict might well return after an eventual pull-out of Syrian dominance in Lebanon.) Nonetheless, the system has been readjusted and reapplied since the Lebanese civil war in the eighties. While all acknowledge its shortcomings, it may be the best formula for now to maintain peace in a society that seeks to remain democratic and open rather than to create "stability" via authoritarian means.

The question then arises whether some form of proportional representation might not provide a formula for transition to a new order in a shattered state like Iraq, or a state under siege from a majority of its population like Bahrain. While far from ideal, it might at least serve to provide the minimal guarantees to all sects or groups within the society that their rights will be explicitly acknowledged and apportioned. Adopting this kind of system is seen as traumatic to some Sunnis in Iraq and Bahrain since proportional representation again involves a strategic shift of the main instruments of power away from the Sunni minority over to the majority Shi'a, regardless of whatever minority guarantees might be given to the Sunnis. Alternatively, proportional representation could serve as a transitional order until a new system of political democracy was stabilized. The problem of course is that proportionalism, once legally enshrined, is difficult to modify or remove since any change involves new winners and losers. Additionally, as Lebanon demonstrates, a system of proportional representation can create inward-looking, segregated communities within the larger society, and eventually breed adversarial relations. Nevertheless, given the severity of problems encountered in Iraq, Bahrain, and Saudi Arabia, the concept—perhaps amended in some form—is worthy of consideration. But there will be no consideration of it as long as the authoritarian regimes in those states find no incentive to change the system.

Secularism. Finally, many Shi'a believe that a secular state is an important goal for the Shi'ite community, especially where Shi'a are a minority. In many Muslim states (Turkey, Syria, Pakistan) the Shi'a (or 'Alawis) fear that it is Sunni fundamentalism that threatens to impose Sunni religious law and values upon the Shi'ite community—implicitly conferring preferential treatment on the Sunnis—resulting in a form of discrimination or second-class citizenship for the Shi'a. In Pakistan in particular this has been the chief cause of vicious Sunni–Shi'a violence. In Turkey, the Shi'a (or Alevis, who represent a heterodox form of Shi'ism) are militantly secular, and leftist, for the same reason. Even in states where they make up the majority, many Shi'a favor a secular system not only out of personal inclination but, more crucially, as the only means of mitigating Sunni fears about the consequences of change and democratization. Secularism would at least foreclose the possible establishment of a Shi'ite Islamic state—although secularism in Iraq did not stop discrimination against the Shi'a under the Ba'th. In both Iraq and Bahrain, rather than trading on their majority status, many Shi'a prefer to establish goals of full Shi'ite participation in society within a meritocracy, as opposed to apportionment of jobs and benefits along sectarian lines. Indeed, many Iraqi Shi'a fear the "Lebanonization" of Iraq. The goal of establishing a secular state would not, however, be likely to be shared by Shi'ite Islamists in a state in which the Shi'a make up the majority, although the Islamists too must recognize the potential friction created if they sought to impose a Shi'ite religious state upon a Sunni minority.

Secularism has much to offer as a principle that seeks legally to separate state and religion, and to keep each out of the other's domain. But such a casually asserted principle is more complicated than simple freedom of private belief; we are dealing with societies composed of well-established sociocultural groups and communities who are differentiated from each other specifically by religion. Differences in religion over centuries (as discussed in Chapter 1 on the Shi'ite identity) have produced differences in social and community life, even in culture and expression, that lie at the very heart of self-identity. While secularism need not, in principle, intrude upon the self-expression of these cultures, it is nonetheless religion itself that becomes the outward expression of community solidarity, becoming a force resembling ethnicity both in its emotive force and its centrality to community identity, and therefore difficult to isolate from the state and its policies. Secularism must be understood and implemented in ways that do not damage community religious identity.

The meaning of secularism must also be clearly defined. On the one hand, secularism that affords freedom of religion to all and absence of state intervention, as in the United States, offers many advantages. On the other hand, secularism as part of the official ideology of Turkey, for example, for many decades has actually meant state discouragement or even suppression of religious expression—indeed heavy-handed state control of religion—in a way that discriminates against Islam, leading to sharp political and social conflict within Turkish society. Turkish secularism is not true secularism, but a distortion of the concept in the interests of the state and its dominant Kemalist elite. Thus the danger of "radical secularism" or "secularist extremism" can also threaten social unity and harmony when it denies the Islamic heritage and its expression.

Shi'ite Strategies

What are the options open to the Shi'a in pursuit of their goals? What strategies do they consider for their attainment? Considerable differences exist among the Shi'a on this issue, from country to country and within specific Shi'ite communities. Different strategies also carry different advantages and disadvantages, particularly as they affect Sunni reactions. Broadly speaking, the Shi'a must choose between a religious and a secular strategy.

The Religious Strategy. Because it is solely religion—and its cultural off-shoots—that distinguishes the Shi'a from non-Shi'a, it is difficult for the Shi'a not to act within the context of a religious movement. What are the Shi'a if they are not religious? How can they avoid using religion as the primary vehicle, symbol, and voice of their community cause? This represents a long-standing dilemma within the Shi'ite identity.

All religious movements have several different strategies open to them in promoting their cause. First, the most cautious, apolitical, and grassroots method of seeking influence and power is the use of *tabligh* and *da'wa*—evangelism and religious propagation, preaching to the community. Tabligh does not seek political power directly through institutions but rather seeks to gradually change the moral environment through education and change within the community. Once the community has been educated and opens itself to the values of the faith, in principle its members will join together in pursuit of a state based on Islamic values. If this groundwork is not prepared, it is fruitless, in this view, even counterproductive and divisive, to seek to impose such an agenda—it simply will not take root and even produce a counter-reaction. Shi'ite educational and religious institutions are thus the primary vehicles for influencing the thinking of the community that over the longer run will make Islam a powerful force.

A second form of action is to create a Shi'ite Islamic political movement, in either democratic or nondemocratic form. Such a movement works at the grassroots level to gain support that can in turn be harnessed to the political system, most likely through a political party. The party can be clandestine and closed, or open and transparent. This choice is primarily determined by the state's willingness to tolerate a religiously-based political party; closed political systems clearly require clandestine organization against the state. The only Shi'ite political parties that exist in an open political system today are Amal and Hizballah in Lebanon. (Hizballah in Lebanon has both a transparent political side as well as a secret guerrilla wing.) Clandestine Shi'ite Islamist parties are Hizb al-Da'wa in Iraq and Hizballah in Saudi Arabia. In general, the more the party is forced into clandestine activity, the more authoritarian its character will be. The ability of such a party to come to power in any authoritarian state obviously depends upon the underground organizational power of the movement, even though popular support is also critical. The goal of such clandestine organizations is usually not to win at the ballot box—indeed the ballot box probably does not exist—but to force change upon a nondemocratic regime through sabotage and political violence. However, in democratic political orders in which Shi'ite religious groups have the freedom to participate (Kuwait, Lebanon), the nature of the political struggle shifts the focus to victory at the ballot box.

The Secular Strategy

Shi'a have a far greater problem in mobilizing their community under a secular banner. If a Shi'i is secular, is one still Shi'ite? (The answer seems to be, yes, but with a much weakened communal identity.) What would the goals of a secular Shi'ite political movement be? If it is to benefit the Shi'ite community, then dispensing with the powerful emotive tools of Shi'ite religious faith and symbolism weakens the appeal of the movement to the broader Shi'ite community. If the goals are broader than just the interests of the Shi'ite community, then why limit the party to the Shi'a instead of seeking a broader coalition? If non-Shi'a join, then it ceases to be a Shi'ite party. Thus fundamental decisions need to be reached early on by the leadership of any secular Shi'ite movement.

Such a secular party could cooperate with Shi'ite religious groups in an effort to strengthen the overall Shi'ite political clout. Even if those Shi'a who are truly secular-minded might feel uncomfortable in a Shi'ite religious organization they could still cooperate on specific goals of interest to all Shi'a. But cooperation becomes difficult if the goal of the religious Shi'a is the establishment of an Islamic state—especially where Shi'a are the majority, making a Shi'ite religious state at least a feasible goal.

Individual secular Shi'a also have the freedom not to work within any Shi'ite organization, but simply to work as individuals in other, broader nonsectarian parties. Indeed, the Shi'a in Iraq, Bahrain, and Kuwait from the 1950s to the 1980s often joined leftist movements, especially the Communist party, which were seen both as antiestablishment and clearly nonsectarian. Shi'a actually made up the majority of the Iraqi Communist party. Shi'ite individuals can also cooperate with non-Shi'ite liberal democratic movements to attain certain democratic gains in the country. This kind of political activity outside the framework of the Shi'ite community is perhaps a viable alternative under two conditions: if the alternative movements accept the Shi'a, and if there is a reasonable chance that the Shi'a will be better off under a new regime led by that movement.

Is a Secular Shi'ite Movement Possible?

As this study tries to show, Shi'ism is more than a theological doctrine and a set of religious beliefs. It also encompasses a culture and a historical consciousness that contribute to the formation of identity. Nevertheless, the bedrock of this identity is the particular religious beliefs and practices that distinguish Shi'ism from other Muslim sects. Diluting the faith inevitably dilutes the identity.

The centrality of religion in Shi'ite political life is demonstrated by the preponderance of clerics at the head of Shi'ite political movements and their instrumental role in the rise of Shi'ite self-awareness in the 1960s. A long list of Shi'ite Imams have led or inspired Shi'ite movements since then, and the lore of Shi'ism has infused the rhetoric of Shi'ite awakening. Secular Shi'a leaders, however, may be seen as lacking authenticity: they are neither one thing nor another. Where do they stand on religious issues? Will they compromise away too many rights and freedoms? In what sense are they Shi'a? Thus there is a striking dearth of secular Shi'ite leadership or movements that do not have an Islamist agenda. Secularism cannot tap into the enormously powerful emotive force of Shi'ism and harness it into political activism. Indeed, secularists tend to shy away from sectarian labeling. This pattern has prevailed over the past three decades, but some interesting changes may be emerging.

Some deviation from the pattern, for example, can be seen in Lebanon, where Amal has developed into a secularist political party with a secular lay leader. Similarly, in Iraq there are signs of a lay and secularist Shi'ite political leadership forming alongside the more traditional clerical Islamist leadership. These emerging secularist Shi'a leaders are not ideological; they are more interested in their constituency than in the establishment of an Islamist state. The goal is not Shi'ism, but the Shi'a: improving the lot of the Shi'a as a community and increasing their participation within the body politic.

The important distinction between the secularist and Islamist is not the depth of personal religious belief but whether the belief shapes political vision and determines political choices. The division between secular and religious Shi'a need not be rigorous, and Shi'ite secularist leaders do form alliances with Islamists, though they may be for limited agendas and temporary durations. The Bahrain Liberation Front (BLF), for example, has a high proportion of clerical leadership, but in all its public statements has consistently propounded only secular goals for Bahrain: restoration of the constitution of 1975 and the reopening of the parliament. This is not to say that religious symbolism is not present in the popular support for the movement, but the movement has avoided articulating any explicit religious agenda over its many years of political struggle. If the BLF should eventually attain power, there will unquestionably be debate among the Shi'a as to the role of clerics or religious institutions in the state. Clerics already work comfortably within a secular framework in Kuwait and in Lebanon. The same type of alliance between secularists and Islamists can be seen within the Iraqi opposition. Islamist groups such as SCIRI (the Supreme Council for Islamic Revolution in Iraq) have been able to build working relations with secularist Iraqi movements and leadership.

The case of Lebanon is instructive, since Shi'ite political parties there have had time to mature and have moreover entered the political life of the country, experiencing firsthand the practical accommodations and choices political engagement requires. Secular and Islamist Shi'ite parties compete.

The Amal movement, first inspired and formed by Musa al-Sadr, initially mobilized both secularist and Islamist Shi'a under one umbrella. By the mid-1970s however, sectarian violence was increasing in Lebanon across the board and the political environment grew more radical and violent. By 1982 a radical Islamist faction, critical of the secular and moderate tendencies of the Amal leadership and encouraged by Iran, split off from Amal to form Islamic Amal, later transformed into Hizballah.[1] Amal emerged after the split as an amalgam of moderate religious and secular outlooks. Hizballah is far more clerically oriented, in part because of its early acceptance of the "Khomeini line" that calls for clerical rule, and because major clerics moved to its support and even offered original ideological leadership (such as Shaykh Fadhlallah). Hizballah is also closely associated with the Higher Shi'ite Muslim Council, al-Majlis al-Shi'i al-Islami al-A'la, led by a senior cleric, Muhammad Mahdi Shams-al-Din, and includes many other clerics in its governing body. The relationship between Amal as a political party (and militia) and the religious Council is symbiotic but preserves the independence of each. Such a model may be practicable among other Shi'ite communities trying to find a balance between a secularist political framework and a legitimating anchor in the religious culture. In Lebanon as elsewhere, however, the balance is difficult to maintain over a long period.

External Patronage

A third alternative also attracts some radical Shi'a who react out of desperation with the status quo: cooperation with a foreign power. At the same time, external states hostile to existing regimes will always try to find internal forces that can help weaken the regime. The Soviet Union sought to influence local Communist parties in the Gulf in the 1960s and 1970s. Iraq, Syria, and Egypt in the same period also tried to influence radical left-wing organizations in the Gulf.

Iran has been the external force to which dissident Shi'a most naturally might turn for support. Obviously Iran's interest lies primarily in supporting Islamist movements rather than left-wing secular forces (although *raison d'état* can never be fully predicted). Iran also needs to balance the gains versus losses for itself in supporting such groups, and to determine the extent and ends of its support. (See Chapter 4 on the Iranian connection in Shi'ite politics.) Iraq, too, in the future will have an interest in the welfare of Shi'ite communities abroad. Depending on the type of government Iraq has, it could likewise come to be seen as a source of support for certain Shi'ite causes. And the Shi'ite Hizballah organization in Lebanon has already provided guerrilla training to foreign Shi'a, also with the blessing of Iran at the time. Thus external support is always a potential option for Shi'ite activists, with Iran at the moment the main, but in the future it will not always be the sole, source of potential support.

Shi'ite communities located in the Middle East are no longer the only external forces that can assist Shi'a under repression. There is a large expatriate Shi'ite community in West Africa, and increasingly in the West, especially in London, that is active on behalf of their co-religionists and their cause in the Middle East. The Bahraini Shi'a have an exiled Bahrain Freedom Movement based in London that has worked tirelessly to publicize the plight of the Bahraini Shi'a, via human rights organizations, the press, nongovernmental organizations (NGOs), and by lobbying parliamentarians, publishing articles and books, lectures, and distributing newsletters by fax and e-mail. The most important international Shi'ite organization outside the Middle East is the al-Khoei (Khu'i) Foundation, which has an active program in support of all Shi'ites in the UK—through education, public programs, outreach groups, seminars, lobbying of the government, and speaking out on the condition of all Shi'a abroad. Saudi Shi'a have worked out of London and even Washington periodically, as do the Iraqi Shi'a.

Is the Target the State or the Social Order?

How the Shi'ite community interacts with the Sunni community is obviously a two-way street. The power of the state or the dominant Sunni community in the end has more decisive impact upon Shi'ite attitudes and policies than the Shi'a themselves have. First it is necessary to distinguish between the Sunni community and the state: the two are not synonymous, even though the Sunnis dominate politics in all the states in question except Lebanon. In Iraq the Shi'a and Sunnis both seek to overthrow the vicious and oppressive regime of Saddam Hussein. The regime tries to stimulate fears among the Sunnis that they will be the first victims of post-Saddam chaos or of a Shi'ite regime. Yet Sunni and Shi'ite opposition groups at least talk of cooperating with each other in bringing an end to the Saddam regime, even if there is not full agreement about the nature of a post-Saddam order. In short, the monstrousness of the regime serves to overcome sectarian differences in working for change, despite the huge implications for change in the Iraqi political and social order in the event of democratization.

In Bahrain, the regime has worked steadfastly to try to portray opposition to the al-Khalifa family as strictly a Shi'ite affair that threatens the welfare of the Sunnis. The regime has to some extent succeeded in isolating the Shi'a from the Sunni liberals who also demand reform and change. Since the status quo for the Sunnis is still tolerable, there is so far little broad Sunni-Shi'ite cooperation to bring change. The Sunnis still hope to maintain the status quo, that is, Sunni rule, albeit with a few concessions to Shi'ite demands. The Shi'ite majority hopes to convince the Sunnis that reform is in the interests of both communities and has scrupulously avoided casting its case against the regime in sectarian terms.

In Saudi Arabia there may be opposition across a wide spectrum to the policies of the House of al-Sa'ud, but the opposition has not yet become a popular movement, nor has dissatisfaction with the status quo for Sunnis reached such a level whereby they would broadly organize against the state. There is no meaningful cooperation between Sunni and Shi'ite opposition. The Saudi case presents the greatest anomaly among all our cases since Saudi Sunnis have far less to lose in granting rights to the Shi'a than do the Sunnis of any other state in question: Saudi Shi'a are relatively few in number, present no threat to the regime, are isolated, and are not contending for political, economic, or social power. Regime hostility must be explained primarily in religious/ideological terms.

In Kuwait the Shi'a have already attained legal equality to a major extent, so the issue is less burning. Kuwait is the only society in which the Shi'a are now working to extract full rights both from the Sunni-dominated system and from the Sunni community itself rather than merely from the regime proper. Sunni-Shi'ite cooperation does exist to pressure the regime to extend liberalization.

In general then, where Shi'a and Sunnis clearly perceive the state, that is, the regime, as the main problem, the potential for Shi'ite-Sunni cooperation grows significantly, although the state will try to play off one against the other. If the state is not the common enemy, that implies that the political order has achieved some degree of liberalization that makes the regime acceptable, even if not ideal, to large numbers of Sunnis. In the absence of joint Shi'ite-Sunni cooperation against the state, negotiations over power between sectarian communities will follow a more political process via existing institutional means, as in Lebanon and Kuwait. Where the state's hostility to the Shi'ite community is strong, the Shi'a will be more inclined to radical or even violent action. The state is again the primary determinant here.

It is interesting to note that an early effort toward healing the sectarian breach within Islam was begun by al-Azhar University in 1948 with the establishment of an "Office for Rapprochement between the Schools of Islam" (*Dar al-taqrib bayn al-madhahib al-Islamiyya*) that brought together a leading Iranian Shi'ite cleric with Hasan al-Banna of the Egyptian Muslim Brotherhood. Delegations from both sides met periodically for many years, and the Brotherhood developed a considerable sympathy for the Shi'ite movement in Iran against the Shah. After the revolution, and after an initial honeymoon between the Brotherhood and the new leaders of the Islamic Republic, a falling out took place, in part due to the emphasis placed by the Islamic Republic on its Shi'ite character, while the Iranian regime perceived the Brotherhood as not sufficiently revolutionary in its approach. Despite the failure of that particular effort at Sunni-Shi'ite rapprochement, many Islamists on both sides place weight on the ultimate unity of Islamist movements and do not wish to have that unity weakened by differences that are not deemed to be essential. As the Iranian regime grows more moderate, it is quite probable there will be further efforts toward a new Sunni-Shi'ite rapprochement in the name of strengthening the clout of Islamist movements internationally. Such a formal rapprochement will undoubtedly affect the position of Shi'a within Sunni-dominated states.[2]

Finally, there has been debate among Sunnis as to whether it is Shi'ite religious or Shi'ite secular movements that are more threatening to the Sunni position. One might assume that Sunnis would perceive Shi'ite religious movements as more zealous and hence more worrisome. However, some Shi'a have commented that in states in which the Shi'a are a minority, Sunnis almost seem to prefer to see Shi'ite political goals expressed through religious vehicles because they know this dooms the Shi'a to isolation and precludes the prospects of Sunni-Shi'ite cooperation against the state. Sunnis also tend to believe "the West will never permit" a Shi'ite Islamist state to come into existence in Iraq or Bahrain.

Shi'ite Avenues for Action

The issue of Shi'ite tactics therefore involves a number of complexities. It is difficult for Shi'ite movements aiming to gain rights for themselves to operate outside of a religious context, since the Shi'a are a religious group and the clergy has always taken the lead in representing community solidarity and its needs. In the long run, we believe secularist Shi'ite movements operate at a disadvantage compared to the religious movements. If secular-minded Shi'a wish to avoid involvement of religion in their political movements, their main alternative is to work with other nonsectarian parties, most likely left-ist, toward the achievement of more open and liberal societies that should benefit the Shi'a in the end as well. The more oppressed the Shi'ite commu-nity, the more likely it will be to turn to the religious vehicle as lying closest to its community roots and identity.

What courses of action can the Shi'a pursue in practice to advance their cause? A great deal depends on the circumstances of the Shi'ite community in each country and the attitude of the government toward them.

First, the strategies that the Shi'a adopt will not be uniform. Even within the ranks of the religious there are differences in conceptualizing the state and defining the type of activism that is required. Like Sunnis, practicing Shi'a are divided over minimum requirements for an acceptable state order. Two prob- . lems make it more difficult to gauge Shi'ite sentiment on this issue. The dif-fering conditions that prevail in the countries of the region mean that their attitudes are conditioned by the particular circumstances of each country. For example, the Shi'a in Lebanon are constrained by the reality of Lebanon's de-mography and social structure and must tailor their aspirations to that real-ity. In a state like Bahrain, where the Shi'a live under a Sunni state system even while forming the majority, there are tactical considerations that may at-tenuate political positions. Thus what might be termed Shi'ite political fun-damentalism is less able, in practice, to express itself than Sunni fundamentalism. Bearing these restrictions in mind, it is nevertheless possi-ble to say that among devout Shi'a there are first, political maximalists who wish to see a state order based on Islam, and second, less doctrinal Shi'a who have more modest aims. To further complicate the picture, the quietist strain of Shi'ism survives in an evangelical school that favors strengthening the faith through grassroots missionary activity, proselytizing, and good works rather than direct political action, thereby building a strong community for a more propitious future. Finally, of course, there are Shi'ite secularists, who have no desire for an Islamic state at all.

In Kuwait and Saudi Arabia, in which the Shi'a are a minority, despite a wave of Shi'ite violence in the 1980s, they have opted for coexistence and negotiation of agreements with the government. These agreements, whether in the context of general democratization, or as specific remedies for Shi'ite grievances, have not necessarily given the Shi'a as much as they hoped for, but they have defused tensions with the government for the moment. A pol-icy of negotiation need not exclude a certain level of continuing political pressure, such as publicizing discrimination or human rights violations against them. These tactics were used to relatively good effect by the Shi'ite minority in Saudi Arabia in propagandizing their fate to the outside world; that tactic, along with other internal events in the kingdom, finally pushed the government into negotiations on their grievances. But, on the whole, the

Shi'a in these countries are more likely to pursue a policy of greater engagement, persuasion, and hope for incremental improvements that may or may
not come. The Shi'ite perception is that the violence of the 1980s did not
necessarily improve their position and possibly undermined it, not only domestically but internationally as well. Additionally, the Shi'ite communities
in these countries can no longer count on the support of Iran and have few
other allies.

In Iraq and Bahrain the calculations are different. There are some broad
similarities between the two countries as regards repression of Shi'a. There is
of course vastly more violence in Iraq and the problem there is far deeper,
more intractable, and pervasive, and the Shi'a are far more politicized and
experienced. The Shi'ite problem in Iraq will emerge as an automatic by-
product of national upheaval against or after Saddam. In Bahrain the problem is still open to peaceful progressive solution, although the government
is moving ever more rapidly toward the formation of a police state vis-à-vis
the Shi'a.

If Shi'ite majorities believe there is no hope of achieving any improvement through negotiated agreements, they may conclude that they have
nothing to lose by turning up the heat, that indeed their situation may deteriorate further unless they do intensify their rejection of the status quo.
Furthermore, their status as majorities gives them wider support in the
country and a stronger case in international opinion, increasing their moral
strength and attracting sympathy as well as possible material assistance. In
both countries the stakes are high for the Shi'a, as their success will bring
major changes in their favor. As they have less to gain by self-restraint, escalating the confrontation with the state could become the only viable alternative. The use of violence and terrorism can become a multipurpose tool:
for expressing frustration and anger, as a political instrument for undermining the regime's credibility and control, and as a red flag that warns the international community of a deteriorating domestic situation.

Conversely, because the Shi'a are a majority in Iraq and Bahrain the
regimes there feel more threatened and are more adamant that there will be
no change or negotiation. This only increases the likelihood of Shi'ite violence and government counterviolence and opens windows for external interference and manipulation of the domestic situation. This escalating spiral
begins to acquire its own dynamic and rationale. Even for the Shi'a such a
rationale acquires its own momentum and internal logic, without reference
to any chances of success.

The logic of upheaval has shown its effectiveness in two of the countries
in this study. The Shi'a of Lebanon gained their enhanced status and power
at least partly as a result of a long and devastating civil war—not initiated by
them. It can also be argued that it took the Gulf war in Kuwait to bring the

Shi'a out of the margins of the Kuwaiti body politic and into the mainstream. More generally, it also appears evident that the upheaval of the Iranian revolution was also responsible for bringing the Shi'ite problem to the foreground in the Arab world and on the international scene, for better or for worse. This does not imply that only war and revolution will improve the status of the Shi'a, but so far it has been the sole way in which the Shi'a's status has changed for the better in the past—and could recur in the future.

CHAPTER FOUR

The Iranian Connection

To Sunni Arabs, the concept of Shi'ism is indelibly linked to Persians. Sunnis have historically regarded Shi'ism as a schism in Islam encouraged and propagated by discontented anti-Arab (Shu'ubi) Persians during the 'Abbasid era. Arab Shi'a correctly contest the traditional Sunni view and stress that the roots of Shi'ism were sown when the succession to the Prophet was erroneously determined in the first years of Islam, long before the Persians became a factor in the Muslim polity.

To listen to the stereotypical views of most Sunnis, especially those in the Gulf, is to believe that all Arab Shi'a owe basic loyalty to Iran. The reality is far from this popular conception. In fact, the relationship between Iran and the Arab Shi'a is quite complex, leaving the Shi'a highly ambivalent about it. Relationships between the Arab Shi'a and Iran are furthermore not written in stone but are susceptible to considerable change and variation. They depend on a whole range of factors: domestic politics within each Gulf Arab state, the nature of regional politics among those states themselves, and, finally, the policies of Iran. Nor is Iran the only major state to affect the Arab Shi'a; their situation and position are further affected by Saddam's brutal policies towards the Iraqi Shi'a, and they will be heavily influenced by Iraq's future course of development and by future relations between Iran and Iraq.

Arab Shi'a variously look at Iran from three different vantage points: as a major center of Shi'ite faith, as the center of an Islamist ideology under the Islamic Republic, and as a state.

Iran as Seat of Shi'ite Faith

There is no inherent or obligatory reason why Iran need be the center of Shi'ite faith at all. There is nothing in the religion that determines it—unlike, say, the role of Mecca for all Muslims of the world. Iran today is simply the most important, but not the sole, religious center of Shi'ism. It happens to rank high today as a place of residence for marji'. Qom has established itself as a major center of learning, but mainly in this century, and there are no religious reasons why Qom must be so favored. As we noted earlier, Iran historically has not even been the basic seat of Shi'ism; it is Iraq that has every reason to be the center of the faith by virtue of its holy sites, which include the tombs of 'Ali and Husayn, the two leading Imams of the Shi'a. Shi'ism came to Iran as the state religion only in 1500 under the new Safavid dynasty, a decision that required a massive campaign to convert most of Iran's Sunni citizens to Shi'ism. Up to then Iran had not been a center of Shi'ite scholarship in the way that Najaf and Karbala in Iraq had long been. As Iran developed its position from the sixteenth to the twentieth centuries as virtually the sole official Shi'ite state in the Muslim world, its power and influence over Shi'ism inevitably grew, and in a process that also began to place a heavy and unique stamp of Persian culture not so much upon the theology, as the practice of Shi'ism. Still, except for Isfahan, no seat of Persian Shi'ite learning matched the dominance of Najaf and Karbala until the late twentieth century.[1]

For Arab Shi'a, then, there had been little question of any "compromise" with their Arabness up until the Safavid period; this was the first time when Iran, as a state power, would have much meaning for Arab Shi'a, given the vastly greater importance of Iraq as the center of world Shi'ism. While Iran had its own shrines of some significance such as Isfahan and Mashhad, and senior Shi'ite clerics and maraji' would often spend time in Iran, Iran did not figure significantly in Arab Shi'ite thinking. It was essentially a foreign culture, albeit Shi'ite.

It was only in the 1970s that the persecution of the Shi'a under the Iraqi Ba'th, and especially Saddam Husayn, closed down the freedom of inquiry and organization of the clergy, and forced most of the key Shi'ite clerics out of the country and into Iran. Under the Ayatollah Khomeini, Qom's influence as a center of Shi'ite religious pronouncements grew greatly, especially as bold new interpretations of Shi'ite theology emerged under his leadership. Today, due to the repressive policies of Iraq, most of the key Shi'ite clerics have been compelled to take refuge in Iran, given the danger of life in Iraq where Saddam has never hesitated to regularly execute or assassinate the top Shi'ite clerics down to today.

In effect, Iraq under Saddam foolishly ended up unilaterally ceding Shi'ite religious authority to Iran. At the same time, other Arab governments with

equal shortsightedness have done nothing to counter Iran's theological supremacy through their own failure to foster domestic centers of Shi'ite learning and marji'iyya in their own countries. If Shi'ite scholarship drastically
declined in Iraq after 1970, it is virtually nonexistent in Bahrain, Kuwait, and
Saudi Arabia and only recently emerging in Lebanon. Shi'a today thus have
little option other than to look to Iran for some degree of leadership in pro-
nouncement on things religious (or even political/religious), and the followers of the various maraji' sometimes travel to Iran to consult with them.

A key problem is how to define the kind of powers a marji' exerts over a
follower. In fact, even within Shi'ite political thought there is a spectrum of
belief among clerical thinkers: it ranges from the strongly authoritarian position that sees the *faqih,* or supreme jurisprudent as selected by God and
whose word must therefore be absolute in almost all spheres of life (represented by the ideas of Ayatollah Khomeini, among others), while more liberal interpretations believe that God, having endowed mankind with reason,
has thus enabled people to select what they believe is right (even through
elections) among disputed interpretations of political thought among various clerical jurisprudents. (Leading modern Shi'ite mujtahids such as
Muhammad Baqir al-Sadr of Iraq or Muhammad Jawad Maghniyah of
Lebanon have provided powerful juridical and theological arguments in support of this latter point—in direct opposition to Iranian official ruling ideology.)[2] In principle, a follower looks to his or her marji' for counsel on
religious matters, or on the application of religious interpretations to daily
life, which can easily spill over into the political arena when it comes to relations between an oppressive Sunni state and the Shi'ite community. Thus
on the formal and theoretical level, some maraji' will be more demanding of
absolute obedience on rulings across a broad spectrum, whereas others will
leave far greater areas open to the discretion of the individual.

On the practical level there is an even greater latitude of behavior. In any
religion, on the level of daily life different believers will bring different degrees of commitment or rigor to their acceptance of the tenets of their religious faith and to the opinions of their religious leaders. One cannot clearly
determine the degree to which religion and its interpretation will affect one's
personal life, the life of the community, and the political stance of the community on issues that affect its welfare. Thus different Shi'a will accept the
weight of their marji's views differently in the various spheres of their lives.
(A rough parallel might be the degree to which a Roman Catholic will accept all facets of Rome's teachings, for example, perhaps ignoring, as do so
many Italians, its teachings on birth control, while all the while considering
themselves serious practicing Catholics.) The marji's word in principle then,
can cover not only interpretations of religious doctrine, but also the interpretation of doctrine as it affects key issues of political life. Some maraji' too,

will pronounce readily and in detail on political issues, while others prefer to limit their pronouncements to religious issues and interpretations.

The problem of "politicization" of religious doctrine has been rendered more complex by the residence in Iran of so many key maraji' today, making it difficult to separate the influence of Iranian political thought or state interest from the religious interpretations and influence of a given marji'. Nonetheless, any Shi'i who chooses to follow a less political marji' such as Ayatollah Sistani today is under no obligation to accept Iranian political or state ideological guidance whatsoever on any topic if his or her marji' does not adhere to that view. Many Shi'a make it very clear they distinguish sharply between what their marji' will say on religious questions and what his views are on current politics. They will think for themselves in deciding what is appropriate and what is not.

Iran as a Seat of Ideology

The second area in which Iran may loom large in Arab Shi'ite eyes is as the seat of contemporary radical Shi'ite ideology. There is often a thin line between theology and ideology in Islam since theology can be taken as the foundation for a given ideology—as has happened in other religions as well. Khomeini, in the years of his residency in Najaf as a senior Ayatollah, propounded a more radical, indeed revolutionary doctrine that called for the state to be ruled with nearly absolute powers by the supreme cleric (Veli-e-Faqih) until such time as the Mahdi, the Twelfth Imam, returns. This was in sharp distinction to long historical practice in which the Shi'ite clergy kept their distance and independence from secular power and institutions, even while speaking out on key political interests of concern to them. (A major exception was the recruitment of the clergy by the Safavid dynasty to serve the state in its the early years. Over time the bulk of the clergy eventually achieved independence from the Safavid state, only to lose it to the state again in the Islamic republic.) After attaining power, Khomeini further articulated a revolutionary ideology toward the region that called for the overthrow of corrupt, despotic, and Westernized rulers and for the pursuit of Islamic social justice in all Muslim lands.

Khomeini situated his radical ideology in Islamic and Third World frames of reference, but the rhetoric struck home more with the Shi'a than with the Sunnis of the Muslim world. His championship of the *mustadh'afin* (the oppressed) against the *mustakbirin* (the arrogant) at a general level reflected the radical ideologies of Ali Shari'ati, who in turn was influenced by concepts of other Third World ideologists such as Franz Fanon in a broader call for a struggle of the Third World to shake off the forces of imperialism and the exploiting West. More specifically, it was heard as a rallying cry to the Shi'a, who regard themselves as the sorest of the oppressed, to assert their rights before (corrupt) Sunni regimes. Even nonreligious Shi'a were lured by the revolutionary call that exhorted the oppressed to reject their status and to take matters into their own hands, as the Iranians had done.

As we noted above, there are theological disputes within Shi'ism about what constitutes the extent of a marji's authority, the proper focus of a marji's views, and the range of his writ. The lines between theology and politics are imprecise and viewed differently by different clerics, but this very imprecision places a dilemma before his followers in interpreting the counsel of the marji'. If one is uncomfortable with the political direction of a particular marji', in principle one is free to choose to follow a different, perhaps more apolitical marji'. That choice is indeed still open today among various ayatollahs. The individual may also choose to ignore certain more politicized aspects of the marji's religious pronouncements, especially if their implementation can bring danger to the individual or the community vis-à-vis a harsh Sunni state. There are, furthermore, differences between theological pronouncements and Iranian state policy, but it may often be difficult or distressing for some followers to draw that distinction. When the follower is the object of persecution by a regime portrayed by Iran as illegitimate, unjust, or corrupt, the advice seems harder to ignore.

The average Shi'ite in the Arab world is likely be flexible, pragmatic, and highly selective in listening to and implementing revolutionary dogma from Tehran. Most individuals may avoid involvement in politics altogether out of lack of interest, commitment, or because it can be harmful to one's health. But for politicized individuals, the ideological line out of Tehran offers a vision of politics with powerful attractions, with some ability to influence and provide a guide to action for those who are inclined to political involvement. Thus Iran as *ideological* center is not binding on the behavior of Shi'a abroad and is actively opposed by large numbers of Shi'a who simply disagree or prefer to stay uninvolved and out of trouble. While the Islamic republic has officially insisted that the "Imam's line" is the official teaching and interpretation of Shi'ism, it is becoming increasingly more evident that there are major, indeed crucial differences among leading Shi'ite clerics on the key issues of state power and leadership. There is therefore no single word from Iran that is necessarily and effectively binding on all Shi'a, although a few truly committed individuals may take such views as binding, and furthermore seek ways to take the requisite actions.

Iran the Country

Finally, Arab Shi'a can think about Iran the country, a major Shi'ite state. For some, state and ideology may be closely linked. For others the country

can mean territory, culture, and national character. Nearly all Shi'a will
have some special regard for Iran as the country where Shi'ism became
dominant, and that encouraged the flowering of Shi'ite culture, a phenomenon usually not possible in the Arab states where Arab Shi'a reside. But
Arab Shi'a also frequently mention that during their trips to Iran (which
many do make), they feel a distinct sense of entering a different culture.
Language is one obvious difference. But the Safavid state made major efforts, especially under Shaykh Muhammad Baqir Majlisi in the seventeenth
century—one of the most important Shi'ite clerics of all time—to Persian-
ize Shi'ite practice and culture in order to facilitate its spread in what was
up to then largely a Sunni Iran. These Persian innovations have influenced
the practice of Shi'ism everywhere, and Arab Shi'a are well aware of its special "Persianness" in Iran. The gulf between Persian and Arab culture thus
persists.

Nor do most Arab Shi'a feel any special commitment to Iran the state. As
we note in the case studies of five Arab countries, many Arab Shi'a resent
Iranian intrusion into the politics of their state, well aware that Iranian state
interests, and not Shi'ism, are the driving force. A comparison of Arab
Shi'ite views of Iran, and Iranian views of Arab Shi'ites, helps reveal the qual-
ity of this complex interrelationship.

Arab Shi'ite Views on Iran

The relationship of Arab Shi'a to Iran is filled with contradictions. Arab
Shi'a respect Iran as the only Shi'ite state in the world and admire the vital-
ity and richness of its culture. Some Arab Shi'a applaud the determination
of Iranians who challenged and defeated the Shah. And many are grateful to
Iran for providing refuge to thousands of persecuted Shi'a around the world
who have no other Shi'a refuge.

Yet many Arab Shi'a who have lived in Iran tell of negative experiences
and acrimonious relations with Iranians. They often find themselves treated
with contempt and discriminated against. They accuse the Iranians of being
arrogant and chauvinist. Some Shi'ite Arabs who took refuge in Iran have
complained that they cannot get jobs and cannot start their own businesses
simply because they are Arabs. Apart from outright discrimination, government bureaucracy is stacked against them, with arcane regulations that bureaucrats can use to deny licenses to non-Iranians. Discrimination also
affects personal life: laws issued in the 1990s prevent an Arab man from
marrying an Iranian woman under Iranian jurisdiction—wildly contrary to
Islamic law. Few Arab Shi'a ever feel at home in Iran, and instead are re-
minded of the powerful differences between Arab and Iranian political culture, society, and national interest.

Arab Shi'a experience the Iranian brand of Shi'ism as a culture apart from their own. They feel its ceremonies are more pagan, more theatrical, that Iranian art is far more depictive and representational—even at times depicting the Prophet himself (without facial features)—than traditional Arab Islamic art would ever allow. The elaborately dramatized ceremonies of 'Ashura that commemorate the martyrdom of Imam Husayn are regarded by many Arab Shi'a as an emotional Iranian theatrical innovation introduced into what has traditionally been a solemn occasion. Iranian miniatures are distinctive examples of an art that cannot readily be found in the traditional Arab world. Its theater, music, and poetry are far more sensual, containing frequent references to wine and sexual overtones in its descriptions of yearning for proximity to God.

All this contrasts dramatically with Arab culture, which is purer, simpler, and more austere in character. Indeed, Iranian Shi'ism is centered more around Husayn and the drama and passion of his death whereas Arab Shi'a are more oriented around the figure of 'Ali himself. (Although both 'Ali and Husayn are buried in Iraq, the shrine of Husayn at Karbala generally draws more Iranian pilgrims than does the shrine of 'Ali at Najaf.) These differences are often characterized as "Safavid" Shi'ism (Iranian) versus "'Ali's" Shi'ism (Arab), and refer to cultural more than theological differences. Some Iraqi Shi'a, among others, speak of the need to "clean up" Shi'ism by ridding it of its Persian accretions in order to get back to its "purer" roots.[3]

Like many Sunni Arabs, nearly all Arab Shi'a respect the fact of the Iranian revolution. Whatever one may think of the policies of the Islamic republic, the ability of its leaders to overthrow the extraordinary power of the Shah and his U.S. backing, to come to power, and to continue to defy the West in the name of indigenous Islamic culture are accomplishments that require respect. In short, "Iran must be doing something right" to have succeeded as far as it has. Iran is thus a potent symbol of anti-Western imperialism to non-Shi'a and even to secular Arabs and Muslims who otherwise despair at Muslim impotence in standing up to Western dominance and power. These individuals are willing to forgive any number of shortcomings of the Iranian regime in the name of preserving the center of anti-Western boldness, vigor, and courage that Iran represents, whatever the cost.

On the one hand, while the West routinely talks about "repressive government" in Tehran, to many Muslims, Sunni or Shi'a, the reality is rather different, certainly in contrast to most Arab regimes. While many secular Shi'a have little interest in Iran as a religious center, they do recognize Iran as a state with a lively and vigorous parliament, regular elections, a lively press, and genuine politics in a way conspicuously absent in so much of the rest of the Muslim world. This level of democratization is far greater than under the Shah and perhaps gradually evolving in the direction of "Islamic democracy."

On the other hand, however much they may admire the Iranian revolution as a model of popular revolt against tyranny, there are still some Arab Shi'a who regard the Khomeini era and the revolution as the worst thing that could have happened to them. They tend to fear the power, intentions, nationalism, and chauvinism of Iran, its often heavy-handed way of treating neighboring Arab states. Arab Shi'a are well aware that Iran is acting first and foremost out of its own state agenda rather than theological or principled motivation. Secular Shi'a and those who follow the quietist religious tradition often say that Iran has disfigured the face of Shi'ism through the religious fanaticism and radicalism it espoused in the first decades of the revolution. Its association with acts of terrorism and sponsorship of Shi'ite use of violence has cast all Arab Shi'a as potential traitors and terrorists. Iran's militant posture and confrontational rhetoric put Arab regimes on the defensive and created domestic tensions that harmed local Shi'ite communities. It increased polarization between Sunnis and Shi'a in the Arab world and exacerbated Sunni doubts about the allegiance of the Shi'a to their native states. Thus the ramifications of the Iranian revolution were a serious setback for Arab Shi'a, damaging their relations with Sunnis and distorting their image in the West.

Many Shi'a who are critical of the Iranian revolution contrast its methods and impact with the very different approach and message of Sayyid Musa al-Sadr, the Iranian cleric who led the renaissance of the Lebanese Shi'a in the 1960s and 1970s. (See Chapter 9 on the Shi'a of Lebanon.) In contrast to Khomeini and his followers among Iranian clerics, Musa al-Sadr strove to build bridges between the communities in Lebanon. He exhorted the Lebanese Shi'a to integrate into Lebanese society by raising their self-esteem, strengthening their community, and building their civic institutions. He preached coexistence and tolerance instead of violence. Musa Al-Sadr is held up by these Shi'a as a model of positive strategies for improving the conditions of Shi'a in the Arab world.

In the end, however, Arab Shi'a recognize that the worse their own conditions of life under various Arab regimes become, the more they may have to look to Iran to provide some counterweight—at least a reminder to the Arab rulers that they would be wise not to oppress their Shi'ite subjects too much. They know they will get little sympathy and even less support from Western governments, who remain conspicuously silent on these issues, despite their protestations of concern for human rights.

As revolutionary drive and religious zeal ebb in Iran, the Arab Shi'a will increasingly see Iran as a state that acts out of national interests. Many Arab Shi'a, including Iraqis, Saudis and Bahrainis, have already started to express skepticism of Iran's commitment to non-Iranian Shi'a and question the motivation of its support in the 1980s.

Iraqi Shi'a who took part in the March 1991 uprising against the regime of Saddam Hussein best exemplify the dichotomy and growing realism in attitudes toward Iran. The secular Shi'a who participated in the uprising blame its failure on the intrusion of Iran, which frightened Iraqi Sunnis and deprived the uprising of essential American and Saudi support. Religious Shi'a, who looked to Iran for support, also blame Iran for failing to support the uprising sufficiently or to help defend the Shi'a, and instead allowed them to be butchered by the Iraqi regime's Republican Guard. Both factions interpret Iran's behavior as the calculated pursuit of state interests and have no illusions that religion, ideology, or even Shi'ite community cohesion were significant factors determining Iranian policy.

Ironically, it is very likely that Arab states who once felt threatened by the religious and revolutionary dimensions of Iran's Islamic republic will now feel more comfortable dealing with a state driven more purely by political self-interest rather than by ideological fervor. Relations between the Arab countries and Iran already began to improve in the early 1990s and have shown dramatic progress since the election of Khatami, especially between Saudi Arabia and Iran. This progress is likely to continue if Iran's policies continue to prove sensitive to the concerns of its Arab neighbors. The relationship that may emerge is likely at the least to resemble the aloof but serious working relations that prevailed between Arab countries and Iran under the Shah. At the same time, greater détente between Arab governments and Iran is a mixed blessing for the Arab Shi'a. It can potentially benefit them by rendering them less suspect in their loyalty their own countries, but it will also rob them of external leverage and may force them to downscale their demands.

Iranian Views of Arab Shi'a

Iran's own views of Arab Shi'a are similarly complex and involve a variety of interests and attitudes at different levels. First, Iranians on the popular level tend to look down on Arabs as a whole, to view them as primitive beduin "locust-eaters" from the desert as opposed to the ancient urbanized Persian culture going back many thousands of years. "A dog in Isfahan lives better than an Arab in Arabia," goes one Persian proverb. A well-known Persian writer in describing his pilgrimage in the 1930s to Najaf reveals typical Persian attitudes towards Arabs:

Ragged Arabs, men with dull faces, wearing fezzes, turbaned men with shrewd faces, shaved heads, henna colored beards and nails, telling their beads, walking around in sandals, loose cotton pants and long tunics. Persian, Turkish, and guttural Arabic spoken from the depth of the throat and entrails deafened the ear. The Arab women had dirty tattooed faces and inflamed eyes, and wore rings in their noses. A mother had forced half her black breast into the mouth of the dirty baby in her arms. . . . In front of the coffee house an Arab was picking his nose and rubbing the dirt out from between his toes. His face was covered with flies and lice crawled all over his head.[4]

Quite recently we, the authors of this book, were gratuitously informed by an Iranian casually encountered that "there is no such thing as Iraq, it is a figment of the imagination." Persians are also fond of saying that in the Middle East in the end "there are only Ottomans and Iranians." Needless to say, Arab Shi'a resent these arrogant views and attitudes associated with Persians.

Second, Iran as a state tends to view Shi'ite communities in the Gulf as objects to be manipulated for Iranian state interests. As the Soviet Union once felt free to sacrifice (or defend) the interests of Communist parties around the world, depending on the immediate tactical needs of the Soviet state, so too, Iran is ready to use, or ignore, the interests of the Arab Shi'a depending on the immediate needs of Tehran's foreign policy. In January 1988, Khomeini issued a stunning landmark fatwa that placed the needs of state above all others: "Our government . . . has priority over all other Islamic tenets, even over prayer, fasting and the pilgrimage to Mecca."[5] This remarkable redirection of Iran away from ideology to statecraft gathered momentum in the 1990s and will increasingly determine Iran's approach to the Arab Shi'a.

Tehran has played sometimes serious roles in the life of Shi'ite communities, most dramatically in Lebanon, even under the Shah when his envoy Musa Sadr literally revolutionized the consciousness of the Shi'ite plurality in the country and forged it into a powerful, self-conscious political instrument that has had more dramatic impact against Israeli and U.S. interests than anywhere else in the Muslim world. (See Chapter 9, "The Shi'a of Lebanon.") There are also persistent allegations that even prior to the Iranian revolution, the Iraqi Da'wa party in the 1970s received indirect support from the Shah of Iran.

Iran has specific links with the Arab Shi'a. Apart from the visits of many Shi'a to Iran, either for religious or cultural reasons, or to visit their maraji', Iran has established ties with Shi'ite political groups, especially those that are in accord with Tehran's own ideological vision. This ideological vision, usually described as "The Imam's Line" (Khatt-e-Imam), is most commonly represented in such groups as call themselves "Hizballah" in various Arab countries. Iran has also provided refuge for thousands of Iraqi Shi'a and has specifically extended support to Shi'ite political groups. Two major groups, the Supreme Council for Islamic Revolution in Iraq and the Da'wa party are either based in Iran or have strong connections with Iran. Lebanese Shi'a who later played a prominent role in the formation of Amal and Hizballah had studied and trained in Iran during the seventies and eighties. Some Lebanese Shi'a are reported to have worked for the Iranian leadership in Iran.[6]

For any Shi'i aspiring to religious education today, study in Iran is almost a must. Thousands of students go annually to Iran, especially to Qom, to pursue religious training. Shi'ite students from Lebanon, Bahrain, Kuwait, and Saudi Arabia, who spend several years at the theological centers in Iran, are likely to pick up more than a theological education, but an entire political world outlook. Iranian seminaries typically offer needy students free education, a stipend, and housing. They create an enveloping environment that facilitates the shaping of political orientation alongside its primary educational goal. One can assume that many of these students are vulnerable to recruitment by Iranian intelligence operatives, although it is an open secret that Arab intelligence services have these schools deeply penetrated by their own agents as well.

Iranian diplomatic missions have normal contacts with Shi'ite communities abroad, and each ayatollah has his own representative (vekil) in each country, where possible, to facilitate open and formal contact between the marji' and his followers. In addition, many Gulf states have a sizeable Persian population, frequently merchants of Iranian origin, some few with Iranian passports, many of whom still speak Persian in the home even after several generations. These merchants are usually prudent and highly apolitical in their desire to maintain unexceptionable relations with the ruling families so that no whiff of disloyalty could affect their positions. In addition to these merchant families, there are often numbers of Iranian laborers on a temporary basis who add to the Iranian political presence, some of whom could possibly be (or have been) easily suborned into violent acts if required.

The Islamic Republic of Iran sees itself in one sense as the "Guardian of Islam," the center of "true" Islam in the Muslim world. It is not that Iran's Shi'ite practice is the only real form of Islam; rather Tehran would like to open new horizons by overcoming the narrowness of past dry scholarly scholasticism and the hang-ups over unimportant differences in theological interpretations that have plagued broader unity among Muslims in the past. A key ideological task of the Iranian regime is political unification of the umma, at least in spirit. It is far from accomplishing any such goal.

Some Iranian government officials in conversation state that the presence of Shi'a in the Arab world actually complicates their foreign policy tasks. According to them, Iranian policy is forced to choose between representing, almost as consuls, the rights of Shi'a abroad, and the national interests of Iran.

Iran is blamed for any and all radicalism that springs from foreign Shi'ite communities. These officials claim that if Iraq, for example, eventually comes to be dominated by Shi'a, Tehran expects that friction between the two Shi'ite centers will not be easily avoided. They say that the Islamic republic seeks to establish a universal vision of Islam; thus any concerns Tehran might show for the parochial interests of local Gulf Shi'a damage that broader image.

Who Owns Shi'ism?

The dominance of Iran today in the Shi'ite world stems from Iran's role as the sole Shi'ite state in the world, its geographical size, its large population comprising at least one-third of the all the world's Shi'a, and its cultural weight. The role as center of Shi'ism as we have seen, is only of relatively recent standing. While it would seem natural for almost any regime in Iran to take a special geopolitical interest in the welfare of all Shi'a, the Shah actually devoted little time to this issue. When he did, it was primarily to organize opposition against regimes or groups propounding radical Arab nationalist ideology, as in Iraq or Lebanon, where the regimes espoused anti-Iranian views. A key consideration in the Shah's preference to avoid strong support to the external Shi'a was his desire not to hand a strong political card to the Iranian clergy, who over the last 200 years of Iranian history had grown increasingly politically independent and outspoken.[7] It was thus the Iranian revolution and its theologically linked ideology that gave Iran the dominant voice in Shi'ite politics that it enjoys today.

But it would be a mistake to think that Iran now "owns" Shi'ism or that events have brought it permanent control over its future course. Over time it is likely that Iran's religious leadership will be increasingly challenged, particularly by Arab Shi'ites themselves who are uncomfortable with Iran's domination of the scene and will seek to contest the course of Shi'ism's future evolution and development. Several factors will probably challenge Iran's attempt to control the leadership of Shi'ism in the future. First, there is a supreme irony in the clerics' takeover of power in Iran. Shi'ism in many senses is the religion of the counterestablishment, of the excluded. It had only rarely been linked with state power until the Iranian revolution and has always flourished in the role of opposition, of independent moral critic of state power, its corruptions and failings. When Shi'ism came to power in Iran in 1979 and the clergy invested the government, where then was the clerical role of opposition to go? The moral independence of the clergy was well on the road to compromise and the clerics' traditional moral critique of power no longer had a locus.

Shi'ism has thus been compromised by coming to power. Whether the world's Shi'a like it or not, the image of Shi'ism on the international level is now being forged on a daily basis by an Iranian regime acting primarily out of its own self-interest. All Shi'a everywhere, whether they wish to or not, are affected by Iran's decisions and actions. The Iranian state furthermore, has been forced to interpret theoretical Shi'ite doctrine in practical ways and to apply it (or ignore it) quite concretely and specifically to real matters of state and society. Just as the Soviet Union ultimately defined communism for most of the world—to the extreme discomfort of millions of communists in other countries—Shi'a too are stuck with the consequences of this regime's actions. They are forced to applaud, to be defensive, or to criticize as the case may be, but any one of these positions are awkward, compromising, and complicating. To the extent that the Iranian regime has failings—and they are many—Iran has come to bear responsibility for the "failure of Shi'ism" as both a state and a society.

The historical phenomenon of the Iranian revolution has importance not only as the first state controlled by the Shi'ite clergy, but also as the first Islamist state, that is, committed to the implementation of political Islam, in the world. Here too Iran bears a certain historic responsibility. First, Khomeini and the Iranian government never called Iran a "Shi'ite state," only an Islamic state—above sectarianism or madhhab (the five schools of Islamic jurisprudence.) Thus the world's Islamists, whether they wish to or not, are also compelled to have an opinion on the Iranian experiment, because the character of Islamic governance will be partly judged by what happens in Iran. The West has formed quite concrete views on the idea of Islamist rule as a result of Iran, regardless of the fact that it is Shi'ite. And all Islamists are required to take some position on the issue of the Iranian experience because of the importance of the phenomenon. Thus the Iranian experiment has an impact on the future of all Islamic politics.

Nor has Iran's theocratic state received the endorsement of many Shi'ite clerics around the world. The Iranian state has muzzled many of its own ayatollahs for views inconvenient to state policy, especially after the death of Khomeini when the Iranian spiritual leadership was heavily contested. In January 1994, the late Ayatollah Muhammad Rouhani, then 70, was arrested by Iranian Security forces.[8] Another prominent marji', Ayatollah Shirazi, is under house arrest, and his sons and followers have suffered harassment by government security agencies.[9]

The political evolution of the Iranian state thus will have a major impact on the course of Shi'ism outside of Iran. The character of the regime and its successes and failures shape the degree of dominance, respect, acceptability, or authoritativeness that the regime possesses in speaking out on Shi'ite issues or influencing the broader Muslim community.

Second, the role of other states will also affect Iran's special relationship with the Arab Shi'a. The single most important alternative player is Iraq,

which has within it the capability to "take Shi'ism back" for the Arab world
if it chooses to. There are several inhibiting factors here, however. The present Iraqi regime has created a hostile environment for Shi'ite scholarship. It
has imprisoned, executed, or deported Shi'a clergy. It has deprived the theological centers of autonomy and undermined their scholarly resources. In
addition, the oppressive dictatorship of Saddam and the Ba'th sharply limit
any role for Shi'ite independent political expression in Iraq; the regime is be
determined to control it tightly. With these policies, however, the Ba'th has
run considerable risk in essentially chasing away its own Shi'ite clergy into a
hostile neighboring state.

Third, as long as Iraq is ruled by a small group of ruthless, paranoid and
sectarian Arab Sunnis, it will never have the confidence to allow the Iraqi
holy cities their former sway as centers of Shi'ism, nor will it give the Iraqi
Shi'a freedom for religious and political self-expression. Iraq was a more important Shi'ite center than Iran until 1970. That year, the preeminent Iraqi
Ayatollah Muhsin al-Hakim died. Simultaneously, the Ba'th began a serious
crackdown on the theological centers, persecution of the clergy, and expulsion of Shi'a. Muhsin al-Hakim's eldest son was accused of being a spy for
Israel and fled. Ayatollahs Rouhani and Shirazi were expelled. In 1969 the
government confiscated Shi'ite foundations *(awqaf)* and closed Islamic
schools.

When Iraq is finally able to achieve more representative government and
democratic practice, its majority Shi'ite population will have an interest in
encouraging Najaf and Karbala to prosper once again and to draw Arab
Shi'ite students from all over the Arab world. At that point there will be
some minor degree of concern again for potential manipulation—this time
by the Iraqi state—of international Shi'ite politics, depending on the nature
of the state and its ambitions. But this kind of problem is always the case
wherever states support religious centers of learning abroad. Saudi Arabia,
too, seeks to influence the politics and theology of Sunni universities and
madrasas all across the Muslim world via major financial support and provision of teaching staff.

Nor will Iraq be alone in the field as a rival to Iran. As Middle Eastern
states continue to evolve, they may find it preferable to encourage the development of local Shi'ite scholarship as a counterweight to external institutions. Bahrain has long had a tradition of Shi'ite learning, on a far more
modest scale, but there is no reason why that should not be resuscitated, especially at such time as the majoritarian Bahraini Shi'a have a commensurate voice in the affairs of the Bahraini state.

Finally, Lebanon has a long and distinguished history of Shi'ite learning;
indeed, it was Lebanon that provided a great number of the clerics and
teachers to the newly founded Safavid Shi'ite dynasty in Iran in 1500, when

it had limited knowledge of Shi'ite theology and practice and required massive external assistance to educate and convert Iran's then-Sunni population to Shi'ism. Today Lebanon has several Shi'ite clerical figures, both radical and moderate, of world-class importance. Shaykh Muhammad Husayn Fadhlallah, the leading Lebanese Shi'ite theologian, has already garnered a respectable following in Lebanon and has aspirations to offer an alternative Arab, Lebanese marji'iyya for Shi'a outside Lebanon as well. As the Lebanese Shi'ite community develops its capabilities, it may pursue avenues not at all in lockstep with Iran, despite Hizballah's early close ties to Iran.

Conclusion

Relations between Iran and the Arab Shi'a are subtle, complex, many-tiered, and fluid. They have exhibited considerable evolution over the past 50 years and are likely to do so again in the next 20 years as well. As Iran moves further away from considerations of religion and revolution and toward the demands of the state, internal reform, and international normalization, its support for Arab Shi'a groups will be selective, understated, and dependent on its national and security interests. Iran is likely to ignore the needs of Shi'a in Arab countries with whom Iran has good bilateral relations. It will not allow defense of Shi'ism to jeopardize its national interests but will probably use the Arab Shi'a card strategically if it can do so. This shift is already apparent in relations between Iran and Saudi Arabia on the one hand, and Iran and the Saudi Shi'a on the other. These problems indeed reflect a broader Arab problem: the welter of political parties of internationalist character, both Arab nationalist and Islamist, whose interests and constituencies cut across borders, and that thus serve as instruments of influence for one Arab state over the internal politics of another. The system of interrelationships among Arab states in fact has no parallel anywhere else in the world: a linguistic, cultural, intellectual, and hence even ideological network that has the effect of sapping the national sovereignty of the individual Arab states. This reality may lessen with time, but it will never completely disappear. Religious links will also matter among Arab states, and increasingly, even among Muslim states more broadly. In a globalizing world, the identity provided by the umma offers a useful cultural antidote to Western cultural dominance. States will thus compete for a chance to influence that umma.

As a counterpoint to changes in Iranian foreign policy, Arab Shi'a too are likely to distance themselves from Iran if they feel there is little to gain by the connection and much to lose, either domestically or internationally. Arab Shi'a who are struggling to gain full representation and equal status in their local body politic may choose to assert their independence from Iran and confirm their nationalism. A certain measure of animosity toward Iran could even emerge, perhaps as an overreaction to Iran's overbearing role of the past. Again, the symptoms of this change are evident in the attitudes of Saudi and Bahraini Shi'a who recognize the shift against Iran and are eager to establish their autonomy from Iranian influence. Iraqi Shi'a are far more divided on this issue because many Iraqis live in Iran, or are dependent on Iran in other ways. However, once the distorted political order in Iraq under Saddam gives way to a system that gives the Shi'a reasonable representative power in the state we are likely to see a rivalry between Iraqis and Iranians over the definition, direction, and management of Shi'ite political activism.

From a Western point of view, Iran's ties with Shi'ite communities could become a positive rather than negative feature if Iran's own policies should undergo moderation and Iran adopt a more constructive role in the region. Under any circumstances, it is in no one's broader interests that any state should possess a dominant voice over the evolution and outlook of the Shi'a community as a whole. A multiplicity of religious centers and a maximum degree of choice among maraji' or different schools of thought will create a more positive climate that is susceptible to modernizing trends. This same thought indeed applies to any religion: theological pronouncements that are highly centralized, potentially hostage to state mechanisms and interests, and somewhat enforceable due to the power of the issuing state can only create tensions. Shi'ism will likely always retain the function of maraji', but with time increasing diversity is likely to characterize the institution.

Thus, Iran's relationship to world Shi'ism is not permanent, but its geographic, demographic, political, and cultural weight guarantees it will remain a major player. In the next century we are likely to see strong Arab contention to restore the influence of Arab Shi'ism as well, thus providing a rivalry to Iran's current role, for better or for worse.

CHAPTER FIVE

The Shi'a of Iraq

The Iraqi Shi'a form the single most important group of Shi'a in the Arab world, both in terms of their number and their intellectual/ideological influence. The Shi'a form 55 to 60 percent of the 22 million population of Iraq, or roughly 12 million people.[1] The majority are Arabs, with a small number of Shi'ite Kurds, Turkomans, and Arabized Persians. Although the Shi'a form an absolute majority, the Iraqi state since its formation has been dominated by Sunnis, and for the past three decades increasingly controlled by a handful of Sunni clans, dominated by Saddam Hussein and his family. Since the late 1970s, Iraqi Shi'a have been leaving Iraq in large numbers to settle in Iran, Syria, Britain, and other Arab and European countries, where they form a vocal opposition to the Iraqi regime. Inside Iraq, Shi'ite groups in the south have kept up a consistent, if weak, armed resistance to the government of Saddam Hussein. Although Iraqis from all communities have expressed their dissatisfaction with the Iraqi regime in a variety of ways, the Shi'ite community, particularly since 1991, has become its most implacable foe.

Should—or when—the Iraqi Shi'a acquire political strength commensurate with their numbers, they have the potential to revolutionize the political landscape in Iraq and to influence significantly the fortunes of the Shi'a in other Arab countries. The impact of a strong Iraqi Shi'ite community on other Arab Shi'a is likely to exceed that of Iran because of shared ethnicity—language, culture, and historical affinity. Moreover, Iraq's importance to the Arab scene means that Iraqi Shi'a can begin to reshape prevailing Sunni attitudes toward Shi'ism and bring Shi'ism into the mainstream of Arab culture as a whole. Iraqi Shi'a thus have community responsibilities that surpass their borders: the choices they make will have profound consequences for fellow Shi'a in the region and can improve or worsen conditions for the Shi'a in Arab countries. The possible consequences of a new Shi'ite prominence in Iraq figured significantly in the considerations of the United States and its allies in the aftermath of the Gulf War and led to allied decisions toward Saddam that Iraqis, especially Shi'ite Iraqis, still deplore and condemn.

Impact of Iraqi Shi'a on Arab Political Culture

At 12 million strong, the Shi'a of Iraq are more numerous than the native populations of the Gulf Cooperation Council countries put together. (In comparison, the Lebanese community, the second largest, is 1.2 million.) This assures them visibility and voice in the region unmatched by any other Shi'ite community. Both Shi'ite numbers and Iraq's place in the Arab world will eventually give Iraqi Shi'a a unique opportunity to shape regional perceptions and even begin to modify the prevalent state-dominated understanding of Arabism and the nature of the Arab state. Furthermore, no other country, even including Iran, is as closely identified with Shi'ism as is Iraq. Southern Iraq in particular is the original spiritual home of Shi'ism and the site of its heroic and tragic events in the early years of Islam. From the early nineteenth century until the late 1960s, the holy cities of Iraq were the preeminent centers of theological scholarship for the Shi'a of the world. Iraq's role and authority in the intellectual and spiritual development of Shi'ism throughout history is undisputed, albeit tarnished and dimmed in the past several decades of Ba'th rule and eclipsed by Iran since the Iranian revolution.

Following World War I, Iraqi Shi'a participated with Sunnis in the process of state-building; the early twentieth-century history of Iraq is closely associated with the Shi'a-led struggle for independence from British colonial rule. The "revolution" of 1920 against the British, which predated and in some ways precipitated the formation of the Iraqi state later under King Faysal, was spearheaded by Shi'ite clerics and tribesmen: At the forefront of the revolution were prominent lay Shi'ite dignitaries, merchants, and tribal shaykhs, supported by Shi'ite clergy. Although the revolution was not an exclusively Shi'ite movement and encompassed many Sunni notables, it propelled to national prominence several Shi'ite leaders, such as the much revered Ja'far Abu'l-Timman, who later founded or took part in nationalist parties and played an active role as an advocate of independence from Britain.[2]

Political Shi'ism had its beginnings in Iraq in the 1950s. The seminaries and schools of Najaf were the crucible in which the ideas of young politicized clerics from the Arab world took shape and gained expression. Muhammad Baqir al-Sadr, a youthful and brilliant Iraqi cleric with family connections throughout the Shi'ite world, was the principal intellectual force and energy behind a Shi'ite project for political Islam. His critique of

Western and communist political philosophies, his construction of an Islamic alternative, and his vision of popular sovereignty in Shi'ism are still
part of the Islamist Shi'ite canon 35 years later—and at odds with much of
the prevailing orthodoxy of Khomeini's Iran today. Non-Iraqi Arab clerics,
such as Muhammad Husayn Fadhlallah from Lebanon (later the spiritual
guide of Lebanon's Hizballah), worked closely with al-Sadr. The influence of
al-Sadr himself and other Najaf-educated Arab clerics was seminal in the
subsequent formation of Shi'ite political movements across the Arab world.

In addition to its Shi'ite credentials, Iraq has been central to the development of Arab identity and Arab history and has contributed critically to
social, political, and intellectual developments in the Arab Mashriq. Iraq was
the first Arab country to gain independence following World War I, albeit
under British mandate.[3] Since independence, it has been at the center of
Arab history and has helped shape Arab discourse and policies. For example,
Iraq in 1940 was a driving force behind the formation of the Arab League,[4]
and Iraqis were engaged in the definition of Arab nationhood from the
1930s onward. In education, the arts, literature, and scholarship, Iraq has
been an important actor, alongside Egypt and Syria, in shaping Arab culture
in its contemporary form. The Iraqi Shi'a see themselves as vital contribu-
tors to this process and regard their contributions as part of the Arab national heritage.

If the Shi'a gain political status in Iraq, they will unquestionably want to
continue Iraq's political and cultural engagement in the Arab world, as the
Lebanese Shi'a have done, but will also want to reshape some of the concepts
that have dominated this world, particularly those prejudices that have been
damaging to Shi'a. The track record they establish in Iraq will be closely
watched by the people and governments of all countries in the region. To the
discomfiture of Sunni elite in the Arab world, they are likely to challenge the
fixed notion that Arab governments must necessarily be Sunni, and they will
break the custom of equating Arabism with Sunnism that has been so long
implicit in the culture of the Arab world. More boldly, Iraqi Shi'a have the
ability to influence the past as well: they can recast Arab historiography to
incorporate Shi'ism as an essential component of that history. The repercussions of Iraqi Shi'ite political revival can be positive or negative for the Arab
Shi'a as a whole, depending on the resolution of intra-Shi'ite and Shi'ite-
Sunni tensions, the choices they make on domestic issues, and their relations
with the countries in the region.

But for the Shi'a to gain a level of participation that is more representative of their numbers, the Iraqi state must undergo structural changes that
are at least as far-reaching as the revolutionary change from monarchy to republic that occurred in 1958. The Shi'a will have to reverse 30 years of per-
sonalized Ba'thist rule as well as 80 years of engrained habits and biases.

More important, they will have to persuade the Sunnis of Iraq that the Shi'a are not a mortal danger to Sunni interests and that democracy is not a "Shi'ite agenda" and an excuse for reverse discrimination. Even assuming the best intentions, this will be a demanding task for the Shi'a.

The World of the Shi'a

Citing historical records, author Yitzhak Nakash argues in *The Shi'is of Iraq* that Iraqi tribes converted to Shi'ism in large numbers only in the eighteenth and nineteenth centuries.[5] While the cities of the south, except the port city Basra, were established Shi'ite centers, the countryside and desert around them were home to nomadic Sunni tribes who traveled back and forth across the Saudi and Syrian borders. Shi'ite conversion was simultaneous with, and a consequence of, their progressive settlement and adoption of agrarian rather than nomadic patterns of association. Thus, according to this analyis, the Iraqi population was not predominantly Shi'a until the end of the nineteenth century, although they numbered 53 percent of the population by the time of the British census of 1919.

In many respects the collective conscious of Iraq south of Baghdad is bound up with Shi'ite history and traditions. Imam 'Ali, the fourth caliph of the Muslims and first Imam of the Shi'a, revered above all others, established Kufa as his capital and is buried in nearby Najaf. His son al-Husayn, the third and most beloved Imam of the Shi'a, was martyred and buried in Karbala, along with his brother, the warrior hero al-'Abbas. The martyrdom of Husayn, with its myriad interpretations and embellishments, is the emotional and intellectual nexus that governs the Shi'ite view of the world. The gilded domes, intricate mosaics, and glittering treasures displayed by the shrines of 'Ali, Husayn, and 'Abbas contrast magnificently with the surrounding flat deserts of Iraq. Just north of Baghdad, the suburb of Kadhimayn houses the extensive shrines of the seventh and ninth Imams. Further north is the city of Samarra, a Sunni city that nevertheless holds the shrines of the tenth and eleventh Imams. However, Samarra is most important for being the birth place of the twelfth Imam, known as al-Mahdi (the Guided One) and al-Muntadhar (the Awaited). Al-Mahdi's occultation, also in Samarra, stands at the center of Shi'ite eschatology and the philosophy of a coming age of righteousness.

Shi'ism in Iraq is not only a religious doctrine; it is also a culture and a geography, and its power derives as much from the richness of the heritage and environment as from religious belief. The Tigris and the Euphrates converge in southern Iraq, and their distributaries, flowing toward a central basin, form the great expanse of the marshlands. This ancient region, with floating villages, forests of reeds, water buffalo, wild fowl, and elaborately constructed reed *madhifs,* or guest houses, is the legendary site of Sumer, the first civilization of Mesopotamia. Below the marsh areas the two rivers flow into a broad estuary that is one of Iraq's grandest palm grove regions. The watery lush landscape of lower Mesopotamia is as much a part of the Shi'ite cultural consciousness as are the shrine cities of Najaf and Karbala.

The communal ceremonies of Shi'ism are performed on a grand scale in the three principal shrine cities, Najaf, Karbala, and Kadhimayn, and more modestly in Shi'ite neighborhoods, houses and husayniyas in other major Iraqi cities. The ceremonies are accompanied by a rich folklore of symbols and rituals performed at mass gatherings, with *qirayat,* or laments for Husayn's martyrdom, group readings from the lives of the Imams, meals for the poor outside the mosques, and sacrificial offerings to the Imams at the shrines. The most powerful ceremonies are held at 'Ashura, the annual commemoration of the death of Imam Husayn, when hundreds of thousands of the faithful converge on Karbala in processions from towns and cities throughout Iraq. The emotional power of this collective ritual permeates the awareness of even those Shi'a who are not particularly religious. The corpus of the Shi'ite tradition—seasonal pilgrimage, religious processions, texts, images and idioms, food and sacrifices—defines the Shi'ite mental landscape equally with religious belief, and it does so on a wider, more popular, scale. The heritage of Shi'ism is a source of pride for Iraqi Shi'a, who like to see a divine grace in their proximity to the Imams and their custody of the holy shrines.

In the ninth and tenth centuries, when Shi'ism was undergoing consolidation, Shi'ite classical texts, history, and tradition were written or codified in Kufa and Hilla, but by the eleventh century Najaf had become the principal center of scholarship, and the great university of Najaf dates back to that period. The history of Shi'ite scholarship in the holy cities is uneven, and Iraqi theological centers vied with Iranian centers such as Rayy, Isfahan, and Qom even prior to Iran's official conversion to Shi'ism in 1501.[6] By the nineteenth century, religious and intellectual dynamism had shifted back to Najaf and Karbala, led by an expanding body of 'ulama and students, many of whom came from Iran as well as from Lebanon, India, and other countries. The lax control of the late Ottoman Empire and later the relative tolerance of the monarchy in Iraq allowed the Shi'a in the south to build mosques, schools, and husayniyas, celebrate Shi'ite festivals, and perform collective religious rituals without interference. Najaf became the home of great religious mentors, maraji', of all nationalities. The two shrine cities again became magnets for pilgrimage, and revenues accrued from the mandatory *khums* (a tithe of 20 percent of profits) that devout Shi'a paid to the maraji', and from the burial of corpses that were carried from all Muslim lands. To a great extent, Najaf and Karbala were autonomous regions in which the writ of the imperial Ottoman administration was secondary to the authority of the great 'ulama.

The world of the Shi'a at the start of the twentieth century was divided between the urban population of towns like Najaf, Karbala, Hilla, and Baghdad and a rural population that is more tribally structured and less controllable.[7] The cities were centers of trade for merchants and craftsmen, and of learning and piety for pilgrims and scholars. They served as entrepots as well as seats of local government and military garrisons. The countryside, by contrast, was populated by semi-settled and nomadic tribes who cultivated the land or raised herds, but who were equally prone to feuding and looting. Relations between town and countryside were regulated by kinships, alliances, and trade, punctuated by periodic tribal raids of the towns. From the early 1900s, Shi'ite merchants began moving northward into Baghdad or south to Basra, and migration accelerated after World War II, when the economic infrastructure and the increasing centralization of government offered greater opportunities for employment in the major cities than did the restricted economies of southern towns. Shi'a peasantry from the rural areas also flocked to Baghdad, congregating in its poor suburbs. The Shi'a in Baghdad and elsewhere outside the shrine cities maintained their connections to Karbala and Najaf through extended family, relations with the senior clerics, and frequent visits to secondary residences, especially during periods of religious observance, for the 'Ashura commemoration, or for family funerals.

Land ownership in southern Iraq, previously fluid and claimed collectively by the tribe, was recorded and consolidated under the Ottoman Land Code of 1869 through the *Tapu*, or land registry. As a consequence of this modernizing measure the rural population was converted into a captive peasant class employed by a small number of large landlords and tribal shaykhs, who controlled the production of grain, rice, dates, and wool in Iraq. These feudal lords were an indispensable pillar of support through the 35-year life of the monarchy, and were awarded prestige and favor by the court. One of the first acts of the revolution of 1958, influenced by leftist and socialists trends in the country, was to promulgate the Agrarian Reform Act, which broke up the large holdings in an effort to distribute land to the peasantry. However, the immediate consequence of the Act was a severe decline in agricultural production, and a resulting migration of poor Shi'a in increasing numbers to Baghdad and other major cities. As in Lebanon, the great migration of Shi'a from the south to Baghdad that has continued since World War II improved economic conditions for some Shi'a but also created impoverished Shi'ite ghettos in the capital. The poorer Shi'a in the cities were an underclass in relation both to the Sunnis and to the affluent Shi'a, and they were therefore doubly disadvantaged in their opportunities for integration into society. The new Shi'ite slums were fertile soil for communism and later for Islamist radicalism.

With the centralization of government in Baghdad after Iraqi independence, and rising oil revenue flowing to the state, Shi'a merchants already established in Najaf, Karbala, and, to a lesser extent, Basra also moved in large numbers to the capital, where they founded trading houses and often amassed considerable financial capital and prestige. Some tribal shaykhs joined the Shi'ite merchant class, creating overlapping interests and multiple community ties. The sons of this wealthy entrepreneurial class went to universities in the Arab world and in the West and formed the Shi'ite intellectual and professional elite that emerged after World War II. In the 1940s and 1950s, the last two decades of the monarchy, this financially secure and educated class became progressively involved in political life. The resulting social fissure within the community is captured by scholar Hanna Batatu: "if in 1958 the richest of the rich were often Shi'a, so were also predominantly the poorest of the poor."[8]

The revolution—some say the military coup—of 1958, led by General 'Abd-al-Karim Qasim, was a setback to this upper class of Shi'a but not necessarily to all Shi'a. The social and welfare reforms of the first Iraqi republic targeted the neediest sectors of Iraqi society, which in practice meant the Shi'ite poor, providing housing projects, expanded education and health care, and jobs in the public sector. Subsequent coups in Iraq, twice in 1963 and again in 1968, were more damaging to Shi'ite interests. In 1964, the government of 'Abd-al-Salam 'Arif, an Arab nationalist Sunni army officer committed to Egyptian-style socialism, issued a number of decrees nationalizing banks, industries, insurance companies, and the import of major commodities.[9] Nationalization directly affected the financial interests of the Shi'ite entrepreneurs, who had by then branched from trade into industry. Additionally, the Aref regime of 1963 and particularly the Ba'th regime that removed it from power in 1968 carried a pronounced Sunni sectarian bias that was detrimental to the social and political interests of a broad spectrum of Iraqi Shi'a.

The Iraqi Shi'a and the State

The rise of the vigorous Safavids dynasty in Iran, newly and ardently Shi'ite, brought Persian imperial ambition face to face with the expanding Ottoman Empire. Nowhere was the contest of these two powers more devastatingly experienced than in Iraq, which from the early sixteenth to the late eighteenth century, became the worn-out battlefield of their contests.[10] Each imperial power, upon capturing Baghdad, would embark on a sectarian revenge to which the Sunnis or the Shi'a would in turn fall victim. The decay of Safavid rule ended any serious Persian claim and confirmed Ottoman supremacy over

Iraq until World War I. After centuries of tenuous rule, Turkish administrative control over Iraq strengthened in the second half of the nineteenth century with the application of the *wilayat* (province) system. Turkish officials formed the corps of senior civil servants and other government officials, but a small cadre of native Iraqis took root in the bureaucratic system, alongside the Turks. Given the long history of rivalry with Persia over Iraq, and the sectarian propaganda that frequently accompanied the rivalry, it was only natural for Ottoman rule to place its trust in urban Iraqi Sunnis as the foundation for a local system of support. The choice for the successive Ottoman governors was made easier by the aloofness and intractability of the Shi'a, whether they were unruly tribes or truculent citizens of the shrine cities. Thus the Sunni community benefited from at least a minimal level of patronage and education, while the Shi'a, especially in the regions south of Baghdad, remained outside the system.

When creating the Iraqi state after World War I, the British colonial power was assisted by a group of Sunni military officers who had earlier served in the Ottoman army and later joined the Arab revolt of 1916 against Turkey. The Arab revolt was launched by the Hashemite Sharif Husayn of Mecca and his sons, but it was encouraged, supplied, and guided by the British, who worked closely with the Iraqi officers. These Iraqi officers accepted the leadership of Prince Faysal, son of Sharif Husayn, joined him briefly in Syria, and then moved back with him to Iraq when he was crowned king in 1921. After brief hesitancy born of religious scruple, the Sunni notables of Baghdad, including former government officials, landowners, and religious leaders, welcomed the Arab revolution and Britain's role. The Iraqi Shi'a had a more ambivalent attitude toward the British during World War I. When British troops were battling Turkey on Iraqi soil, Shi'ite clerics and tribal shaykhs balked at supporting an infidel against a Muslim power, particularly as the presence of British forces and administration in southern Iraq threatened to limit the authority and economic advantages of both clerics and shaykhs.

Once Turkey had been firmly evicted and British presence had became a fact of life, the disposition of Iraq's future occupied the attention of Iraqis. The Shi'a were in the vanguard of *Thawrat al-'Ishrin*, or revolution of 1920, which demanded independence from Britain and indeed precipitated the declaration of the Iraqi monarchy. As a result of what they considered a pivotal role in the revolution, the Shi'a saw themselves as at least equal partners in a future Iraqi state, and they were severely disappointed when the British handed Iraq over to the Sunni military elite. The British decision stemmed from several factors, the most important of which was the history of relations between the British occupying forces and the two confessional groups. For religious considerations, the Shi'a had been largely hostile to the British during the War and fought alongside Turkey when British troops took over Basra and began moving north through the Shi'ite heartland. Only a few Sunni leaders were opposed to the British, and in fact many of them had worked closely with them and sought their support. Additionally, the Sunnis were an urbanized society, more predictable and easier to understand and control. The majority of the Shi'a, in contrast, still followed an unruly and arcane tribal social order that was far less fathomable and manageable for the British. Sunni society also offered a cadre of relatively educated civil servants who had trained in Ottoman government services and were familiar with the administration of the provinces.

Another factor that swayed Britain toward Sunnis was the political activism of Shi'ite clerics and their influence over the Shi'ite population. The Shi'ite senior clergy in Iraq, many of whom were of Iranian origin, had been particularly damaging to British interests in Iran in 1891, when their decisive opposition forced the Iranian government to repeal a tobacco monopoly granted to Britain. Again, in 1909, the Shi'ite clerics supported the constitutional movement in Iran that brought about the downfall of the Qajar Shah. In Iraq, the grand marji' Mirza Muhammad Taqi Shirazi, based in Karbala, issued a fatwa in November 1919 forbidding Muslims from choosing or electing a non-Muslim to rule Iraq.[11] In August 1920, Shirazi issued another fatwa that legitimized the 1920 revolt against the British.[12] The involvement of the Shi'ite clergy in anti-British political activism, their defiant independence, and their power over the Shi'ite community rendered the Shi'a unattractive partners and tilted the British toward support of the Sunnis as a less troublesome community and easier to handle.

The overlap of Sunnism with military authority and with state formation that began during the war was consolidated after independence and remained unaffected by the modest measures taken during the monarchy to include Shi'ite tribal shaykhs and notables in parliament or in the cabinet. The increasing power of the Iraqi armed forces and the rise of militant Arab nationalism in the 1930s and 1940s served only to entrench Sunni power. Extreme forms of Arab nationalism, culminating in the Ba'thist seizure of power in 1968 and the eventual restriction of authority to a handful of Sunni allied clans, reversed previous efforts by the state to include the Shi'a in Iraq's power structure. For their part, most Shi'a distrusted government and shunned public office. The clergy discouraged the Shi'ite population from entering into the service of a government that they regarded as illegitimate and a threat to their authority. Thus, for example, in the 1920s the 'ulama frowned upon attendance at the newly established government schools because they took children away from the supervision of the clergy and taught a secular curriculum. When the Iraqi army was formed in 1921 the Shi'ite clergy opposed it, and in the next few decades few Shi'a entered military academies.

During the early years of the monarchy, King Faysal I and some political leaders were aware that a system in which a Sunni Arab minority ruled a Shi'ite Arab majority (and a large Kurdish minority) was flawed and unstable. In a confidential memorandum of March 1933, shortly before his death, King Faysal warned against the dangers and the inherent instability of such a system.[13] As a result, the monarchy wooed prominent Shi'ite tribal shaykhs and landowners, creating a narrow segment of Shi'ite allies whom it could control through benefits and privileges. Additionally, the government followed a relatively enlightened but slow course of spreading education among the Shi'a and bringing them into government service. During the life of the monarchy, from 1921 to 1958, there were 4 Shi'ite prime ministers out of 23 (all of whom took office after 1947), though there were several Shi'ite cabinet members and a large number of Shi'ite parliamentarians.[14] Despite these steps by the government, participation among the Shi'a was limited to a narrow class, and sensitive state sectors such as defense, the police force, and finance were reserved for Sunnis. Because measures to include the Shi'a moved slowly, were strictly controlled, and affected a limited group, reform only grazed the surface and had little effect on the Shi'ite population at large; thus the stark political imbalance between the Sunnis and the Shi'a was only partially redressed during the 35 years of Hashemite rule.

Instead, Iraqi Shi'a, like their Lebanese and Bahraini counterparts, gravitated toward revolutionary parties outside the existing political framework. Politics with a strong ideological content drew newly educated and restless Shi'ite youth from the rising middle classes. Communism in particular was attractive to this sector of the Shi'a because it drew on ideals of social justice, class equality, and equitable wealth distribution—all notably deficient in Iraq, especially where the Shi'a were concerned. The Shi'a formed the bulk of the Iraqi Communist Party membership in the 1950s and 1960s, to such an extent that Communism became identified with them (hence the linkage of *Shi'i, shiyu'i, shu'ubi*—Shi'ite, communist, non-Arab—cited in Chapter 2). The Sunnis, by contrast, and despite their rivalries, saw the state as "their party," and themselves as the party of the state, with room for collective self-expression and achievement within the existing state system, even when they were opposed to a particular government at a given time. Opposition politics within the political framework was largely an insiders' competition for power among Sunni factions, in which the Shi'a played only a secondary role.

Arab nationalism in its Ba'thist translation also attracted disaffected young Shi'a when it was in its revolutionary phase, though to a far lesser extent than Communism. Ba'thism offered an indigenous ideology grounded in Arab identity, with a promise to transcend sectarian differences and disengage from Western colonialism. The Shi'a were sufficiently attracted to the Ba'th to be in the civilian leadership of the fledgling party at the time of the first Ba'th coup d'état in 1963. However, after the Ba'th seized power briefly in 1963, and once the second Ba'th regime was instated in 1968, that is to say when the Ba'th itself became the party of the state, Shi'ite presence in the party declined sharply and Shi'ite leadership was virtually eliminated. A breakdown of the composition of the Ba'th Party Regional (Iraqi) Command in this period is illustrative. While in 1963, 6 out of the 13 members of the Ba'th Regional Command were Shi'a, there were none by 1970. Similarly, the Revolution Command Council of the first Ba'th regime in 1963 included 6 Shi'a among 18 members. The 15-member Revolution Command Council established by the second Ba'th regime in 1968 included not a single Shi'ite member.[15] After 1964, the Shi'a progressively lost any political gains they had made in the 1940s and 1950s and under the brief regime of 'Abd-al-Karim Qasim between 1958 and 1963. After 1969, the new Ba'th government began a severe curtailment of Shi'ite cultural and religious life, confiscating endowments, closing down seminaries, and banning religious processions.

Secular Arab nationalism had the potential to transform political practice by advancing a system that rises above sectarianism and religion. However, Arab nationalism, and especially the intellectually circumscribed Ba'th, failed in this task in Iraq, and instead consolidated the existing Sunni political culture. At least in theory, the Ba'th regime sees Iraq as part of the larger Arab world rather than an end in itself, and it draws heavily on the lore, imagery, and traditions of mainstream Arab history, which usually ignores or actively denigrates Shi'ite contributions. In practice, adopting a pan-Arabist position in Iraq was an easy solution for the Ba'th because it avoided the question of minority Sunni rule and grounded legitimacy in Arab rather than Iraqi credentials. Thus, during the 1970s and 1980s, the Ba'th regime coined an abstract political language that addressed the Arab world at large, rather than the specific conditions in Iraq and the nature and needs of Iraqi society.[16] When the Kurdish issue forced itself upon the attention of the Ba'th leadership in the 1970s through continued armed resistance by the Kurds, the regime responded with a mixture of violence and lip service to Kurdish demands: the Kurds, as a non-Arab minority, were deemed a peripheral presence that could do little damage to the Arab Ba'thist government in Baghdad. The Shi'a, however, present a more dangerous problem that does not permit any compromise: as Arabs and as the majority, they are at the heart of the Iraqi nation and in a position to dramatically alter the political landscape of Iraq. Any acknowledgment that the Shi'a are marginalized and neglected and that redress is necessary would threaten the regime's base of power. Understandably, therefore, making the political system better represent the demographic composition of Iraq and improving opportunities for the Shi'a is not part of the Ba'th political program.

Of particular relevance to Iraqi Shi'a, Arab nationalism for long defined itself by its enemies and viewed the Persians as the historical foes of the Arabs who pose a perennial threat to Arab civilization. The equation of Shi'ism with Persia and the long presence of Iranian theologians and families in Iraq placed the Shi'a under the spotlight of suspicion. The notion of shu'ubiya as the convergence of Shi'a and Persian (that is, anti-Arab) influence was revived in the political discourse of Iraqi Arab nationalists, reaching extremes of jingoism in the writings of Khayrallah al-Tulfah, Saddam Hussein's uncle, father-in-law, and mentor. Because of the intimate association of Persia with Shi'ism, the Shi'a suffered guilt by association in a dogmatic interpretation of Arab nationalism.

In addition to its ideological straightjacket and its vested interests, Ba'thism since 1968 has been manipulated by the Iraqi regime into a tool for exclusion and concentration of power in the hands of a few. Although the exclusion increasingly affects urban Sunnis, it has been near total for the Shi'a. As mentioned, in 1970 there was not a single Shi'ite member in the Revolution Command Council, the only decision-making body in the state. Yet during the 1970s the Iraqi government made decisions that were to affect Iraq's future for decades: a new provisional constitution was drafted, a landmark autonomy agreement with the Kurds was signed—and then broken by the regime in a new war against the Kurds—the maritime border between Iran and Iraq was redefined—then abrogated by Saddam—and Iraq's oil sector was nationalized. The Shi'a had no voice in any of these decisions. The discrimination against the Shi'a by the Ba'th of 1968 was due in great measure to a visceral prejudice felt by the new regime's leaders, who came from the lower-middle classes of small Sunni towns in Iraq's central provinces and represented an insular segment of society far less tolerant and integrated than residents of the major cities. The discrimination also reflected a determination by the regime to restrict political power to an ever-diminishing group of people, eventually forcing out the military and the party itself, limiting power to a handful of allied clans.

Under the guise of secularism, the Ba'thist regime of Saddam Hussein denies sectarian bias while it pursues vigorous political and religious discrimination against the Shi'a. The policy of the Iraqi regime has been to (1) deny pursuing sectarian considerations in its domestic policies, (2) condemn Shi'ite demands as sectarian, divisive, and inspired by Iran, (3) bring a token number of Shi'a into minor or ceremonial posts to forestall criticism,[17] (4) enfeeble and stunt Shi'ite religious institutions, and (5) strike hard at Shi'ite activism. While the regime permits the private practice of Shi'ism, it fights any corporate or public expression of Shi'ism and manifestation of Shi'ite solidarity, and it undermines the autonomy and academic strength of religious institutions. Execution of Shi'ite clerics is only one manifestation of the regime's repression of the Shi'a. In 1979, the year Saddam Hussein became president of Iraq, at least 14 Shi'ite clerics were executed, and in 1980 a further 13.[18] A far larger wave of executions and "disappearances" of Shi'ite clerics occurred in 1991, when, among many others, 96 members of the al-Hakim family and 28 members of the Bahrul Ulum family were seized by the regime and "disappeared."

Finally, it should be noted that the problem for the Shi'a in Iraq is with the state rather than with the rest of Iraqi society. The larger cities, particularly Baghdad and Basra, have long had a relatively high measure of integration and amicable relations between the Sunni and Shi'ite communities. Most neighborhoods in Baghdad, and especially new ones, have a mixed population, although there are also predominantly Sunni neighborhoods and predominantly Shi'ite neighborhoods, just as there are predominantly Christian and Kurdish ones. On the whole, demographic distribution is more dependent on economic status or profession than on religion and ethnicity. This is particularly true of neighborhoods that were built after 1958 to house members of specific professions, such as teachers, army officers, or others. Similarly, social relations within the Shi'ite community itself and between the Shi'a and Sunnis are determined largely by class and professional association, rather than on a confessional basis. Shi'a-Sunni intermarriage has become commonplace, and mixed business partnership are equally accepted and practiced. However, even in the mixing bowl of Baghdad, Shi'ite communitarian ties persist through collective religious observance and domestic customs. Shi'ite customs are socially tolerated but considered "quaint" by the Sunnis.

Radicalization of Shi'ite Attitudes Toward the State

Whereas the Iraqi state practiced active repression of the Kurds to varying degrees throughout its history, its policy toward the Shi'a until the 1960s was one of discrimination to the extent that the state was overwhelmingly controlled by the Sunni community, with all the administrative advantages that follow from such domination. As in other countries, discrimination against the Shi'a is disguised and undeclared: in theory they are an integral part of the state rather than an accidental addition, yet in fact they have no part in the state. Thus while the government of Iraq in 1970 accepted the principle that the Kurds have a right to local autonomy, it is inconceivable for the Shi'a to present an argument for Shi'ite rights, or for the central government to accept such an argument. As a result, many Iraqi

Shi'a are afflicted with a "victimhood" mentality and are burdened with a unresolved conflicts.

Decades of discrimination, combined with dissatisfaction with social, political, and economic conditions, galvanized a circle of Shi'a in the 1960s into adopting a radical platform that was perceived as a more serious threat to the state than Kurdish demands. As Arabs and Muslims, the Shi'a could not seek separate status on religious, ethnic, or linguistic grounds. While the Kurds, Turkomans, or Christians can negotiate a set of rights and immunities as minority groups, the Shi'a are in a sensitive position because their platform is global; it assails the very nature of the state and questions some of the fundamental assumptions of power in Baghdad.

During its formative years in the 1950s and 1960s, the revival of Shi'ism as a personal belief and practice came in reaction to the increasing secularism of Iraqi society and the gains made by the communists among young, educated Shi'a. But the conflict with Communism, whose influence on Iraq's political institutions was at best limited, was on the level of ideology and did not present a physical threat to Shi'ism or the Shi'a. The nature of the threat to Shi'ism altered when the Ba'th assumed power in Iraq in 1968. The new regime was an imminent danger to Shi'ism at every level, and it threatened the security and welfare of the community.

Toward the end of the 1950s, Shi'ite clerics began to formulate an Islamic alternative to Communism, surpassing it in passion and authenticity. Although this Islamic alternative aspired to pan-Islamic status, in practice it was promoted by Shi'ite clerics, especially Sayid Muhammad Baqir al-Sadr and Sayid Mahdi al-Hakim, son of the great marji', Ayatollah Muhsin al-Hakim. It employed Shi'ite terminology, addressed itself to the Shi'a, and recruited in the southern provinces and the poor Shi'ite areas of Baghdad. Apart from expressing sympathy for the emerging movement, the affluent, urbanized Shi'ite classes resisted recruitment. The Da'wa party, the first Islamist Shi'ite political organization, was first conceived in 1958 in Najaf but formally declared itself only in 1968.[19] The members of the Da'wa looked to al-Sadr and al-Hakim for intellectual and spiritual inspiration, but al-Sadr was never a member and there is doubt about Mahdi al-Hakim's exact role in the formation and propagation of the party. The Da'wa originally confined itself to *tabligh,* calling the people to the faith, educating, and reviving religious commitment. Eventually, it became an activist political party, operating underground and developing an intellectual content to set against the doctrines of Arabism and Communism.

The radicalization of Shi'ite self-awareness in Iraq after 1968 was a natural outcome of the clash between increasing state discrimination and restriction of Shi'ite religious freedom on the one hand, and Shi'ite clerical interests and popular sentiment on the other. The Ba'th seizure of power in 1968 was followed by a crackdown on Shi'ite institutions, curtailment of the autonomy historically enjoyed by the clerical establishment, prohibition of many of Shi'ite practices, and deportation of thousands of Shi'ite families. The Iraqi regime pursued the Shi'ite Islamists with ruthless brutality through the 1970s and 1980s, targeting Da'wa members, their families, sympathizers, and the clergy who were their spiritual guides. As early as 1969, the regime arrested and tortured Sayid Mahdi al-Hakim, accusing him of being an Israeli spy.[20] Between 1970 and 1985, the regime executed at least 41 clerics, including Muhammad Baqir al-Sadr and his sister, Bint al-Huda, in 1980.[21] In 1988, the regime assassinated Mahdi al-Hakim in Khartoum. Hundreds of other clerics were arrested in the two decades, many of whom have never been released and are included in the ranks of thousands of "disappeared" Iraqis. In 1980 the Iraqi Revolution Command Council issued an edict retroactively making membership in the Da'wa party a capital offense. The edict was somewhat superfluous: the regime had been arresting, torturing, and killing people accused or suspected of being Da'wa members and sympathizers for at least eight years by then. Indeed the methods of torture inflicted on Da'wa suspects became the stuff of fearful whispering and instilled terror and dread among Iraq's Shi'a.

Government repression was not confined to the Da'wa or to religious Shi'a but afflicted the community at large. A campaign of forced expulsion of Shi'ite families got under way in the seventies, when thousands of Shi'ite merchants were accused of being of Iranian descent despite their Iraqi citizenship. The government confiscated their businesses, assets, and properties; stripped them of their citizenship; and dumped them and their families at the Iranian border. Frequently, the security forces took away young sons between the ages of 15 and 25 and held them in detention centers while their families were forced to leave. These young men were rarely seen again by their families. In all, the Ba'th government is conservatively estimated to have deported 150,000 people from 1970 to 1981. In 1977 a religious procession 30,000 strong traveling between Najaf and Karbala and chanting religious as well as anti-Ba'th slogans, was attacked by the army on the ground and by military helicopters from the air. It took two days of killing and arrests to crush this popular defiance.[22] Inevitably, the harsh repression of the Shi'a and the religious movements prompted retaliatory violence. Cells of Islamists fighters, from Da'wa, the Islamic Action Organization, and other smaller groups, carried out acts of sabotage against the regime. Their guerrilla tactics targeted government security officers, Ba'th party buildings, and senior officials. There were spectacularly ambitious attempts on the lives of Deputy Prime Minister Tariq 'Aziz in 1980 and on President Saddam Hussein in 1980 and 1982. However, these failed attempts only resulted in more executions, expulsions, and detentions.

It is difficult to estimate how many people enlisted in the Islamist parties. Often young men joined against the wishes, and sometimes without the knowledge, of their families. As the level of government brutality rose, the Islamic parties gained sympathizers if not members. On the popular level, many in the Shi'ite community were critical of the religious zeal of the Islamists and feared that their militancy was detrimental to the interests of the community. Despite their criticism and fears, however, all Shi'a could identify with the grievances expressed by the militants and deplored the brutality of the regime's retaliatory measures. Following the execution of Muhammad Baqir al-Sadr and other clerics in 1980 and the outbreak of the Iran-Iraq war, many Iraqi clerics moved to Iran, along with a large contingent of adherents. Sayid Muhammad Baqir al-Hakim, son of Ayatollah Muhsin al-Hakim and brother of Mahdi al-Hakim, was among the clerics who fled to Iran. In Tehran and under the aegis of the Iranian government, he and other lay and clerical leaders formed the Supreme Council for Islamic Revolution in Iraq (SCIRI) to coordinate the activities of the Shi'ite groups that had by then proliferated. As the radius of repression expanded to include people unconnected with the Islamist parties, increasing numbers of Shi'a, as well as Sunnis, felt threatened and voluntary left Iraq to forestall becoming victims of the regime's suspicions. In addition to Iran, Syria, the Gulf countries, and Britain saw a large influx of Iraqi Shi'a in the early 1980s.

The Iran-Iraq war made it necessary for the Iraqi government to adopt a two-track approach to the Shi'a. In the early years of the war, when Iraq was scoring gains against its Iranian adversary, the regime intensified its persecution of Shi'ite clerics and the religious parties and speeded up deportation of Shi'ite families to Iran. By 1983, however, Iraq had lost its military edge, and the regime was forced to modify its strategy. The regime recognized that it needed to maintain the loyalty of the Shi'a, who formed the overwhelming majority of soldiers and noncommissioned officers in Iraq's armed forces, and to bolster its Islamic credentials in the face of Iran's propaganda. Visits by senior Iraqi officials, including Saddam Hussein, to the Iraqi shrine cities of Najaf and Karbala increased markedly and acquired all the trappings of national ceremonies. Buildings in these cities were renovated and embellished even as the Shi'ite theologians were being intimidated and repressed. To improve his credentials with the Shi'a especially, Saddam Hussein invented a genealogical tree that claimed descent from the Prophet Muhammad through Imam Husayn, and thus proclaimed him a sayid, a member of the venerable Ahl al-Bait, or family of the prophet. Thus Saddam Hussein tried to establish both an emotional tie to the Shi'a and a highly respected religious status.

The Iraqi government took great pains to paint the war with Iran as an episode in the ancient conflict between Arabs and Persians, rather than a war between Iraq alone and its Iranian neighbor, or as a sectarian war between Sunni and Shi'ite political orders. The regime injected a religious dimension by calling the war the Qadisiyya of Saddam, in reference to the 637 A.D. battle that brought Persia under Arab Muslim rule. The name implied that the Arabs were the true Muslims whereas the Persians were *majus*, a generic name for Zoroastrians and other ancient Persian religions. The regime, partly out of fear of Shi'ite subversion of the war in favor of Iran, thus played on the pan-Arab and pan-Muslim sentiments of Iraqis. In fact, despite Iran's hopes and exhortations, and the occasional guerrilla attacks by Shi'ite militants against government targets during the war, no Shi'ite revolt was forthcoming in Iraq. Indeed, once the war shifted to Iraqi soil in 1982, patriotic sentiment among Iraqis overcame all other considerations, desertions from the army declined, and the Shi'a fought as vigorously as the Sunnis. The conflicting sentiments of the mass of Shi'a toward the war arose from other considerations than their confessional affinity with Iran. Rather, the Shi'a believed the Iraqi regime had launched a needless and devastating war for the sole purpose of its own aggrandizement, yet as Iraqis they had no choice but to defend their country. Their condemnation of the regime's folly grew as the war dragged on, the casualties (mainly Shi'ite) mounted, and the economy bled. The dilemma for the Shi'a was not the choice between the regimes of Iraq and Iran. They were caught between their hostility to the Iraqi regime on the one hand and their patriotism on the other, and in the end their loyalty was expressed not to the regime but to their country.[23]

But the later years of the Iran-Iraq war were only a temporary truce between the regime and the Shi'a. In 1988 and 1989, confrontations between Shi'ite guerrilla groups and the Iraqi government resumed and the regime attacked the southern marshes of Iraq where army deserters and dissidents were believed to have taken refuge. In December 1988, the Iraqi government issued a highly classified "Plan of Action for the Marshes," which imposed an economic siege on the southern region and ordered the burning of villages and crops and the arrest of suspects.[24]

The watershed in the confrontation between the Shi'a and the regime was reached in the massive uprising in southern Iraq that broke out on March 3, 1991, immediately after the Gulf war, and was followed by the uprising of the Kurds in the north.[25] The rebellion in the south was a spontaneous, leaderless eruption of Shi'a of all political colors that brought together Islamists and leftists but was made up largely of politically unaffiliated Shi'a who fought out of anger and hatred for the regime and not for a particular ideology. The uprising swept through the provinces south of Baghdad in a matter of days. The Iraqi regime labeled the dissidents *ghawgha'* (hooligans) and the uprising mob violence. The regime reacted brutally, using tanks, artillery, and helicopter gunships to bombard the cities and shrines of the south.

Under the supervision of Husayn Kamil, Saddam's son-in-law, army tanks rolled into Karbala with banners that proclaimed *La Shi'ata Ba'd al-Yawm* ("No Shi'a after today").[26] There is some evidence that the regime used napalm in its attacks. According to Saddam Hussein's cousin, 'Ali Hasan al-Majid, the regime killed 300,000 citizens in its three-week campaign to squash the uprising.[27] Even if the figure is exaggerated, eyewitness reports describe mounds of corpses lining city streets and highways. After the uprising, seven articles, believed to be written by Saddam Hussein, appeared in the official Ba'th newspaper, al-*Thawra*, denouncing the Shi'ite dissidents as Iranian agents and pronouncing the Shi'a of the marshes non-Arab primitive aliens, morally depraved, and repugnant.[28]

The atrocities committed by the regime resulted in universal Shi'ite anger. Immediately after the March 1991 uprising, some 33,000 Shi'a sought refuge with Allied forces in Saudi Arabia. At least an equal number fled to Iran. The exodus of Shi'a from Iraq has continued since the war, creating large communities of dissident Iraqi Shi'a in Iran, Syria, Britain, other European countries, and the United States. The violence of the regime's retaliation against the Kurds added to the general outrage. Since March 1991, opposition to the regime has spread to hitherto apolitical Shi'a and to an expanding group of Sunnis.

Since the Gulf war the Iraqi regime has tried to follow a multiple approach toward the Shi'a. To enforce security measures in the restive southern region, it has singled out some tribal shaykhs for special favor and armed them against the population in the south. On a propaganda level, it has repaired the damage to the shrines and reopened them for foreign pilgrims, including those from Iran. At the same time, the regime has continued to persecute, and at times assassinate, prominent clergy, including those who have no political activity. In 1991, 90-year old Grand Ayatollah Abul Qassim al-Khoei, the most prominent Shi'ite marji', was interrogated and placed under house arrest, despite the fact that he had never been politically active. In 1994, his son, Mohammad Taqi al-Khoei, was assassinated, and two senior clerics, al-Gharawi and Burujurdi, were assassinated in 1998. The regime has also implemented harsh preemptive measures against any Shi'a suspected of hostility to the government and has forced Shi'a families to leave Baghdad, where they pose a special threat. To cut off refuge for dissenters and deserters, the "Plan of Action for the Marshes" went into draconian implementation in 1992, with a military campaign to depopulate the region combined with an economic and environmental devastation of the area through drainage. An estimated 500,000 Shi'ite marsh inhabitants were forced to flee to Iran or to other parts of Iraq, many were killed by government forces, and the environmental damage has rendered the region uninhabitable.

In the towns and countryside of southern Iraq, intermittent armed resistance to the Iraqi government has nevertheless continued, and there are weekly reports of confrontations between Shi'ite groups and paramilitary forces and attacks on government buildings or officials. These are always followed by retaliation from government troops. The reports of village burnings, arrests, executions, and forced displacement have risen since 1994. On February 19, 1999, a popular cleric, Mohammad Sadeq al-Sadr, and his two sons were assassinated by gunmen in Najaf, almost certainly by the regime. The backlash from the Shi'ite community has been widespread, intense and continuous, further raising the level of violence between the Shi'a and the regime.

Although SCIRI, Da'wa, and other Islamist parties claim to hold political sway in the region, antiregime activities in the south are not necessarily linked to any of the known traditional parties. Accounts of participants and witnesses indicate that the present resistance is carried out by local groups acting independently or in loose association, and that leadership is localized. Cooperation among these guerrilla groups arises from family and clan ties and personal friendships, not through an organizational framework.

In the past three decades, the Iraqi state has moved from a policy of discrimination to one of active repression of the Shi'a. Repressive policies have triggered a Shi'ite anger at home and abroad that will be very difficult to reverse or contain. One Shi'ite secularist expressed the view of many when he said that the regime had become "an existential threat" to the community. Southern Iraq since the Gulf war has been simmering with a continuous low-intensity armed conflict between Shi'ite dissident groups and government forces. The government is unlikely to relent, and there is no prospect of any negotiated solution. For the Shi'a, the only solution lies in the removal of the regime of Saddam Hussein, and it is unlikely that they will accept a continuation of their current underclass status in the state once the present order in Iraq changes.

Divisions and Unity

In Hanna Batatu's encyclopedic work on Iraq, *The Old Social Classes and the Revolutionary Movements of Iraq,* a short chapter is titled "Two Iraqis, Three Parties"—and there is much truth in his quip. Among the 12 million Shi'a in Iraq, the differences exceed the points of accord. These differences, like those of Shi'a elsewhere, are a product of political history and social and economic variables. Unlike the situation in countries such as Lebanon, the Iraqi Shi'ite picture must be examined through the statements and actions of groups outside Iraq as well as conditions and actions of groups within. During the March 1991 uprising, many dissidents carried posters of Shi'ite clerics, such as Khomeini or Muhammad Baqir al-Hakim, the leader of SCIRI, accompanied by Islamic slogans.[29] However, personal accounts of the uprising also indicate that most participants had no strong ideological inclinations and were motivated only by opposition to the regime. Indeed, the latter groups blame the religious zeal of Islamists for the failure of the uprising.[30]

The 1991 Gulf war mobilized Shi'ite opposition to the regime as never before, invigorating the traditional Islamist parties and dramatically expanding the secular opposition in all its forms. All Iraqi Shi'a agree on the issue of discrimination and the need for greater equity in the distribution of power. They also agree on the problems of repression, the absence of even a modicum of human rights, and the importance of radical political change in Iraq. This latter belief is not unique to the Shi'a: it is shared by Sunnis, though less universally.

Beyond these broad issues, Shi'ite disagreements emerge over the nature of change and its mechanisms, the shape of Iraq's future, and Iraq's political orientation. The principal fault line lies between Islamists and secularists. As described earlier, Iraq has a strong tradition of Arab nationalist and leftist ideologies that attracted the Shi'a from the 1940s through the 1970s. The education of many Shi'a in the West and their long domicile in Europe and the United States has, additionally, produced a corps of liberal Shi'a Westernized in their political thinking. While secular Shi'a claim that they are the silent majority in Iraq, the Islamic groups maintain that they are the true representatives of Shi'ite interests and enjoy the support of the majority of the Shi'a. Neither of these claims can be verified under current conditions in Iraq.

Inevitably, the Shi'a carry their ideological biases into the political debate, attributing different interpretations to fundamental concepts such as democracy, representative government, civil rights, and majority rule. No term in this debate is more vexed than democracy, which has been argued over, in speech and writing, more than any other, especially by Shi'ite Islamists. For secularists, and particularly leftists and liberals, the definition of democracy is close to the European model, embodying a set of political and cultural norms that govern most aspects of public life. The Islamists for their part approach the term cautiously. They attempt to confer legitimacy on the concept through reference to Islamic notions of *shura* (consultation) and *bay'a* (rendering an oath of allegiance), cited in the Qur'an and other Muslim texts. Islamists are also averse to the Western associations of democracy and its perceived liberalism that implies political and social permissiveness. Especially, they reject the possibility that democracy itself can provide an alternative political ideology to set against other ideological systems. Consequently, they have traditionally preferred to speak about "democratic mechanisms," such as elections, the rule of law, and accountability, rather than democracy. However, this hesitation over democracy is dissipating among Shi'ite Islamists, and increasingly the term is used without qualification.

One of the consequences of the Gulf war was to terminate the isolation of Islamists from mainstream Iraqi opinion, and Islamists groups are now an indispensable component of the overall Iraqi opposition. The Supreme Council for Islamic Revolution in Iraq, an umbrella organization established in Iran in 1980 and headed by Sayid Muhammad Baqir al-Hakim, takes a prominent place in opposition alliances. It joined the umbrella group of the Iraqi National Congress in 1992, and has engaged in dialogue with the United States despite its physical dependence on Iran. The older Da'wa party, which has taken more hard-line stands, has suffered from splintering and lost its former vigor, but it is more amenable to cooperation with other Iraqi opposition groups now than in earlier periods. The Da'wa, however, views the United States with suspicion and has avoided talks with U.S. officials. In the process of rapprochement with the Iraqi opposition, Iraqi Islamist groups have been engaged in far-reaching exploration of the principles of democracy, prompted in part by their need to conduct a dialogue with secular Iraqis, and possibly by the transformations occurring in the Iranian state itself, so long regarded as the Shi'ite Islamist prototype.

As early as 1989, SCIRI and Da'wa were holding talks with other Iraqi opposition groups in Damascus. By December 1990, prompted by Saddam Hussein's invasion of Kuwait, a group of 17 political parties had formed the Joint Action Committee and signed a statement condemning the regime and advocating democratic change in Iraq.[31] The Joint Action Committee was significant because it brought together SCIRI, the Da'wa party, the Islamic Action Organization, and smaller Shi'ite Islamic groups, as well as the Iraqi Communist party, dissident Ba'thists, Arab nationalists, socialists, the principal Sunni Islamic groups, and the major Kurdish parties. In 1992, most of these groups joined forces in the Iraqi National Congress (INC), a broad-based opposition coalition, and endorsed the political platform and statement of the Congress. The statement, agreed to by all the parties present, declared the opposition's commitment to " . . . pluralist parliamentary rule . . . achieving equality for citizens, preserving democratic rights and freedoms, providing security and stability, and instating the rule of law and basic human rights, especially civil and political rights, and respect for the nation's creed represented by Islam."[32]

In addition to the secular-Islamist split, there are disagreements within the ranks of the Islamist camp itself. Many of these differences are less doctrinal than personal, as parties coalesce behind particular clerics or lay leaders and rarely switch allegiances. Where there are ideological differences, they frequently revolve around the concept of *wilayat al-faqih*, the rule of the jurisconsult applied by Khomeini in Iran, which is rejected or disputed by many devout and committed Shi'a. In fact, not all Islamists agree on the leadership role of clerics. While the 'ulama have a guiding spiritual and counseling function, their assumption of leadership in the political arena is far from universally accepted. Islamists also vary in their perceptions of Iran, their tolerance of the West, acceptance of democratic norms, and the strategies they favor for Islamizing society and state. SCIRI, though based in Iran, has demonstrated greater pragmatism in dealing with the West and the United States in particular than have other Islamist groups such as the Da'wa and the Islamic Action Organization. These divergences are matters of degree only, and in the "period of struggle" the Islamic groups can and often do achieve a measure of cohesion and share a common purpose.

The disagreements among secular Shi'a arise principally from their multiple ideological backgrounds. Arab nationalists and Ba'thists continue to view the Iraqi situation within the traditional matrices of the Arab struggle, in which Arabs must strive for true independence from neocolonial powers such as the United States. Communists and other socialists are more Iraqi-centric but share the nationalists' distrust of the United States. The relevance of Arab nationalism as an ideology for the problems in Iraq is a topic of debate within the circles of the secular opposition. Similarly, the legacy and role of the Ba'th party in Iraq and tolerance for Ba'th ideology are sources of tension between Shi'a of different political stripes. Ba'thists and nationalists argue that it is Saddam Hussein and not the Ba'th that is responsible for Iraq's predicament, and that the party itself has been turned into a mere tool of Saddam Hussein. Other secularists counter that the regime of Saddam Hussein is the product of Ba'th ideology, which of itself is "fascist" and totalitarian, and of the authoritarian nature of the Ba'th party's structure.[33]

Unlike Islamists, secular Shi'a have not formed their own organizations, and no Shi'ite party similar to the Lebanese Amal has emerged. However, the Shi'a are numerically dominant in all Iraqi political organizations that are not ethnically based (such as the Kurdish, Turkoman, or Assyrian parties). For example, the Iraqi National Accord, a nationalist group comprising former Ba'thists and bureaucrats, is commonly dubbed "Sunni" in the Western press, whereas in fact many of its senior members are Shi'ite. The confusion indicates a dangerous tendency in the West to equate secular with Sunni and Islamist with Shi'ite. The ability of secular Shi'a to find common ideological ground with Sunnis is a promising factor that can help Iraqi society heal and recover from the ravages of decades of repression.

Notwithstanding ideological differences, Shi'ite secularists recognize the importance of the Islamic Shi'ite groups in the framework of Iraqi opposition, and the two sides are prepared to cooperate in their common struggle against the Iraqi regime. During this stage at least, Sunnis as well accord the Shi'ite Islamist parties importance. The short-lived Joint Action Committee of 1990 and the Iraqi National Congress (INC) that succeeded it are evidence of the willingness of various groups to temporarily bury their differences for a common cause. Eventually, the tensions inherent in such a broad and disparate alliance came to the surface and dissipated the energies of the Joint Action Committee and later of the INC. However, it is noteworthy that the cracks and disputes within the INC were not sectarian, but were caused by personal, partisan or strategic differences.

The above two umbrella groups provided a valuable forum where Iraqi Shi'a could talk to each other and to Sunnis. Of continuing importance in the intra-Shi'ite and the Shi'ite-Sunni dialogues is the al-Khoei Foundation, a charitable and educational organization that was established by the late Ayatollah Khoei and is currently headquartered in London, with branches throughout the world. The Foundation has become a focal point for discussion of issues relating to Islam and democratization, Sunni-Shi'ite rapprochement, and relations between secularists and Islamists.[34] The Foundation preserves the late Ayatollah's distance from politics, but strongly upholds the Shi'ite intellectual and cultural tradition and defends the welfare of the Shi'a on humanitarian grounds. By eschewing the turmoil of politics and addressing political issues from an intellectual standpoint and in the spirit of rapprochement, the al-Khoei Foundation has succeeded in commanding the respect of a broad range of Iraqi and other Arab Shi'ite intellectuals.

The Iraqi Shi'a and Iran

The Shi'ite heartland in Karbala and Najaf has long attracted Iranian clerics and students, many of whom settled in these urban centers, became Iraqi citizens, and married into Iraqi Shi'ite families. Many of the maraji' in Iraq were of Iranian origin and took an equal interest in Iranian and Iraqi affairs. Because of their status as "sources of emulation" and spiritual guides, this class of senior clerics in particular exerted strong influence on Iraqi Shi'a, both theologically and politically.

Iraqi Shi'a admire the culture of Persia and the scholarship of Iranian clerics, and Shi'ite life in the holy cities contains elements of Persian folk influence such as cuisine, artifacts, and vocabulary. Since the first deportations of Iraqis in 1972, Iran has granted refuge to nearly 700,000 Iraqi Shi'a, and they are immensely grateful that Iran has opened its borders to them when they have been deported, persecuted, or forced to flee. But there is also an Iraqi Shi'ite tendency to view Iranians as untrustworthy and unduly arrogant. Anecdotes about "Iranian deviousness" compared to "Arab forthrightness" are part of the lore. Shi'ite Iraqis, moreover, maintain an attitude of moral superiority, regarding themselves as "chosen" by the Imams and the as repository of true

Shi'ism. The fear of Iranian hegemony is a constant theme even among Iraqi Shi'a. These ambivalent attitudes underwent a shift with the rise of the Islamist movement in Iraq, and were reversed after the Iranian revolution.

The Iranian revolution, which occurred at the height of confrontations between the Iraqi Shi'ite Islamist movements and the Iraqi government and helped to intensify the conflict, dramatically reversed the balance of the relationship between the Iranians and the Shi'a of Iraq. Whereas Iraq had served as host to Iranian clerics and trading families for decades, after 1980 Iran became the protector of Shi'a fleeing the Iraqi regime. The Da'wa, SCIRI, and other Iraqi Islamist groups found new bases in Iran under the aegis of the Islamic Republic. Qom and Tehran supplanted Najaf and Karbala as centers of theology for students from around the Arab and Muslim worlds. The Islamic revolution in Iran gave a temporary boost to Iraqi Islamists movements, and in March 1980, for example, the Islamic Action Organization felt bold enough to attempt the assassination of Tariq Aziz, the deputy prime minister.

Iran offered three contrasting faces: the revolution, the religion, and the state, and Iraqi Shi'a saw the face that suited their interests. Like many others in the Arab world, including many Sunnis, the Iraqi Shi'a admired the Iranian revolution as a successful challenge to despotism supported by Western imperialism. The Islamists admired Iran's revolution and religious rigor, as a vindication for Islam and for Shi'ism. Iran as a state, however, was a challenge because it pitted its Persian nationalism against Arabism. The attitude of most Iraqi Shi'a changed as Iran exhibited more or less of each feature, and as the interests of Iraqis merged with or diverged from the interests of Iran.

Ayatollah Khomeini, who had lived in exile in Najaf since 1965, seems to have been isolated from Iraqi Shi'a and to have exerted far less influence than Sayyid Muhammad Baqir al-Sadr. Nevertheless, after the Iranian revolution, Khomeini acquired heroic stature among Iraqi Islamists, although their emotional allegiance remained with al-Sadr and increased after his execution by the regime in 1980.

The Iran-Iraq war demanded difficult choices from Iraqis. The Iraqi Shi'a who had fled or been forcibly deported to Iran condemned the Iraqi state for initiating the war. The Shi'a inside Iraq were more prepared to perceive the nationalist nature of the conflict than the religious, and they supported their own state. However, the prevailing sentiment was one of disenchantment with a war that was not of their own choosing and over which they had no control. The war with Iran in fact considerably restrained the activities of Shi'ite Islamists in Iraq, partly because of continuing arrests and executions and partly because of the patriotism that the war engendered. Activities of the Da'wa party thereafter moved to other countries, including Lebanon and Kuwait.[35] Despite its painful effects on Iraqis in general, and on the Shi'a in particular since they formed the bulk of the lower ranks of Iraq's armed forces, the Iraq-Iran war created no permanent rift within the Iraqi Shi'ite community.

By contrast, the dependency of Islamist groups on Iran has engendered a reaction among Iraqi Shi'a. Many resent Iranian control over the Islamist movement and its manipulation to serve Iranian national interest. In addition, the experiences of Iraqi exiles in Iran have often been difficult or downright negative. Many complain that the Iranians discriminate against them because they are Arabs, and that they are treated with scorn and condescension. They find it difficult to find jobs or set up businesses because of bureaucratic discrimination. Iranian law prohibits the marriage of Iranian women to Iraqi men except under very limited conditions. Further, Iran has come under criticism for what the Shi'a inside Iraq regard as Iran's failure to support the Iraqi uprising of 1991 that followed the Gulf war. Because many of the Islamist groups have no other refuge, they are constrained to accept Iranian tutelage. Nevertheless, a few have tried in recent years to loosen their ties and take steps toward a measure of autonomy from the Iranian state and clerical establishment. Since the Gulf war of 1991, thousands of Iraqis have left Iran and moved to Syria or Europe. Elements of the Da'wa leadership have also shifted their bases to other Arab or European countries. SCIRI has expended considerable effort to gain the sympathy of Arab governments, particularly in Saudi Arabia and Kuwait. In practical terms, Iran still offers financial and strategic assistance; the personal and spiritual ties between Iraqi clerics and Iranian clerics also continue to play an important role.

A significant development in recent years has been the effort by some Iraqi Shi'ite Islamists to reform Shi'ism out of its Iranian mold. Some currents of the Iraqi Islamist movement see the need to reclaim Shi'ism from Iran and strip Shi'ism of what they regard as superfluous "Safavid" accretions; they advocate a return to a purer and more intellectual form of "'Alawi" Shi'ism more closely related to Iraqi tradition. They stress the importance of restoring Najaf and Karbala to primacy in theological training and scholarship, and of developing an indigenous Iraq marji'iyya that will both stem the flow to Iran and attract new Shi'ite scholarship to Iraq.

While the Shi'a around the Arab world as a whole now see Iran more as a state than an ideology, this new assessment is more relevant to Iraq than to any other Arab state. The idealism that propelled Iraqi Islamists to Iran after the revolution is now tempered by recognition that Iranian policies arise from its own state interests rather than pure Islamic ideology or disinterested defense of the Shi'a. The Shi'a also recognize that conditions in Iraq are far different from those prevailing in Iran on the eve of the Islamic revolution. Finally, they also accept that Iraq is a multicultural society with particular problems that do not lend themselves to an Islamic revolution, and that they have to adopt cautious political strategies in order to enhance their appeal.

On the non-Islamist Shi'ite front, the Iranian question is clearer. Although many leftists and liberals value the Iranian revolution as a triumph against oppression and Western hegemony, there is no spiritual or doctrinal draw to the Iranian regime. Indeed, there may be a lingering tendency to refashion Iran as the historical rival of Arabism and of Iraq in particular, and the concern of many Iraqi Shi'a, along with Sunnis, is how to arrive at a modus vivendi with the Iranian state. There is one sentiment shared by both Islamists and secularists: In comparison with the totalitarian nature of the Iraqi state, most Shi'a admire the ability of the Iranian state to institutionalize, to tolerate some diversity of opinion, and to engage in democratic elections, albeit within limited parameters.

Political Challenges

Under the present regime in Iraq, the Shi'a lack leverage over the central government and have no negotiating power. Although active resistance to the regime continues in the south, at its present level it presents only a manageable irritant that the regime can endure for the time being. Therefore, while Baghdad may find it necessary to negotiate with the Kurds, there is no imperative to negotiate with the Shi'a, and the government is unlikely to give in to any of their demands. The Shi'ite resistance may escalate and expand, but it cannot pose a serious threat to the formidable striking power of the regime without external support. For the moment, the Shi'a have no acceptable sponsors: Iranian support of some Islamists groups is less certain now than in the 1980s, and in any case it is a liability rather than an asset in the eyes of Sunnis, most Shi'a, all of Iraq's neighbors, and the West. The Arab countries of the region and the United States are hesitant to strengthen the domestic Shi'ite opposition. Meanwhile, neither the Shi'a nor the regime have any desire to negotiate on neutral terms, and the only opportunity for improvement in the conditions of the Shi'a is removal of the regime.

One of the consequences of the Gulf war has been the "coming out" of the Iraqi opposition en masse. The universal disaffection with the regime of Saddam Hussein means that Shi'ite opposition has become only a component, though perhaps the largest, of a nation-wide call for change. Because of their greater numbers the Shi'a tend to have dominant roles even in secular groupings. Almost any scenario for change will bring tremendous benefits to the Shi'a, if only because they start from such a disadvantaged position. But the extent of their gains will depend on the mechanism of change and the choices that the Shi'a themselves make. As described in this chapter, internal divisions and political difference among the Shi'a mean that there is no unifying "Shi'ite platform" that can determine a common course of action or define one Shi'ite vision for Iraq's future. As a result, the Shi'a are far from reaching consensus on issues that pose serious challenges both while they are in opposition and in the event of change in the political order.

These challenges fall in three broad areas. The first challenge is whether the Shi'a should strive for community identity or try to integrate. The second challenge is how to approach the Sunnis, and what assurances, if any, the Shi'a need to offer: How will relations between the two communities be structured, given the sense of grievance of the Shi'a and the fears of the Sunnis? Third, how will the Shi'a deal with the legacy of 30 years of dictatorship, of which they were one of the primary victims? The dramatic events, and the failure, of the March 1991 uprising demonstrate the seriousness of these challenges and their impact on the aspirations of Iraqi Shi'a.

The first choice that the Shi'a must make is whether to speak from the Shi'ite perspective, articulating Shi'ite grievances, expressing Shi'ite demands, and pressing for redress from decades of discrimination and repression. Should Shi'ite leaders be the voice of their community exclusively, as Kurdish leaders are, or speak on behalf of a wider constituency of Iraqis? The alternative to the sect-driven agenda is for the Shi'a to adopt a pan-Iraqi posture and hold the specifically Shi'ite concerns in abeyance while advocating universal Iraqi demands for human rights, participation, and representation. The choice between the two options is a matter of debate within the Shi'ite community outside Iraq, and, while it is impossible to draw hard and fast dividing lines, in general Islamist parties tend to express a Shi'ite-centered platform and advocate Shi'ite interests, while secularists favor a more universal outlook. This does not imply that the Islamists ignore such universal demands—indeed, within the opposition the Shi'a Islamists have been at the forefront of human rights advocacy because their share of suffering has been great, and they have been particularly sympathetic to Kurdish suffering at the hands of the regime. It is more a question of emphasis and perception. Shi'ite Islamists tend to stress the violations of human rights against the Shi'a, deplore the exclusion of Shi'a from power, and call for representation and participation of the Shi'a in the political system. Shi'ite Islamists justify this emphasis on multiple grounds: first, because they believe that they represent the community and therefore their first duty is toward their constituents; second, because they believe the Shi'a have been more oppressed than other communities in Iraq and, unlike the Kurds, have not benefited from advocates; and third, because the Shi'a are the majority that has been defrauded of its natural majoritarian rights and requires specific redress. Indeed, the Islamist language on democracy and representation is often articulated as a call for majority rule, without specifying whether such a majority is defined by sectarian affiliation or political belief. Intensified state persecution of the Shi'a since 1991 gives added energy and credence to the Shi'ite-centered platform, and undermines the more broad-based alternative.

Secularist Shi'a are keenly aware that their community has been relegated to second-class status in the Iraqi state structure and that despite the alleged secularism of the state their opportunities for participation in the prevailing structure are limited by their Shi'ism. Nevertheless, secularists are reluctant to adopt an overtly Shi'ite perspective and are more inclined to follow a universalist approach that subsumes their demands within demands made by all Iraqis, since their political views often share common ground with those of non-Shi'ite groups. Furthermore, many non-Islamist Shi'a regard identity politics as detrimental both to Shi'ite interests and to Iraq's social unity. They situate the Shi'ite grievance within the context of a national problem affecting all sectors of society, originating in the monolithic structure of the state—its exclusivity, centralization, and absolutism. They advocate a national agenda to change the political culture toward participation and pluralism within a system based on meritocracy rather than religion or ethnicity. Their prescriptions, however, may be idealistic and beg the question rather than answer it: in order to be implemented, they require a politically mature acceptance of pluralism and democratization throughout the state and society, and such acceptance cannot be guaranteed.

The choice between assimilation, integration, or assertion of identity is not straightforward, as each option presents its own drawbacks. On the one hand, as described earlier, Shi'ite attempts to assimilate in the 1960s and 1970s by joining the Ba'th party or working for the state led to few personal gains and failed entirely to shift an entrenched state system toward greater recognition of Shi'ite rights. On the other hand, whenever the Shi'a adopted a specifically Shi'ite agenda, usually via Islamist parties that argued openly for the interests of the community, the state and Sunni society accused them of sectarianism, divisiveness, and foreign clientism, and they were easily ostracized on that basis. Integration advocated by secularists may help preserve identity while blending the Shi'a with the other communities, but it assumes commitment to democratic rules of conduct and a strongly developed national identity that overcomes religious and ethnic differences and alleviates mutual suspicions.

As in Bahrain and Lebanon, advocacy of even a sect-neutral democratic system in Iraq will favor the Shi'a and so is suspected by the Sunnis of being a disguised "Shi'ite agenda." The divisive and unresolved issue that arises from sectarian differences in Iraq concerns the future relationship between the Shi'a and the Sunnis should a democratic and representative system be established. Although many Shi'a dismiss this as a nonissue because the democracy and equality they advocate encompasses all, it remains an incipient and potentially explosive problem in the future relations between Sunnis and Shi'a. It was an important underlying issue in the failure of the March 1991 uprising in the south, which received minimal Sunni support inside Iraq and alienated the United States and its Arab allies. The Sunnis, who have dominated Iraq's politics, armed forces, and bureaucracy for the past 75 years, are reluctant to relinquish their privileged status. The Sunnis also fear that any concessions they make will result in a Shi'ite backlash—that they will be summarily stripped of all power and relegated to minority status, and perhaps in turn suffer discrimination and persecution. The most pressing problem facing the Shi'a is how to calm Sunni fears and persuade Sunnis that democratization and Shi'ite participation will not lead to a Shi'ite monopoly that practices reverse discrimination against Sunnis.

The Shi'a have chosen to gloss over this issue rather than meet it head on. Thus they have not proposed any confidence-building measures—such as constitutional arrangements, administrative allocations, or electoral mechanisms, as currently exist in Lebanon—that can provide guarantees or safeguards to the Sunnis. Expatriate members of the two communities who share an opposition to the Iraqi regime have not sought a dialogue on this critical issue confronting Iraq's future. Their reticence can be attributed to an attitude of letting sleeping dogs lie: it is in part a refusal to acknowledge openly that a problem exists, in part a worry that a dialogue may even exacerbate the problem. Additionally, there may be a strategic decision on both sides that such discussions will detract from the common purpose of confronting the regime, to which all energies should be directed at present.

However, dangers do lie ahead. There is a narrowly held Shi'ite view, for example, that speaks of Iraq as "our country" and drives certain Shi'a to speak of reclaiming Iraq. Within this same political outlook, Shi'ite leaders, and especially the Islamists, refer to their constituency as *al-sha'b*, "the people," making the part stand in for the whole. The state is expected to transform rapidly in favor of the Shi'a. One former (secularist) Iraqi politician, speaking of the necessity of rapid transformation, advocates changing the composition of the armed forces immediately by dismissing Sunni officers and replacing them with Shi'a.[36] Regardless of the justice of these demands, the Sunni community is likely to resist them vigorously.

One facet of the debate on Iraq's political identity and the role of the Shi'a is revealed in the disputes over the mechanism for removing the current Iraqi regime. Two routes for change are presented: the first is the classic coup by the Iraqi armed forces, led by (Sunni) army and air force officers; the second is a popular uprising, better organized than in March 1991, triggered by the Shi'a in the south. Some Shi'a accept the likelihood (favored by most Sunnis) that change in Iraq will probably come from the armed forces or from the Ba'th party and that it will be incremental, without the dramatic reversal from a Sunni state order supported by the army to a Shi'ite order supported by the masses. Others, particularly Islamist Shi'a, believe in the necessity of revolutionary change led by the Shi'a masses, *al-sha'b,* who only then can freely express their will. SCIRI and the Da'wa party are very clear in their insistence on a popular insurrection rather than a military or palace coup that leaves little room for Shi'ite participation.

These different scenarios touch on the pace of any future change in Iraq. At the opposite ends of the spectrum, the hard-line Sunni scenario sees minimal change from the status quo that preserves much of Sunni authority, while the counter Shi'ite scenario anticipates revolutionary change to sweep away the status quo and vault Shi'ite interests to the surface. Thus while Sunni army officers have tried to hatch numerous coup plots since 1988, relatively few have joined the opposition umbrella groups, which they perceive as overwhelmingly Shi'ite. The absence of a Shi'ite–Sunni consensus has weakened both sides and, unless there are prior accords and mutual concessions, the likelihood of disagreement in the future will increase.

An associated problem confronting the Shi'a is how to deal with the legacy of 30 years of dictatorship closely identified with the Ba'th party. This issue will be faced by all Iraqis, but it will be especially acute for the Shi'a because of the extent of the persecution they have suffered, comparable only to that endured by the Kurds. The number of Shi'ite deportees and refugees alone is in the hundreds of thousands, and many have been stripped of citizenship, property, and assets. Thousands of Shi'a have been killed at the hands of the regime, leaving orphans and widows who present a lingering social problem. The religious institutions, endowments, and heritage of the Shi'a have been usurped or destroyed by the Iraqi regime. What type of restitution will the Shi'a accept if they become an equal, or a dominant, partner in Iraq's future power structure? Rightly or wrongly, the three decades of the regime are perceived to be linked to the Ba'th party and Sunni clans who for a long time supported the central government. During the uprising, there was no wholesale revenge against Ba'thists, but there were many incidents of individual reprisals against government officials. Shi'ite political leaders do not advocate collective punishment of the regime, but the Ba'th party and at least some of the military and paramilitary forces of the regime may be subject to severe political, social, and moral condemnation. At the very least, there will be demands for quick action to redress the ills of discrimination and compensation for material and intangible losses.

Notwithstanding their real worries, Sunni fears that all the Shi'a will speak with one voice in the future and share common goals is unwarranted. In fact, the political landscape of the Shi'ite community, already very diverse, is likely to be more fractured in an open democratic system than under a repressive regime. At present, the only specifically Shi'ite leadership resides in the Islamist parties. A secular Shi'ite leadership may develop in time, as it did in Lebanon with the Amal movement, and it is likely to compete with Shi'ite Islamists for the support and votes of the Shi'ite community. Should the Shi'a achieve some gains and make progress in a politically tolerant environment, the pressure that crystallizes sectarian identity may diminish, and differences are as likely to revolve around ideology and domestic and regional policies as they are around sectarian belief. As we see now in Kuwait and Lebanon, greater political freedom may lead to alliances between Shi'ite Islamists and Sunni Islamists for a common social and legislative agenda. Arab nationalists, for whom sectarian differences are less important than regional and international policies, will congregate to counter any tendencies toward isolationist Iraqi policies. The development of the nascent liberal movement will also contribute to political cooperation across sects, and it may emerge as a strong counterbalance to the Islamist platform.

In contrast, a limited change in the political order that ignores Shi'ite demands, perpetuates discrimination and confirms Sunni dominance will lead to increased polarization in society, political radicalism, and a strengthening of the Islamist parties as the only true representatives of Shi'ite interests. Shi'ite secularists will be condemned as irrelevant and indifferent to Shi'ite concerns. Because the Shi'a have already been radicalized by 30 years of repressive Ba'th rule, including military brutality since March 1991, it is unlikely that the Shi'a will remain passive if a new, weaker regime attempts to preserve the status quo. The potential for violence is likely to rise, pitting Shi'ite dissidents against the central government in escalating confrontations. In such a polarized climate, the clashing parties may seek external support, and foreign interests will have ample windows for interference in Iraq's internal affairs.

CHAPTER SIX

The Shi'a of Bahrain

The situation of the Shi'a in Bahrain—who represent a majority of the population—is one of the most unfortunate in the Arab world, and it has substantially deteriorated in the past decade. A Sunni ruling family, the al-Khalifa, dominates an autocratic political order that excludes the Shi'a from participation in public life and discriminates against them economically. They are freer than the Saudi Shi'a (a distinct minority) to practice their faith in public, and they are not subject to the incredible brutality of anti-Shi'ite campaigns of Iraq. Nonetheless, as they have sought to redress their predicament of exclusion and discrimination via legitimate, peaceful, and democratic means, they have been rebuffed, repressed, and driven to despair by ever more repressive measures of the minority ruling family, which brooks no democratic reform that might loosen their grip on power and over the economy.

Because the Shi'a are a majority, any demands they make for democratization or equal opportunities are automatically perceived by the ruling oligarchy as a threat to the established order. The Bahraini government has no intention of accommodating the legitimate demands of the Shi'a (or of Sunni liberals), and has every incentive to try to isolate them. The predicament of the Bahraini Shi'a, unlike the Iraqis, has received only modest international attention. And unlike Iraq, the only other Arab country with a Shi'ite majority, the Bahraini government enjoys the support and friendship of its neighbors and world powers, while heavily dependent of the patronage of Saudi Arabia for survival. As a consequence, the Bahraini Shi'a have few champions and face powerful domestic and regional opponents. Increasing violence has been the result.

When the Shi'a, together with the Sunnis, called for restoration of the constitution and parliament in 1992, the al-Khalifa responded with a non-negotiable rejection and a policy of heightened Shi'ite repression. As a consequence, the Shi'a, frustrated and repressed, have turned to illegal demonstrations and sometimes even violent confrontations and a few acts of bloodshed, which in turn draw yet more government violence. The ruling family has so far successfully sought to portray all Shi'ite calls for reform, democratization, and constitutional government in the country as a "radical Shi'ite agenda" bent upon destabilizing the island. As a result, today the island has become the scene of a small Shi'ite *intifada* confronting a heavy-handed government crackdown, which is polarizing sectarian sentiment on the island. Simultaneously, most of the secularists and liberals on the Sunni side have been silenced.

The accession of Shaykh Hamad al-Khalifa as Emir of Bahrain in March 1999 could perhaps pave the way for some easing of the government's draconian measures against the Shi'a and allow for greater openness in system. Several hundred political prisoners were recently released in the spring of 1999, including the leading Shi'ite cleric, Shaykh Abdul Amir al-Jamri, indicating readiness on the part of the government to adopt a calmer approach, at least to counter the negative publicity its policies have attracted in the West. However, it is too early to predict whether measurable improvement will in fact occur.

The growing opposition movement among the Shi'a is headed by a cleric-dominated leadership, but one whose political program is noteworthy for its proclamation of secular goals. However, the regime has deliberately cultivated a polarization of the country's political forces in an effort to salvage its personal rule over the country. The result is damaging the longer-term prospects of Bahraini stability and prosperity for all. In short, all future political reform would seem to be hostage to the sectarian problem by deliberate choice of the regime.

The overall population of Bahrain is approximately 600,000 people, small and highly concentrated on a small island. Approximately one-third of the population are noncitizen expatriate workers, mostly from South Asia, but there is also a group from other Arab countries and a smaller group of Western expatriates. The Shi'a represent approximately 70 percent of the total native population. Thus Bahrain, along with Iraq, is one of two Arab states in which the Shi'a constitute an absolute majority yet are excluded from a share of power.

The Bahraini Shi'a can themselves be divided into native Bahrainis (Baharna), who have a very old history and make up about 50 percent of the total population, and the Shi'a of Iranian background ('Ajam), who are some 22 percent of the total population. (Others sources suggest the 'Ajam may be no more than 10 percent of the overall population.) The social positions of the two Shi'ite groups also differ. The Iranian-origin Shi'a are well represented in the professions and pointedly stay out of politics. Indeed, the Iranian Shi'ite families see their permanent residence in Bahrain as contingent upon the tolerance of the ruling family, on whom they are utterly dependent; as a result they fully support the ruling elite.

Unlike other new cities in the Gulf spawned by twentieth-century oil wealth, Bahrain is actually the seat of one of the earliest civilizations in the ancient Middle East, Dilmun, which was contemporary with the ancient Indus civilizations of Mohenjodaro and Harappa in the second millennium B.C.E. It was converted to Islam very early in the period of the Islamic conquests of the Arabian Peninsula. From early Islamic times, however, it had a significant Shi'ite community. This community was initially dominated by the then radical Isma'ili sect of Shi'ism that for several centuries posed a major threat to Sunni states in the region.[1]

By the eleventh century, large numbers of mainstream (Twelver) Shi'ite communities had sprung up in the Gulf where there had formerly been Isma'ili Shi'ite communities, who probably converted in the face of a general collapse of Fatimid/Isma'ili power in the whole region.[2] The Shi'a of Bahrain were invigorated and strengthened by Iran's adoption of Shi'ism as the state religion in 1500, followed by an interlude of Iranian control of Bahrain starting in 1602 that enabled the Shi'a to set up centers of study.[3] Bahrain was actually one of the centers for Shi'ism in the Arab world at this time, along with Jabal 'Amil in Lebanon and Kufa and Najaf in Iraq. All of these Arab centers helped supply trained clerics to the new Shi'ite Safavid state in Iran, which needed guidance in the Shi'ite faith in order to propagate it throughout the country. The first Safavid Shah even cleared his early *fatwas* (religious edicts) with clerics in Najaf and Bahrain to ensure theological correctness. Bahrain was also known as a prosperous island due to its pearl trade and agriculture, based on good sources of fresh water.[4]

Shi'ite control in Bahrain was overturned in 1782 with the conquest of the island by the al-Khalifa tribe, launched from neighboring Qatar off the east coast of Bahrain. Most Shi'a on Bahrain's east coast were then killed or expelled—even now the east coast is entirely Sunni except for the town of Sitra. Most of the Shi'a then retreated north and west on the island—today the main Shi'ite stronghold. In the 1820s the Khalifa also called upon the Dawasir tribes in Saudi Arabia to assist in further displacing the Shi'a by sending forces to land on the western side of the island. As a result the Shi'a lost further territory and the Dawasir were given special privileges in return for helping alter the sectarian balance in Bahrain. A total of 313 Shi'ite villages that had existed at the time of the al-Khalifa conquest are reduced to 50 today. Some Shi'a comment that the mentality of the minority Sunni ruling family continues to require a relationship of dependency upon neighboring Saudi Arabia and to import outsider Sunnis as a means of weakening the Shi'a's demographic power.

The al-Khalifa thus brought an end to the flowering of Shi'ite culture in Bahrain. This development

> resulted in a gradual attrition in the position of the Shi'i community. Sunni Arabs were brought in from other parts of Arabia and soon formed the urban population including the ruling class, the military and many of the traders. The Shi'a were relegated to the villages. There they gradually lost ownership of the land through a system of heavy taxes and other extortions and were reduced to cultivating the palm groves as feudal peasants of their Sunni overlords.[5]

According to Shi'ite accounts of the feudal period, a Shi'ite uprising in 1928 broke the bondage of the Shi'ite community to a system that had required them to work without compensation for the al-Khalifa in a state of near serfdom and without any rights to testify in court to their grievances. Highly revealing of the character of the al-Khalifa conquest is the fact that the ruler took the title "Fatih," or Conqueror, a term used in reference to conquest of non-Muslim peoples, implying that Shi'ite blood could thus be legitimately shed and their lands confiscated.[6] The Shi'a of Bahrain in turn tend to view the al-Khalifa to this day as outside Sunni conquerors and oppressors, and modern events have done little to change this mindset. Sunnis often refer to the Shi'a as *hala'il,* or "chattel."

In terms of a political and social pecking order in Bahrain, the Shi'a rank last: the ruling family receives the highest position, followed by tribal (Sunni) groups, merchants (among whom the Shi'a are only modestly represented), the technocrats, Iranian Shi'a, and finally the native Bahraini Shi'a.[7] Discrimination is easily perpetuated by the fact that even today most Bahraini Shi'a are readily recognizable from their names and home village and sometimes even from their accent.

The Shi'a have a largely separate social life from the Sunnis although there has been some mixing among professional classes and even occasional intermarriage before the disorders began in 1994. The center of Shi'ite political and social life is the *ma'tam,* or meeting place—paralleling the *husayniya* of the Shi'a in Iraq, Saudi Arabia, and Kuwait. These centers teach Shi'ite history, customs, and lore to the population and are centers of festivals and celebrations, passion plays, and community gatherings. Today they are also the centers of agitation and political demonstrations that usually grow out of religious celebrations or funerals.

The arrival of the British marked a significant turning point in the status of the Shi'ite community. British rule sought to put an end to the persecution and killing of Shi'a on the island and improved their opportunities for entry into the civil service. Despite their low social position, the Shi'a under British rule in the 1930s actually made great social strides, especially through their recognition that education was vital to their future position in society. The level of literacy in Bahrain in general has been one of the highest in the Arab world—over 80 percent, accompanied by a high rate of high school graduation. As a result, Shi'ite men and women rank high among the top graduates of high schools and universities. In virtually the only Gulf state with a native workforce, the Shi'a represent nearly 90 percent of the labor force, especially since the Sunnis look down upon physical labor and prefer to go into business or government administration, as do most of the populations of tribal origin in the other Gulf states.

The Shi'a of Bahrain have always maintained a strong Arab identity. They did sympathize with the Iranian revolution when it took place, but primarily as a mark of new Shi'ite power in the region; most of them indicated no desire to associate with it politically. In the past there have also been clear theological differences between Iran and Bahrain, stemming from two different Shi'ite schools of legal thought: the Akhbaris and the Usulis.[8] In addition, there has never been any warmth between the Bahraini Shi'a of Iranian origin ('Ajam) and the native Arab Shi'a (Baharna). No 'Ajam live in Baharna areas and there is little intermarriage. In the 1950s and 1960s, the Arab Shi'a were actually sympathetic with Nasser's Arab nationalist movement, the sworn enemy of Iran at the time.

The Roots of Shi'ite Political Activism

Democracy activists in Bahrain trace the beginning of the democratic movement in the country to the mid-1930s when pro-democracy organizations, including the National Youth (Shabab al-Umma) emerged. Shi'a and Sunnis both joined, as did even a few members of the ruling family, including the then crown prince. Among other things this movement called for an end to the political police. Democratic movements were linked to a broader struggle for liberation from colonial rule as well, a goal shared equally by Shi'a and Sunnis.[9]

Further disorders took place among the Shi'a in 1953 to 1956, stemming from alleged affronts to the community during their Ashura mourning period,[10] but quickly found expression and common cause in Nasserist pan-Arab ideology; Nasserist ideas above all were antimonarchy across the Arab world, and hence a suitable vehicle for anti–al-Khalifa activity. But if many Shi'a turned to Nasserist movements as a nonsectarian way of expressing a desire for domestic change, the Nasserist movement was even more strongly supported by the Sunni population. Shi'a and Sunnis cooperated in this movement without sectarian overtones. In effect then, the Shi'a had not seriously created a modern political resistance movement on their own until the Iranian revolution.

Political demands by the Shi'a, starting with the labor unrest of 1970, served to weaken their job positions. The Shi'a had also made up a high proportion of the Bahraini Defence Force (as enlisted men, not officers), but they were increasingly let go as a Shi'ite political movement came into being. It was the significant downturn in the Bahraini economy in the 1980s, brought on by a sharp fall in the price of oil, that had an even greater impact on the course of Bahraini politics—as it had in most of the rest of the Gulf. Oil went from a high of $35 a barrel in the 1970s to a low of $6 (when adjusted for inflation). Government revenues were sharply reduced. Major investment in infrastructure projects—hospitals, roads, water, telephone, electricity, and schools—had to be reduced or eliminated. Large workforces were reduced by as much as 50 percent, in which the brunt of the pain was felt by the Shi'a. The government had been a key employer and had developed huge personnel cadres as a means of full employment and redistribution of income. Many white-collar jobs were cut. Shi'a, who constituted the chief labor force in major Bahraini companies such as Bahrain Petroleum (Bapco) and Aluminium of Bahrain (Alba), were let go in large numbers in efforts to reduce expenses; full national employment no longer was an affordable goal. With near total government ownership of everything, there was no significant private sector to take up the slack. In fact, of a total of $226 billion private investment in the world in 1995, for example, .02 percent went to GCC states and none to Bahrain. Unfortunately the government has failed to create strong conditions for direct foreign investment.[11]

As elsewhere in the Gulf, the Shi'ite communities during the 1970s also came under heavier economic and social pressures stemming from rapid social change, lower oil income, widening economic gaps between Shi'a and Sunnis, and a growth in imported labor that further increased Shi'ite unemployment. With population growth especially high among the Shi'a, jobs that once were able to keep most of the older generation employed were insufficient to keep the younger generation employed. Indeed, today the Shi'a can be divided between the few who are rich and the many who are poor, those who have jobs, and those who do not. Shi'ite community discontent was intensified by the impact of external ideology—primarily radical Arab nationalism coming from Egypt, Iraq, and south Yemen, but also by Marxist or Communist movements to which Shi'a as well as Sunnis were drawn. After 1979, Iran provided the new wave of ideology imported into Bahrain.

It is significant that the character of the al-Khalifa's position in society was also changing drastically in this period, parallel to the regimes of most other Gulf oil states. These ruling families have ruled largely by consensus on the basis of tribal support. Before their dependence on oil revenues, most of these families, including the al-Khalifa, had been dependent upon large merchant families to provide financial support to them. With the discovery

of oil and the sudden influx of rapidly rising oil revenues in the 1970s, however, the economic and political position of these ruling families was transformed as they became independent of local merchant support and even the
need for rule by consensus. A shift toward greater authoritarianism was the
result. In Bahrain, as elsewhere, the al-Khalifa were the first beneficiaries of
the oil income since the oil by definition belonged to the family. The wealth
of the state was the al-Khalifa's to distribute as largesse to grateful citizens.
In Bahrain today, the word "government" in common parlance still refers to
the family. Most of the land on the island belongs to the al-Khalifa family.
There has been no institutional accountability of the family to the public for
25 years since the suspension of the parliament.

The presence of an elected parliament in Bahrain stems from the 1973
parliamentary elections, held two years after independence and for the first
time in Bahrain's history. There were 30 elected members offset by 14 cabinet ministers answerable to the ruling family. By 1975, however, the parliament was seriously challenging ruling family prerogatives, demanding
greater government accountability, and seeking to put limits on the family's ability to exercise absolute power. A majority of the parliament insisted that the 1973 constitution, with its broad range of human rights,
civil liberties, due process, and protection of citizens from arbitrary action,
be fully implemented. Behind Bahraini internal politics was a sharp ideological struggle across the Arab world in general between radical Arab nationalists and conservative, mostly monarchical regimes. The al-Khalifas
were probably more concerned with the activities of Nasserite or pro-Ba'th
leftists in the parliament than with the Shi'a. As a political stand-off grew,
any possible political détente between the al-Khalifas and civil society
came to an end in 1975 when the parliament refused to pass a State Security Measures Law sponsored by the regime that "authorized arrest and imprisonment of up to three years without charge or trial for undefined 'acts'
or 'statements' that could be construed to threaten the country's internal
or external security."[12] The government then dissolved the parliament by
decree and ignored constitutional provisions that new elections be held
within two months.[13] Thus ended Bahrain's brief experiment with representative parliamentary government.

The Iranian Revolution and the Iran-Iraq War

It was perhaps the Iranian revolution of 1979 that was the major turning
point for the status of the Shi'a in Bahrain. Large segments of the Shi'ite
population saw in the emergence of a new revolutionary power in Iran a
force that would lend weight to expression of Shi'ite grievances on the island—the hope that the Shi'a would no longer be "alone" in the Gulf and

abandoned to their fate. Very quickly radical Shi'ite groups sprang up, undoubtedly influenced by Iran both directly and indirectly. Iran chose first
to try to galvanize the quiescent Shi'ite population through radical preaching by Iranian clerics whose words generally enjoyed respect among the
bulk of the population. An Iraqi-Iranian cleric, Hadi al-Mudarrisi (who,
with his brother Taqi, led the Islamic Action Organization earlier in Iraq),
was sent to Bahrain as Khomeini's personal representative, followed by a
second Iranian cleric, Ayatollah Sadegh Rouhani. Several Shi'ite demonstrations took place in the summer of 1979 as a result of Mudarrisi's preaching, leading to his expulsion along with Rouhani several months later.
Apart from the incitement from these clerics, the Bahraini Shi'a also had
other grievances stemming from long-standing regime treatment of their
own clerics by the regime.[14]

This Shi'ite unrest in Bahrain was paralleled by simultaneous Shi'ite unrest in Saudi Arabia and Kuwait, reflecting close ties and sentiments among
these three Shi'ite communities. The atmosphere of instability was intensified by Sunni fundamentalist disorders in Saudi Arabia when the Grand
Mosque was seized by Sunni dissidents. All of these events reflected long-
standing Shi'ite grievances and served to stimulate a general expectation of
change around the Gulf.

The waves of protest and unrest moved into a new phase of terrorism in
much of the Gulf in 1981 as Iran began to take a more direct hand in stim-
ulating subversion. The much bolder and more revolutionary approach by
Tehran at this juncture stemmed less from ideology and more from the harsh
realities of the Iran-Iraq war. Despite Iraqi initiation of the aggression, all
Gulf regimes lent full and unstinting support to Saddam Hussein's Iraq
throughout the eight-year conflict. Iranian-sponsored violence in the Gulf
primarily reflected a determination to diminish or even end Gulf-state support for Saddam Hussein during the war—not merely a show of some newfound sympathy for the Gulf Shi'a.

A Bahraini Shi'ite movement, the Islamic Front for the Liberation of
Bahrain (IFLB), was set up in Tehran by Mudarrisi, who had by then also
taken over the Gulf section of Iranian radio, a key voice in Iranian influence
over the Gulf Shi'a. In 1981 the Bahrain government announced the un-
covering of a Shi'ite conspiracy directed by IFLB to overthrow the regime
and set up an "Islamic Republic": a group of Shi'a from Bahrain and other
parts of the Gulf had reportedly been trained in Iran and were to be supported by Iranian hovercraft in the attempt. Iran's role as a source of
weapons, training, and ideological support had thus become central to the
most radical of the Shi'ite groups in a struggle in which it was difficult for
the Shi'a to avoid being dragged into the vortex of a broader Iran-Iraq struggle whether they liked it or not. The actions of the most radical Shi'a directly

affected the status of even the moderates, who began to be viewed as potential fifth columnists for Iran. Thus the Shi'a of Bahrain, as elsewhere, had essentially failed to create a sustainable and effective political resistance movement for themselves partly out of fear of the vulnerability of their own situation in their society.

The Petition Struggle

Two simultaneous and overlapping, but distinct, processes are under way in Bahrain today. First, there is a broad demand for liberalization and democratization that is supported by nearly the entire Shi'ite population and by Sunni liberals. Second, there is a movement by the Shi'a to secure their own just place in the Bahraini political, economic, and social order. Tragically, it is by default that the Shi'a have become the chief force behind the democratization campaign, because the state has successfully driven a wedge between the Shi'a and the bulk of the Sunnis. Support for liberalization and democratization among the Sunnis has thus been marginalized.

With the general lessening of regional and global tensions by 1992, and the hospitable climate for democracy, reformers in Bahrain were emboldened to launch a new democratization campaign. Approximately 14 reformers—a majority of them Sunni—resolved to present a petition to the Emir with over 300 signatures calling for restoration of the elected parliament and the restitution of the constitution. A key consideration was the need to liberalize, modernize, "rationalize," and streamline the government to make it more responsive to change and economic development. Virtually every minister in government had been there unchallenged for 25 years, with only a few exceptions. The petition's goals were reformist and called for no change of emir or removal of the al-Khalifa but simply a return to the democratic political order abrogated in 1975. Kuwait was seen by the petitioners as a conscious model. The Emir, however, rejected the petition.

The reformers regrouped and came back in 1994, led again primarily by Sunni secular liberals, this time with a petition carrying 23,000 signatures, of which a majority were Shi'ite, reflecting their numerical dominance in the country.[15] Petition leaders say that many more signatures could have been obtained, but the petitioners did not want to escalate the confrontation unnecessarily with the government. The secularists were proud of the fact that they had initiated this movement and had even brought the Shi'ite clerics around to the value of this approach to reform. Only two Shi'ite clerics were actively involved in the leadership of the petition movement at this stage: 'Abd-al-Wahhab Husayn and Shaykh 'Abd-al-Amir al-Jamri. Two Sunni clerics, Shaykh 'Abd-al-Latif al-Mahmud and 'Isa al-Jawdar, were also part of what was primarily a secularist movement.

The government reacted more sharply to the second petition. Security services raided many of the petition signers in their own homes, and in the villages they often confiscated their property. But the chief regime strategy was to polarize the petition movement by labeling it as Shi'ite—a destabilizing movement representing special pleading on the part of Shi'a. As a result the Shi'ite population was made the primary focus of punishment for having presented the petition, while the Sunnis remained largely untouched—as if to prove that the movement had only a narrow Shi'ite sectarian character. A prominent Sunni dissident lawyer and leader of the petition movement, Ahmad al-Shamlan, was jailed but quickly released in an effort to build the anti-Shi'ite case. (Al-Shamlan has been in and out of jail repeatedly.) In a few cases, members of prominent Sunni merchant families sympathetic to the petition movement had to retract their support because their families were seriously harassed. In contrast, al-Jamri, the popular Shi'ite cleric, was held in jail for four years with only a brief interruption.[16] The Shi'a perceive the beginning of heavy political discrimination by the regime against them as dating from the petition movement.

The petition movement, at least as a nominal presence, has not died. At present there still exists a Popular Petition Committee (Lajna t al-'Arida al-Sha'biyya), which seeks to keep it alive and that has attained some degree of international recognition in legal and human rights circles. It is a nonsectarian group once made up of nine (five Sunnis and four Shi'a) but now of seven members: Hisham Shihabi, Muhammad Jabir al-Sabah, Ahmad Shamlan, 'Ali Qasim Rabi'a, Ibrahim Jamal-al-Din, 'Isa al-Jawdar, Sa'id al-'Asbul. The Sunnis on the committee are willing to work with the Shi'a because they believe that they share similar reform goals and that their demands are realistic. They believe that the country would not "fall under Shi'ite control" even with an elected parliament, given all the natural differences among the Shi'a. They fault the regime for having encouraged Shi'ite clerics in the 1970s against the leftists, who were then strong. The Petition Committee is, however, quite independent of the religious Shi'ite resistance movement and has no control over its activities. The committee hopes that its goals will gradually gain greater support from the Sunni community, which shares the unhappiness with economic conditions and political deadlock, but which avoids involvement in the movement out of fear of government harassment. The committee's hope seems unrealistic in the short-term, however, and its influence is weak.

The committee maintains secular, nonsectarian goals and does not agree with the violence practiced by Shi'ite youths, but it believes that the regime has not handled the problem well and that the Shi'a have been driven into a corner. The secularist Sunnis say they do not view Shaykh al-Jamri, who has been specifically targeted by the regime, as a fundamentalist or radical and believe he is flexible in dialogue. The Sunni secularists are likewise generally dismissive of the government's case about Iranian involvement; while they agree that Iran has helped stir the pot in the past, they do not see the Iranian factor as a significant aspect of the problem. Sunni liberals also doubt the seriousness of government charges that the Bahrain Liberation Movement (BFM—see below) has been engaged in serious coup plotting against the regime.[17]

The regime is particularly galled by the Petition Committee since its very existence demonstrates that the grievances are national and nonsectarian; the regime has consistently refused even to discuss the petition. Although the regime has avoided officially punishing Sunni members in order to portray the issue as a sectarian conflict, it has subjected many Sunnis to harassment, encouraging people to label them as "Shi'a" and encouraging harassment of their children in school. The ruling family is determined to ensure there is no revival of petition.

In a diversionary move, and to avert the issue of restoring an elected parliament, in 1993 the regime established a Consultative Council (Majlis al-Shura), all 30 (later 40) of whose members were appointed by the ruling family. To most Bahrainis this council is seen as a distinct step backward from the 1975 elected parliament and represents continuing regime determination to ignore the existing constitution. Shi'ite secularists point out that a return to the 1975 parliament is a moderate call. The 1975 parliament consisted of 40 members directly elected plus 14 members of the cabinet, mostly members of the ruling family. No parties were permitted in the parliament, but there were factions. Some eight members were leftist/socialist, five were religious (including al-Jamri and his supporters), and there was a middle group of nationalists, most of whom had government support, and who were augmented by cabinet members appointed by the government. In this situation the government had major control over what happened in the parliament. In the liberals' view, the regime can easily afford to reopen that body. Liberals note that this constitution distinguished Bahrain from many neighboring states that have no constitution. The new Consultative Council is meanwhile viewed by most Bahrainis as an empty gesture, a rubber stamp. It has neither legislative nor oversight authority, and its discussions and agenda are said to be carefully scripted by the office of the prime minister or the Emir. Conservative Sunnis acknowledge the weakness of the Shura but suggest that it could be the vehicle for gradual reform if the regime should appoint more broadly representative members or permit it to have some elected members in the future.

The government has taken advantage of the crisis with the Shi'a to appeal to Saudi Arabia and other Gulf states for support against the violence ("terrorism") and to request funds to create employment. The assistance received from the Gulf states is significant.

Pro-regime Sunni sympathizers base their case against the Shi'ite activists on the idea that their early demonstrations in 1994 represented deliberately contrived incidents. They claim the government has evidence of telephone contacts between Shi'ite clerical leaders on Bahrain and 'Isa Qasim, a key Bahraini Shi'ite cleric then in Qom, about these demonstrations. Some pro-government spokesmen admit that the government may have erred in deporting the leading Shi'ite activists as a means of solving the problem; they believe the government probably could have negotiated with the Shi'ite leaders and found them suitable positions in government.

By comparison with truly authoritarian police states in the Arab world such as Iraq, the Bahraini regime has been relatively restrained with these opposition leaders, who could have been jailed for life or simply murdered or executed. Instead, these figures—especially Mansur al-Jamri (son of Shaykh al-Jamri), 'Isa Qasim, and 'Ali Salman—have undertaken leadership of the BFM against the regime from London. Pro-government figures point out that the initial release of Shaykh al-Jamri from prison after the early demonstrations was exploited by the BFM, which went on to make inflammatory pronouncements and to encourage violent activities such as the burning of tires, cars, and houses. They state that many Shi'a themselves were disturbed at the violence; some had their cars burned for not supporting the movement. Some of the Shi'ite slogans were particularly worrisome to the Sunnis, such as "Through knowledge and numbers we'll rule the country" (Bi'l 'ilm wa'l 'adad sanahkum al-balad). The family saw an even greater direct threat to its rule in slogans calling for "death to the al-Khalifa"—the most violent slogan yet to have appeared.

Some pro-government Sunnis concede that both Shi'a and Sunnis may support the democracy movement but that their "cultural roots are different," creating political problems. These Sunnis point out that the Shi'a bear a sense of long-term oppression as a community and have always wanted self-rule; this is their fundamental agenda behind all the talk of democracy. They say the last parliament, in the 1970s, demonstrated broad differences not readily reconciled, especially between the leftists and the religious groups. Failure of the Shi'a and the liberals to compromise with the regime and their attempts to block passage of the regime's security laws led to the parliament's closure. The Islamists have thus profited from these differences. In the Sunni view, much of the recent Islamization tendencies has been "imported from abroad," for example, when upper-class girls come back from Western education wearing the veil (hijab). These government sympathizers maintain a great political caution that they say reflects their awareness of the fragility of the Bahraini state and its position in the middle of the Gulf, which is aswirl with ideological competition and competing international interests. While in their view change must come, it must come only gradually; Bahrain, they say, is not ready for a parliament yet.

The regime in the meantime characterizes the Shi'ite clerics as having been "captured by Qom." In reality, the regime may fear the influence of Qom and the clerical inspiration from Iran far less than it fears the currents of democratization in the Arab world. In a revealing statement, a regime sympathizer stated that the Kuwaiti system, with its elected parliament, open debates, and free press, is the most dangerous threat to Bahrain.[18] Thus the bogies of Iranian influence and Shi'ite sectarian fanaticism may be a cover for what the Bahraini regime really fears: a universal call for restraints on the regime's powers.

Shi'ite Leadership

Several Shi'ite political movements exist, all of them illegal by Bahraini law. The dominant Shi'ite movement is the Bahrain Freedom Movement (BFM), also known as the Bahrain Liberation Movement, many of whose leaders live in forced of self-imposed exile. In Arabic it is popularly known among the Shi'a as Harakat al-Bahrayn al-Islamiyya, or Bahrain Islamic Movement, but the BFM seeks to downplay any religious or sectarian angle that is not part of its formal agenda. The BFM enjoys a broad sympathy among most Shi'a because it is the only force seriously fighting for Shi'ite rights, has broad emotional appeal, and is led by educated people who know how to present the cause on the international level. Some Shi'ite leftists maintain, however, that the BFM and its partially clerical leadership does not have to be the inevitable or sole vehicle of Shi'ite demands; they say that if the Communist party, for example, as a nonsectarian ideological party, were to take up the same issues the Shi'a might flock to them again. The Communist party has been largely eliminated, however. Many Shi'a believe that if the political scene were to open up the moderate Shi'a (not excluding clerics) would easily win over the support that the more radical elements currently enjoy. These moderates believe it is the very violence of regime police action against the broader Shi'ite community that is the primary factor contributing to the growing strength of the radicals. Confrontational marches and clashes that once numbered perhaps 3 a year, for example, rose in frequency and size after 1994, and came to involve anywhere from a few hundred to 25,000 people.

In its role as an umbrella organization the BFM also maintains contacts with the leftist, nonsectarian National Front and Popular Front movements that operate both inside Bahrain and in exile. The government has avoided cracking down on either of these two organizations since it would prefer not to alienate the left as well—particularly since it no longer presents the threat that it once did in the 1960s and 1970s. Harshest government treatment is reserved for the Shi'ite Islamists, then for the Shi'ite secularists, and only after that for the Sunnis.

The BFM particularly respects modernist Islamist thinkers such as the Tunisian Shaykh Rashid al-Ghannushi (Sunni) or modernist clerics in Iran. It is also in touch with Shaykh Mahdi Shamseddin in Lebanon, the leader of the Higher Muslim Shi'ite Council of Lebanon who maintains an interest in the welfare of Gulf Shi'a. Shamseddin has expressed an interest in mediating between the Shi'a and the Bahraini government but has been given no opening to do so. He has met with the BFM in London but has said he is unwilling to come to Bahrain unless he can come in a completely independent capacity. Shamseddin reportedly has commented that it is easier to deal with the al-Sa'ud family in Riyadh than with the al-Khalifa in Bahrain, and that the Saudi Shi'a are easier to deal with than the Bahraini Shi'a (perhaps because they are a majority in Bahrain).

Within Bahrain, the old town of Muharraq north of Manama is important to the BFM since it is half Sunni, half Shi'a, and an area of some cooperation between the two communities. It is almost a bellwether for such cooperation since if Sunni professionals there cannot be urged to cooperate then Sunnis elsewhere on the island are very unlikely to do so.

The leadership of the BFM is divided between an internal and external leadership. The internal leadership is underground and little is known about it, but it is probably connected to Shaykh 'Abd-al-Amir al-Jamri who has been in and out of prison several times. The BFM inside Bahrain has the major day-to-day, hands-on control of the community's resistance activities, and the external leadership is more likely to serve as adviser and channel of information than as shaper of activities on the ground in Bahrain.

The BFM leadership in exile is gaining in importance over time under the leadership of Mansur al-Jamri, son of Shaykh 'Abd-al-Amir al-Jamri, Sa'id Shihabi, and a number of others. Another significant figure in the external opposition is the cleric Shaykh 'Ali Salman, whose relationship to BFM is less formal. Salman began his career as a reader at ceremonies held in ma'atim. He was sent to Qom for religious training by the community and, like many others, was radicalized in his views while there. He nonetheless requested that the government allow him to return to Bahrain after his theological training. Upon his return he turned quickly to politics and was a key figure in arranging the first disorders by the Shi'ite community in 1993, against international marathon runners who ran through Shi'ite neighborhoods. As a result of his agitational activity he was expelled by the government—as was the younger al-Jamri—and now lives in London.

Liberal Sunni observers note that both these figures were initially young, inexperienced, and unrealistic about politics. Today, Salman, despite his Qom education, has grown politically wiser while living in London, learning English and becoming exposed to Western political thinking. Both al-Jamri and Salman have gained a greater understanding about the international and domestic political order and how best to politically orient the movement. From this point of view it has probably been beneficial for the BFM to have part of its leadership expelled to London, where it is subject to a more sober and practical environment. Indeed, a key role of the BFM in London is to bring the Bahrain situation to the attention of the international community and make it more sympathetic to the BFM's goals. In this area it has already had some success (see below).

The BFM seeks consensus among Shi'a to the maximum degree possible and avoids policy stands on controversial issues that go beyond its call for restoration of the constitution and parliament—such as the issue of the role of the Shari'a (Islamic law). It has not even called for an end to the ruling family, although it does seek constitutional limits upon it.

The BFM leadership in exile in London has devoted considerable attention to the media struggle and an information campaign against the al-Khalifa regime. For several years it has been producing a short daily newsletter distributed to a wide variety of addressees both in Bahrain and abroad to keep the realities of the struggle prominent in people's minds. The newsletter, distributed both by fax and through the internet, is soberly written, presenting information about riots, incidents, police brutality, the state of various trials, and the condition of the imprisoned, especially Shaykh 'Abd-al-Amir al-Jamri. It presents information on al-Khalifa policies and tactics; statements from the BFM itself on its views, policies, goals, and successes; and publicizes other international reporting about the situation that is favorable to their cause. It does not attack other organizations, figures, or groups, or talk about Iran.

The BFM believes it realized considerable success in 1997 in the struggle to make its case in the West. Some of its accomplishments include:

- The new Labor Party foreign minister in the United Kingdom declared that the Bahraini opposition is a "moderate" one with a moderate set of demands.
- A major 109-page report was issued by the U.S.-based Human Rights Watch on July 24, 1997, that described human rights abuses in Bahrain as "wide-ranging." The report speaks of "the broad denial of such civil and political rights as freedom of expression, freedom of association and assembly, and the right to participate in the conduct of public affairs, directly or through freely chosen representatives. . . . It is the Bahraini government's systematic violation of these fundamental freedoms and political rights that has contributed to the conditions of confrontation in Bahrain today."[19]
- An important and historic U.N. Human Rights Sub-Commission resolution, passed on August 21, 1997, condemned the government of

Bahrain for its gross violations of human rights, including discrimination against the Shi'ite community.

- The European Parliament issued another historic resolution calling on the Bahraini government to release political prisoners, to facilitate the return of exiles and institute due process of law according to accepted international standards, and to open negotiations with opposition forces immediately, with a view to holding democratic elections, open to both sexes, at the earliest opportunity. Moreover, the parliament called on the European Union member states to refrain from supplying arms or security support to the government of Bahrain.[20]

In the view of the BFM, these condemnations reflect the failure of the Bahrain regime's policies, which assumed that using the Shi'a as a scapegoat would continue to be a winning game with cautious European powers. Such sharp criticism emanating from Europe and especially London has led the al-Khalifa regime to claim that London now seeks to destabilize the Bahraini government and is interfering in Bahrain's sovereignty.

The case of the Bahraini Shi'a again illustrates the problem of creating secular leadership within a Shi'ite movement. The leadership of Shi'ite opposition has been dominated by clerics since the 1980s with the eclipse of the left. Clerical leadership, however, does not necessarily denote a radical or hard-line approach. The explicit public agenda of the BFM, despite its mainly clerical leadership, is secular in its political goals and above narrow sectarian interest; except for the IFLB (see below) in Iran, none of the clerics speak of Iran, of the Shari'a, or even of Islam in their political pronouncements. The IFLB, which has very little following on the ground, reportedly does have the explicit goal of an Islamic state. (As in other countries, hard-line Bahraini Sunnis argue that democracy is a Shi'ite agenda, rendering any democratic compromise virtually inaccessible).

In one sense it is even difficult to speak of "leaders" in the Shi'ite movement since there are few clearly dominant figures. Shaykh al-Jamri, who was a member of the short-lived 1974 parliament, is the most prominent Shi'ite leader in Bahrain now, but he achieved his position as primary leader in the last few years and in the absence of other leadership figures on the island. His stature has also risen as a result of his prominence in the petition movement and his incarceration. Because the remainder of the leadership is in London, it has less clout on the ground and must play its cards carefully in order to maintain a voice in the evolving situation on the ground.

A smaller but more radical organization is the Islamic Front for the Liberation of Bahrain (Al-Jabha al-Islamiyya Li Tahrir al-Bahrain). The IFLB was founded by the Iraqi/Iranian cleric Hadi al-Mudarrisi in 1980 (see above), a key figure behind a great deal of the violent revolutionary activity in the early 1980s, operating out of Iran after his expulsion from Bahrain. The IFLB infrastructure was badly damaged in the government's crackdown in 1981 to 1982. Today the IFLB has little support among the senior Bahraini clergy, only some measure of street support. Its leadership remains based in Iran. In the eyes of one liberal Sunni activist, the IFLB represents no real challenge to the BFM, even if it were incorporated into the broader BFM, which it has so far resisted. Indeed, the BFM sees itself as a comprehensive Shi'ite political organization with an inclusionist policy. It maintains ties with the IFLB but claims it finds that organization difficult to deal with because of lack of any clear-cut political program with which the BFM could cooperate. The IFLB reportedly does not call for restoration of the constitution, as does the BFM, since it sees that constitution as "incomplete" in Islamic terms.

A third group may exist among the Shi'ite radicals that is referred to as "Hizballah." As we have noted elsewhere, the term "Hizballah" as used by various Arab governments has different meanings. In this case the Bahraini government uses it to refer to Bahraini Shi'a with close ties to Iran, and who are committed to terrorist operations. In June 1996, 51 Bahrainis were arrested and charged with plotting against the government. They were accused of being members of "Hizballah," trained and armed in an Iran-backed plot. The BFM acknowledges the presence of a small minority of radicals among the Shi'a, although it claims the 51 were not linked to Iran. Several of these figures were in fact educated in Qom—the only place where aspiring Shi'ite clerics can study today—and are revolutionary firebrands. Three were sentenced to death. The BFM claims that the evidence for the bulk of those tried was circumstantial, that the accused had no adequate defense, and that confessions were extracted by torture. Other Shi'ite clerics state there is no such thing as a "Hizballah" organization as such, but they acknowledge that there are a few extremists who advocate violence. Other credible observers support this view, including the Human Rights Watch.[21]

Shi'ite observers as well as Sunni liberals dismiss the importance of the 1996 "Hizballah plot" to overthrow the regime that was uncovered by the government. They state that the number and type of weapons found by the security forces was hopelessly inadequate to start a revolution or even to stand up to Bahrain security forces. These same groups point out that the somewhat fabricated and exaggerated 1996 plot contrasts dramatically with the situation in the early 1980s when real terrorism was indeed operating in Bahrain in the full flush of the Iranian revolution and its unambiguous support to revolution abroad. Today most Shi'a have lost their idealism for the Iranian regime. There nonetheless exists some concern among Shi'ite and Sunni liberals that the "Hizballah" element, that is, radicals, could grow in prominence over time if the Shi'a are unable to attain minimal satisfaction of their grievances.

Shi'ite Grievances

While the BFM has embraced nonsectarian goals for the future of Bahrain fully compatible with the goals of liberal Sunni activists, the Shi'a do have specific grievances as a community that they seek to redress.

- They point to a complete unwillingness of the government to listen to any of the Shi'ite grievances or to engage in any dialogue.
- They state they have no significant representation within the government bureaucracy—the minister of labor is the only Shi'ite.
- They complain of job discrimination across the board, but especially in the major industrial complexes with substantial government ownership.
- They call for the release of some 1,500 to 2,000 Shi'ite political prisoners.
- They call for cessation of harassment of Shi'ite communities, which they claim is one of the leading causes of antiregime demonstrations and resentments. This harassment is widely reported by Shi'a of almost all walks of life. It is usually conducted by expatriate police who often speak no Arabic and treat the Shi'a insultingly, rudely, and often with physical violence. They routinely raid Shi'ite homes, ransack them, beat the inhabitants, mock them, insult the women, and create an overall climate of insecurity, fear, and violence. With the government's decision to affix responsibility for the petition movement on the Shi'ite community, it moved to suppress Shi'ite activity in various areas of civil life and society. For example, a new president, a military man, was brought in to head Bahrain University, and he proceeded to fire most of the leading Shi'ite professors under various pretexts.
- They call for the elimination of the special security courts in which the Shi'a have been prosecuted. These courts were established by amendment of the Penal Code, and the judiciary cannot be considered independent. According to lawyers, court judgments are based on confessions. Informers provide information against the accused but are not brought to court proceedings and the defendants cannot confront their accusers. No witnesses are called and there is no cross-examination. The defense counsel is not permitted to read the charges in advance. The defense attorney is usually summoned to the court knowing nothing of the case, and is able to meet with the accused for perhaps half an hour after six months of detention and a signed confession. Non-Bahraini (usually Egyptian) judges are often brought to the prison cell to hear a confession and offi-

cially accept it; its veracity is not established by court procedure. Confessions cannot be renounced in court under oath. If the accused speaks up during the court procedure he is often taken back to his jail cell and tortured further. Security court decisions cannot be appealed. One Sunni lawyer stated that there are approximately 2,000 Shi'a now under detention without trial.

- They protest discrimination in university education: Even Sunni liberals speak of discrimination against Shi'a in the higher levels of education; many Shi'a in the top 10 percent of their class do not gain entrance to university, whereas less qualified Sunnis do. Government policies have also encouraged rising antipathy between the Sunni and Shi'ite communities, which is visible now even in secondary level education.
- They maintain that until the early 1990s, the Shi'a had been relatively free to practice Shi'ism and perform its rituals. Since the crackdown, however, the government has repeatedly attacked or closed *ma'atim* (religious centers) and religious schools and practiced close surveillance on Shi'ite religious activities.

Unemployment and Labor Policies

The Shi'a form the bulk of the poor in Bahrain. The modern high-rises in the capital, Manama, and the elegant garden villas in the outskirts are only a stone's throw away from, and often flank, the run-down, shabbily built and dusty villages of the Shi'a, with few paved alleys and hardly any amenities.

The rate of unemployment among Shi'a is very high compared to very low unemployment among Sunnis. A key factor in this is a particularly pernicious regime practice of importing foreign expatriate labor which is favored for three reasons. First, senior government officials (ruling family members) and large businessmen are able to "sell" work permits and visas abroad to poor Bangladeshis, Filipinos, Pakistanis, Sri Lankans, and other South Asians and make a profit on bringing them to Bahrain where they then "sell" their labor to employers. Second, expatriate workers are willing to work for less money and fewer protections than the local wage system would require for native workers. Third, expatriate laborers come without family and for specified periods of time and are totally beholden to the system for maintaining their jobs and salaries, the bulk of which is repatriated to their families back home. This makes for an exceptionally docile labor force. The least whisper of dissent, dissatisfaction, or labor agitation and the worker is on the next plane out. Thus Bahrain, one of the few places in the Gulf in which a genuine native labor force exists—since most Gulf citizens are unwilling to engage in physical labor—is spared the labor problems and strikes that were a feature of antiregime disorders and leftist organizing in earlier decades.

Even the outside observer in Bahrain can hardly fail to be struck by the virtual sea of South Asians encountered in the bazaar and small shops, and their presence in even the most traditional fields of labor. The fishing trade, for example, long monopolized by Shi'a, today has been taken over by Filipino labor. Small shopkeepers, workers in the tourist trade, and service sector employees are predominantly South Asian.

The cost of these labor policies is rampant unemployment among the Shi'a, who have traditionally carried out such jobs involving few skills or physical labor. Some Bahraini businessmen argue that only these policies help keep Bahraini wages low and the island attractive and competitive for foreign investment. If the cost is the alienation of the majority of the native population, however, the cost is indeed high. The government has gone so far as to ask the Kuwaiti government not to permit Bahraini Shi'a working in Kuwait to receive wages any higher than they might receive in Bahrain— a request that was ignored. The government is fearful that Shi'ite labor unrest could lead to bad publicity for the country; there are even allegations that in its major contracts with foreign firms the government stipulates that they are not allowed to hire native (that is, Shi'ite) labor, including drivers.

With growing pressure on this volatile issue, the government has taken some steps to lessen the amount of expatriate labor that can be brought into the country, and it has taken away permits from small businesses to import them. While this practice exerts hardship upon the smaller importers, it leaves a major loophole open by which large firms still maintain labor importation permits. These firms benefit financially by taking a cut of the laborers' modest pay and at the same time are rendered beholden to the government and more obligated to support its policies.

Labor policy is not an entirely negative picture, however. The government has appointed a Shi'ite, 'Abdul-Nabi al Shu'ala, as minister of labor, and he has been empowered to deal with the unemployment problem among the Shi'a—although without full voice over broad expatriate labor hiring practices. The Labor Ministry is engaged in a training and education program that is designed to qualify more Shi'a for work in the economy— although the government argues that as long as the intifada continues, opportunities for hiring Shi'a will not markedly increase. The intifada has also had the effect of depriving greater numbers of Shi'ite youth of educational opportunities, as the government clamps down on their entry into the state-run colleges. Thus the government is holding jobs and education hostage to "improved" Shi'ite behavior.

The Shi'a hope that a return to an elected parliament will benefit them. Shi'ite leaders have suggested that any attempt to impose a purely democra-

tic system—one person, one vote—upon the country now would be counterproductive, given Sunni sensitivities and fear for their own status in the
future. These leaders suggest that a 50–50 split of parliamentary seats between Sunnis and Shi'a would be an acceptable arrangement that would
bring far greater voice and benefits to the Shi'ite community than anything
it has now. There would thus appear to be some flexibility among the Shi'a
in the interests of changing the intolerable status quo.

Due to regime efforts to cast the liberalization campaign in purely sectarian terms, most Bahraini Sunnis have abandoned active support for the
issue and by default have allowed it to be largely coopted at the popular level
by the Shi'a as a means of political and social mobilization of the community. In reality, however, despite strong BFM support for the constitution
and parliament, one may question whether these are inherently ringing issues to the Shi'ite masses. They have become symbolic vehicles for Shi'ite
ambitions and grievances, however. And the BFM both at home and abroad
wisely focuses on these issues in the belief that they are free of sectarian character and help lend domestic and international legitimacy to their cause.

A trip to the Shi'a villages, however, offers rawer insights into the character of Shi'ite thinking and imagery at the local level. The villages demonstrate the degree to which Shi'ite communities are now living in almost total
isolation, cut off from the rest of the island by security forces and under
heavy police guard. Poverty and poor conditions are widespread; houses are
poorly built and in a state of serious disrepair. Slogans, nowhere visible in
Manama, are everywhere in the Shi'ite villages and have not been removed.
The most common slogans are particularly revealing of popular sentiment:

- parliament or destruction! (*al-barlaman aw al-damar!*)
- death to the al-Khalifa! (*al-mawt li'l Khalifa!*)
- we're not concerned about execution! *(La nubali al -i'dam!)*
- parliament is the solution! (*al-barlaman huwa al-hall!*)
- there is no religious holiday as long as al-Jamri is jailed and 'Ali Salman
  is exiled! (*La 'Id wa 'l-Jamri sajin wa 'Ali Salman mub'ad !*)
- the constitution is the solution! (*al-dustur huwa al-hall!*)
- there are no Shi'a or Sunnis, we are an Islamic ummah! (*La Shi'a la
  Sunna, nahnu umma Islamiyya!*)
- we have won through martyrdom! (*fuzna bi'l-shahada!*)
- we won't kneel! (*lan narka'!*)
- no to humiliation! (*la li'l dhill!*)
- If you kill, we kill, a soul for a soul and an eye for an eye! (*in qataltum
  qatalna, wa al-nafsu bi al-nafs wal-'aynu bil-'ayn!*)
- Al-Jamri won't bargain, he will struggle for us! (*al-Jamri la yusawim,
  min ajlina yuqawim!*)

- where is the just trial? (*ayn al-muhakama al-'adila!*)
- manhood doesn't derive from spilling blood or beating prisoners, you mercenaries! (*laisat al-rujula bi safk al-dima' wa halk al-masajin, ya murtazaqa!*)
- why are people unemployed? (*limadha al-sha'b 'attal?*)
- let our generation learn vigilance at all times! (*fa li tata'allam ajjaluna al-istiqadh fi kulli lahdha!*)
- Al-Jamri + the parliament = governance (*Al-Jamri + al-barlaman = al-hukm*)
- the people won't rest! (*Al-sha'b lan yahda'!*)
- the Shi'a live by calamities! (*Al-Shi'a tahya bil masa'ib*)
- there is no Sunnism or Shi'ism—the people just want freedom! (*la sin-niyya la shi'iyya—al-sha'b yutalib bil hurriyya!*) [22]

Despite their emotionalism, the slogans generally are remarkably moderate in what they call for (with the exception of "Death to the al-Khalifa"). Particularly striking is the minimal emphasis on Shi'ism; when it does occur it is more in the communitarian than the ideological sense. There are no calls for Shari'a, for an Islamic state, for Iran, or denunciation of imperialism, Zionism, the United States, or "the arrogant of the world." The slogans reflect almost nothing of the kind of slogans used by the Islamic Republic and its external supporters—such as by Hizballah in Lebanon. To this extent, most of them are broadly within the guidelines of BFM policies. There is a major focus on legalism. There are no pictures of Khomeini as there are in the Shi'ite districts of Beirut. Pictures of al-Jamri and 'Ali Salman, the two top leading clerics, are widespread, however.

Older and conservative Shi'a are concerned at the latent or real radicalism that they perceive in some of the Shi'ite violence. They don't see clashes with the Sunnis as wise or inevitable, and they point to past periods of Sunni-Shi'ite cooperation against the British. The Shi'a believe that they must be loyal to the state, but only if the state is loyal to them in meeting their needs as citizens and treating them equally. Few conservative Shi'a believe that Iran is a significant force in the violence that is under way; they see the violence as flowing directly out of local circumstances and frustrations and provoked by the government in order to avoid examining the genuine domestic roots of discontent. They see the ruling family as out of touch with reality, prone to listen to the advice of the bad-intentioned and the security services. They point out that whenever discussion comes up about the security budget there are always disorders that demonstrate the case for major security expenditures. In the meantime the government maintains a news blackout on almost all events relating to the Shi'a so no one is informed and the outside world is unaware of events. Many Shi'a state that if the government were to allow the return of the BFM leadership from London it would see that they are not radicals.

These conservative Shi'a also point out that elections are a dangerous idea in the present climate of polarized thinking and emotions. Elections are suitable after the society has attained some degree of calm, when economic conditions are better, when there is equality of treatment for all, with good government and accountability and freedom of speech that will allow proper debate of issues. In their absence, impressionable and frustrated youths will be carried away by radical rhetoric. Some Shi'ite liberals also believe that the situation must be improved before there can be any real elections. If they are held prematurely, with emotions running high and other elements of the Shi'ite community not politically organized—as they cannot be under present conditions of repression—then the more radical or religious forces will win out.

Even the conservative Shi'a want local elected government and an end to discrimination, which they see as the primary problem. Under the rule of the late Shaykh Issa, many saw the prime minister, Shaykh Khalifa, (the Emir's brother), and the crown prince as dominating the government, bent on inflexible policies, refusing any dialogue, and intolerant of serious discussion or dissent within the cabinet. Only the Emir was seen as a benevolent figure within the regime, but as essentially reigning without power in the face of his brother's control of government. With the death of Shaykh Issa and the accession of his son, Shaykh Hamad, in March 1999, the balance of power between the new Emir and his uncle, the prime minister, is uncertain, and it is unclear yet whether Shaykh Hamad will prove more sympathetic to Shi'ite grievances and more willing to introduce democratic reforms into the state system.

Sunni Attitudes

As we have seen, the Sunni population in Bahrain itself has participated in liberalization and democratization movements—usually movements from the left and associated with external Arab ideologies such as Egyptian-led Arab nationalism, or Iraqi- or Syrian-led Ba'th parties, or even the Communist party. These movements, free of any sectarian character, enjoyed an overlap of Shi'ite and Sunni interests and participation. With the fading of the left on the Arab political scene and the emergence of Islamic revivalism the sectarian factor has emerged more strongly in the contemporary movement for democratization in Bahrain.

The attitudes of the Sunni population toward the Shi'ite community range from hostile to sympathetic. The ruling family had ties with Shi'ite merchants for many years, but those have deteriorated. A leading source of anti-Shi'ite feeling are the Hawala tribes, originally from the northern (Iranian) coast of the Gulf that had themselves experienced historic oppression from the Shi'a in Iran and carry hostility toward them to this day. Unlike the Shi'a, the Sunni population has not suffered economically since the 1950s. And unlike the Shi'a, they have very little unemployment and receive good salaries. The Sunni upper class has little sympathy for the Shi'a and remain loyal to the al-Khalifa family out of concern that the growth of Shi'ite political, social, and economic power will undermine their interests. They are afraid of al-Jamri and fear that a Shi'ite victory will make the Sunnis second-class citizens. They are upset by the violence. They see Shi'ite leaders opposing "terror" in words, but doing nothing about it.

Only the moderate Sunni reformers and leftist secularists share the BFM's goals on the constitution and parliament. The National Front and the Popular Front are both leftist Sunni movements of Marxist origin in past decades. Today they still maintain general Arab nationalist views but have lost almost all grassroots ties and are generally prepared to work within the system. The Bahrain Liberation Movement seeks their support, however, as Sunni allies for the nonsectarian reform cause. In the eyes of Sunni liberals a key part of the problem is the failure of the Sunni population to support the petition movement. The struggle for a return to the constitution has thus become a de facto Shi'ite issue, which it need not be. "The Sunnis are asleep," one Sunni liberal commented.

Among upper-class Sunnis—except those on the left—one hears comments that "the government has done everything for the Shi'a," including affirmative action, but that the Shi'a "show no gratitude." Some Sunnis even hint that the Shi'ite riots stem from a U.S.-Israeli plan to destabilize Bahrain in punishment for Bahrain's failure to establish diplomatic relations with Israel. These Sunnis believe that "Hizballah" is running wild in the country and that the government should crack down even harder "to teach the Shi'a a lesson." Sunni intellectuals, including lawyers and other professionals, who tend to have leftist or Arab nationalist sentiments, are far more sympathetic to the plight of the Shi'a and critical of the Bahraini government. Several Sunni lawyers, such as al-Shamlan, have represented Shi'a detainees and have been in turn charged by the Bahraini security courts. Many middle-class Sunnis are also openly contemptuous of the al-Khalifas and their corruption, even if they do not support the Shi'ite movement. In the period of 1950 to 1970 there was considerable intermarriage between Shi'a and Sunnis, a phenomenon that has largely disappeared today, signaling a progressive breakdown along sectarian lines. Lower-class Sunnis, however, are less happy with their social and economic position, express greater hostility toward the ruling family, and therefore are reportedly more sympathetic to Shi'ite efforts to reform the existing political and social order.[23]

Religious attitudes are also on the rise among the Sunni population, although not as much as among Shi'a. Several Sunni Islamist tendencies exist:

- Jam'iyat al-Islah (Association for Reform), which is linked to the Muslim Brotherhood;
- al-Jam'iya al-Islamiyya (The Islamic Association) led by Shaykh 'Abd-al-Latif al-Mahmud, a liberal movement that basically supports government positions on many issues (although al-Mahmud was originally on the Petition Committee, he was later persuaded to leave it);
- Jam'iyat al-Tarbiya al-Islamiyya (Islamic Association for Education)—a more Wahhabi or Salafi movement that is strongly anti-Shi'ite and antidemocracy. Bahraini Wahhabis have been given some leeway by the government for their activities. Those under Saudi influence are quite active among the Sunni population but focus primarily on religious, cultural, and moral questions and stay out of politics. They are particularly strong in the Ministry of Education and receive a lot of Saudi financial support.

Whatever Sunnis may feel about the Shi'a, many are also quite disturbed at government policies that import Jordanian and Syrian Sunni beduin into Bahrain, who are perceived as aggressive and uneducated. Many of them are already active in the police force and have negative interactions with Sunni Bahrainis as well. Bahrainis fear they are changing the nature of a society that has little sympathy with or roots in beduin culture. With a crunch in domestic resources and a desire to limit population growth, it makes no sense to bring outside Sunnis in.

The Question of Violence and "Terrorism"

Despite the fact that an insurgency of sorts is under way with frequent confrontations and demonstrations—an intifada, as it is sometimes called—one is struck by the relative lack of violence in terms of actual deaths. By March 1996 a total of 24 people on both sides had died; in the single worst case a fire bomb in a small restaurant resulted in the death of seven Bangladeshi expatriate workers. The overall figure also includes three policemen, and several unaccounted "jail deaths." One Shi'a died in a blast at a branch of the National Bank; he was believed to have been the perpetrator of the explosion.[24] Considering that the confrontation has been under way since 1994, the overall casualties and damage to either side on a relative scale has been modest. The Shi'a have employed disorders or disturbances—illegal assemblies, illegal demonstrations, stone throwing, Molotov cocktails, burning tires, exploding cooking-gas bottles, the burning of empty cars, and so forth—mainly for symbolic purposes. Astonishingly, there has been almost no use of guns of any kind by the Shi'a. From the regime side, it may be significant that the director of Public Security since 1966 has been Ian Henderson, a British expatriate with a lifetime of security experience starting with fighting the Mau Mau in British Kenya. As a Western professional, Henderson is probably able to keep the instruments of state repression within certain limits of violence that would not be observed, for example, by Saddam Hussein or other authoritarian regimes in the Middle East. Henderson is bitterly resented by the Shi'a and by many Sunnis as the foreign enforcer putting his repression skills in the service of the al-Khalifa. Henderson's deputy is also a British citizen, but in 1998 the government appointed a member of the al-Khalifa family as acting director.

The Bahraini government makes the case that politically motivated violence is unacceptable, intolerable, and punishable by the standards of any government. This is undoubtedly true and the Shi'a have embarked on a dangerous course in escalating the issue to street violence. On the other hand, long-term inflexibility by the government and provocative and intimidating police action will have its social consequences in any country, regardless of the legalities. Serious abuses of human rights are taking place and have been documented at length by Middle East Watch, the U.S. State Department Human Rights office, and other organizations. But the regime has perhaps avoided crossing a certain threshold that would drive the Shi'a to the absolute brink of desperation.

More important, despite regime accusations of "terrorism," the BFM has in fact studiously avoided the use of what is commonly called "terror" in common parlance. If the movement were to decide to embark on acts of genuine terrorism, it is likely that bombs in city centers and assassination of government or security officials, foreigners, and members of the ruling family would be part of the pattern and would pose a formidable threat. The targeting of select foreigners for assassination alone would have a devastating impact upon the economy. All this has been eschewed by the moderate leadership of this movement—at least to date.

What accounts for the relative moderation of the dominant Shi'ite Islamic movement? Several factors come to mind. First, the Bahraini Shi'a as a political culture have not been violent; they stem from settled agricultural stock rather than warring beduin traditions. Second, the Shi'a have always been aware that the al-Khalifa family and the Sunnis exercise dominant power, including control of all the mechanisms of security and repression, thus leaving the Shi'a as a community quite vulnerable. The mass of Shi'ite villages in Bahrain are exposed to security forces, large numbers of whom are foreign mercenaries with little sympathy and no stake in the future of Bahraini society. More broadly, the Shi'a are aware that they live in the middle of a Sunni-dominated Arabian peninsula where neighboring regimes are hostile to them as well. Third, the expulsion of much of the BFM leadership abroad (primarily to London) has placed it in a politically moderate milieu in which the chosen instruments of struggle relate more to information and persuasion of foreign governments—especially the United Kingdom and the United States—of the validity and justice of their cause. However, this political approach could give way over time to genuine violence if it has no success.

Finally, most Shi'a are aware that life could get a great deal worse for the community and for Bahrain as a whole if the situation were to utterly deteriorate. To date the violence has largely been confined to the Shi'ite sections of the island, while life goes on more or less normally in the capital city where one might scarcely be aware that an insurgency is going on. Whether by choice or for lack of opportunity, Shi'ite acts of violence in the business sectors of the capital have been minimal, thus shielding foreign residents from a full awareness of the tensions on the island and making it hard for Western observers, including journalists, to take stock of the situation. All Bahrainis emphasize that the economy of the island is highly vulnerable; if a total breakdown of law and order were to occur, with widespread violence in the capital and among foreigners, foreign investment would quickly depart and leave the island with no resources. No one so far is willing to push the situation to the breaking point. In short, life could become even more difficult for the Shi'a over the longer run were they eventually to take over an island that has lost its central place for foreign banking, trade, and investment in the region.

The Iran-Bahrain Connection

When Britain was preparing to leave the Gulf area in 1970, the question of Bahraini independence was clouded by Iranian claims to the island. To resolve the dispute, in 1970 the United Nations carried out a plebiscite in which Bahrainis overwhelmingly rejected the choice of joining Iran and opted for their own state. Bahraini Shi'a often cite this fact to prove their independence from Iran and their commitment to their Bahraini citizenship and the state.

According to the opposition, there are some 200 Bahraini students studying in Qom. There is no legal barrier against going to Qom to study; indeed it is virtually the only place aspiring students can go for serious study of Shi'ite theology and law, especially since the Najaf seminaries no longer function under Saddam Hussein's regime in Iraq. Students generally receive funding from the religious centers (ma'atim) within the Shi'ite community in Bahrain to go abroad for religious studies, and like other seminary students, they receive stipends from the religious philanthropic institutions in Iran.

Once there, however, they become objects of great suspicion for Bahraini security organizations. Bahraini intelligence (and other regional intelligence organizations) is reported to have heavily penetrated student circles in Qom and hence to be aware of who is there doing what. There is probably little activity at the Iranian seminaries that is unknown to foreign governments.

The BFM leadership makes no secret of the fact that both Najaf and Qom matter very much to the Shi'a as important centers of religious thought—Qom being currently the more prominent center. The BFM believes it is under no compulsion to renounce religious ties with Qom simply to please the Bahraini regime or the West since the movement remains committed to its own independence from any foreign power. It distinguishes sharply between Iran the state and ideology, and Iran as a center of Shi'ite scholarship and learning.

Some leftist Shi'a believe the importance of the Iranian connection with the Bahraini Shi'a lies primarily in the arena of ideological support and encouragement, especially through Iran's radio broadcasts in the 1980s. They believe that the specifically religious flavor of the opposition movement would be more muted were it not for Iranian provision of religious and ideological education to young clerics. However, Shi'ite leftists do not automatically equate clerical leadership with radicalism, recognizing that even among Shi'ite clerics there is a spectrum of belief.

Shi'a leftists tend to think of the BFM as basically a political movement in which religion is used as a symbol to define identity, provide ideological fervor, and buttress its strength. The leftists recognize that the clerics, more than any other political group among the Shi'a, are able to "deliver the masses" to support what might otherwise be a more middle-class and professional movement. These leftist professionals are worried that if the regime at some time strikes up a dialogue with the Shi'a, it will be with the BFM leadership in London rather than with secularist professional Shi'a on the island. In short, the moderates are aware that they are being deliberately marginalized by the state in its efforts to portray all opposition as radical, fundamentalist, and Shi'ite. Some secularists have been directly told by the clerical elements that they respect secular efforts on behalf of the Shi'a, but ask that they not stand in the way or cooperate against the religious leaders. In any case, the regime clearly believes that the moderates can be intimidated and neutralized, whereas the radicals cannot. The wisdom of this policy, of course, is open to question.

The Regime's Strategy Against the Shi'a

The regime has developed a multifaceted, broad strategy to deal with the Shi'ite intifada:

- Government policy ensures that all reform movements are denied any nationwide character and are portrayed as strictly part of a Shi'ite agenda at Sunni expense. The regime has been largely successful in breaking off the bulk of any potential Sunni support for the Shi'a.
- The Shi'ite opposition movement is painted as radical, terrorist, and an instrument of Iran, thereby relieving the government of any responsibility to negotiate with the Shi'ite community. References to "terrorism," Hizballah," and "Iranian backing" have tended to carry some weight in U.S. policy circles, deterring the United States from any serious criticism of regime policies toward the Shi'a.
- The Shi'ite movement has been largely confined to areas of high Shi'ite concentration where the violence is kept out of sight; the intifada has had little impact on the capital. The foreign media has been excluded from any significant coverage of the conflict; foreign news correspondents that stray from the government line have been permanently expelled for unauthorized reporting on the intifada. The outside world thus has little information on internal Bahraini events. The domestic press is completely under government muzzle and offers almost no reporting on the intifada whatsoever, much less objective reporting.
- The regime has enlisted the assistance of numerous neighbors to provide financial support, (mainly Saudi Arabia and Kuwait), or manpower (Syrian and Jordanian militia) to assist in keeping order and to prevent the contagion of political liberalization and change from spreading beyond Bahrain. Sunni tribals have also been brought into the labor market, but their presence has alienated even the Sunni population, who resent the privileged housing these new arrivals get and their rougher tribal ways that conflict with the Bahraini way of life.
- The government has imported foreign elements to expand its security capabilities. For example, the Bahrain Defense Force has Syrian and Jordanian beduin troops that complement Bahraini tribal elements; the security forces, which are used to quell riots and demonstrations, include Belushis and Yemenis. The regime uses foreigners to isolate the communities and to makes it easier to use harsh measures, which may otherwise be objectionable to native Bahrainis.
- The government has established an iron grip over the educational system in order to control all youth, the chief street fighters of the intifada. A general has been appointed chancellor of the University of Bahrain to deal swiftly with any dissent or political discussion on campus by bringing in the police immediately in the event of any irregularities. Teachers and professors report that all classrooms have informers in them. There are strict de facto limits placed on the number of Shi'a admitted to the university and Shi'a students are no longer given scholarships to study abroad.

- The regime has moved to take control of some Shi'ite religious institutions, mosques, and ma'atim, and it practices close surveillance over others. Mullahs can be appointed only by the state, and the contents of their sermons are controlled. The government has not been able to completely control illegal or unofficial religious centers and preaching, but it has seriously crimped the freedom of action of the clergy to mobilize the population. Illegal processions and marches still take place, however, stemming out of private ceremonies such as funerals, religious festivals, and other observances.

- The al-Khalifas have moved to establish firm family control over key financial posts in the country to lessen the ability of the Shi'a to gain funding for community political purposes.

- The regime has divided the country into governorates that report directly to the minister of the interior. Governors have no discretion to handle local disorders; all problems are immediately handled by calling in the security service troops. Collective punishments are imposed when communities are unable to keep their youth under control.

These sets of controls have been effective in keeping the situation on the ground largely within controllable parameters. The intifada is not likely to get worse unless the Shi'a change their tactics and are willing to escalate to major violence and genuine terrorism, which so far they have not been willing to do. The BFM and most Shi'a have so far been concerned to maintain an image of moderation before the world in an effort to gain support abroad and to place pressure on the regime. Europe indeed has shifted to a far more critical position on Bahrain over the past year as we have seen above. As a result the Bahrain government has now accused the British of seeking to destabilize Bahrain and "treat it as a colony," in the words of a prominent Sunni. The United States has been reluctant to acknowledge either the general moderation of the BFM or the excesses of regime policies; it has not dissented in any public way with the regime's handling of the problem and has spoken of its support for the regime in confronting "terrorism." Only in private has the United States urged the regime to seek a dialogue and find a political solution. Bolstered by this reticence, the regime has so far felt no need to compromise on its tactics.

Who Is Winning the Struggle?

Any judgment about whether the regime or the Shi'a are winning or losing the political struggle depends on the criteria used. But the regime is "winning" in several respects. First, it has succeeded in confining the intifada to a limited area populated primarily by poorer Shi'ite villagers where its turmoil and noise has little direct impact on the capital or its important sectors. It has broken off any significant Sunni support for the parliamentary movement. The regime has also succeeded in creating some divisions among the Shi'a, nearly all of whom sympathize with a Shi'ite effort to gain greater political and economic voice in the country, but many of whom, especially the affluent classes, are nervous that the BFM may lead to a dominance of radical clergy and an Islamist agenda over the future leadership of the community. Some others fear that the confrontational nature of the intifada will in the longer run not only damage the existing position of the Shi'a, but could fatally damage the larger economy and future of the entire island.

The regime, furthermore, so far has not had to weather significant pressure from abroad and it has maintained rock-solid support from neighboring Arab regional states who share both goals of containing the Shi'a and limiting any democratization processes. And since the election of President Khatemi in Iran in the summer of 1997, Iran itself has moved to improve its ties with Bahrain; its foreign minister visited Manama in the fall of 1997— broadly perceived in Bahrain as an encouraging sign that Iran may no longer lend any kind of direct support to the Shi'a, in the interests of breaking out of its broader international isolation.

Thus the Bahrain regime has achieved a certain degree of containment of the situation for the foreseeable future. It believes that the Shi'a will gradually grow tired of the sacrifices they are making with little to show for it, and that the situation will eventually return to normal. The regime reportedly has privately stated in the past a willingness to have a dialogue with Shi'ite leaders and to release most of its political prisoners. It did release Shaykh al-Jamri from prison for a period until his presence became the occasion of further demonstrations and a sense of tactical victory among his supporters. The regime wanted the Shi'a to apologize for all that they had done so far, but the BFM refused. When the BFM made public such a possible government "deal" the regime backed down. Al-Jamri was re-arrested in 1996. By January 1999, al-Jamri had been in detention without trial for the full three years allowed under the State Security Measures Law.[25] In early July 1999, four months after the new Emir took over in Bahrain, al-Jamri was, in the space of three days, tried, sentenced to ten years' imprisonment and payment of a huge fine, and released from jail. His release, however, is reported to have been heavily conditional and even humiliating.[26]

On the negative side for the government, however, there are a number of disturbing indicators that make it difficult to say that it is "winning" over the longer run. Even while financial aid from regional states was stepped up in recent years, overall foreign investment on the island has dropped. The Shi'ite population is growing much faster than the Sunni, in spite of the importation of Sunni tribals from the peninsula. The regime is doing little to seriously alleviate the chief sources of Shi'ite grievance in the areas of economic life, unemployment, just and equitable representation in the bureaucracy, and dignity of status. A legacy of Shi'ite bitterness persists from the al-Khalifa conquest of Bahrain two centuries ago. This negative trend showed some signs of change and improvement in the 1960s and 1970s, particularly as symbolized by a degree of intercommunity socializing and even intermarriage. But the Shi'a have since grown even more alienated, as evidenced by the rising demands for change, the emergence of the parliamentary and petition issues, and the subsequent intifada. It will take a long time for trust to be reestablished on either side, assuming that the regime will ever be willing to take major steps toward improvement. The Shi'a are not likely to abandon their quest for satisfaction of their grievances. The problem is that the steps necessary to satisfy Shi'ite grievances require a liberalization of the political order that will inevitably lead to a weakening of al-Khalifa rule and to opportunities for Sunni opposition to emerge as well.

Nor is the regime likely to be permanently successful in dividing the Sunni population off from the Shi'a as long as major Sunni grievances exist that are shared with the Shi'a. While it is still a small minority of Sunnis who are active in their critique of the regime, the grievances of the Sunnis over al-Khalifa misrule will not diminish and will likely grow. Most Sunni professionals believe that the regime is archaic in its determination to run the island as a family-owned business under mechanisms of tribal loyalty. The economy cannot seriously modernize until a more modern and rational form of governance emerges. The Shi'a fully share these beliefs. Indeed, Sunni willingness to push more forcefully for these political goals has been tempered only by fear that political liberalization has now become a "Shi'ite issue."

How long will the Sunnis abstain from participation in a quest for change in an unsatisfactory political order? As long as the Shi'a limit their quest to terms of rule of law, a constitution, and an empowered parliament, growing numbers of Sunnis are likely to eventually gravitate toward that same agenda, perhaps on their own. In the eyes of non-Shi'ite observers interested in the modernization of Bahrain, the al-Khalifa themselves represent a serious obstacle to that process, with their failure to distinguish among the government, the family, and the state. Prime Minister Khalifa bin Salman al-Khalifa has been the power behind the throne for decades, and could truly say, "L'état c'est moi," though his dominance is now likely to be challenged by the new Emir. We also witness this impasse in Iraq, but there the stakes between a criminally vicious regime and the Shi'a have been raised to point at which only the elimination of the regime and its political apparatus can alleviate the crisis. The situation in Bahrain, however negative, does not involve such high stakes.

The regime may thus be "winning" in the short term, but if it is, the country is the loser. Success against the Shi'a simply builds pressures for a greater explosion later, hostilities run deeper, morale sinks, and grievances and wounds are harder to bind. The overall morale, economy, and reputation of the country suffers. Even if the United States is unwilling to step up public pressure on the Bahraini government, Western Europe is, most notably the United Kingdom with its long-time relationship with the country. Thus, even if the regime is succeeding in wearing down Shi'ite resistance for now, the grievances will inevitably rise again soon. Key elements of the next generation of al-Khalifa in the line of power are reputed to be more arrogant in their outlook than their fathers and even more determined not to yield to the Shi'a, whom they see as depriving the family of its birthright. The intransigence of the younger generation of al-Khalifa may be stiffened by the fact that their number is rising and the financial benefits, in a nationally retrenching economy, will have to be distributed more thinly within their ranks.

In short, the level of confrontation, the tendency to see the struggle as a zero-sum game, and a determination to play it out to the bitter end is likely to grow rather than diminish with time. The only hope is that more moderate members within the al-Khalifa, who may see the need for change even from the point of view of enlightened self-interest, will dominate. Under either circumstance, the future of the country cannot rest indefinitely upon government by clan and upon a minority Sunni community that itself is increasingly less well served by the status quo.

As time runs out on this type of traditional regime in Bahrain, it simultaneously lacks the cushion of oil wealth that some of its neighbors have relied on to fend off reform. So far only the ruling al-Sabahs in Kuwait have bowed to the new order, and that with the cataclysm of the Iraqi invasion. The al-Khalifa's only hope is that Saudi largesse may be able to support it for some time to come. In the end it will probably be the Sunni merchant class itself in Bahrain that will push for serious limitations to ruling family power, and demand that it stand aside and allow a more modern and rational political order take its place. The degree of moderation of the Shi'ite opposition will be a key factor in determining how much fear the Sunnis have of Shi'ite political ambitions. This rationale has been a key factor behind the moderation of the BFM to date.

If the Shi'a continue to make no progress against the regime with the present moderate tactics, the pressures for them eventually to escalate the violence will be powerful. Terrorism is an obvious alternative for the frustrated, from which the Bahrain scene to date has mercifully been spared. Yet the regime—and the Sunnis—need to fear Shi'ite reversion to true terrorism because it would be the kiss of death for the economy and domestic stability so critically needed by the state. Such a terrorist scenario sadly would cast

Bahrain into political convulsions whose outcome cannot be foreseen. The first requirement would be for the Bahraini Defense Force (BDF) to be brought in to control the population. So far this has not happened since the regime prefers not to have Bahrainis punishing or abusing other Bahrainis; that work is carried out by mercenary security forces recruited from abroad, as we have noted. While the good news is that the use of such forces avoids a civil war situation, the bad news is that the mercenaries have little incentive to handle the situation with any sensitivity and have no stake in the future of the country.

The Saudi Factor

The first probable reaction to any loss of control by the Bahraini regime in the face of terrorism would be the dispatch of Saudi troops to Bahrain to maintain a military grip on the island. The Saudis are in fact already deeply involved in the Bahraini situation. Riyadh bolsters Bahrain's hard-line policies on three counts: first, it is unalterably opposed to any spread of democratic governance in the region that might pressure the Saudi regime itself. Second, the Wahhabi ideology of the Saudi kingdom sets it in strong opposition to the Shi'a and would never comfortably live alongside Shi'a in power in neighboring states if it can be avoided. Third, the Bahraini Shi'a have close ties to Saudi Shi'a, so that any success of the Bahraini Shi'a would have immediate impact upon the aspirations of the Saudi Shi'a, however different their own political situation is as a small minority. Saudi Arabia reportedly provides up to 45 percent of the Bahraini budget, a critical consideration. Large numbers of Saudis visit Bahrain, with its more tolerant social practices and availability of alcohol and night clubs, over the new causeway that now physically links the two countries. This is a boon for the Bahraini economy and a useful social outlet from the point of view of Riyadh and gives the Saudi government a direct stake in the internal affairs of Bahrain.

Bahraini Shi'a believe that Saudi riot troops briefly came to Bahrain in 1975, although the Bahraini regime today relies more on Syrians and Jordanians for such police and militia work. Saudi intelligence reportedly permeates the island. At least one leading Shi'ite cleric believes that if it were not for Saudi support of the al-Khalifa, they would have been forced to negotiate some time ago. Such views are impossible to verify, but they are plausible. But in the end does Riyadh have a veto over al-Khalifa concessions to the Shi'a? Are there differences between them on how to resolve the situation? Such questions are hard to answer, but it seems reasonable to assume that the Saudis are a strong factor in encouraging al-Khalifa intransigence, although obviously Saudi Arabia would like to see an end to this problem festering on its doorstep.

Many Shi'a see Saudi Arabia as the source of a great many of Bahrain's problems, especially in its harsh view of how to handle the Shi'a. The Saudis send Wahhabi literature to Bahrain to influence Sunni thinking. They also dump a lot of their excess domestically produced goods in Bahrain at below cost, which damages Bahraini products and prospects for export markets. Saudi Arabia is perceived by many Bahraini Shi'a as a more violent and intractable society, with a heavy beduin overlay that makes internal reconciliation difficult, unlike Bahrain's more sophisticated and historically more tolerant environment.

Any Saudi occupation of Bahrain to keep control of the situation would come at a high cost of bloodshed on both sides and over the longer run would be untenable—even to the Bahraini Sunnis. The existence of such a seething situation would inevitably intensify the connections between the Saudi Shi'a in the neighboring Eastern province (al-Hasa) and the Bahraini Shi'a and would negatively affect security in the Shi'ite areas of Saudi Arabia. Thus, while force can keep the lid on for a certain period, the cost grows constantly and the likely outcome seems increasingly negative and bitter in tone, with wider international repercussions. Many Bahrainis state that most of the weapons coming into Bahrain are coming from Kuwait (where huge stockpiles remain from the Gulf War) and from Saudi Arabia (where arms are allegedly readily attainable).

If real violence comes, visited directly against the capital city or regime figures, Bahrain will be badly damaged. However, such a development need not automatically mean that Bahrain would come to resemble Iran, Lebanon, or Algeria. The key uncertainty is whether the Sunni community will of its own accord move to bring about reform and democratization, or whether its fears of losing out are so great that it will assume a fortress-like posture toward any political progress by the Shi'a. As in Iraq, the future development of Bahrain involves a Sunni problem more than a Shi'ite problem. In the end, Bahrain's ability to solve its Sunni problem could be a bellwether for eventual political change in Iraq, despite that country's more intractable dilemma. (Bahrainis as a whole tend to have a great fondness for Iraq as a country, although not for Saddam Hussein or the Ba'th regime.)

U.S. Interests

The United States has several key interests in Bahrain that will be affected by a rising security crisis. First and foremost, if reforms do not come and the Shi'a continue to be radicalized, the U.S. presence on the island will be an inevitable target of violence. The Fifth Fleet maintains its regional administrative headquarters in Bahrain, and the island is a key port of call for rest and recuperation of U.S. naval forces. So far the Shi'a have not attacked the

United States, even in slogans, and have not called for the pullout of the U.S. naval facility. The BFM still hopes that the United States can help in bringing about reform in Bahrain, as it has done in Kuwait with much success. But if over time the Shi'a perceive that the United States is not part of the solution but part of the problem, hostility toward the U.S. presence will inevitably grow. The Shi'a could eventually call for the pullout of the U.S. military forces in the Gulf. While not a fatal blow to the U.S. military presence, this would be a considerable political setback and would vindicate those elements in Iraq and Iran who call for a Gulf free of U.S. forces. It would make the U.S. military presence—already a politically sensitive issue—that much more sensitive in the region.

U.S. business interests in the region could also suffer. U.S. businessmen could be targeted in any terrorist campaign, with a guarantee of CNN and global attention. As noted above, Shi'ite discontent in Bahrain might spread to Saudi Arabia—although probably not to Kuwait, where the Kuwaiti regime has handled the Shi'ite problem intelligently and effectively through an opening up of the political order. (Interestingly, the Kuwaiti parliament, with its Sunni majority, strongly supports the call for a return to an elected parliament in Bahrain, even aware that the Shi'a are a majority. In short, democrats are supporting democrats, regardless of sect.) If U.S. policies spur Shi'ite hostility in the region, the eventual political orientation of the Shi'a in Iraq could also be affected. Thus the Bahraini issue could represent a defining point in U.S. policies in the region on questions of liberalization and change. Will Washington prefer to act while the situation is still susceptible to change and amelioration? Or will it prefer the false stability of standing by the al-Khalifa through thick and thin, thereby perpetuating the root of the problem and ensuring a greater explosion down the road? These are some of the choices which confront U.S. policymakers today.

CHAPTER SEVEN

The Shi'a of Kuwait

The case of the Shi'a of Kuwait represents the one success story, the one bright spot in what is otherwise a fairly dismal survey of the conditions of the Arab Shi'a in the Gulf. The Shi'a of Kuwait are better off than any other Shi'ite community in the Gulf region. Constituting about 25 to 30 percent of the country's population, they encounter little visible persecution at the official or social levels. They are free to practice Shi'ism and observe its rituals openly, while their economic status and professional opportunities are better than anywhere else in the Gulf. There is a high degree of Shi'ite social and political integration into Kuwaiti society. Most important, the Shi'a have a sense of belonging and a vested interest in the fortunes of the state—which is not true anywhere else in the region. Kuwait is almost the only country in the region that does not have an exile opposition, either Shi'ite or Sunni. Nevertheless, this basically healthy situation often conceals subtle, complex forms of discrimination that are recognized by the Shi'a, acknowledged by many Sunnis, and represent areas in which the Shi'a seek to improve their standing.

The Kuwaiti Shi'a After the Gulf War

As elsewhere in the Gulf, the 1980s were a turbulent period for relations between the Shi'a and the Kuwaiti government. Throughout the decade, Kuwait was the target of extremist Shi'ite groups who carried out a series of bombings and assassination attempts, including attempts against the life of the Emir of Kuwait. As a consequence, the Kuwaiti Shi'a were subjected to heightened government security measures, including arrests and deportations, that split society along Shi'ite-Sunni lines. The conditions that led to Shi'ite activism in Kuwait are manifold: the Iranian revolution, which provided inspiration and support; the decimation of the Iraqi Da'wa party, many of whose members fled to Kuwait; the emergence of Islamic Amal and Hizballah in Lebanon; and above all, the strong support given by the Kuwaiti government to Iraq in the Iran-Iraq war. The relatively open society of Kuwait and the presence of large numbers of Arab workers, including Palestinians, Lebanese, and Iraqis, opened a wide window for the infiltration of extremist elements into Kuwaiti society. The Shi'ite community felt that the measures adopted by the Kuwaiti government against extremists were unnecessarily harsh and broad, that they needlessly alienated the Shi'ite community (which generally condemned the terrorist acts) and further contributed to the polarization of Sunnis and Shi'a along sectarian lines.

The role of the Kuwaiti Shi'a during the Gulf war against Saddam, however, contributed to a dramatic change in the acceptance of the Shi'a back into the Kuwaiti body politic, including the political establishment. Many wealthy Kuwaiti Sunnis were vacationing abroad in August 1990 and were caught outside the country when Iraqi forces swept in to occupy Kuwait. Because the Shi'a are less affluent and less Westernized, the larger part of the Shi'ite community was in Kuwait at the time of the invasion and was forced to remain there throughout the occupation. With the departure of so many Sunnis, the demographic balance in the country was tipped in favor of the Shi'a; there are some estimates that the Shi'a made up at least half the resident population during that period. The Shi'a thus found themselves in the vanguard of the resistance against the Iraqi occupation, helping to organize clandestine relief and resistance activities alongside their Sunni compatriots. Many of them were killed or imprisoned by the Iraqi occupation authorities for their activities.

This Shi'ite display of patriotism had two beneficial consequences: it allayed Sunni suspicions about Shi'ite loyalty to Kuwait and fused the Shi'ite and Sunni communities into a common solidarity. Additionally, there was an unconcealed measure of vindication for those Kuwaiti Shi'a who had opposed the unrestrained support given by the Kuwaiti government to Iraq during the Iran-Iraq war. In sum, the shared ordeal of the Iraqi occupation helped create a stronger feeling of nationhood among Kuwaitis than one can find in most Arab countries today. The new national solidarity was reflected in the combined Shi'ite/Sunni calls immediately after the Gulf war for restoration of the constitution and the National Assembly. Indeed, even during the occupation of Kuwait by Iraqi forces, prominent Shi'a and Sunnis joined forces in bargaining with the ruling al-Sabah family, sheltered at the time in Saudi Arabia, for the restoration of the constitution and parliamentary life following the liberation of Kuwait.[1]

However, many Shi'a and Sunnis in Kuwait acknowledge that the sense of solidarity and the benefits the Shi'a gained in terms of credibility and acceptance began gradually to erode a few years after the Gulf war. By common admission, this is not due to any decrease in loyalty among the Shi'a, but to a Sunni reversion to previous patterns of behavior once the war trauma had subsided, accentuated by latent Sunni resentment of the gains made by the Shi'a as a result of their struggle against Iraqi occupation.

For the time being, the ties that hold the Kuwaitis together are stronger than their divisions, despite the fact that these ties are negative in nature, arising out of common fear and defensiveness against the perceived threat from Iraq. Nevertheless, the temporary sense of siege gives the Shi'a an opportunity to confirm their patriotism and their solidarity with the Sunnis and to institutionalize the gains they have made.

Divisions Among the Shi'a

The Kuwait Shi'ite community is more demographically heterogeneous than other Shi'ite groups in the region. There are three distinct groups: the first two, the Hasawi and the Baharna, are Arabs, with roots in Saudi Arabia, Bahrain, southern Iraq, or the Ahwaz (Arabistan) region of southwest Iran. The third, and largest, group is the 'Ajam, Kuwaiti Shi'a of Iranian descent who have lived in Kuwait for several generations. Within these groups there are even subtler distinctions between "old settlers" and "new settlers," the latter comprising the less affluent, less integrated members within each group. Disparate economic status also divides the Shi'a. While it is hard to speak of "poor" Kuwaitis (in comparison to the poverty of the Shi'a in Bahrain, for example), there are nevertheless visible disparities in affluence among the Shi'a that have become a politically sensitive topic.

Allegiance to different maraji' provides other demarcation lines that cut across the Shi'ite community, particularly among the 'Ajam and the Baharna. Kuwaiti society and the Kuwaiti regime recognize these socioeconomic and religious distinctions and tend to deal with the groups accordingly. Non-Kuwaiti Shi'a, including Iraqis and Lebanese who lived in Kuwait during the 1980s, are no longer a significant factor in the Shi'ite community of the country.

Broadly speaking, the Hasawis are a self-contained and politically quietist community that is distinctive for having its own native marji', Ayatollah Mirza al-Ihqaqi, a Kuwaiti citizen living in Kuwait. The Hasawis stay outside the communal and sectarian fray and rarely intermarry even with Shi'a from the other groups. The wealthy 'Ajam trading families have long been allied with the ruling al-Sabah family and, as part of the "government bloc," are careful not to jeopardize their gains and privileges. Other than the powerful 'Ajam families, most Shi'a are part of the middle class of professionals and civil servants whose livelihood depends heavily on the public sector, either as employees of government bureaucracy and affiliated agencies, competitors for government contracts, or beneficiaries of government social services. What can be termed the lower-middle class of Kuwaiti society also has a large Shi'ite component of small shopkeepers and semiskilled workers who are for the most part recent settlers in Kuwait and who may or may not have Kuwaiti citizenship.

Traditionally, the wealthy merchant families close to the regime acted as intermediaries and spokespersons for the Shi'ite community. The increase in Kuwaiti oil wealth in the 1960s and 1970s and the expansion of education, scholarships, and foreign travel changed the character of the Kuwaiti Shi'ite community. Educated young Shi'a were no longer content with the traditional representation offered by the privileged merchant families, who were increasingly discredited for having failed to serve the community's interests or to protect the community from harsh government measures. The younger generation of Shi'ite professionals, businessmen, or state employees had ambitions that could not be fulfilled by the old system of patronage and needed new avenues for expression. The politically engaged sector of the Shi'a is drawn largely from the rising class of 'Ajam and Baharna, and it is among these groups that one finds the greatest diversity of beliefs and political orientations, and where dissatisfaction and aspirations are likely to emerge. This more active political role of the 'Ajam in Kuwait is in sharp distinction to the 'Ajam of Bahrain who maintain a distance from Shi'ite community politics.

The Shi'ite community exhibits the familiar diversity of political opinion that divides secularists from Islamists and Islamists from each other. Political opinion among the Shi'a covers a spectrum ranging from leftist/liberal/secular views to conservative Islamist ideology. As in other countries, Muslim observance among the Shi'a and Sunnis is more prevalent than it was two decades ago, when it was confined to small pockets of the population. Religious adherence does not necessarily translate into a political doctrine, and for most Kuwaitis Shi'ism is a matter of personal piety and observance rather than a political agenda. Nevertheless, a general rise in religious adherence does affect outlook on social issues and a broad array of domestic and foreign policies. Greater religious adherence broadens the constituency of Islamists and buttresses their platform in the national debate.

Difference in religious mentorship (marji'iya) among the Kuwaiti Shi'a is another factor of diversity. Apart from the special case of the Hasawis, Kuwaiti Shi'a follow several maraji', including Khamenei (usually followed by those who originally followed Khomeini), Sistani in Iraq, Shirazi in Iran, Fadhlallah in Lebanon, and other clerics in Iran. To a certain extent, the choice of a marji' sets the tone for a political outlook, or at least is perceived to frame political leaning. Thus Kuwaitis, both Sunnis and Shi'a, tend to

draw careful distinctions between those who follow the official Iranian marji'iya, regarded as more activist and doctrinaire, and those who follow Sistani
or Shirazi, who are deemed less outspoken or even quietist.

No clear leadership has evolved within the Kuwaiti Shi'ite community.
Unlike Lebanon where the Shi'a have several options, and Bahrain and Iraq
where al-Jamri and al-Hakim respectively command broad respect, in
Kuwait there are few prominent Shi'a who enjoy wide recognition as leaders. In large measure this is due to the greater reluctance of the Kuwaiti
Shi'a—compared to Shi'a in Saudi Arabia, Lebanon or Bahrain—to engage
in explicit identity politics and to confine themselves to narrow sectarian interests. As evidence of their desire to behave as Kuwaiti citizens, Kuwaiti
Shi'ite parliamentarians, both Islamist and secularists, are at pains to portray
themselves as representatives of mixed Sunni-Shi'ite constituencies, with responsibility toward all sectors of their electorate.

Kuwaitis estimate that about 30 to 40 percent of the Shi'a are "Imami,"
or *khatt al-imam* (followers of the "path of the Imam"): they accept the
teachings of Ayatollah Khomeini and his doctrine of an Islamic state ruled
by clerics (wilayat al-faqih). In other words, they are conservative Shi'ite Islamists with a stronger connection to the Iranian establishment than other
Shi'a. The designation "imami" is loosely applied, however. It does not define what adherence to khatt al-imam precisely means in the context of
Kuwait, where the Shi'a are a minority and thus cannot reasonably aspire to
a political system similar to that of Iran. Nor does it adequately describe the
nature of the relation of the imamis to the Iranian political institutions, as
opposed to the religious establishment. Some Kuwaitis suspect that there is
a Hizballah network in Kuwait, but Western observers believe there is little
evidence of such a network.

The decentralization of political power and fragmentation of spiritual authority in Iran after the death of Khomeini contributed to the ambiguity of
the imamis' relationship to Iran as a state and as a spiritual authority today.
The leaders of the Kuwaiti khatt al-imam group have strong links with the
Iranian religious institutions in Qom and Tehran, making them the group
most identified in Kuwaiti eyes with the official Iranian outlook on politics
in the Gulf. The followers of khatt al-imam insist that their religious adherence to the Khomeini doctrine does not lessen their loyalty to Kuwait, any
more than Nasserism among Kuwaiti Sunnis in the 1960s meant disloyalty
to Kuwait—indeed, Nasserism at that time actually implied negative attitudes toward the ruling family, whereas imamis do not challenge the political system or its leadership in Kuwait.

The majority of the Shi'a in Kuwait follow the teachings of religious scholars unconnected with official Iranian institutions. Apart from the Hasawis,
whose marji' comes from within the community, large numbers of Kuwaiti

Shi'a follow Ayatollah Sistani, a quietist cleric in Najaf who has inherited the mantle of the late Ayatollah Khoei. Others are followers of Ayatollah Shirazi, who is under house arrest in Iran and whose sons have suffered harassment by the Iranian political-theocratic establishment. Both of these groups are in fact critical of Iranian official doctrines and policies and view Shi"ism as a religious devotion and not a political ideology. They are thus careful to distinguish themselves from the imamis, whom they regard as hard-line on social and political issues and more confrontational in their advocacy of Shi'ite rights. Furthermore, they worry that the proximity of the imamis to Iran casts a shadow over the entire Shi'ite community and gives rise to suspicions that the Shi'a are motivated more by sectarianism than national loyalty.

At the other end of the political and ideological spectrum are secularist Shi'a who object to the adoption of a political platform based on any religion, whether Sunni or Shi'ite. As in other Arab countries, secularism in Kuwait, encompassing Sunnis and Shi'a alike, is rooted in a long history of Arab nationalist fervor with mildly leftist overtones that dominated the Arab world from the early 1950s to the late 1980s. If Shi'ite religious ideology is influenced by Iran, Arab nationalism in Kuwait was likewise fed by huge numbers of Egyptian and Palestinian educators, civil servants, and professionals who formed the backbone of the Kuwaiti economy and educational system from the 1950s and well into the 1980s. Indeed, throughout this period Arabism was the dominant political force in Kuwait and the challenges to the Kuwaiti regime came, sometimes violently, from this end of the political spectrum. But notions of Arabism were harshly dispelled when Iraqi troops invaded Kuwait and Kuwaiti citizens failed to get wholehearted and unqualified condemnation of the invasion from all Arabs. Unlike Iraq, Lebanon, or Bahrain, there was no Communist party in Kuwait to attract the Shi'a, and, not surprisingly, socialist sentiment is less pronounced here than in other Arab countries.

Arab nationalism and other secular ideologies have been transformed in Kuwait into a Western-style liberalism that is more deeply rooted than anywhere else in the Gulf region. Liberalism, however, is increasingly challenged by two emerging forces: political Islam in its Sunni and Shi'ite forms, and a conservative tribal force encouraged by the Kuwaiti ruling family. These two rising political trends threaten all liberals, but they represent a particular threat to secular Shi'a. Since the sectarian label is inescapable for Shi'a whatever their political views, liberal Shi'a are twice jeopardized by Sunni conservatives, first for being Shi'a and then for being liberal/secularist.

Shi'ite Islamists present a different kind of threat to the Shi'ite liberals by undermining their credentials to represent the community. Thus in the parliamentary elections of 1996, it was liberal Shi'ite candidates who sustained losses in voter support.[2] The immediate fear among Shi'ite liberals is that a rising trend in Shi'ite Islamism will emphasize sectarianism and reverse the processes of integration and acceptance that the Shi'a literally fought for during the Iraqi occupation, and that it could return the community to the suspect status of the 1980s. On a broader scale, they also fear that the rise in conservative Sunni orientation—tribal and Islamist—will in time adversely affect the entire Shi'ite community, despite temporary and tactical alliances made between conservative Sunnis and Shi'ite Islamists. The Shi'a feel particularly vulnerable before the conservative forces because they know that the burden of proof of their loyalty, their good conduct, always lies upon their shoulders, and that the gains they have made are so fragile that they need constant caution and demonstration of "good behavior" to retain them.

The Shi'a in State and Society

The Kuwaiti Shi'a enjoy a religious freedom unequalled anywhere in the region except in Lebanon. Unlike the Shi'ite minority in Saudi Arabia, Kuwaiti Shi'a have freedom to build mosques and *husayniyat* (community centers), observe the rituals of Shi'ism, and teach their children the *Ja'fari madhhab*, or Shi'ite creed. Mosques operate schools and libraries, and social and religious occasions are freely organized around the husayniyat. The Sunni majority takes the public expressions of Shi'ism in its stride, perhaps regarding them as attractively quaint and intriguing. Even during the Iran-Iraq war, Kuwaiti Shi'a were able to travel to Iran to study at the seminaries of Qom or Tehran. Kuwaiti Shi'a of Iranian descent have also been able to maintain continuous contact with their relatives in Iran despite strained relations between the two governments.

For most of Kuwait's history, the Kuwaiti Shi'a were not viewed as a threat to the regime. Indeed, the Shi'a have long been treated as allies in the al-Sabah family's constant and shrewd game of divide-and-rule to maintain control over a politically energetic society. In the 1930s, when the family was under pressure from other Sunni clans and merchants, it found a useful ally in the Kuwaiti Shi'ite merchant class, who were, for the most part, 'Ajam, and who felt protected by the al-Sabah from the tribal Arab Sunni majority. Although the Shi'a were barred from the first legislative assembly formed in Kuwait in 1938, the laws were amended in 1962 following Kuwaiti independence. During the ascendancy of Gamal Abdul Nasser in Egypt and the revolutionary Nasserite brand of Arab nationalism, the 'Ajam merchants again stood by the regime in the 1960s to mitigate the impact of Nasserite zeal spreading into Kuwait. This repeated Shi'ite support has in fact often drawn the anger and resentment of Kuwaiti Sunnis—especially from the liberals and the left—who stood at times against al-Sabah family power or in opposition to its policies. Today, some Shi'a claim that the government has consistently tried ,to use the Shi'ite community to prevent the emergence of political solidarity against the family and to deepen divisions between Sunnis and Shi'a.

It was, however, militant Shi'ite activity during the Iraq-Iran war in Kuwait that raised the most serious tensions between the community and the government. This militancy had roots that did not spring entirely from the internal situation in Kuwait but were linked to other broader events involving the Shi'a in the Arab world. In the mid-1980s a dramatic increase in Shi'ite militancy and terrorist activity was inspired by Iranian revolutionary fervor and was guided by the Iraqi and Lebanese members of the Iraq-based Da'wa party. Terrorist acts were motivated by Kuwait's unflagging support for Iraq in its war against Iran. The persecution of the Da'wa in Iraq led many of its members to flee to Iran and Kuwait, as well as to Lebanon, where they played a significant role in the formation of the Lebanese Da'wa and later the Hizballah movement.[3] Iraqi and Lebanese members of Da'wa were active in Kuwait, setting up clandestine cells and recruiting local Shi'a.[4] Thus, from 1983 to 1988 Shi'ite groups in separate incidents bombed American and European interests in the country, sabotaged oil installations, hijacked Kuwaiti aircraft, and, in May 1985, carried out an assassination attempt against the Emir of Kuwait, Shaykh Jabir al-Sabah. Evidence suggests that, at least initially, Iraqis and Lebanese were the leaders in the violence. For example, of the 25 people arrested for bombings in 1983, there were 17 Iraqis, 3 Lebanese, 3 Kuwaitis, and 2 stateless persons.

Further arrests of Shi'a were carried out in 1985 and 1987. In March 1989, 18 Shi'a were arrested for an alleged plot to overthrow the regime, and in July of the same year 20 Kuwaiti Shi'a were arrested in Saudi Arabia for involvement in bombings in Mecca during the season of pilgrimage. Saudi Arabia beheaded 16 of them and returned 4 to Kuwait in 1991.[5]

Although the majority of the Shi'ite community condemned these acts, the Kuwaiti government responded with a campaign of arrests, deportations, and convictions of Kuwaiti citizens and other nationals.[6] Many Shi'a working in the country's sensitive oil industry lost their jobs, and there was increased surveillance of the Shi'ite community as a whole. Today many Kuwaiti Shi'a complain that these measures by the government were harsh and indiscriminate, antagonizing many Shi'a who were opposed to these acts of violence. Nevertheless, the Kuwaiti government demonstrated a more mature and wise policy than that of Iraq or other Gulf states. It did not pursue a wholesale policy of persecution against the Shi'a as a result of the violence. For example, although a half dozen Shi'a were sentenced to death following the attempt on the Emir's life, no executions were carried out. In contrast, Saudi Arabia publicly executed 16 Shi'a in 1989. In Iraq, membership in the Da'wa party was a capital offense, and members there were brutally exterminated. The policy of the Kuwaiti government continued to be comparatively restrained, and it was thus able to isolate extremist groups and restrict their penetration into Shi'ite society.

The calibrated policy of the Kuwaiti regime to the issue of the Shi'a was partly a consequence of the government's overall pragmatic and flexible approach in domestic politics, which relied on shrewd manipulation rather than crude force. Additionally, Kuwaiti society—outward looking, oriented toward commerce, and permanently overshadowed by much larger and more powerful neighbors—has the mercantile capacity for accommodation and bargaining. The Shi'a have benefited from this more hospitable environment. Merchant societies of course exist elsewhere in the Gulf, but in Saudi Arabia the strongly doctrinal Wahhabi ideology and intensely tribal nature of Najdi politics overcomes any mercantile tendency to moderation, while in Bahrain the narrowly based Sunni minoritarian regime must always be vigilant to maintain its control over the Shi'ite majority.

There are lingering fears of Shi'ite extremism even today in Kuwait, with some Shi'a and Sunnis suggesting that Kuwait still has a small and clandestine Hizballah network with close ties to Iran.[7] Except in the case of Hizballah in Lebanon, however, the designation "Hizballah" is ill-defined in the Arab world, and it need not indicate an organizational superstructure or direct collaboration with Iran. It is therefore hard to gauge the accuracy of allegations about potential "Hizballah activism," or what it might mean in practice in the Kuwaiti setting. There may well have been efforts during the 1980s to organize Kuwaiti Shi'a into a formal Hizballah movement, but there are no traces of success for such a possible attempt. Indeed, the demographic and political features of the country, unlike those of Lebanon, are not conducive to the unique military and social conditions that created and strengthened Hizballah in Lebanon.

The Hizballah allegations are largely based on the fact that some prominent Shi'ite Islamists, including at least two Shi'ite members of parliament, travel frequently to Iran and have good relations with a number of Iranian centers of religious and political authority. There are no suggestions that any Kuwaiti Shi'ite leaders receive their instructions from the Iranian political establishment, or that there is official sponsorship from Iranian authorities. Whatever the nature of these relations, the Hizballah label in Kuwait (or even Saudi Arabia and Bahrain) is unlikely to denote anything similar to the organized party structure of the Lebanese Hizballah, or to have comparable objectives and strategies. Furthermore, there have been no terrorist acts in Kuwait since 1989.

In practice, the Kuwaiti Shi'a are politically more attuned to moderate Shi'ite clerics, such as Sayid Mahdi Shamseddin in Lebanon, than to

Lebanon's Hizballah. Whatever their truth, the allegations disturb some Kuwaitis and are perhaps exploited to keep the Shi'a in check. The Shi'a certainly worry that these allegations contribute to their vulnerability to accusations of sectarian extremism and extraterritorial allegiance.

Because of the relative tolerance in the country, the Shi'a are broadly supportive of the Kuwaiti regime, although they may be critical of regime policies and of the lack of transparency and accountability. Despite general criticism or specific Shi'ite grievances, they acknowledge that the Shi'a are better off in Kuwait than anywhere else in the Gulf, and they may ultimately see the regime as a protector against the tyranny of the Sunni majority. Equally, the state does not view them as an inherent domestic threat to its security, but rather as a "management issue" on a par with the challenges the regime faces in managing other sectors of a politically energetic society. Indeed, Sunni criticism of the regime is far more vocal and its impact can be far more damaging to the government's authority than any Shi'ite activism, which is easily contained and isolated.

Nevertheless, the Shi'a are uncomfortably sandwiched between the state and the prevailing social system. The state keeps a watchful eye on them, alternately courting and manipulating them. Politically, the Shi'a form one component of the complex system of mercantile, tribal, and ideological alliances and divisions that the state must constantly juggle to maintain its own political advantage. While the regime allows the Shi'a a high degree of personal and community freedom, it is careful to set certain boundaries that limit full Shi'ite access to state institutions. Kuwaiti society, dominated by powerful Sunni interests, tends to be condescending, even if tolerant. Sunnis display, alternately, resentment of the gains the Shi'a have made in recent years and their past support of the al-Sabahs, and fears that the Shi'a are "too close to Iran." Socially, too, there is a concern that the Shi'a may "exceed their limits." As a result, they are watched with wariness by conservative Sunni sectors of society, such as the Kuwaiti tribes and the growing number of Wahhabis in Kuwait, who nourish deep doctrinal opposition to Shi'ism. However, both the more moderate wing of Sunni Islamists, the Islamic Constitutional Movement (associated with the Muslim Brotherhood), as well as Kuwaiti liberals often find common political ground with the Shi'a in the context of Kuwait's newly invigorated parliamentary life following the Gulf war.

Parliamentary elections in 1992 returned three Shi'ite members in what were by most accounts free and fair elections. In 1996 five Shi'ite members won parliamentary seats, including (for the first time) a Shi'ite cleric, two other Islamists, and two non-Islamist Shi'a. Unlike the elections of 1992, the 1996 campaign did raise sectarian sensitivities and Sunni fears regarding the candidacy of Shi'ite Islamists deemed too close to Iran. Specifically, the electoral victory of Sayid Husayn al-Qallaf, a Shi'ite cleric who had studied in Qom, over a secular Shi'ite and a Sunni candidate, raised Sunni concerns about the emergence of sectarian politics in Kuwait.[8] For their part, the Shi'a accuse the government of having gerrymandered the electoral districts to minimize the impact of the Shi'ite vote and complain that the electoral system itself is designed to fragment society. Despite some sectarian friction during the campaign, however, there is every indication that Shi'ite parliamentarians have been accepted as participants in Kuwaiti political life by the regime, the public, and other members of the National Assembly. The Shi'ite representatives have engaged in parliamentary life wholeheartedly, and the National Assembly has proven a powerful forge for welding together electoral alliances on various concrete issues regardless of potential ideological differences among the members.

Ironically, fearful of just such Sunni/Shi'ite parliamentary coalitions, the regime has actually tried to persuade Shi'ite leaders to represent sectarian Shi'ite interests and to weigh issues in the light of Shi'ite concerns.[9] The Shi'a view such advice as part of the complicated maneuvers of the regime to isolate the Shi'a and to prevent alliances with Sunnis. Additionally, since the Gulf war the regime has promoted the conservative Sunni tribes as a political force to counter both the liberal Sunnis and the Shi'a.

Thus the Shi'ite population of Kuwait has had to maintain a sensitive balance between often conflicting necessities: allaying latent government and Sunni suspicions regarding their loyalty, securing the good will of the al-Sabahs, and improving relations with the Sunnis. Skillful management of these difficult and sometimes conflicting relations has been essential for the security and well-being of the community. The precise configuration of relations between Shi'ite groups and the Sunni sectors of society varies according to political belief, social status, and financial interests. As noted earlier, the wealthy 'Ajam families have traditionally controlled Kuwait's substantial trade with Iran and have preserved at the same time the good will of the Kuwaiti regime by asserting their loyalty to the family. The Shi'ite Islamists joined forces with the moderate Sunni Islamists in the national debate over adopting Islamic Shari'a law as the basis for a new Kuwaiti constitution; however, they disagreed with the Sunnis on women's voting rights, which the Shi'a welcomed.[10] Similarly, Shi'ite and Sunni Islamists voted together in favor of a bill, not enacted, to segregate university education.

Secularist Shi'a have found significant difficulty in establishing viable political parties on a secular foundation. As a professional liberal Shi'a complained, a Shi'ite secularist party suffers double-barreled criticism: it is superfluous in the eyes of the Shi'a, and it is a sectarian statement to Sunnis. A Shi'ite secular party has less appeal to the Shi'ite community than a Shi'ite Islamist party, but it is equally suspected by Sunni voters for being Shi'ite.

Thus Shi'ite political candidates have an impossible choice: if they campaign for Shi'ite votes through religious and sectarian interests they will lose the Sunni vote; if they adopt a secular, nonsectarian platform, they will lose the Shi'ite vote and will still be uncertain of persuading the Sunni voters. There is thus a "damned if you do, damned if you don't" predicament for Shi'ite politicians who consider venturing away from their religious identity. The problem is somewhat mitigated by the fact that a number of Shi'ite MPs have been elected in mixed Sunni/Shi'ite constituencies, and over time the sectarian differences may lose their edge if Kuwait can continue to develop in a stable environment.

Cross-sectarian cooperation, though perhaps limited and tactical, already provides some evidence that the political landscape in Kuwait is tentatively moving toward modern forms of alignment based on political issues and individual interest rather than on primordial allegiances. The Islamist and liberal blocs in the National Assembly include both Sunni and Shi'ite members and are clearly based on ideology. Non-ideological independent merchant groups also cut accross confessional lines. Only the tribal bloc comprises Sunnis only and is defined by its social and class background. Needless to say, the groups are not rigidly separated. For example, some of the Sunni Islamists come from tribal backgrounds and are influenced by Wahhabi doctrine, making them less inclined to work with Shi'ite Islamists. The loosening of primordial allegiances and their replacement with issues-oriented politics will benefit the Shi'a by blurring the sectarian lines and expanding the dialogue between Sunnis and Shi'a. However, it is too early to draw any conclusions regarding a breakdown of sectarian or other social barriers, as Kuwaiti society remains predominantly organized around tribal and family ties, and principal allegiances go to these primary connections.

The Limits of Equality

In most countries of the region, the Shi'a suffer from violations of their human rights to varying degrees as well as from severe limitations on their civil rights. In Kuwait, by contrast, the Shi'a fare well in terms of enjoying freedom of worship and community organization, freedom from persecution, and relatively high levels of integration. But the issue of loyalty dogs the Kuwaiti Shi'a as it does other Shi'a, and they still suffer from disparity of opportunities.

There is of course a second and important distinction to be made about "loyalty" that complicates the picture in Kuwait and elsewhere in the Gulf. In Gulf societies there still remains little clear distinction between the government and the ruling family; in common parlance in Kuwait the two terms are used almost interchangeably. But there is a clear political and conceptual difference between loyalty to the family and loyalty to the state and country in a broader sense. To remain loyal to the family may be viewed by reformers, liberals, and Islamists as nonpatriotic and self-serving. Yet the family is most likely to base its criterion of "loyalty" on loyalty to the family as well as the government. As Kuwait develops, the concept of loyalty will take on subtler connotations that could include serving in the opposition ("loyal opposition") and working with other Kuwaiti parties or movements to liberalize the state in ways that may run counter to the interests of the ruling family. Thus Shi'ite political activists are in a bind when it comes to deciding on how "loyalty" is to be expressed within Kuwaiti politics.

The practice of marji'iya and the emulation of a marji' is a key reason for the distrust felt by the Kuwaiti establishment toward the Shi'a. With the collapse of Iraq as a center for Shi'ite spiritual authority, most of the Shi'a in the Arab world, including Kuwaitis, have perforce turned to the centers of learning in Iran for spiritual guidance and education. Shi'a aspiring to careers as jurisprudents must graduate from one of these institutions. Yet extensive travel to Iran, or pictures of Khomeini or other leading clerics in Shi'ite homes, intensify the anxieties of Sunnis. Many Kuwaiti Sunnis, both inside and outside official circles, are suspicious of the "dual loyalty" this may create for the Shi'a, but the Kuwaiti government has nonetheless significantly not banned the Shi'a from travel to Iran. The Shi'a contend that their religious connection to Iran does not diminish their allegiance to the Kuwaiti state. Making a very important political point, the Shi'a refer to the fact that Kuwaiti Wahhabis turn to eminent Wahhabi clerics in Saudi Arabia for similar guidance. For example, the Shi'a claim that the Wahhabis asked senior religious authorities in Saudi Arabia to rule on whether a Kuwaiti parliament was even legal in Islamic terms prior to running for election in 1992. The Shi'a interpret this as serious interference in the domestic affairs of Kuwait by a non-Kuwaiti authority and point out that they sought no such authorization from the maraji' in Iran.

Disparity in opportunities and subtle forms of discrimination still exist and are keenly felt by the Shi'a, even those who appear most integrated into Kuwait's social and professional life. The Kuwaiti Shi'a have benefited from Kuwait's oil wealth and the services of a generous welfare state made possible by oil revenues. Unlike in Bahrain or Saudi Arabia, there are no pockets of Shi'ite poverty although there are disparities of income, with the Sunnis holding most of the country's wealth. Nevertheless, the Shi'a suffer from discrimination in government employment: the Shi'a are excluded from "sensitive" areas of government or, more commonly, tend to hit a "glass ceiling" in promotion to senior posts. Although the army chief of staff in Kuwait is Shi'ite, this is a rare example of tokenism rather than an indication of "sect-blind" equality in government service. Kuwaiti Shi'a have also complained that since the 1980s they have been excluded from the oil industry, the sector most important to Kuwait's economy and security. This exclusion is probably related to acts of sabotage against oil installations in the 1980s that were blamed on Shi'ite groups. Employment in the government sector is further restricted by the system of nepotism and patronage that is endemic to a clan-based society: officials are far more inclined to employ and advance relatives and clan members than strangers with merit. This practice puts the Shi'a at an added disadvantage, because it feeds Sunni fears that a job that goes to one Shi'ite employee means many more jobs to other Shi'a.

Another area of clear bias against the Shi'a is in the funding of charitable institutions. Political parties are prohibited in Kuwait, but social charitable organizations—often in fact thinly disguised political parties—are legal and have proliferated. The Kuwaiti government plays a major role in funding Sunni charitable organizations and in permitting them to raise public funds. The Sunni Islamists in particular have benefited from government largesse and the ability legally to campaign for contributions to establish wide-ranging educational, social, and media services that carry a political message. No Shi'ite organization gets funding from the government for similar activity, nor are the existing institutions that are supported by the Shi'ite community allowed to raise funds publicly. Shi'ite mosques and publications receive no grants from the government, as do similar Sunni institutions. This is one of the principal grievances of the Shi'a, as it stacks the cards against them and hinders peaceful forms of community solidarity and education. The absence of government funding would not be detrimental if it were universal. It is the selectivity of official funding that is resented by the Shi'a, who argue that their institutions should receive equal government support and be allowed to raise funds freely.

The Shi'a, along with many Sunni liberals, also accuse the regime of bias in its naturalization policies. In recent years, but especially since the Gulf war, the Kuwaiti government has selectively granted citizenship to "bidoun," tribes that straddle the Kuwaiti-Saudi and Kuwaiti-Iraqi border. The Shi'a complain that the government has granted citizenship to Sunni tribes but has withheld it from Shi'ite tribes, in an obvious effort to influence the demographic structure of the state in favor of the Sunni tribal elements. More broadly, both Sunnis and Shi'a complain that the government has promoted and favored tribes that are loyal to it, while discriminating against other tribes whose loyalty to the al-Sabah is in doubt.

In the most glaring demonstration of inequality, the Shi'a have only 10 percent of the National Assembly's 50 seats, whereas they represent between 25 and 30 percent of the population. In a democratically level playing field, the number of Shi'a in parliament would not be an issue, but in a polity in which discrimination is customary, the low figures carry special significance. In some of the five electoral districts, voting occurred along strict sectarian lines, the Shi'ite vote being the majority. The disparity between these figures is large enough to raise troubling questions: Are Sunni voters unprepared to vote for Shi'ite candidates? Are the electoral districts deliberately gerrymandered, as some Shi'a claim, to prevent the Shi'a from winning elections? If so, why does the government feel it needs to restrict the Shi'a? What is the profile of a Shi'ite candidate who can hope to win over both Shi'ite and the Sunni voters?

It should be noted that neither the Shi'ite MPs nor other Shi'a have pointed to their small share of Assembly seats as an indication of discrimination, despite accusations of gerrymandering prior to the 1996 elections that put specific Shi'ite candidates at a disadvantage. Furthermore, notwithstanding the low level of Shi'ite representation, nowhere among the Shi'a is there a call for proportional representation. This reluctance is consistent with the effort of Shi'ite MPs and candidates to stand as representatives of their (mixed) constituencies, rather than their coreligionists, and to subordinate sectarian interests to those of the constituency.

The Kuwaiti Shi'a are aware of the dangers inherent in creating Shi'ite solidarity groups in a country that otherwise practices relative tolerance and in which the Shi'a enjoy uncharacteristic advantages. The Shi'a are delicately poised between gaining more for the community and risking what they have. Shi'ite parliamentarians, for example, insist that they represent their constituents, whether Sunni or Shi'ite, rather than the Shi'ite community at large, and that they are motivated by the interests of the voters rather than by ideological or communitarian considerations. While this is true to a large extent, it is an oversimplification of the situation. For example, the reaction of the Shi'ite members of parliament to the situation of their fellow Shi'a in Bahrain went beyond the stated policies of the Kuwaiti government on the issue and caused it diplomatic embarrassment.

In a promising sign of changing attitudes, Sunni liberals and members of the Islamic Constitutional Movement acknowledge and deplore institutional discrimination against the Shi'a and accept the necessity of greater equality of professional and economic opportunities for the Shi'ite community. However, this sector of Sunnis situate the Shi'ite problem in the context of the evolutionary process under way in Kuwait, and not as an isolated issue.

Issues and Strategies of Integration

It is to the credit of the Kuwaiti government and society that the issue of the Shi'a can be raised at all, let alone debated openly. In Saudi Arabia, Bahrain, and Iraq, the discussion of sectarian discrimination is socially and officially taboo, condemned as divisive and subversive. In Kuwait, by contrast, the place of the Shi'a in the Kuwaiti polity was discussed even during the difficult decade of the 1980s, when the majority of the Kuwaiti Shi'a sought to distance themselves from the violence of the few. The process of mutual confidence-building was hastened by the Iraqi invasion and occupation of Kuwait, which bound the Shi'a and Sunnis in a unified national battle against the occupiers.

Given that Kuwait is the only society in which the Shi'a as a minority enjoy a large measure of rights and recognition, the goals of the Shi'ite community are significantly different—indeed, more "advanced"—from those of the other countries in the region. For example, whereas the Shi'a of Saudi Arabia still lack basic recognition of their creed and the freedom to practice Shi'ite ceremonies or to build mosques, the Kuwaiti Shi'a are under no comparable restraints.

The Shi'a in Kuwait want equal opportunities and equal participation on the political, economic, and social levels. Their principal complaints are the low numbers of Shi'a in senior government posts, their virtual absence from what are deemed sensitive sectors, and their inability to benefit from government sponsorship and funding as Sunni institutions do. As a minority, their leverage is limited, and they are caught between the need for integration and the desire to preserve a strong Shi'ite identity. Whether these two goals are reconcilable and can be accomplished in tandem is the central long-term question for the Kuwaiti Shi'a.

The changes in Kuwait following the Gulf war have tended toward representation, pluralism, and civil liberties, albeit heavily orchestrated and calibrated by the ruling family. Kuwaiti Shi'a hope to remain part of this evolutionary process and benefit from it in equal measure with other groups instead of falling behind and losing out. The primary target for the Shi'a is greater integration and equality of opportunities through the very avenues opened up by the changing political culture of Kuwait. Kuwait is almost the only country in the region that does not have an exile opposition, either Shi'ite or Sunni. Opposition politics, of which there is a good deal, has a reasonable operating margin within the country.

As noted earlier, there are no Shi'ite political organizations in Kuwait. The prohibition on political parties makes it difficult for the Shi'a to organize, as they have done within Lebanon or among the Iraqi or Bahraini exile communities. In addition, the Shi'a, as a minority, are fearful of segregating themselves from the majority and isolating themselves from national issues in favor of community issues. Shortly after the Gulf war, Islamist Shi'a gathered within an informal group called the Islamic National Coalition, but this was disbanded in late 1996, either because of internal divisions or to avoid sectarian labeling.

Many Shi'a in Kuwait believe that their community was until recently inward-looking and had deliberately segregated itself in an effort to keep its identity from dissipating in the face of the Sunni majoritarian culture. The 1980s placed enormous pressure on the Shi'ite community and put it on the defensive. All Shi'a resent the fact that they are "less equal" citizens in the Kuwaiti system, that they come first in the line of suspicion but last in access to opportunities. Yet they readily acknowledge their advantages over fellow Shi'a in Saudi Arabia, Iraq, and Bahrain, and the tenor of all debates favors integrative policies over a minoritarian agenda.

One can say that integration has become the "Shi'ite agenda" in Kuwait. Kuwaiti Shi'a say that the first steps toward integration should be greater openness to Kuwaiti society and participation in civic and political life. However, to be successful, an effort by the Shi'a to move into the mainstream has to coincide with a willingness by the majority Sunnis to receive the Shi'a as equal citizens. Obtaining such reciprocity is not assured: for most Sunnis, retaining undiminished economic and political clout is more tangible than abstract concepts of building shared citizenship among Sunnis and Shi'a. Many Sunnis continue to suspect that Shi'ism is not only a personal religious faith, but a system of political and social attitudes that determine the behavior of the Shi'a. According to a secularist Shi'ite liberal academic, the political label of Shi'ism transcends a person's own sense of affiliation—even if a Shi'ite were to become a Sunni and adopt Sunni beliefs and customs, he or she would still be perceived as a Shi'a.

Shi'ite and Sunni secularists are concerned that the rise in religious adherence in Kuwait is likely to further divide the communities at certain levels because it deepens awareness of difference and shifts attention away from common bonds. Thus it works against forms of social blending, such as intercommunal marriage. At the political level, however, Kuwait is a clear demonstration of shifting alliances, in which interests of Sunni and Shi'ite Islamist groups often coincide. Thus in the parliamentary politics of Kuwait, the bloc of parliamentarians representing the view of the traditional Sunni Ikhwan (Muslim Brotherhood) frequently works in concert with the Shi'ite Islamists. Similarly, Sunni and Shi'ite liberals share a common ground on social policies affecting domestic issues, such as the segregation of university education. Politically, we see in Kuwait new alignments arising not from sectarian affiliation but from differences over liberal versus conservative policies, secularism versus Islamism, and support for versus criticism of the regime. These emerging alignments are likely to have a positive impact on the capacity of Kuwait to move toward greater integration, and they offer the Kuwaiti Shi'a one of their best opportunities to be accepted by the Sunnis as partners.

The greatest impediment to the acceptance of the Shi'a in Kuwait may be the dramatic increase in Wahhabism and the number of Salafis, strict observers of Wahhabism, who study in Saudi Arabia and follow the authority

of Saudi shaykhs such as Bin Baz or Bin Jibrin. Whether with active or pas-
sive endorsement of the Saudi government, Wahhabism is spreading in
Kuwait, as it is in Iraq and Bahrain. The official doctrinal position of the
Wahhabis, expressed in a fatwa by the Saudi shaykh Bin Jibrin, is that the
Shi'a are heretics who have corrupted the unitarian message *(tawhid)* of
Islam. Moreover, Wahhabism appears to be spreading fastest among the tra-
ditionally conservative tribal Sunni groups in Kuwait, reinforcing existing
social prejudices with an underpinning of religious intolerance.

The different attitudes of the Ikhwani Islamists and the Salafis toward the
Shi'a is illustrated in the debate over adopting a new constitution based on
Islamic Shari'a, which would become the principal source of legislation.
Both Sunni and Shi'ite Islamists are advocates of a Shari'a-based legal code,
but the Shi'ite Islamists want this to be accompanied by a formal recognition of the Ja'fari madhhab (the Twelver Shi'ism creed) as one of the Muslim sects of Kuwait, and by extending the teaching and inclusion of the
Ja'fari code to family law. The Ikhwani Sunnis are willing to accept this
recognition as a condition of applying the Shari'a. The Salafis, however, are
opposed to it on doctrinal principle since they refuse to accept the legitimacy
of Shi'ism as an Islamic school at all, and they have in fact inadvertently
strengthened the hand of liberals, both Sunnis and Shi'a, as well as the
Kuwaiti government, in impeding any change in the constitution. Politics
thus makes strange bedfellows.

Another problem that may impede the integration of the Shi'a is the attitude of the Kuwaiti government. The Kuwaiti regime may perceive greater
social cohesion as a threat to its interests, especially if it fears that the Shi'ite
community can no longer be counted on as an ally looking to the ruling
family for special protection. Such concern by the government is unwarranted, however, because Shi'ite attitudes toward the regime are not uniform; they are as diverse as Sunni attitudes. Indeed, it can be argued that the
Kuwaiti government stands to gain from encouraging greater participation
by the Shi'a in public affairs in order to strengthen their allegiance and their
commitment to the state.

One option for Kuwaiti Shi'a is to demand proportional representation
in parliament and in the civil service, as there is in Lebanon. Very few Shi'a
regard this quota system as a desirable alternative at present. Most believe
that sect-blind equality is the best path for integration, provided integration
recognizes pluralism and the Shi'ite right to their own personal and group
identity. However, if the share of the Shi'a in the civil service and in the National Assembly should deteriorate, or if there is a rise in discrimination,
opinions in favor of proportional representation may increase.

The fortunes of the Shi'ite community in Kuwait are as much determined by the social forces of the predominantly Sunni society as by under-

lying suspicions of the regime. As political freedoms grow, the opposition to the regime is likely to come from confident and secure Sunni elements, both liberal democrats and Islamists, rather than from the Shi'a. In theory, the Shi'a can take advantage of this situation by acting as "the government party," as they did in the 1930s and at other times when the al-Sabah family faced challenges. In practice, however, such a course is perilous. It will reignite hostility from the sectors of the Sunni population that form the opposition parties and potentially are more liberal on the Shi'ite issue, while at the same time making the Shi'a vulnerable to the unpredictable shifts of government policy. In the framework of an increasingly open and pluralist political system, the Shi'a benefit more by allowing their own political diversity full expression than by isolating themselves. If the democratization process that is under way in Kuwait continues, the Shi'a will only lose out if they stay aloof and are perceived as a self-enclosed community that draws its support from the government rather than from society at large.

The abiding challenge for the Kuwaiti Shi'a will be to balance these conflicting forces within the community on the one hand, and between the community and the forces of state and society on the other. It will not be an easy task for the Kuwaiti Shi'a to steer clear of the pitfalls that threaten their progress if they miscalculate. Nevertheless, given the nature of Kuwaiti society and government and the present direction of the Kuwaiti polity, the difficulties faced by the Kuwaiti Shi'a are negligible in comparison to the immense hurdles confronting the Shi'a in Saudi Arabia, Bahrain, and Iraq.

External Factors

Additionally, the Shi'ite community in Kuwait is likely to be affected, positively or adversely, by external factors, chief among them political changes in Iraq and Iran, and the possible influence that Saudi Arabia may exert on Kuwait.

The Role of Iran

For the foreseeable future, the marji'iya for most Kuwaiti Shi'a will remain in Iran, and to a lesser extent Iraq, and the religious training of Shi'ite clerics will continue to take place in Qom and Tehran. This will maintain at least a strong spiritual and physical connection with Iran. Whether this religious dependency translates into political influence will be determined by several factors both within and external to Kuwait, including the policies of the Kuwaiti government toward the Shi'ite population and Iran's need to gain leverage over Kuwait's foreign policy. In turn, the policies of the two governments will present the Shi'a with alternative courses of action from which to choose.

The policies of the Kuwaiti government will be the strongest determining factor in the relations between Kuwait's Shi'ite population and Iran. To the extent that the Kuwaiti system can treat the Shi'a as equal to all others in the rights of citizenship, it will increasingly incorporate the Shi'a into the state and society, minimize grievances, and diminish the need of the Shi'a to reach outside Kuwait's borders for support and validation. Although this holds true for the Shi'a throughout the region, it is especially necessary in Kuwait where most Shi'a are of Iranian descent and commercial relations with Iran are deep. Well after the effects of the solidarity created by the Gulf war have receded, the Kuwaiti government needs to confirm that it regards the Kuwaiti Shi'a as Kuwaitis first and Shi'a only second, and that their loyalty is not constantly questioned.

The fact that revolutionary fervor in Iran has abated lessens but does not necessarily eliminate Iran's long-term interest in cultivating special relations with Kuwaiti Shi'a—just as Israel seeks to cultivate ties with Jewish communities around the world in the interests of the Jewish state. Iran's role as the source of revolutionary Islamist and Shi'ite inspiration is gradually evolving into the role of a state with regional "great power" aspirations. This changes the nature of its relationship with Shi'ite groups and its motivations behind establishing such relationships. The support that Iran provided for extremist Shi'ite groups in the 1980s is unlikely to be repeated under present Iranian policies.

As a regional power, Iran aspires to a leadership role in the security arrangements and international relationships established in the region. Under such circumstances, Iran will need to choose whether it gains greater clout via state-to-state relations with regional states, or via the back door of influence with the local Shi'ite populations. At present, relations between Iran and Kuwait are cordial, and Iran has backed away from earlier efforts to manipulate local Shi'ite communities to its advantage.

Indeed, the Kuwaiti Shi'a can always serve as a pressure point for Iran in Kuwaiti external politics. But how productive will such an approach be? And how susceptible will Kuwaiti Shi'a be to such an approach from Iran if they are well on their way to integration into Kuwaiti society and politics and might only suffer from excessive Iranian interest in their community? Are the Shi'a prepared to risk their nationalist credentials to gain an external advocate that compromises their loyalty? In this respect, Shi'ite opposition to government policies will always stand at a disadvantage to Sunni opposition. Sunni motivations will not be impugned in ways that Shi'ite motivations will, and they can be portrayed as springing from national interest. Shi'ite criticism of the state, especially on foreign policy, will raise suspicions of a foreign (Iranian or Iraqi) agenda.

Finally, relations between the United States and Iran will have an impact on the Shi'a. At present, the most likely reason for Iran to use the Shi'a as a pressure group is to oppose the presence of U.S. troops and military bases in Kuwait. When image of Iran as a "rogue state" recedes and relations with the United States improve, Iran will have less of a need to cultivate support within Gulf states and in fact will lose some of its allure among Shi'a and Muslims generally as champion of the *mostaz'afin* (the oppressed). Iran will increasingly be seen as a state rather than a revolution or a religion. The American need, too, for military facilities in Kuwait will diminish as relations between Iran and the West improve and as the Iraqi threat diminishes.

The Role of Iraq

Relations between Iraq and the Kuwaiti Shi'a are likely to be more complex and ambiguous. So long as the regime of Saddam Hussein continues in power, it will draw hostility and suspicion from all Kuwaitis; indeed, Kuwaiti Shi'a may feel a special antagonism in the light of Saddam's particularly oppressive policies toward Iraqi Shi'a.

In a post-Saddam era the situation will be shaped by several variables. Assuming the emergence of a more moderate, less militarist regime in Iraq, there is likely to be a relative easing of tensions and some rapprochement between Kuwait and Iraq. However, the Kuwaitis will continue to regard Iraqis, both Shi'a and Sunnis, with suspicion and wariness, and there will be a large number of disputes over territory and financial obligations that will have to be resolved.

A change in government in Baghdad will have the immediate effect of opening the Shi'ite shrine cities of Iraq. There is likely to be an influx of Kuwaiti Shi'a to Najaf and Karbala, the two holiest shrines of Shi'ism, which have been out of bounds to most non-Iraqis for two decades. To the extent that Najaf and Karbala can be gradually reestablished as places of pilgrimage and learning, they will attract Arab Shi'a away from Qom and other Iranian centers. However, the restoration of Najaf and Karbala as centers of theology and scholarship will be an arduous and prolonged process, and it will be some time before they can serve as something more than places of pilgrimage. Their pull will be largely emotional; Qom and Tehran will continue for a long time as the main centers for serious students. In this capacity, their role in shaping doctrine as well as political thought is likely to last beyond the opening up of the Iraqi cities.

If political liberalization in Iraq gives substantial power to the majority Iraqi Shi'a, the fears of the Kuwaiti government may shift from territorial concerns toward worries about a new patron for Kuwaiti Shi'a; these fears will either be mitigated or deepened by the conduct of the Iraqis. The Shi'a of Iraq will represent a more credible and less assailable patron for the Shi'a of Kuwait than the Iranians. As fellow Arabs, the Iraqi Shi'a are free from the historical Arab-Persian rivalry that stigmatized the Iranians. A common Arab language and culture, a shared history, and a large common border argue for closer ties, easier access, and stronger affinities between Kuwaiti and Iraqi Shi'a. Altogether, should Iraqi Shi'a gain a larger role in the Iraqi state, they are in a position to exert influence over the Shi'a of Kuwait as well as those of other areas in the Gulf. Whether the influence is salutary or adverse will depend on how the Iraqi Shi'a choose to define their Shi'ism, their relations with Iraqi Sunnis, and their regional role. If the Iraqi Shi'a tend toward integration and moderation there is likely to be a healthy ripple effect that will reach Kuwait first. However, if Iraqi Shi'ism moves toward militancy and intolerance, the impact on the Shi'ite populations of the region will be detrimental, and the backlash from regional governments will be commensurately negative. For Kuwait in particular, a militant Shi'ite Iraq is far more dangerous than a militant Shi'ite Iran.

Conclusion

The Kuwaiti Shi'a have moved further along the path of integration into the polity than any other Shi'ite groups in the Arab world, except for the Lebanese. This is partly a result of a relatively open and tolerant social and political system, but the traumatic occupation of Kuwait by Saddam Hussein's forces in 1990 made a major contribution to strengthening a sense of common citizenship. The invasion, resistance, subsequent liberation, and pressures for reform served to create an entirely new environment in which democratic process was greatly advanced, giving the Shi'a—but not just the Shi'a—an opportunity for deeper participation in Kuwaiti society and politics. This reality has its disturbing side: does it take a cataclysm of this order to create the conditions for moving toward democracy and greater equality among citizenry? The only other case in which Shi'a have greatly advanced their position is Lebanon, which also underwent its own trauma of the civil war, in some ways worse than the Kuwaiti experience. In any case, it has been the democratizing process in Kuwait that has made the difference, suggesting that this process, apart from contributing to better governance, also has a therapeutic effect on sectarian relations. Conversely, a retreat in the democratic process will diminish the chances of integration of the Shi'a and weaken the sense of citizenship shared by all sectors of society.

It is also evident that with the introduction of limited but real democracy, the Kuwaiti Shi'a are now confronted with a dilemma that will face all other Shi'a seeking integration into their respective political orders: choosing between preservation of community identity and integration into the political and social order. The two are not incompatible, but they suggest different orders of emphasis on the part of political leaders: Are they to seek a better deal for the Shi'a, or are they to work for the improvement of the political order overall, largely eschewing sectarian interests? Different Shi'a will have different answers to this question—as all minorities do—and politicians themselves will present differing views on the issue. A key indicator to watch will be the extent to which politicians among the Kuwaiti Shi'a feel they must run on either a secular or a sectarian platform to get elected. But over time we argue that a community that feels relatively secure and an equal participant in the system will probably turn ever greater attention to the workings of the whole system and not just to its own sectarian interests. This perception is further reinforced by a strong sympathy on the part of many Kuwaiti Shi'a for a merit-based system as opposed to proportional communal representation or a confessional quota system.

Another encouraging feature of the Kuwaiti case is the ability of highly disparate political forces to work together and cooperate within the parliament. Thus Wahhabi Salafis sit with Shi'ite Islamists to reach agreement on selected common goals, even when they are ideologically deeply uncomfortable with each other. We should point out, however, that we are witnessing only the very beginning of this process of cooperation among various sects. It is also uncertain whether the overall political order will lead to overall reduction of radicalism among the various elements or not. Will Islamists—Shi'ite and Sunni—combine to weaken or eliminate the secularists in power? Or will there be a gradual shift toward the center on the part of all? Alternatively, a dramatic rise in Sunni Islamist fanaticism could put new restrictions on the Shi'a, alienating them from the social and political order.

Additionally, as the Shi'a gain the recognition and confidence of Kuwaiti society, how much can they afford to demonstrate interest in the welfare of other Shi'a in the region? Kuwaiti Shi'a in parliament have already spoken out against the repression of the Bahraini Shi'a, stirring the ire of the ruling family in Manama. However loyal Kuwaiti Shi'a are to Kuwait as their homeland, they will probably never lose interest in the welfare and position of Shi'a in other neighboring countries. The future of the Iraqi Shi'a in particular could have a major impact on Kuwait and the Kuwaiti Shi'a.

Finally, the question of loyalty remains a critical one in the Kuwaiti context. Is loyalty owed to the ruling family—the traditional criterion—or to the state and country? Will the two loyalties come into increasing conflict? The Shi'ite community faces a dilemma, in this transitional period between family rule and evolution toward a constitutional monarchy, in selecting the objects of its loyalty. Whereas this may be a strategic choice in the eyes of many, it may resemble more a tactical day-to-day choice on the floor of the parliament.

CHAPTER EIGHT

The Shi'a of Saudi Arabia

The Shi'a of Saudi Arabia make up the largest Arab Shi'ite community in the Gulf except for that in Iraq. Among all the Arab Shi'a they are the least integrated into Sunni society. They are highly disadvantged in the sense that they are the only Shi'a to suffer not only from de facto, but even from de jure discrimination within the country, and are almost entirely denied public expression of their religious traditions. As a small minority they cannot in any case ever aspire to gain much political influence in the country. They are concentrated far away from the capital of Riyadh and the commercial center of Jidda, thus removing them from public focus—except for their presence near the oil center of Dhahran. If the Shi'a's daily existence is relatively quiet today, it is only because they have never dared—with few exceptions—to struggle publicly for their cause in the way that the Bahraini Shi'a, in a much more open environment, have done. Any public expressions of Shi'ite identity have been harshly and regularly repressed. Indeed, of all the Shi'a in the Arab world, the Saudi Shi'a are truly the "forgotten Muslims." The issue in the Kingdom is made more delicate by the fact that they live in the heart of the Saudi energy sector in the eastern part of the country—a sensitive strategic area. The Saudi Shi'a present no actual political threat to Sunni dominance in the country and their political goals are modest, but if their frustration drives them to extremes, they are capable of violence and terrorism that could be quite destabilizing within the country.

Who Are the Shi'a of Saudi Arabia?

There have been Shi'a in the al-Hasa region (or al-Ihsa', now known as the Eastern Province) of today's Saudi Arabia from the early days of proto-Shi'ism in the Arabian peninsula. Shi'ite communities along the Gulf have been closely linked since that era and have exercised self-rule for long periods of time. As primarily a settled agricultural and merchant people they have remained relatively untouched by the Sunni beduin culture emanating from the desert fastnesses of inner Arabia.

The numbers of Shi'a in the Kingdom today are disputed. The Saudi government places them at around 2 to 3 percent of the population, in the neighborhood of 300,000. Most accounts list them as numbering between 200,000 and 400,000.[1] Shi'a dispute this however, pointing out—correctly—that many Shi'a often conceal their status because of the disadvantages that accrue from such association. Many of these Shi'a, they claim, pass for Sunnis and thus are able to maintain their jobs in the bureaucracy, which would otherwise be impossible. Some Saudi Shi'a thus state that overall they number one million people,[2] but this figure seems highly suspect. The numbers are nonetheless probably well over half a million. Furthermore, in their main region of concentration, the Eastern Province, or al-Hasa', the Shi'a are believed to make up 33 percent of the overall population. (They constitute nearly 95 percent of the population in the al-Qatif oasis, and half the population in al-Hufuf oasis.)[3] Other, more modern cities in al-Hasa, such as Dhahran and al-Khobar, are majority Sunni. In the al-Qatif and al-Hufuf areas Shi'a are able to live within a fully Shi'ite environment.

From the Shi'ite point of view, the Saudi Wahhabis represent the greatest calamity to the their community in their entire history. Starting in the late eighteenth century, with the first of three campaigns of harsh Wahhabi military conquest of the Shi'ite regions led by Ibn Sa'ud, the Shi'a were subjected to raids and the destruction of their mosques, shrines, and even their culture and way of life. Zealous Wahhabi beduin swept across the sands to the Gulf and spread northward, determined to "purify" Islam from all impure and alien influences. The Shi'a were considered distinct heretics, "polytheists" because of their veneration of saints (a practice well known among many non-Wahhabi Sunnis as well) and thus guilty of the sin of *shirk,* or splitting the oneness of God.[4] Austere Sunni Wahhabi practice was imposed upon the Shi'a's public life.

The Wahhabis spread on up north into Iraq in 1803 and 1806 and sacked the tomb of 'Ali's son Husayn in Karbala—an act of incredible desecration to the Shi'a; Wahhabi forces were only then driven back by the Ottoman Turks, retreating into Central Arabia. Wahhabi warriors erupted a second time in the mid-nineteenth century, again to attack Shi'ite "heretics" and to take over much of the Gulf coast. This time most of the country was united by conquest under the Wahhabi forces of King 'Abd-al-'Aziz. The third conquest took place in 1913.

Scholar Jacob Goldberg points out a gradual evolution over time in Saudi policy toward the Shi'a. The fiercest and most ideological trend was represented by the beduin forces committed to the pure fire of Wahhabi belief, the driving energy behind the conquests. As the royal family took on responsibility for governing the areas under conquest, however, a more pragmatic attitude developed that would let the Shi'a conduct their religious practices in private, but not in public. Shi'a would not be forcibly converted or killed for the crime of apostasy or polytheism, even though elements of the Saudi 'ulama actually urged this approach. The criterion would become political loyalty rather than religious orthodoxy.[5] But Shi'ism as a faith has never been sanctioned; implicit in Saudi belief is that Shi'ism is an illicit faith, which, if not extirpated, then is only to be tolerated in isolation and in private.

From 1913 to 1985 the Shi'a were under the direct rule of the Bin Jiluwi family, provincial governors who ruled in the name of the royal family. The Minnesota Lawyers International Human Rights1996 report on Saudi Arabia describes this rule as "stern, brutal, and characterized by their hatred of the Shi'a."[6] The same report describes the economic condition of the Eastern Province as follows:

> Despite the wealth of natural resources, however, the Eastern Province is one of the most impoverished regions in Saudi Arabia. Compared to other regions in Saudi Arabia, the government has spent much less on construction projects, roads, medicine, and education in the Eastern Region. One journalist observed that houses are unimaginably poor by modern Saudi standards. Shanties were commonplace until the early 1980's, and Shi'a cities and towns still lack the modern medical facilities available in cities like Riyadh and Jidda. It was not until 1987 that the Saudi Government built al-Qatif Hospital—the first modern hospital in the Eastern Province.[7]

The Shi'ite Critique of the Saudi State

In an incisive, anonymously written critique of the Saudi state,[8] a leading Shi'ite activist criticizes the Saudi regime in more sweeping political terms, specifically for failing to unite the country's population under any concept of commonly shared citizenship. No sense of identification with the state, or loyalty to it—as part of a commonly accepted ideal—has been achieved. On the contrary, national "unity" exists only in a legal and administrative sense and has been imposed strictly by force, primarily for the benefit of the Wahhabis living in the central Najdi heartland. Any so-called national vision and national ideology is really only the imposed agenda of a ruling minority in accordance with its narrow Najdi Wahhabi vision, which is not shared by most of the country. Even other Sunni schools of jurisprudence, apart from the Shi'ite, have been suppressed: both Hanafi practice in the Hijaz (Red Sea coast) and in the northwest (Jordan border area), as well as Zaydi Shi'ite practice in the 'Asir (southwest coast). The distinctive cultures of these regions have all been subordinated to the Najd that produces the ruling class of the country headed by the royal family.

This Shi'ite critique readily recognizes that over the past three decades the Kingdom's incredible new oil wealth and communications infrastructure has brought about a considerable degree of physical integration of the country in an economic, administrative, and infrastructure sense. Oil wealth has benefited nearly everyone in the country—although the Shi'a far less—but the state has signally failed to create any psychological sense of citizenship or shared national experience. It has not managed to create a true nation-state. The very fact that one must call oneself a "Sa'udi" after the royal family's clan name, still rankles most Saudi citizens deeply. The name may not survive the royal family; many Saudi dissidents abroad already refuse to refer to the Kingdom as "Saudi Arabia" but only as "Arabia" or the "Kingdom." These Shi'ite charges are broadly shared by many other non-Najdi Saudis in other regions. This failure to instill a sense of common citizenship exposes the country to potential separatist trends in all regions in the future—movements that already exist in nascent forms.

In this context the Shi'a feel that Shi'ism is indeed the only identity open to them in the Kingdom today. They are not really "citizens" of Saudi Arabia, and as subjects of the Kingdom they are alienated, mistrusted, and rank at the bottom of the social order. There simply are no other serious identities open to the Shi'a as a result—they thus automatically revert to the principal Shi'ite identity by default. Only when the political and social order of the Kingdom changes will the Shi'a have the option to adopt the broader identity of the country within the context of Saudi society.

The Shi'a are also confronted with the same problem that Shi'a in other Arab states face: if they are to be loyal, to whom should they be loyal? To the state that marginalizes them? To the royal family in the hopes that it will "protect" them from the excesses of social and religious discrimination of Saudi state and society? Or do they owe first loyalty to their own local community, or even to a broader Shi'ite regional culture? Shi'ite exclusion and assertion of their parochial identity is not the choice of the Shi'a, but of the regime.

Shi'ite Grievances Today

Under Saudi rule, the Shi'a have consistently been the object of formal discrimination, their community rights denied. Chief grievances are the following:

Religious Discrimination

In religious terms Saudi Arabia's Shi'a are the object of systematic, official, legal religious discrimination—the only Shi'a in the Muslim world who are formally denied the status of Muslims. In 1927 Sa'udi senior 'ulama issued fatwas declaring *takfir*, that is, condemning the Shi'a as apostates or nonbelievers, which can be punishable by death. The declaration stated that the Shi'a "should not be allowed to perform their misguided religious practices, and if they violated the prohibition they should be exiled from Muslim lands."[9] In 1991 there was a fatwa from a senior cleric *('alim)*, Bin Jibrin, reasserting the Shi'a's status as nonbelievers *(kuffar);* by such law it was not juridically illegal to kill them. On the popular level, there is a widespread traditional belief among Saudi Sunnis that all Shi'a nourish the deep-seated goal while on the pilgrimage to Mecca, to smear human excrement on the holy Ka'ba; indeed at least one Shi'ite from abroad was allegedly executed several decades ago for this crime. Shi'a are also believed to curse the first three rightly guided caliphs *(al-Rashidun)* or successors to the Prophet, who were selected over 'Ali from within the Prophet's family. (Such curses have in fact been practiced by some Shi'a in the past, although Iran's senior clerics have officially banned any such expression.)

Shi'ite rights to build mosques or maintain religious community meeting houses *(husayniyyat)* have been severely circumscribed. The building restrictions imposed by the government have meant, for example, in Safwa—a city of 100,000 and predominantly Shi'ite—that only three or four husayniyya are permitted and no new building permits granted. In 1990 the Saudi authorities also closed down the Hawzat al Mubaraza, a religious school that had been operating for 16 years, and arrested some of its teachers.[10]

Shi'a report that they are not allowed to have any written religious materials about Shi'ism in their possession and can be arrested for attempting to bring it into the country. The call to prayer is not allowed in its Shi'ite form but must conform to Sunni practice. The morals police *(mutawwa'in)* often harass Shi'a in the streets, although technically Shi'ite practices are permitted in private. Saudi Sunnis are formally forbidden to eat the food of the Shi'a during the Shi'ite ceremonies of the holy day of 'Ashura, and strict Wahhabis will not buy meat slaughtered by Shi'a because it is "unclean." According to Wahhabi practice, Shi'ite men are not allowed to marry Sunni women.[11]

Since the Iranian revolution the regime has banned any travel of Shi'a to Iran. Yet, denied the right to study Shi'ism inside Saudi Arabia, Shi'a have no alternative if they wish to gain a religious education. Shi'a are caught between having no opportunities for religious education at home and being punished for seeking such education abroad.

Although official ideology against the Shi'a has lost much of its fervor from earlier in the century, a pervasive anti-Shi'ite mood still dominates conservative religious circles in Saudi Arabia. For example, a memo was sent in 1993 to the then head of the Committee of Higher 'Ulama, Shaykh Bin Baz, that excoriated Shi'ite behavior in the Kingdom and in outraged terms demanded a crackdown against those very things that lie at the heart of the Shi'a's demands. The memo stated that the Shi'a are becoming increasingly bold, challenge "our *tawhidi* [here, Wahhabi] traditions in schools, refuse to participate in our religious traditions, proselytize in their offices, demand recognition of Shi'ism as a legitimate juridical school, call for freedom of religion and sanctity of their religious places, demand the right to build husayniyat, to teach Shi'ism in their schools, to publish Shi'ite books, and for the government to end to the state's campaign against Shi'ism."[12] Thus orthodox Wahhabi belief treats as outrageous the very list of Shi'ite goals required to alleviate discrimination against them.

Cultural Discrimination

In cultural terms the Shi'a feel strongly repressed. Shi'ite books, music, and religious tapes are banned and their possession is punishable; certain Shi'ite given names are prohibited. The regime has sought to wipe out local Shi'ite culture, even by renaming the ancient province of al-Hasa with the culturally sanitized designation of "Eastern Province." The Shi'a are forbidden to publish books about their history or culture.[13]

The Wahhabi doctrine has also been forced upon them in education: the Shi'a not only are forbidden to teach Shi'ism but are required to study Wahhabism—including its official denunciation and distortions of Shi'ism. Religious education, an important part of the school curriculum from elementary to high school, teaches Wahhabism exclusively and overtly condemns Shi'ism even in the Shi'ite areas. Textbooks on religion stress the puritanical tenets of the Wahhabi faith and denounce as *kufr* (heresy) and *shirk* (polytheism) those beliefs and practices that run counter to Wahhabism. Thus a government-issued textbook taught to ninth graders in the Eastern Province condemns the (Shi'ite) practice of visits, gifts, and sacrifices offered to shrines because they allegedly contravene the principle of *tawhid* (oneness of God); people who commit such acts are guilty of polytheism and apostasy. Textbooks also condemn "excessive attachment" to Ahl al-Bayt (the family of the Prophet) as a form of idolatry. Shi'ite children are taught that *rafdh* ("rejectionism," the pejorative Wahhabi term for Shi'ism) arose from the attempt of atheists and subversives to defame the Prophet and to destroy Islam.[14]

According to several sources, anti-Shi'ite religious indoctrination has led to the conversion or attempted conversion of some students away from Shi'ism, especially adolescent girls. The Shi'a are therefore afraid of the dissipation of their culture and identity, and fear assimilation into the culture imposed by the state, including the erosion of Shi'ism as a faith and tradition in favor of Wahhabism.

Legal Discrimination

The Shi'a have been denied any significant positions in the government and lack autonomy or self-rule even in their regional affairs. Shi'a are excluded from at least 50 percent of Saudi universities and research institutes. Shi'ite testimony is not permitted in courts, nor are the Shi'a equal to Sunnis in court. There are no Shi'ite judges in Saudi courts.

Economic Discrimination

Al-Hasa province has not shared in the general level of prosperity that characterizes the rest of the country. The situation has improved somewhat over the past decade but the gap is still significant. The Shi'a have been systematically let go from employment in the area, especially from ARAMCO (Arabian American Oil Company) where they constituted one-third of the workforce and professional-technical jobs. Shi'a have few government jobs. Shi'ite women were traditionally banned from being teachers—one of the few jobs open to women in the Kingdom; more recently this ban has been lifted, but those women who have received teachers training are often deliberately offered jobs only far away from the home province—a particular hardship in austere Saudi society in which it is difficult for women to work, much less live apart from their families. Yet many Shi'ite women have taken these jobs anyway as an act of defiance and an expression of community self-reliance.

Shi'ite Representation in the Government

The Shi'a have almost no clout at all within the Saudi government. There has been an occasional Shi'ite cabinet minister in a technical area, but otherwise almost no representation within the upper echelons of government. They are excluded from the judiciary, the military officer corps, the security forces, and the National Guard. They are reportedly also barred from positions in the Hajj Ministry and the Ministry of Islamic Affairs.

In 1993 the regime finally established a Consultative Council *(Majlis al-Shura)* that had been under consideration for over three decades. Its members are entirely appointed and have no legal or legislative authority; their function is to advise on problems, and to suggest potential legislation in certain areas when asked. Its members are well educated, largely professional in background, with a high number of foreign Ph.D.s. In the first Majlis there was only one Shi'ite member, Dr. Jamil al-Jishi, who is a university professor.

In July 1997, King Fahd expanded the Majlis from its original 60 members to 90; of the original 60, half were replaced with new faces. Press reports stated that the new Majlis contained four Shi'a. One of the rationales mentioned by commentators for these appointments was that four Shi'ite members came closer to reflecting the official Saudi statistics that the Shi'a make up approximately 4 percent of the population.[15] But the Shi'a themselves claim that of the four so-called Shi'ite members, in reality only two of them are actually Shi'a, despite the fact that the other two have names that could be taken as Shi'ite.[16] The press also speculated that an increase in Shi'ite representation was perhaps a gesture to counterbalance the security crackdown against the Shi'a in the aftermath of the 1996 al-Khobar bombing—which the government blamed on the Shi'a. While the Shura has very little power, the representation of any Shi'a at all within the Majlis is almost surely highly distasteful to the conservative Wahhabi 'ulama.

Shi'ite Political Organizational Activity

Shi'ite opposition to the Saudi regime before the Iranian Revolution largely came in the form of Shi'ite participation in leftist movements, such as the illegal Saudi Communist party, or other illegal radical leftist movements, such as the Arab Socialist Action Party in the Arabian Peninsula *(Hizb al-'Amal al-Ishtiraki al-'Arabi fi'l-Jazira al-'Arabiyya)*. We have seen this same trend elsewhere in the Gulf where the Shi'a, in quest of a universalizing nonsectarian movement that will accept them, formed ties to Ba'thi movements in Iraq or Syria, or to other similar movements operating in the Gulf.

The 1960s also saw the creation of the Organization of the Islamic Revolution *(Munadhdhamat al-Thawra al-Islamiyya)*, which was reportedly part of a broader regionwide Shi'ite group known as the Organization of Vanguard Revolutionists—linked with similar groups in Bahrain and Iraq.[17] It was founded under the influence of the ideas of Ayatollah Sayyid Muhammad al-Shirazi and called for "educating and enlightening the masses" rather than advocating violence. While the group was strongly antiregime in Saudi Arabia, there was no evidence of violence by this organization, which remained quiet even during the 1987 riots in Mecca when Iran called for a jihad against Saudi Arabia. The Saudi branch went public in 1975 and renamed itself the Organization of the Islamic Revolution in the Arabian Peninsula (*Munadhdhamat al-Thawra al-Islamiyya fi'l Jazira al-'Arabiyya*). One scholar, Mamoun Fandy, describes the period of 1975 to 1985 as the "militant phase" of the Shi'ite movement, characterized by scant attention to the realities of the regional political environment within which the group was working, a focus on purifying Islam from Sufi practices, and an uncompromising view of the Saudi state, which they viewed as illegal, reflecting the Iranian revolution's own views as well.[18]

The Iranian revolution of course stirred renewed Shi'ite hopes and ambitions across the Gulf. The seizure of the Grand Mosque by Sunni Najdi dissidents under Juhayman al-'Utayba in 1979 shook the Kingdom and helped transform long-festering resentments into severe and widespread rioting in the Eastern Provinces by Shi'a late in the year; at least 20 people were killed during brutal suppression of the riots and hundreds were arrested. But the shock of these events caused the Kingdom to reconsider the situation. While continuing the crackdown against any form of Shi'ite dissidence, for the first time Saudi Arabia decided to try to improve the poor economic situation in the province with the construction of more schools and roads. Significantly, the first modern hospital in the province was finished only in 1987.[19] One of the king's sons, Prince Muhammad bin Fahd, was appointed governor in 1984, replacing the notoriously corrupt, heavy-handed, and discriminatory Bin Jiluwi. Some lessening of discrimination took place, although the Shi'ite workforce in ARAMCO has been consistently reduced, even though the Shi'a constitute the main workforce in the Eastern Province.

According to Fandy, a major shift in Saudi Shi'ite thinking took place in 1988 among Ayatollah Shirazi's followers that brought an end to revolutionary rhetoric and a turn toward an agenda calling for democratization and human rights in the Kingdom.[20] Thus in 1990, after the Iraqi invasion of Kuwait, this group formally broke organizationally and ideologically with other Shi'ite organizations in other countries and renamed itself the Reform Movement (al-Haraka li'l-Islah), of which the major goals were independence from Iranian policies,[21] and a focus on bringing about reform within the Kingdom, with special appeal to the West on this issue. Political action and media pressures were to be its primary instruments. Ayatollah Shirazi's group to this day has continued to avoid involvement in political violence.

In accordance with the new strategy, in 1991 a number of leading Shi'ite dissidents with offices in both London and Washington, calling themselves the International Committee for the Defense of Human Rights in the Gulf and the Arabian Peninsula (ICDHR-GAP), began to publish antiregime materials. This organization produced publications in both English and Arabic

such as *(Al-Jazira al-'Arabiyya)* that exposed human rights problems in the
Kingdom and presented an overall critique of the regime. These materials
were both mailed and faxed back into the Kingdom as well as disseminated
in the West, representing the first open opposition movement not linked in
some way to other Arab radical movements in the Middle East. This information campaign disturbed the regime considerably, especially with its focus
on a Western audience as well, thereby undercutting the monopoly on information about the country that the regime has long sought to maintain. The
publications deliberately aimed at presenting issues in Western political
terms, including a focus on human rights. This unprecedented flow of information besmirched the dignified and peaceful image of the Kingdom that
had been so well preserved in the past.

Saudi policy toward the Shi'a took another major turn after the 1991
Gulf war with the first emergence of serious organized religious opposition
from Sunni Saudis themselves. The stationing of U.S. troops in the Kingdom constituted a highly controversial act that created divisions even among
the Sunni 'ulama. At issue was whether non-Muslim troops were in fact required for the defense of the Kingdom—permissible according to Islamic
law only under certain legal conditions of "necessity." The duration of such
foreign troop presence also became an issue, since the regime had declared
the presence to be "temporary," yet U.S. troops did not leave after the end
of the war. In the eyes of dissident Sunnis, the Qur'anic criteria for a non-
Muslim military presence were not met, and the regime was charged by
more radical clerics with having railroaded the requisite fatwa through a pliant and "state-owned" Council of Senior 'Ulama.

Additionally offensive to the dissident Sunni clerics was the perception
that the United States was propping up the royal family, whose rule was increasingly interpreted as illegitimate in Islamic terms. They charged the
regime with engaging in a self-serving relationship with Washington
whereby Riyadh would acquiesce to large arms purchases from the West and
provide a plentiful supply of oil at low prices—all in return for a Western
commitment to help maintain the royal family in power. Widespread corruption within the royal family added to clerical dissatisfaction with its rule.
Many of these Sunni dissidents—most notably Muhammad al-Mas'ari and
Sa'd al-Faqih—both from religious families in the heartland of the Najd—
escaped abroad, where they set up information/propaganda offices in London. The most prominent such organization, the Committee for Defense of
Legitimate Rights (CDLR), and later the Movement for Islamic Reform in
Arabia (MIRA), drew on the methods of the earlier Shi'ite ICDHR-GAP to
publish materials on the human rights violations and other corrupt practices
in the Kingdom. Both these organizations named names and otherwise
washed Saudi dirty laundry in public, faxing such information back into the

Kingdom at all levels including the press, and reportedly even in the royal palaces. They provided secure telephone lines in London by which Saudi citizens could call up and send in reports and news of malfeasance within the government structure for publication by MIRA. For the first time this Sunni opposition, based in London and in Washington, began to use e-mail and web sites extensively as a way to propagate their message to a wide audience including press, scholars, and foreign government officials.

Under these broad pressures, in a surprising strategic move, the Saudi government sought to ease the pressure from the Shi'ite opposition. The leading Shi'ite cleric, Shaykh Hasan al-Saffar, resident outside the country, had already publicly signaled a willingness to negotiate with the regime as long as substantive issues were discussed and steps toward alleviation of anti-Shi'ite discrimination taken.[23] The Saudi regime had also noted that the Saudi Shi'a had been strongly hostile to Saddam Hussein's invasion of Kuwait in 1991 and had supported Saudi policies during the war. In short, the "threat" from the Shi'a, heightened from the Iranian revolution, was perceived to be diminishing. In an unprecedented step, in 1994 the regime invited many of the leading Shi'ite dissidents back to the Kingdom for discussions on calling a truce to the Shi'ite antigovernment campaign. The Reform Movement presented an important list of demands, reflecting their discontent within the Kingdom.

- An announcement by the government that it respects the Shi'a as a recognized Islamic sect and acknowledges their right to practice their beliefs.
- Freedom of worship, including the right of Shi'a to build mosques and husayniyyas and to rehabilitate the tombs of Shi'ite Imams.
- Shi'ite religious education to be taught in state schools in Shi'ite-populated areas.
- Freedom of expression, including the right to publish and import Shi'ite books, and permission for the Shi'a to publish newspapers and magazines.
- Freedom to establish Shi'ite seminaries and religious schools as existed in the past.
- Cessation of anti-Shi'ite campaigns and denunciations of the sect, and recognition of the right of Shi'a to defend their beliefs.
- Shi'ite religious courts to be granted the same powers as Sunni ones (in matters of family law).
- Freedom to practice Shi'ite rites.
- Equal opportunities, particularly the abolition of anti-Shi'ite discrimination in terms of access to universities and educational establishments, civil service employment, and political, military, and security jobs.
- The construction of better infrastructure in neglected Shi'ite areas.[23]

It is interesting to note that only one out of these ten items relates directly to economic interests—improvement of the infrastructure of the Shi'ite areas of al-Hasa province. The bulk of the grievances relate directly to questions of cultural identity and religious freedoms. The list focuses exclusively on Shi'ite grievances; it does not encompass broader general grievances among the Sunni population that the Shi'a also share. But unlike in Bahrain and Kuwait, the Saudi Shi'a clearly felt that the Sunnis would not accept any effort to make common cause with the Shi'a and that the best they could hope for was alleviation of their own sectarian grievances. The list of requirements is exceptionally modest in that it calls for no reforms in the nature of the Saudi regime, government, institutions, or even ideology. While religion is naturally central to the Shi'ite identity, their document is secular in nature—it seeks no religious goals other than freedom of religion and equal rights with Sunnis in the practice of religion. In short, it is a thoroughly community-oriented document without ideological or broader political overtones.

That said, however, the changes called for are nonetheless extremely difficult for the regime to accommodate because their acceptance runs entirely counter to the Wahhabi ideological basis of the Saudi state. For the Wahhabi 'ulama, most of these demands are offensive and unacceptable. To the regime's credit, however, it embarked upon long negotiations with the Shi'ite Reform Movement—negotiations that were boycotted by the Saudi Shi'ite group known as "Hizballah." The regime reportedly finally agreed upon only four points for immediate action but failed to address the ideological elements of Shi'ite grievances relating to freedom of religious practice:

- Forty Shi'ite political prisoners were freed, including some who had been sentenced to death.
- Passports were issued to Shi'ite exiles who wanted to return home. (The Reform Movement insisted that this measure should apply to members of all Shi'ite groups, not just its own followers, in a bid to counter anticipated opposition of other Shi'a to the deal.)
- A review was begun of the travel bans imposed on some 2,000 Shi'ites inside the Kingdom.
- The Reform Movement's demands were forwarded to the concerned government departments and measures were taken to reduce discrimination. It was agreed that Shi'ite publications or books by Shi'ite authors would be permitted to enter the Kingdom, and that school history books would be amended to remove disparaging references to Shi'ism and acknowledge it as one of the Kingdom's Islamic sects alongside the four Sunni schools of thought.[24]

In return, the Shi'ite dissidents agreed to cease their propaganda efforts against the Kingdom. Most of the dissidents then returned to Saudi Arabia.[25]

But the Shi'ite dissidents had themselves been split along ideological lines, as noted above. The more radical group, known as Hizballah, criticized the more moderate group for making excessive concessions to the regime and, in effect, for giving away its major leverage against the regime by curtailing its propaganda instruments. The Hizballah group did not believe the regime would honor its commitments and felt that the regime should be required to prove its own good intentions before the heat was removed from it. The more moderate group, the Reform Movement, was willing to make these concessions to the regime to test its good faith. Significantly, the Reformers remained in consultation with the moderate Ayatollah Shirazi in Iran as their primary marji'; Shirazi reportedly stated that any agreement with the Saudi state was up to the Saudi Shi'a themselves and that he would not pronounce on the issue. (This policy is at odds with the political line pursued by Iran's leader, Ayatollah Khamene'i. Shirazi himself has long had a falling out with the Iranian regime; many of his followers have been arrested, and his own freedom of action in Iran has been under constraints.)[26]

There is reportedly a third, smaller group among the Saudi Shi'a led by two brothers and leading clerics, Shaykh Hasan al-Radhi and Shaykh Husayn al-Radhi. Both of them look to Iran in the religious sense but do not subscribe to Iranian leadership in the political sphere and are nonviolent. One of them has been accused of involvement in the Khobar Towers bombing of U.S. forces in 1996, but most Saudi Shi'a in exile scoff at this prospect, given the group's quietistic bent.[27]

Saudi Shi'ite activists today remain divided about the course of events in the Kingdom. Many believe that the regime has not seriously honored its agreement and that conditions have not improved sufficiently for their communities. Other Shi'a believe that, despite government failure to entirely deliver on its promises to the community, it is better to accept the current slightly improved conditions rather than return to confrontation. Shi'ite leaders who express more radical views on the problem are mainly under arrest or outside of the Kingdom.

The bombing of a U.S. military housing facility (Khobar Towers) resulting in 19 American deaths in June 1996 drew dramatic attention to the Saudi Shi'a once more and placed renewed pressure upon the community. Saudi officials initially claimed they had evidence that Shi'ite groups backed by foreign forces—clearly implying Iran—were behind the bombing, but no official government statement was issued confirming these claims. Notwithstanding, the bombing was followed by a wide campaign of arrests of Shi'a. According to Amnesty International, over 200 Shi'a were detained by Saudi security forces,[28] and Saudi sources say that at least

35 of these remain incarcerated. In a quite remarkable turnabout, in May 1997 the Saudi minister of the interior announced publicly that the government had concluded that there was no foreign involvement in the bombing and that all the actors were Saudis.[29] No further comment about their identities was made, and the Saudi government has kept a tight lid on the investigation and interrogation of suspects.

The Shi'a have all along vehemently denied involvement in the operation, arguing that it would be against the interests of such a weak community to engage in major acts of terrorism against both the Saudi state and against U.S. personnel and installations. This does not exclude the possibility that maverick elements of the Shi'ite community took part in the bombing. Intriguingly, the Saudi government notably refrained, however, from issuing charges against any specific individuals or groups, including those in custody, despite the deep frustration of the United States in its inability to proceed with prosecution of the case. The investigation seems to have effectively been closed. The fact that the Saudi government has not sought to publicize the alleged Shi'ite perpetrators—strongly in the interests of the regime to do so—leads one to suspect that the evidence is lacking, or that the perpetrators may be Sunni. There is also a distinct possibility that the Saudis decided to shut the door on the investigation, even though they may have had evidence of some direct or indirect backing from Iran. Such a decision would be based on the subsequent rapidly warming relations between Saudi Arabia and Iran starting with the election of President Khatami in 1997, who indicated a strong desire to start relations afresh.

Interestingly, both the Shi'a and the Sunni Saudi dissidents have all along stated their joint belief that the 1996 Khobar Towers bombing of the American military was carried out by dissident Sunnis, not Shi'a. However, both groups have their own agenda in claiming this: the Shi'a seek to reduce suspicion and pressure upon their own community, while the Sunni dissidents would like to demonstrate that heartland Sunni opposition to the regime is growing in its ability to hit both the regime and the United States.

In organizational terms, one should avoid attributing too much importance to apparent distinctions among the different dissident organizations and trends. The leading Saudi Sunni Islamist dissident in London, Muhammad al-Mas'ari, suggests the possibility that the Shi'a may have agreed in 1993 that it would be prudent to divide their forces: some key elements of the Reform Movement would return to the Kingdom, while others, perhaps those more skeptical of the agreement, would remain abroad as a reserve, maybe with a different organizational name, to retain a few pressure points against the regime, and to protect the movement in the event of a breakdown of the agreement.[30] Yet others suggest the organizational and philosophical differences are indeed meaningful.

Opposition forces are still represented abroad. An external arm of the Shi'ite Reform Movement is based in Washington and does not accept the 1993 agreement; it works to continue publicizing the plight of the Shi'a and the failings of the regime. This group has several publications—one is *al-Kalima*, a periodical designed to research and promote Shi'ite history and culture. Other organizations have surfaced in the press, but it is hard to learn whom or what they specifically represent among the Shi'ite community: a Hijaz Human Rights Defense Committee,[31] a Haramayn (the two Holy Places) Islamic Information Center, as well as a Hijaz 'Ulama Association.[32] Muhammad al-Mas'ari has suggested that these various groups could all be basically diverse elements or arms of the Reform Movement, each created to draw attention to different issues, or to seek cooperation with different groups.[33]

Clerical Leadership

As we have seen in other states in the region, Shi'ite clerics in Saudi Arabia have taken a prominent leadership role over the last 20 years in the search for greater rights. The leading Shi'ite clerical figure within the Kingdom is Shaykh Hasan al-Saffar. Radical in his early years, since 1988 Saffar has moved toward a much more moderate position vis-à-vis the regime. In taped sermons and writings analyzed by Fandy, he actively calls for dialogue with liberal Sunni and secular opposition forces in the country; he urges reforms of an essentially secular nature and for broad-mindedness in accepting plurality of ideas.[34] He has published several works including *Pluralism and Freedom in Islam* (*al-Ta'addudiyya wa'l Hurriyya fi'l Islam*), as well as a body of taped sermons on a variety of issues relating to Islam and political thought. His thinking reflects much influence of liberal Sunni thinkers outside the Kingdom such as Yusif al-Qaradawi, Fahmi al-Huwaydi, Hasan al-Turabi, and the Iranian thinker Abdol Karim Soroush.[35]

Under severe conditions of repression, Muslim minorities everywhere can drift into frustration and violence. But in the absence of repression it is worth considering that Muslim minorities may otherwise generally produce thinkers who gravitate toward a liberal conception of Islam, democratic processes, and human rights—precisely because they are the primary victims of the absence of these rights. Thus al-Saffar's liberal vision reflects the only workable long-term political strategy for Saudi Shi'a, who can never aspire to the establishment of a Shi'ite Islamist state, and who must therefore come to terms with the state in which they live—even while preserving their community's minoritarian culture.

The Saudi regime has so far been unresponsive to the calls of al-Saffar and other Shi'a for fundamental reform and change of the nature of the state.

The state has preferred to deal piecemeal with some of the most pressing Shi'ite grievances and not to deal with their broader calls for change in the philosophy, structure, and makeup of Saudi governance.

Relations Between the Sunni and Shi'ite Opposition

Historically, the Saudi Shi'a have only been able to cooperate with leftists within the Kingdom, not with the rightist religious opposition. The same holds true today, except that there is little leftist-liberal opposition anymore in evidence.

The Sunni religious opposition is largely negative about relationships with the Shi'a. At the purely secular level, in past decades, Shi'a in Saudi Arabia have been participants in leftist movements, especially Communist, as they have in other Arab countries. Arab nationalist groups have also included Shi'a in various Arab countries at certain times, but there is often a strong Sunni flavor to Arab nationalist movements that celebrate mainstream interpretations of Arab history in which the Shi'a do not really figure or figure negatively. The Shi'a sometimes may not be perceived as "fully Arab" in Arab nationalist eyes, or they are seen as having "uncomfortable" religious ties to Iran. There is thus much ambivalence among Sunni religious dissidents towards Shi'a dissidents, even if they share the common goal of changing the Saudi regime.

Among the Sunni opposition to the Saudi regime, it is Hijazi nationalists who feel most comfortable with the idea of potential cooperation with the Shi'a. Hijazi culture, that includes the holy cities of Mecca and Medina, is far older and deeper than that the Najd; its nationalists nurse grievances about their loss of cultural independence and their conquest and domination by Wahhabi culture and religion, although they have not apparently organized into any coherent movement. At a minimum they seek far greater cultural and religious autonomy and call for a state that is not based solely on the culture and domination of Wahhabism and the Najd. Hijazi nationalists are therefore predisposed to talk to other groups in the Kingdom who share these same goals of change and have less religious antipathy to Shi'ism.

But the Shi'ite and the Hijazi communities are geographically far from each other, separated by the Najd—except for a small and timorous community of Shi'a in Madina, the Nakhawila, who maintain a very low profile out of fear of repression. Furthermore, mainstream Sunni Islamist opposition groups in the Kingdom essentially derive their thinking from *salafi* (conservative fundamentalist) or Wahhabi concepts and apply the Wahhabi critique and vocabulary to their sharp criticism of the royal family and the regime. For these Sunni opposition groups, cooperation with the Shi'a from an ideological point of view ranges from the awkward to the unacceptable. If they made common cause with the Shi'ite opposition, they could bring down upon themselves the ire of both proregime elements and radical 'ulama in the Kingdom who see the Shi'a as apostates or heretics in Islamic terms.

Among Sunni religious dissidents, the Bin Ladin group has not spoken out specifically on this issue, but is one of the most salafi-oriented; in 1998 its London spokesman was strongly anti-Shi'ite. After the CDLR split apart, its successor, the Movement for Islamic Reform in Arabia (MIRA), led by Sa'd al-Faqih, stated that it would be "difficult" for them to cooperate with Shi'a against the regime, but that he would not rule it out flatly in certain circumscribed areas. The rump CDLR under Mas'ari, however, initially stated a clear willingness to cooperate even with the Saudi Shi'a against the regime and actually announced a forthcoming historic cooperation agreement between Sunni and Shi'ite opposition groups. Mas'ari at that time stated he had no problem with cooperation with the Shi'a since the CDLR is "not a sectarian movement but an Islamist one."[36] Mas'ari suggested that the importance of the Shi'a also lies with their geographical location athwart much of the energy resources of the Kingdom, which the Najd will always need.[37] Mas'ari's initial willingness to work with the Shi'a may have been among the factors that cost him much support in the Kingdom. He has since reconsidered and said that a Hanbali-Islamist state could not accord full citizenship to the Shi'a since they constitute a dissident sect.[38]

For their part, the Saudi Shi'a see little benefit from cooperation with Wahhabi salafi groups. In their view, the Wahhabi dissidents will gain from such cooperation, but the Shi'a will lose. The Shi'a fear that the Wahhabis will use the them as added leverage against the Saudi government to strengthen their own position, whereas the Shi'a will then lose even the minimal gains they have made in the 1990s and will sink back into conditions of active persecution. Indeed, the conduct and statements of several Wahhabi dissidents, both lay and cleric, give little comfort to the Shi'a that an alliance would benefit them.

The Shi'a so far remain isolated among the opposition, suggesting a future that is problematic. The Saudi Shi'a, like other Shi'ite activists in other countries such as in Pakistan and Turkey, are uncomfortable with Sunni Islamist movements since they believe that such movements are unlikely to be tolerant of Shi'a; as a result it is clear the Shi'a would be better off in a secular regime than a Sunni Islamist one. (And where Shi'a are minorities they know that a Shi'ite Islamist regime is out of the question.) For this reason many Saudi Shi'a are skeptical about their future in the Kingdom and state that only when a democratic and secular regime comes to power will the Kingdom stand any chance of staying together. Some are inclined to the view that the Kingdom may not be capable of staying together over the longer run except by force, in view of Najdi chauvinism and domination.[39]

Links to Bahrain

The Shi'a of the Eastern province of Saudi Arabia are geographically located next to Bahrain and are closely linked by blood ties. Both these communities are very old and consider themselves in many ways as one community. There are also Shi'ite groups in other Gulf states such as in Kuwait known as Hasawi, revealing their origins from communities in al-Hasa Province—further highlighting the Saudi rationale of renaming the area Eastern Province in order to extirpate the old Shi'ite cultural name. Shi'ite communities in both Bahrain and Saudi Arabia are under heavy pressure from their respective regimes and are concerned for each other's welfare. Contact is frequent. The Saudi regime is equally firmly committed to the suppression of any trends toward democracy in Bahrain under the al-Khalifas; they see this as the only barrier to prevent the Shi'ite majority in Bahrain from becoming dominant, at which point they could lend state support to the Saudi Shi'a. In a similar vein, the charge is made that weapons are reaching the Bahraini Shi'a from Saudi Arabia, since the Kingdom is known to have a plentiful domestic arms supply that can be smuggled into other Gulf states. The interrelationship of these two communities is thus important to the future politics of the Gulf, especially when the Bahraini Shi'a eventually attain some kind of political role reflecting their numerical majority on the island.

Shi'ite Options

The Shi'a of Saudi Arabia today feel their options are limited essentially to four:[40]

- Active opposition to the Saudi regime using all means, including violence, in order to force drastic change upon the political order. This strategy could involve a range of violent actions including bombing, assassinations, riots, and other forms of resistance. The Shi'a have already engaged in some of these activities over the past decades. By most accounts, the community is not well armed and has not used weapons against the regime—with the possible exception of the al-Khobar Towers 1996 bombing in which Shi'ite complicity has not been declared. But observers in the Gulf report that Saudi Arabia actually has a lot of weapons floating around that the Shi'a conceivably could acquire. Kuwait, furthermore, is reportedly awash with arms as a result of the Gulf War. So acquisition of at least small arms by the Saudi Shi'a should not be impossible. The more important question, however, is whether the Shi'a actually wish to arm and to engage in a violent confrontation with the state. Clearly the vast majority do not, and there has been no hint of anything like an intifada (such as now dominates Bahrain) ever since the extensive rioting in 1979 to 1980—when arms did not figure prominently. The major reality for the Shi'a is the well-developed Saudi state security apparatus that dominates the country. Unlike in Bahrain, the Shi'a in Saudi Arabia are relatively few in number and isolated; they could not on their own seize power in any way. From a regime point of view the most worrisome scenario would involve Shi'ite violence and terror that attracts world attention—just as the Khobar Towers bombings did—thus creating an environment of instability and a belief abroad that the regime is losing its grip on internal security. Under these circumstances, Sunni opposition forces or terrorist groups might themselves feel emboldened to act against the state in ways even more threatening, at the outside eventually even sparking a palace coup or military takeover. Violence against Americans in particular could have major political impact—and already has in forcing U.S. troops to move to isolated desert bases far from population centers and in intensifying regime sensitivity about the continuing U.S. military presence. American deaths constitute high-profile events in the international media, with clear political impact on the Kingdom. But the vast majority of Saudi Shi'a have little or no grievance against the United States per se. On the contrary, the Shi'a flourished in their association with ARAMCO from the earliest years, in which time they encountered no discrimination in employment. The Shi'a perceive no harm to their community stemming from past U.S. policies. There are, however, three other possible grounds on which the Shi'a could come to nourish anti-U.S. feeling in the future:

1. in accordance with broader Arab world thinking, deep resentment against near-unqualified U.S. support for Israel
2. anger at the United States for backing the Saudi regime and for exhibiting no significant interest or pressure about the condition of the Shi'a in the Kingdom
3. adherence to the Iranian ideological vision of the United States as an enemy of Islam.

Only a small handful of quite radical Shi'a across the region actually think in these terms. Iranian backing for such adventures has swiftly diminished since Khatami was elected president of Iran in 1997. But a destabilizing atmosphere could be created in the Kingdom by a small number of terrorists even without any Iranian support. One might hope that attendance to Shi'ite grievances by the state will further discourage a turn in these violent directions.

- Continuation of the struggle through opposition by peaceful means. This strategy involves a return to more active information and propaganda activity of the kind that marked the ICDHR-GAP in the early 1990s. It includes an effort to cooperate with any other elements of Saudi society that seek change in the Kingdom. This would obviously include Sunni liberals and secularist opposition forces, many of whom are also operating outside the Kingdom today. It could include Saudi religious opposition as well, although as we have seen, ideological issues make it difficult for Saudi Sunni Islamists—even if not Wahhabi—to cooperate closely with Shi'a.

- "Withdrawal" from Saudi life. This option essentially represents only a survival strategy until better days come along. It recognizes the overwhelming coercive power the regime possesses to do great damage to Shi'ite lives and welfare, and a preference not to run those risks. Withdrawal *(in'izal)* would focus on a turning inward of the community, basic preservation of Shi'ite culture and way of life, self-help, and reliance on external financial support where possible to survive. It would involve no confrontation of any kind, including political, with the regime—and indeed, it suggests virtual nonengagement with the regime beyond bare necessities.

- Cooperation and coexistence. This is the current strategy of the Reform Movement, and probably that favored by most Saudi Shi'a: in short, to live with the situation, avoid confrontation, and seek openings for change and improvement. Coexistence *(ta'ayush)* does not have to imply submission, however. It can leave room for dialogue and negotiation, perhaps at the edges of the problem rather than at the heart of it, and a gradual erosion of discrimination. However, the problem with the strategy of coexistence is its complete dependence on the good will of the other parties, the state and the Wahhabi religious establishment, as well as their stated or tacit agreement not to worsen their treatment of the Shi'a or deepen discrimination against them. Should the powers of the state for any reason intensify their pressure on the Shi'a, coexistence will become an untenable strategy.

What Does a Solution Require?

If improvement in the predicament of the Shi'a in Saudi Arabia is to come about, leading to their integration into Saudi society, what must happen? The solution is almost exclusively in Sunni hands. First, in Saudi Arabia, as in Kuwait, the problem is about improving the lot of a minority group— far easier than in states where the Shi'a constitute the majority. In principle, addressing the needs and grievances of the Shi'a and integrating them into Saudi society should not be a major challenge to the state—if it wished to do so.

In reality, however, the problem in Saudi Arabia is perhaps deeper than it appears. To meet the key Shi'ite grievance—the accordance of legitimacy to their faith, culture, and religious practice—requires abandonment of the founding religious/ideological principles of the Saudi state, that is, Wahhabism. It is Wahhabi belief that casts the Shi'a into outer darkness as non-Muslims. Mere suspension of Wahhabi teachings about them, a willingness to look the other way and to let the Shi'a practice their faith, is the best the Shi'a can today hope for in terms of their identity and faith. Indeed, most Shi'a for now would be greatly relieved if the regime would simply leave them alone. But over the longer run, such "tolerance" is not enough in the eyes of religious minorities, who believe they should not be merely tolerated, but accepted in legal and social terms. Such an acceptance is anathema to the ruling religious convictions of the Kingdom today.

Issues of reform or change in ideology and dogma go beyond the condition of the Shi'ite community alone, of course; it affects all non-Wahhabi groups in the country, that is, the majority of the population in all regions except the Najd. How easily could such change come about?

The Saudi state since 1929 in principle has limited the ability of radical Wahhabi dogma to fully determine the policies of the state. The central power structure of Wahhabi faith was the Brotherhood (Ikhwan)—unrelated to the Muslim Brotherhood of the same name—who constituted the spearhead of Wahhabi military conquests over two centuries. With the enforced disbanding of the Brotherhood in 1927, the state has been under far less pressure to conform to their harsh orthodoxy. But while the 'ulama remain bearers of Wahhabi faith and teachings, the state has long learned to deflect, manipulate, cajole or coopt the majority of the 'ulama in the interests of the state. These strategies make possible Saudi Arabia's acceptance of multiple forms of modern technology, close ties with non-Muslim states, dealings with prominent Jewish leaders, the presence of foreign non-Muslims in the Kingdom, and toleration of the many small hypocrisies of Saudi daily life that make life livable for native and foreigner alike. Nonetheless, in times of stress in the Kingdom, ruling family legitimacy is bolstered by renewed emphasis upon its religious orthodoxy, usually asserted by the time-honored devices of publicly attacking the Shi'a, and granting greater scope to the religious morals police (mutawwa'in, or "enforcers")—signs that the country still preserves its core values.

But the regime cannot totally ignore or reject the 'ulama either. 'Ulama acceptance of the royal family and its policies constitutes the essential underpinning of legitimacy for the regime. The regime must thus cooperate with

the 'ulama, bargain with them, or concede here to gain there. The formal acceptance of other forms of even Sunni schools of jurisprudence and religious
practice in the Kingdom—much less Shi'ite—would constitute a sharp af-
front to Wahhabi belief. At a time when the royal family is under pressure in
many respects—diminishing national income, corruption, the high cost of
the privy purse of the house of al-Sa'ud, the interference of ubiquitous princes
in most aspects of the country's commercial life, close association with U.S.
military policy—the regime is not ready to do ideological battle with the
'ulama over the legal position of Shi'ism in Saudi life. To ask for such a thing
would damage the foundations of broader al-Sa'ud legitimacy in the eyes of
the 'ulama. Simply put, it would constitute a revolution in Saudi practice to
suddenly recognize the existence of the three other *madhahib* (schools of jurisprudence) apart from the Hanbali (of which Wahhabism is a radical deriv-
ative). Acceptance of the Shi'ite school *(Ja'fariyya)* as a fifth legitimate school
of Islam is a liberal view even to non-Wahhabis, and is not juridically widespread even in some other predominantly Sunni countries.

In short, can the Saudi regime change its religious base of orthodoxy or
"national ideology" and still remain the Saudi state? How can the state ideologically integrate the non-Wahhabis of the Kingdom? On what new ideological basis would the state reorganize itself, and what would be the
implications for the royal family and the traditional foundations of its
power? This transition would seem to be exceedingly difficult to negotiate.
But until this fundamental issue is resolved, there can be no serious talk of
Shi'ite integration into Saudi life; the fundamental Shi'ite demand for acceptance of their presence, faith, and culture will go unmet.

None of this means that other grievances cannot be met, however. In the
economic realm, for example, a great deal can be done to lessen Shi'ite discontent. Greater investment in the infrastructure of al-Hasa province has
been a long-standing demand, one that the state has moved to meet somewhat more seriously over the past decade. The state can also do more to employ Shi'a in the bureaucracy, especially in al-Hasa. It can permit more
construction of mosques and *husayniyya*s without any serious compromise
of state ideology, especially in those regions in which Shi'a are the majority.
Shi'a detainees can be released from prison and greater freedom granted for
Shi'a to travel abroad. If Shi'ite loyalty is suspect, such suspicions lead to
policies that become a self-fulfilling prophesy; loyalty is a two-way street.

What happens if the Saudis take no more serious steps to alleviate Shi'ite
grievances? First, leading Shi'ite clerics and activists will again seek to leave
the Kingdom to begin anew their campaign of exposure of human rights and
injustices in the Kingdom as they did earlier. The regime showed unusual
sensitivity at that time to such activity by taking unprecedented measures to
try to reach accommodation with them. With a Sunni opposition abroad

today also engaged in an active antiregime political and informational struggle, would the addition of the Shi'a make much difference to the Kingdom? Has the regime perhaps grown used to the nuisance factor of an external opposition that they cannot fully buy off or shut down, but that has not yet become regime-threatening? By any standards, Sunni opposition, especially coming as it does from the Najd itself, is far more threatening than Shi'ite opposition. As we noted above, any cooperation between the Shi'ite and Sunni opposition depends almost entirely upon Sunni willingness to do so.

If the situation does not markedly deteriorate further in the Shi'ite regions, the community as a whole will probably not move toward greater violence. But a small radical minority is still capable of practicing violence or terrorism. Moderation of Iranian policies abroad and the increasing integration of Hizballah into the state in Lebanon remove two key external factors that could assist violent aspirations among a Shi'ite minority. But the Shi'a may not require major external patrons in order to carry out certain types of violence, such as assassinations or bombings, if they feel heavily pressured.

In the end, the Shi'a by themselves constitute no major security threat to the regime, but under conditions of general discontent in the Kingdom they could contribute to overall instability, or even help spark more serious action on the part of violent Sunni opposition that would have major impact. If Bahrain continues to mismanage its Shi'ite majority population, or when Bahraini Shi'a eventually come to dominate the Bahraini government as a majority, this too can have serious impact on the behavior of the Saudi Shi'a toward continued regime oppression.

When the day comes that Saudi Arabia moves toward truly liberalized rule, the Shi'a will still represent only a modest voice in the country's political order. As Arabs, they have no inherent reason to maintain a pro-Iranian orientation if there is hope for the future, and in the absence of oppression. In the extreme case of a breakup of the Kingdom along regional/religious lines in the future, the Shi'a there will inevitably gravitate toward close association with their kinsmen in adjacent Bahrain, a long-standing natural link.

CHAPTER NINE

The Shi'a of Lebanon

The Shi'a of Lebanon possess a political and ideological dynamism that makes them the most significant Shi'ite community in the Arab world today. In absolute numbers the Lebanese Shi'a make up only a modest 1.3 million,[1] but they represent perhaps 30 to 40 percent of the population, the single largest sectarian group in the country. The story of the Shi'a's rise to power, while containing a number of features unique to Lebanon, offers some general insights relevant to the future of Shi'ite communities elsewhere in the Arab world. Indeed, the story of change in Lebanon has relevance to the broader evolution of more open political systems in the region. What are the most striking features of the Lebanese Shi'ite experience?

The Lebanese Shi'a are the first Shi'ite community to have achieved significant political power as a group in the modern Arab world. They are the only Arab Shi'a who have pulled themselves up by their bootstraps from an oppressed, despised, isolated, and marginalized community to achieve major political power within the political order of their state. The Shi'a over a 30-year period have become quite simply the most powerful political force in Lebanon today. But even as the single largest community in the country, their success is noteworthy by contrast with the Shi'a of Iraq and Bahrain, who constitute absolute majorities of the population, yet who remain deprived of a significant political role in the states in which they live. And Shi'ite minorities in other Arab states—except Kuwait—have no significant political voice of their own.

The Shi'ite community in Lebanon displays much of the diversity of Shi'ite communities elsewhere and is divided by the same types of ideological, class, and educational distinctions that characterize Shi'ite communities in other countries, particularly in Iraq. In addition to the presence of traditional baronial families, the *zu'ama,* feudal strongmen, the Shi'ite population has been exposed to the various currents of socialism, Arab nationalism, and Westernization, as has the rest of the population of the Arab world, whatever their religious affiliation. In his study of Amal and the Shi'a, A. R. Norton points out that "the race to mobilize the Shi'a community during the early 1970s was a race between secular creeds and a distinctly sectarian movement."[2] Economic disparities have also created a class of Shi'a with a vested interest in stability and an aversion to revolutionary currents. Within this vested class, and the thin class of zu'ama, cross-sectarian alliances to preserve the established order figure more prominently than affiliation to Shi'ism. Because Lebanon has been more exposed to Western influences than any other Arab country, large sectors of the population, including many Shi'a, are secular in their politics even though the country's political system is based on sectarianism.

Perhaps not surprisingly, the secular, vested elements in the Shi'a community have not established their own political organizations or formed a political front that can exert pressure on or influence the political system. Instead, it was left to Amal and later Hizballah, groups avowedly based on a Shi'ite agenda, to take the lead in spearheading the Shi'ite revival in Lebanon and to advocate Shi'ite rights, whether in south Lebanon or the Biqa' valley to the west. Neither Amal nor Hizballah between them have universal Shi'ite support, and many Shi'a remain out of the range of the two groups. Nevertheless, if some sectors of the Lebanese Shi'ite community do not support either Amal or Hizballah, they have not created an alternative, and in any case they have benefited from the success of these two movements in securing a greater share for all Shi'a.

The Rise of the Lebanese Shi'a

The story of the rise of the Lebanese Shi'a has been well told in several excellent studies[3] and need not be repeated here. The most dramatic single feature of the process was the crucial role of "Imam" Musa al-Sadr, an Iranian cleric of Lebanese extraction, who came to Lebanon in 1959 to replace the recently deceased Shi'ite *Mufti* (religious authority) and to act as shepherd to the community. Musa al-Sadr was the catalyst, during an extraordinary 20-year career in Lebanon, for the mobilization of the Shi'a in the social and political realm. Through al-Sadr's charismatic personality and tireless efforts, he was able to crystallize for the Shi'a a sense of identity, a pride in and connection with the broader Shi'ite tradition in the Muslim world. He generated a sense of indignation among the community about their lowly position in Lebanese society and stimulated the belief that they could indeed do something about it through nonrevolutionary political action. Al-Sadr devoted his early efforts to raising the self-esteem of the Shi'a by establishing schools, professional training centers, hospitals, and other social service institutions, to bring the Shi'a in line with the rest of the educated and trained sectors of Lebanese society.

The populist nature of this Shi'ite awakening in Lebanon is particularly important: it was from the start a movement from the grassroots up, rather than a narrow reformist effort led by a coterie of elite. Its energy derived from emotive sociological forces rather than out of ideological justifications. This may be one reason why it succeeded where Communism among Shi'ite communities, for example, ultimately failed to mobilize the community. Until the Lebanese civil war broke out in 1975, the Shi'a had been an important component of nonsectarian, transnational movements—Communism, Arab nationalism, and Syrian nationalism—as a means of entering into the political process in Lebanon. However, these movements remained marginal to the traditional conservative power structure in Lebanon before the war, which was dominated and manipulated by an old boys' club composed of a handful of Maronite, Sunni, and Shi'ite baronial families. The nonsectarian parties could not crack this tight circle or provide their members or agendas a serious voice in Lebanese politics. For the Shi'a in particular, these movements proved a dead end and failed to address the problems specific to the Shi'a of underrepresentation, underdevelopment, and governmental neglect.

Indeed, a sad irony of al-Sadr's remarkable role in Lebanon was that just as he had begun to register real progress by the mid-1970s in bringing the Shi'ite community into the state order in Lebanon, the Lebanese state itself began to self-destruct as the country devolved into a proxy battleground between Syria, the Palestinians, and Israel—part of a 15-year civil war that all but destroyed the country's political and social order. Al-Sadr then mysteriously "disappeared" in 1978 during a visit to Libya, almost certainly killed at Qadhafi's orders because of al-Sadr's opposition to spreading Palestinian guerrilla power in the Shi'ite regions of southern Lebanon (after the Palestinian guerrillas' expulsion from Jordan in 1970).

Lebanese Shi'a today show signs of vigor, confidence, and drive that indeed worry other elements of the population—Christians and Sunni Muslims—whose former power and position have been threatened by Shi'ite gains within state and society that are more commensurate with their numbers. This Shi'ite rise to power emerged from several conditions—some of them unique to the Lebanese scene. First, a prerevolutionary Iranian cleric played a decisive role in creating community cohesion and identity.[4] Second, the terrible Lebanese civil war—abetted by the interests of external players such as Israel, Jordan, Syria, Iraq, Libya, the Palestinians, and the United States—led to the virtual collapse of the centralized state as such. Third, this weakening of central state power and the beginnings of civil war facilitated the rise of the first Shi'ite militia organization, Amal, in 1975 and later a second militia under Iranian tutelage, Hizballah, in 1982. Amal served to protect the community first against PLO guerrillas in southern Lebanon, later against Israeli forces who invaded from the south repeatedly in response to Palestinian guerrilla activity, and against Christian and even Sunni Muslim forces, all of whom were seen as threatening the heretofore weak Shi'ite community. The Amal militia thus helped give the Shi'ite community a place and voice in the overall violent politics of the 1970s and 1980s. Hizballah, with its greater focus on elaboration of a religious ideology inspired by the Iranian revolution; on spectacular guerrilla and terrorist operations, especially against American military and diplomatic presence; and on resistance against Israeli forces in Lebanon, played a major role in imprinting the presence of the Lebanese Shi'a upon the consciousness of the world.

The growing weakness of the Lebanese state and the chaos of civil strife and war seem to have been crucial conditions for permitting the emergence and flourishing of a self-help civic program among the Shi'a. It is important to note that external states had little to do with the emergence of Shi'ite power in Lebanon in its first two crucial decades. While Imam Musa al-Sadr came from Iran, the power of his role depended almost entirely on his personal genius in organizing and creating a voice for the Shi'a and winning strong financial support from Lebanese Shi'ite merchants; early funds from the Shah were limited and no weapons were involved. The split in Amal that gave rise first to a splinter group, al-Amal al-Islami, and soon after to Hizballah, brought to the fore the role that Iranian funds and weapons later played in forming the radical phase of the Shi'ite emergence. However, had it not been for the sociopolitical base created by al-Sadr long before the Iranian revolution, Iran would have found little hospitable soil for inserting itself into Lebanon after the revolution. That entree too, was considerably facilitated by the conditions of the Israeli invasion of Lebanon and the ongoing civil war. In short, the assertive rise of a formerly marginalized sectarian sociopolitical group like the Lebanese Shi'a probably cannot readily be replicated in most other Arab states. Such Shi'ite movements, even when mobilizing on a strictly peaceful political basis, have been routinely repressed or crushed elsewhere, in Iraq and Bahrain in particular.

Furthermore, weight should also be given to Lebanon's own unique form of representation based on the allocation of political power along preestablished sectarian proportionality. While this system may be far from a Western ideal of how to manage a democratic process, it provided an essential precondition in which the existence and rights of diverse communities were formally recognized and enshrined. This facilitated the Lebanese Shi'ite task at the outset in that they did not have to battle for formal political recognition of their communal existence and legitimate community rights as Shi'a have had to do in other Arab countries.

Finally, The Ta'if Accord, negotiated in October 1989 by the major Lebanese warring factions under the auspices of Syria and Saudi Arabia, formalized the gains made by the Shi'a during the civil war in asserting their presence on the Lebanese political stage. The new, enlarged Shi'ite participation in government is written into the Ta'if Accord, which serves as the basis for a new constitutional arrangement, as part of a larger share for all the Muslim communities of Lebanon. In a break with convention, the Shi'ite representation at Ta'if included not only the traditional old guard, but also the leadership of the relatively young and vigorous Amal Movement.

For the first time since independence in 1943, this accord gave the Muslims parity with the Christians in parliament, cabinet posts, and senior civil service posts. Also for the first time, the Shi'a received a share equal to that of the Sunnis in all these areas. Thus the accord provided a more equitable distribution of state functions, one more closely reflecting demographic reality. In a remarkable reconfiguration of high authority, the term of the speaker of parliament, a Shi'ite, has been extended from one year to four, giving him unprecedented power and maneuverability. In a further dramatic departure from the past, the speaker is now on an equal footing with the prime minister and president, a position that the current speaker, Nabih Birri, exploits to the full.

How the Shi'ite Movements Have Galvanized Their Community

The two Shi'ite movements, Hizballah and Amal, have managed to galvanize, modernize, and transform the character of leadership within their own community over the last several decades in ways that neither Sunni Muslim nor Christian movements have been able to do within their own communities. The two movements by no means command the loyalty of all the Lebanese Shi'a, and in fact many Shi'a disapprove of both for different reasons. Nevertheless, all Lebanese Shi'a have benefited from the energetic surge of Amal and Hizballah into the political arena in Lebanon.

Within a period of 30 years, the Shi'a in Lebanon have managed to transform their role in society and, more important, the character of their leadership in a dramatic fashion. A community that had languished under an essentially feudal order dominated by *zu'ama* (traditional local strongmen), managed to eliminate these feudal and clan-oriented leaders in favor of "modern," populist, mobilizing leaders with a clear sense o f community and goals bolstered by ideology and linked to traditional Shi'ite values.[5]

This was not simply a "revolutionary process"; indeed, Musa al-Sadr, while transforming his society, did not have a revolutionary agenda in the literal sense, since he did not seek to overturn the existing order in Lebanon, but simply to claim a more just share within that society. The identification with Iran in an ideological sense came rather late in the process of regeneration of the Shi'ite community, after al-Sadr's mission and the Iranian revolution, and affected only a small part of the community.

Comparison with Sunni and Maronite Evolution

By contrast, the Sunni community of Lebanon had undergone a radicalizing phase at an earlier time with its identification with pan-Arabism starting with Jamal 'Abd-al-Nasir in Egypt in the 1950s. The intellectual/ideological roots of Sunni radicalization linked the Sunni community with broader Arab nationalist movements outside Lebanon in a long-established common identity. The Sunni movement was not a quest for identity in the way it was for the Shi'a. The Sunni identity was well formed and was directly linked to neighboring Sunni populations in Syria, Palestine, and Jordan. Nor did the Lebanese Sunnis ever develop a true community militia during the civil war as did the Shi'a, except for the politically insignificant "Murabitun," largely a creature of Libya. In reality the PLO in Lebanon served functionally as the primary Sunni militia, serving its general interests vis-à-vis regional powers. The Sunni community failed to develop a body of robust young leaders that could galvanize Sunni support. While new, younger personalities were emerging in the Shi'ite milieu, the Sunnis continued to rely on customary figures and on the long-established Sunni families. Because Sunnis were already established within the affluent and intellectual strata of Lebanese society, they showed few signs of significant new social development during the war years, unlike the vigorous emergence of Shi'ite businessmen, intellectuals, and new politicians to replace the old feudal barons.

Finally, the Maronite Christians throughout this period were in the hands of their own feudal or baronial clans, who were engaged in internecine quarrels for leadership and for preservation of Maronite national privilege, by force if necessary. The Maronites underwent far less development than the Shi'a during this period of chaos and civil war in Lebanon, despite the appearance on the scene of younger, more radical warlords, such as Samir Ja'ja'. It has only been in the last decade or so that the old Maronite families have been almost totally discredited and have left the country, leaving de facto leadership of the Maronites largely in the hands of the Patriarch, Cardinal Nasrallah Sfeir. If the social structure of the Maronite community did not change dramatically, its relative position of power over the Lebanese government did decline significantly, mainly due to the rise of the Shi'a. Many in the Maronite community now feel that "the old Lebanon" has gone and wonder if they have a place in the new Lebanon. Indeed, the Maronite community may itself be ripe for dramatic social change in the future, such as the Shi'a underwent, in response to the challenges the new political order has placed before their once-dominant position.

How is the dramatic change in the position of the Shi'ite community to be understood? The Shi'a admittedly started from a much lower base of social development than the other major communities, making their gains comparatively more vivid in a short period of time as they caught up with the more advanced Christians and Sunnis. Every community in Lebanon has of course sought or enjoyed an external protector at one or another time. While the external factor for the Lebanese Shi'a has been Iran, the Shah's Iran cannot take major credit for the remarkable early metamorphosis among the Shi'a. While the Shah had some interest in utilizing the Lebanese Shi'a as a bulwark against leftist tendencies in the Arab world during the 1960s, and the Iranian government had played a role in facilitating al-Sadr's appointment to the Shi'a in Lebanon, Iranian support was marginal to his success, which came almost entirely on the basis of his own personality and ability to draw on the resources of the Shi'ite community itself.

The Shi'ite community was ripe for development by the time of al-Sadr's arrival. It had begun to build a significant financial base of its own, supported by the large Lebanese Shi'ite merchant diaspora settled primarily in West Africa that remitted monies back to south Lebanon. The Shi'a had also pursued education since the independence of the country in 1942 and had developed a significant professional class that was ambitious. By the late 1960s, many Shi'ite families had returned to Lebanon with fortunes made in Africa and were ready to assail the traditional bastions of Lebanese society and money in Beirut.[6] In this sense al-Sadr's arrival came at any extremely opportune time when his impact was greater than it would have been had he arrived 20 years earlier or later. But apart from the extraordinary role of Musa al-Sadr in winning the confidence and loyalty of most of the Shi'ite community and the acceptance of even of the leadership of Lebanon's Maronites, it was the turmoil and chaos of Lebanese politics, including the weakening of the state and the subsequent political free-for-all, that created the conditions in which the Shi'a were able to build a strong community and eventually to challenge the traditional system of sectarian division of power.

Why Have the Lebanese Shi'a Succeeded While Other Shi'a Have Not?

The Shi'a of Lebanon managed to transform their situation in a way that no other Shi'a of the Arab world have been able to do. This phenomenon is of interest well beyond any parochial concern for the welfare of the Shi'a. As we noted earlier, this book is interested in the implications of the Shi'ite political problem as it affects the broader issue of democracy and liberalization in the Arab world as a whole. What the Shi'a have or have not been able to accomplish on a broader level in Lebanon and elsewhere suggests something about the process of change in the region.

Are the conditions of Lebanon unique, or do they bear some relevance to the position of Shi'a elsewhere? Among the key factors shaping these developments in Lebanon are the following:

- the demographic power of the Shi'a as the single largest sectarian element;
- an existing confessional system of which the Shi'a are already recognized as a component;
- the foundations of a quasidemocratic electoral order, albeit flawed;
- the unique role and personality of al-Sadr in helping galvanize and unite a new Shi'ite identity;
- a 14-year civil war that led to the collapse of the state;
- the emergence of militias backing each sectarian community;
- the Israeli invasion of Lebanon in 1982, which further radicalized the Shi'a and gave them the dominant role in the guerrilla war against Israeli occupation in the Shi'ite heartland;
- major support from revolutionary Iran;
- Syrian interest in periodically backing the Shi'a as part of its balance-of-power politics in Lebanon—a factor still valid today;
- the Ta'if Accord, which brokered an internationally sponsored post–civil war redistribution of sectarian power in Lebanon that benefited the Shi'a.

The central fact is that the Shi'a represent the biggest single sectarian group in Lebanon. But the size of the Shi'ite community has had two results. First, it has provided them with a sense of confidence (after attaining a certain degree of political consciousness) that they have a right to a major role in the Lebanese political order. They will continue to pursue that right in the future. But second and more important, their demographic strength gives them a stake in the benefits of any longer-term weakening of political sectarianism and steps toward nonsectarian democratization (one person, one vote on the basis of universal Lebanese citizenship for all). Thus the Shi'a stand to benefit both under a system of political sectarianism and under nonsectarian democracy.

In principle, this same dynamic should apply to the Shi'a of Iraq and Bahrain where they actually constitute an absolute majority. As in Lebanon, in Bahrain or Iraq the Shi'a should be able to demand either a form of proportional political sectarianism or nonsectarian democracy and know that they will be the primary beneficiaries. At the present time, however, neither option is open to the Shi'a in those two states due to entrenched and inflexible authoritarian rule by Sunni minorities. Lebanon has passed beyond that stage: the Lebanese Shi'a had suffered considerably under Ottoman Sunni rule in Lebanon in a previous era, but their position improved under European colonialism, as did the position of the Shi'a in Iraq and Bahrain. In Lebanon, postcolonial independence brought a measure of democratic process to Lebanon that was not reversed by later regime action, but only suspended by civil war. In Iraq and Bahrain, however, postcolonial regimes also started out on a democratic basis but soon retreated to an authoritarianism that canceled most gains the Shi'a might have made.

Outside powers have not affected the position of the Shi'a in Bahrain or Iraq in the way that Syria, Iran, and Israel have done in the Lebanese case through their major intrusions into Lebanon. And unlike the government in Lebanon, authoritarian regimes in Bahrain and Iraq have not yet broken down to give way to the emergence of a new order and a redistribution of power on a more equitable basis. The collapse of the old state order into civil war in Lebanon almost seems to have been the prerequisite to the emergence of a more equitable state order. It is disquieting to think that similar violent state breakdown and extreme civil conflict may have to occur in Bahrain and Iraq as a prerequisite for change and liberalization to take place.

The Lebanese case is also distinct in that the Lebanese Shi'a have not been pitted against the state per se for the attainment of greater rights because the state was never fully captive to any one single group as it is in Iraq or Bahrain; in Lebanon, control of the state has been contested among differing groups.

Finally, do the Shi'a of Bahrain and Iraq require a Musa al-Sadr to stimulate their community's quest for an equal political role in their societies? The Shi'a of Iraq already have a well-developed sense of identity that does not require an outsider, much less an Iranian, to help awaken it—although there is at present no single commanding figure. The situation of the Shi'a in Bahrain perhaps more closely resembles that of the Lebanese Shi'a 40 years ago as an oppressed and marginalized element in the political order. At present in Bahrain there is neither a system of sectarian proportionalism, which would consolidate the position of the Shi'a in the political order, nor is there any move toward more democratic rule, which would also benefit them as a majority.

It may be that in both Iraq and Bahrain, however, some form of political sectarian proportionality will eventually be required to preserve a proportional balance between the two (or more) sects in order to overcome the communal crisis. Proportional representation as exists in Lebanon could serve as an intermediary phase toward longer-term democratization on a nonproportional basis. While the Sunni communities in Lebanon, Iraq, and Bahrain all have anxiety about any political change that alters the balance of power that now favors Sunnis, the Sunnis have the broader sense of community confidence that comes from being by far the preponderant force in the Muslim world by a factor of nearly nine to one. Or does this broader preponderance make concessions to Shi'a in their own home states all the more distasteful? And, more positively, can the Sunni communities rise above sectarian considerations to look toward a broader fusion of "co-Muslims" or even co-citizens within the state?

Hizballah and the Power of Islamist Resistance

Hizballah has been the most effective Shi'ite guerrilla organization in the Arab world in waging a struggle against Israeli occupation and against U.S. policy in the region for over a decade and a half. Hizballah's emergence as a guerrilla movement was essentially the product of several differing impulses:

- While major emphasis is placed on Iran's impact on Hizballah's formation, it is important to remember that the ideological roots of the party preceded the Islamic Republic by at least a decade with the political ideas of the Iraqi cleric Sayyid Muhammad Baqir al-Sadr and the launch of Shi'ite political activism in Najaf. Baqir al-Sadr, executed by Saddam Hussein in 1980, provided the intellectual and religious impetus for the Iraqi Da'wa (Religious Call) party and was mentor to several Lebanese Shi'ite clerics, including Sayyid Muhammad Husayn Fadhlallah, who, with others, carried the ideas of Da'wa to Lebanon. It was members of the Lebanese Da'wa who later made up an important part of the Hizballah movement, and who looked on Fadhlallah as their spiritual guide.[7] The continuing interrelationship of clerical circles across the Shi'ite world is thus striking.[8]
- Radical Lebanese Shi'ite clerical opposition to the secularization of Amal caused a group to break away from Amal and found an Islamic Amal, a forerunner of Hizballah.
- The massive Israeli invasion of Lebanon in 1982 radicalized many Shi'a in the Israeli-occupied south.
- Revolutionary Iran's entry onto the Lebanese scene after the Iranian revolution radicalized many Shi'a and provided ideological and material support that enabled Hizballah to extend its influence.

It is naturally a source of major discomfort, indeed anger, for Americans to recall Hizballah's lethal guerrilla and terrorist operations (often under the name of "Islamic Jihad") against the American presence in Lebanon between 1983 and 1986. In 1983 alone these operations included the blowing up of the American embassy, killing 69 people; the blowing up of the U.S. Marine barracks in Beirut, killing 241 Marines; the blowing up of Israeli military headquarters in Sidon, Lebanon, killing 67; and the blowing up of French paratroop headquarters, killing 58—to name only the most spectacular cases.[9] In 1984 Hizballah altered tactics to focus upon kidnappings of foreigners, including the CIA station chief, journalists, diplomats, and others, to intensify the drive to expel the foreign presence. Many of these captives were killed.

The rationale was clear: by 1984 foreign forces, and especially American, were perceived as actively participating on the side of Israel and against the Shi'a. In 1983, the United States brokered an agreement between Lebanon and Israel that was regarded by most Shi'a and Sunnis as a sellout and contrary to their interests.[10] The U.S. Marine Corps presence, originally designed to support the U.N. multinational forces in Lebanon to keep the peace, had by 1984 actively taken sides in the conflict, and were facilitating US bombardment of Druze villages in the mountains.[11] These actions on the part of the United States, perceived as de facto serving Israeli interests, triggered the violent reprisals from Hizballah that eventually led to the withdrawal of U.S. forces entirely and to the retreat of Israeli forces to a narrow "security zone" in south Lebanon. No other political/guerrilla group in the Middle East has managed to achieve such dramatic withdrawal of American and Israeli troops by force.

This is not the place to debate the complex differences of the spectrum between guerrilla warfare and terrorism. Clearly, many of Hizballah operations fall into the terrorist side of the spectrum, but the attacks on military targets, American and Israeli, would be considered by most observers as acts of guerrilla warfare against foreign troops on Lebanese soil. In either case, terrorism or guerrilla warfare was clearly sanctioned by Shaykh Muhammad Husayn Fadhlallah and other top Shi'ite clerics at the time as acts of legitimate defense—classically as the operations of the weak against the strong.[12]In the eyes of most Lebanese Muslims, those operations were probably perceived as dangerous to Lebanon, but also as a natural response of a broader Muslim guerrilla resistance against Israeli and U.S. intervention in Lebanese national affairs. At least as important in Hizballah's success was the role of Syria and Iran. The national interests of Iran and Syria especially were both clearly hostile to Israeli-U.S. interests; both states contributed powerfully to the success of Lebanese guerrillas to check Israeli and American goals in Lebanon that in any case were supported only by a small part of the Lebanese population, mainly Maronite factions.

The fact remains, however, that Hizballah guerrilla operations and suicide bombings were spectacularly successful in their political-military impact.

They blocked the U.S. project of imposing upon the Lebanese government a peace treaty with Israel in 1983 that was also opposed by a majority of the country. They forced an eventual withdrawal of U.S. military forces, the abandonment of most of Lebanon by Israeli forces, and the reestablishment of Syrian power over most of the country for strategic purposes. Regardless of how Hizballah may be viewed in the broader context of Lebanese politics, it is respected, if not feared or admired, by most citizens of Lebanon and the region for its remarkable successes against such powerful adversaries.

To what can these remarkable successes by Hizballah be attributed? Several factors contributed: first, Syrian acquiescence, facilitation, and support of such guerrilla activities; second, Iranian ideological inspiration, financing, training, and logistical support; third, the anger of a large number of Shi'a themselves who felt they were participating in a just struggle for their homeland against occupation by Israel-a country whose general goals were backed by the United States. The success of Shi'ite operations represented a first in Middle East politics, in that suicide operations were routinely employed against foreign enemies, with devastating and decisive effect.

Much is made in the West of Shi'ite tendencies toward fanaticism as a way to explain these suicide bombings. Yet Lebanese Muslims generally feel that these actions are not inherently "Shi'ite" in character but simply reflect the reality that the Shi'a had been harder pressed than any other component of Lebanon's population. Iran indeed contributed the language of martyrdom to the struggle, but the idea of self-sacrifice is hardly unknown in Sunni Islam either, in which to die in the cause of Islamic struggle, *istishhad,* is a familiar concept. Guerrilla or terrorist operations in which the attacker faced likely if not certain death were a part of earlier Palestinian modus operandi. The Muslim Brothers in Egypt in the 1950s had employed political violence, and the Shi'ite Da'wa organization in Iraq also carried out such operations, giving some inspiration to the Lebanese Shi'a as well. Suicide operations in Israel by Palestinian terrorists have also become more common in the late 1990s. (Indeed, the United States had experienced suicide operations from the Vietcong during the Vietnam War, and they have been practiced by the Sikhs in India and the Tamil Tigers in Sri Lanka.) In sum, while there is nothing uniquely Shi'ite about these operations, they did serve to give suicide operations—and especially the modus operandi of the car bomb—a new prominence in Middle East guerrilla warfare. For better or for worse, depending on the vantage point, the instruments of Middle East struggle against foreign powers have been expanded and proven effective.

More important than any Shi'ite-Sunni distinction, all these operations share a common Islamic character. The language of Islam has served to elevate political resistance to a high level of idealism and morality that exceeds that of the secular nationalist cause. The Islamic vocabulary even combines

with and reinforces the nationalist cause. Thus the Iranian contribution to
the prominence of this kind of struggle was to renew emphasis upon the religious element in political struggle. Iran did not invent these concepts; they
are latent in the annals of political struggle in Islam, indeed in any religion,
and have been used over centuries in countless conflicts.[13] The elevation of
political struggle to the religious arena found its most powerful and practical expression first in Iran and then among the Shi'a of Lebanon, while
going on to be part of the vocabulary of nearly all other Islamist political
struggles in the Middle East.

Guerrillas in Transition to Political Parties

Hizballah and Amal are the first guerrilla groups in the Arab world—except
for the PLO—to have made the transition to political parties and participants in the governing process.

Amal began in 1975 not as a political party, but as a militia organization,
designed to defend the Shi'a under conditions of growing civil war and the
militarization of all Lebanon's factions. It was the armed wing of the *Harakat
al-Mahrumin* (Movement of the Dispossessed), which was Musa al-Sadr's
original political movement, designed to lift the Shi'a from the status of un-
derdog and to integrate them into society. The immediate military threat to
the Shi'a was the confrontation in southern Lebanon with Palestinian guerrillas who had fled to Lebanon after expulsion from Jordan in 1970, and
who sought to pursue the guerrilla war against Israel from southern
Lebanese territory where a majority of Shi'a lived. The name "Amal" (Hope)
is in fact an acronym for the Lebanese Resistance Brigades (Afwaj al-
Muqawama al-Lubnaniyya)—a name that significantly possesses neither
Shi'ite nor religious content. The absence of a declared religious agenda was
one of the factors that facilitated Amal's eventual move toward secularism as
a party after 1980.

Amal's initial focus thus was a military one as an adjunct to al-Sadr's political movement. Musa al-Sadr by this time had also established a Higher
Muslim Shi'ite Council (*al-Majlis al-Islami al-Shi'i al-A'la*), which had been
recognized by the state as the formal body representing the full spectrum of
the Shi'ite community at large. But as the civil war progressed in intensity
and with Musa al-Sadr's own disappearance, Amal gradually took on the role
of primary political vehicle for the Shi'a, until challenged by breakaway religious factions in the early 1980s that eventually formed Hizballah.

By this time, Amal had set itself up as a defender of Shi'ite interests in the
south against Palestinian and Israeli attacks, and also as a protector of hundreds of thousands of Shi'a who had to escape the repeated onslaughts of Israeli forces and seek shelter in the crowded neighborhoods of south and

southwest Beirut. Amal also acquired political recognition and status within the chaotic Lebanese political-military scene and by the vestigial central government. In 1982, when a National Salvation Committee was formed, Amal was invited to participate; in 1989, Amal was one of the Lebanese parties involved the negotiation of the Ta'if Accord. Hizballah, however, did not attend the Ta'if meetings.

Hizballah's transition from guerrilla movement to political party was far more complex and difficult than Amal's transition, mainly due to its vital links to Iran and subordination in many respects to Iranian pressures and policies. Israel's invasions of Lebanon, first in 1978 and more massively in 1982, offered Iran the first serious opportunity, via Lebanon, to engage in a confrontation with the Zionist state. Lebanese Shi'a had previously had little to do with Israel, and indeed initially many of them believed the Israelis could even be helpful in lessening or eliminating Palestinian pressure upon them in southern Lebanon. The Israeli invasion, however, rapidly changed the complexion of Shi'ite political attitudes toward Israel. In a massive miscalculation and misreading of the Shi'ite community, Israel actually managed to turn the Shi'a from being a community potentially sympathetic toward Israel into one of the chief victims of Israeli actions in the regional conflict, and eventually broadly hostile to Israel. Hundreds of thousands of Shi'a were forced to flee their homes and lands and to take refuge in the ghettoes of southern Beirut. It was in this environment that Hizballah was formed.

In 1982 the Islamic Republic of Iran was still deep in its original revolutionary fervor and relished an opportunity to take a direct part in the struggle against Israel. Israel's invasion of the south, the destruction of much of the region in the conflict, and the long-term Israeli occupation of one-eighth of Lebanon's territory presented Iran the perfect opportunity. Iran provided weapons to the newly formed Hizballah militias, provided training from the large presence of Iranian Revolutionary Guard in the Biqa' valley, and financing, that enabled Hizballah to conduct guerrilla operations as well as social programs for large parts of the Shi'ite population.

Iran's influence over Hizballah reflected not only Iranian ambitions in the confrontation with Israel, but also factional struggles within Iran itself. Amal's long-time Iranian supporters had lost out politically in Iran in the early 1980s, leaving Iranian radical activists in strong support of the Hizballah alternative. Iran had initially sought to take over Amal by infiltrating it with radical clerics in order to make it more responsive to Iran's agenda; indeed, Islamic Amal was a breakaway organization from Amal that eventually became Hizballah. Where Amal had opposed PLO activities in southern Lebanon, Iran supported the PLO—as did Syria even more—as an instrument against Israel. Whereas Amal was growing more secular, Hizballah called for an Islamic state in Lebanon. When Amal agreed in 1982 to join the National Salvation Committee to try to solve Lebanon's deepening crisis, the more radical Islamist members, supported by Iran, denounced participation in the committee as capitulation to Western and Israeli pressure. Amal under the new leadership of Nabih Birri had also grown dependent upon and highly responsive to Syrian policies, whereas Iran sought to make Hizballah responsive to Tehran's agenda. Hizballah's own policies—particularly as related to later kidnappings of Westerners in Lebanon—demonstrated the ascendancy of the radical Khomeini faction in Iran and its arm, the Revolutionary Guard (Pasdaran) in Lebanon. Thus Amal-Hizballah rivalries came to reflect, among other things, a degree of Syrian-Iranian rivalry even as the two countries shared a common anti-Israeli policy and supported one another for common tactical goals.[14]

The personal, ideological, organizational, and international rivalries led Amal and Hizballah to confrontation during most of the 1980s, and the two militias fought a particularly bloody conflict from 1988 to 1990, in which allegedly more people were killed than in any intersectarian fighting. In addition, throughout the 1980s Hizballah was engaged in resistance to the Israeli occupation in the south, while Amal also became involved in major battles around Beirut to protect Shi'ite turf and community interests against other sectarian groups. Maronite Christian militias were intent upon expelling the Shi'a from key areas of both northern and southern Beirut, and Amal was the primary armed Shi'ite force to resist this effort, eventually losing out in north Beirut, but keeping the south. However, Hizballah soon displaced Amal from many areas of south Beirut that Amal had fought hard to retain. South and southwest Beirut have settled into a tense mosaic of Amal and Hizballah enclaves.

It was only in October 1989 that the deadly 15-year civil war in Lebanon was brought to an end with the Ta'if Accord, brokered by a coalition of Arab states and Syria—the most important political event in Lebanon since the outbreak of conflict; Ta'if continues to provide the foundation for the evolving but still peaceful relations among all sectarian communities. The war had involved all major sectarian communities of Lebanon, most of whom had also been assisted (or manipulated) by external forces with an interest in Lebanon's internal struggle and in the international implications of its outcome. Leading the states interested the Lebanese conflict were Syria, Israel, Iran, and the United States, as well as Iraq, Libya, and Saudi Arabia to a lesser extent. Amal participated in the Ta'if process, whereas Hizballah condemned the accord as "a deadly repetition of the sin committed in 1943"—a reference to the National Pact crafted under the auspices of the French mandate. In 1992, however, Hizballah implicitly accepted the provisions of Ta'if when it decided to run in the national elections.

By 1989, when Amal had already developed into a clear-cut political party, Hizballah was still a radical movement outside the mainstream of Lebanese politics. Hizballah's transition to the political arena was more painful than Amal's, reflecting a need for greater ideological and strategic changes. In 1989 the emergence of Rafsanjani as president in Iran, with his more moderate agenda, began to put pressure on Hizballah to end its hostage-taking policies. Even more important, Syria no longer had need for these tactics by Hizballah, since it was in the process of securing its Pax Syriana over Lebanon. A deal was struck among Iran, Syria, and Hizballah that would bring an end to hostage-taking, would permit Hizballah to retain an armed capability (Iran's goal), but would limit its armed activities to confronting the Israeli occupation of Lebanon (Syria's interest).[15] By 1992, with a change in the leadership of Hizballah due to the assassination of its leading cleric by the Israelis, Hizballah decided to strengthen its hand in the political arena as well, by fielding candidates for the new parliamentary elections. Hizballah calculated that such a shift was necessary for its survival and legitimacy in the post–civil war environment. This shift also indicated increasing skepticism on the part of many leading clerics within Hizballah about the appropriateness of seeking an Islamic state in Lebanon, a skepticism endorsed by Sayyid Husayn Fadhlallah, whose views on an Islamist agenda in Lebanon were becoming less doctrinal and more pragmatic during this period.

Both Amal and Hizballah participated in the parliamentary elections of 1992 and later in 1996 and sent deputies to the parliament. Hizballah's participation in these elections had not been, of course, a foregone conclusion, since it had been critical of the Ta'if Accord and had never officially abandoned its long-range goal of making Lebanon an Islamic State. Doctrinally, Hizballah was opposed to the status quo which provided the framework for the elections. Yet actual participation in the elections by Hizballah indicated de facto acceptance of the existing political order, or at least a willingness to work within its framework to pursue change. Hizballah candidates actually gained eight seats in the 1992 elections and had support from a further four unaffiliated deputies, in part bolstered by its formidable social programs, which had been funded by Iran.

A further sign of Hizballah's shift into the "establishment" was its signal to the Lebanese government that it would be acceptable to use military force to oppose a breakaway leader of Hizballah who attempted a showdown with the government in the Biqa' Valley. Shaykh Subhi al-Tufayli, its former secretary-general, broke ranks with Hizballah over its participation in parliamentary elections in 1992. In mid-1997 his "Movement of the Hungry" sought to rally the poor and the jobless in the Biqa' region, one of the poorer parts of Lebanon dominated by Shi'a, seriously challenging both Hizballah and the

Lebanese government.[16] Tufayli's tactics included efforts to block the roads to the Lebanese military in a civil resistance movement. After many months of negotiations, Hizballah gave the green light to the government to permit it to use force to end the civil disobedience and to open the highways. The army would never have attempted to move against Tufayli if he had still been part of Hizballah or if Hizballah had backed him. Thus Hizballah ended up cooperating with the government against one of its own renegades who still sought to pursue a radical agenda.

On a more worrisome note, however, neither Amal nor Hizballah has abandoned its militia. In classic accordance with its own complex political agenda, Syria permits Hizballah to remain armed because of the great interest that Damascus has in maintaining the resistance and pressure against Israel. At the same time, both militias are also operating in a fully political mode within the political system. For Hizballah the armed resistance remains its chief source of legitimacy and domestic support among the Shi'a, a role grudgingly accepted even by Hizballah's opponents and by nearly all elements of the country who acknowledge that elimination of the Israeli occupation is a national task; in 1998 there were still some 1,200 Israeli Defence Force (IDF) soldiers and 3,000 South Lebanon Army (SLA)—Israeli-supported Lebanese Christian paramilitary forces—militiamen in Southern Lebanon. And as long as Syria has no peace with Israel, the Israeli presence can only be eliminated by resistance or unilateral Israeli departure rather than by a peace treaty. This reality gives Hizballah a continuing stake in the Israeli presence.

A key political question remains: What will be the position and role of Hizballah in Shi'ite and Lebanese politics on the inevitable day that Israel unilaterally withdraws from the south—or that a peace treaty is signed? (That day may be approaching, as Israeli politicians debate ever more sharply the army's presence in the south in what has been a costly and largely failed operation in the eyes of large numbers of Israelis. Casualties on both sides—Israel and its Christian militia versus Hizballah—have been nearly equal in recent years.) What will be the source of Hizballah's political strength once the guerrilla activities—widely recognized in Lebanon as both brave and effective—have come to an end?

Syria almost certainly will not permit Hizballah to remain indefinitely the sole armed faction within Lebanese politics. Yet Hizballah spokesmen speak confidently of their already deep involvement in Lebanese politics—with six engaged and active members of parliament after the 1996 elections and possible inclusion in the cabinet in the near future. They also point to their ideological strength of offering a coherent vision about the role of Islamic ideals in governance, particularly as they affect the popular welfare. At this point Hizballah enjoys major strength in its dedication to social programs and its challenge to the largely corrupt spoils system of the current Lebanese political order. In short, Hizballah feels that its base of political action and support will remain unaffected by an end to the resistance—especially if the resistance is successful in achieving its aim of driving out the Israelis. Hizballah will attempt to carve a niche for itself as the "moral conscience" of the Lebanese political system, championing the needy and dispossessed and advocating welfare programs. Israeli specialists believe Iran has already withdrawn financial support from all but Hizballah's guerrilla activities in the south, leaving it on its own in its political programs as a Lebanese party. Political and ideological differences nonetheless remain within Hizballah, and not all members accept pragmatic choices. With the 1997 election of President Khatami in Iran, Tehran is likely to play a restraining and moderating role within Hizballah, unlike the radical role it had played in the 1980s.

Thus we see over a nearly two-decade period an interesting and important transition of Hizballah from guerrilla movement to political party, an evolution not often witnessed elsewhere in the Middle East, apart from Palestinian politics. While so far a limited phenomenon, it perhaps offers some encouraging reflections on the influence of democratization on political movements.

Amal as Part of the Mainstream

Through participation in the post-Ta'if Lebanese political order, Nabih Birri, the leader of the Amal movement and currently speaker of the Lebanese parliament, has now become the most powerful Shi'ite official in the Arab world. Amal is far more deeply involved in the political process than Hizballah, with 8 official members of parliament and an additional 13 deputies who support Amal, and are largely committed to the Amal program (the Amal bloc is said to be the largest in parliament). Additionally, Amal has cabinet seats and representation throughout the bureaucratic system. Birri, a charismatic and energetic individual, is a full member of the ruling national troika and in some senses may wield more sheer political power than the other two (the Maronite president and the Sunni Muslim prime minister). In his role as speaker of parliament—guaranteed for four years, unlike the prime minister, who could be defeated at any time—Birri is able to initiate or block all legislation and to oversee nearly all distributive functions of the government in terms of finances and appointments. He is the gateway to any political office in the country for any Shi'ite. Amal's strength, then, has become firmly institutionalized and already firmly established within the redistributive functions of the political order, even if it lacks any clear ideological vision. (It is possible that this powerful role may yet be challenged by some Maronite groups aspiring to restore some of the early Maronite domination of the system.)

While Birri is still critical of the system, he works solidly within it. Part of Amal's strength derives from the close relationship developed between its leader, Birri, and the Syrian regime. The relationship with Syria originated with Musa al-Sadr, but Birri maintained and deepened it through the years of conflict and after 1989. It is not insignificant that Birri heads the Board for Reconstruction of the South (*Majlis I'mar al-Janub*), the government-funded agency that is charged with rebuilding and improving the infrastructure of southern Lebanon, which is backward at best and battered by decades of Israeli incursions and factional Lebanese warfare. The board has authority for improving roads and communication networks, schools, hospitals, and other social service sectors. The board not only allocates funds but awards contracts to Lebanese contractors. Birri's control of the board places him at a unique advantage in dispensing patronage and favor to actual and potential supporters, and in portraying himself as the benefactor of the southern Shi'a. Thus Birri has backed into the pattern of patron-client relationship that dominated Lebanese politics prior to the civil war (and still does to a certain extent), and his image is in danger of shading into the traditional profile of the Shi'ite barons whose grip on the south he helped to break.

The contrast between Amal's political strategies and the strategies of Hizballah is reflected in their respective constituencies. Amal appeals to the generation of Shi'a who have had a longer history of settlement in Beirut and its suburbs and have already acquired a vested interest in the system by enrolling in the government bureaucracy or building their own enterprises. This sector of Shi'a is relatively more ambitious, more integrated into Lebanese society, and certainly less doctrinally Islamist. Hizballah's following is predominantly in southern Lebanon and in the newly created Shi'ite enclaves in south Beirut, populated by recently arrived refugees from the south, who are economically disadvantaged and usually direct victims of Israeli raids on southern Lebanon. Hizballah provides a financial safety net for this constituency through health and education services, subsidies, and direct stipends to families of *shuhada*, martyrs who have died as a consequence of the conflict with Israel.

The transition made by both Amal and Hizballah from a predominantly militia role into politics and governance is highly unusual in the Arab world. What has made this possible in Lebanon? First, the longtime relative deprivation of the Shi'ite community made it a candidate for rapid and dynamic evolution when given the right leadership. Its sheer momentum in moving to assert its rightful place (in accordance with its demographic weight) has provided it an élan that is worrisome to more static communities anxious to preserve the benefits of the status quo. Yet redress of grievances is not enough to provide ongoing power and authority to a community. The development of armed Shi'ite militias—parallel to the various Christian,

Druze, and Sunni militias—also played a key role in the emergence of Shi'ite power in the context of the harsh and violent events the country has undergone. These military confrontations were galvanizing actions that helped create social, political, and military responses among the Shi'a.

The quasi-democratic character of Lebanon's past and the inability of any one faction in the country to prevail over the others have been additional important factors enabling these militia movements to evolve into political organizations. In short, the opportunity for community mobilization and action has led to a natural transition from militia to political party. Finally, Syria's role in Lebanese politics should not be underemphasized. Syria's obsession with maintaining the balance of power within Lebanon has led it to be alternately permissive toward the Shi'a in some circumstances, and to limit any unbridled quest for Shi'ite sectarian power in others.

The Transition Away from an Islamic State

Hizballah is the first Shi'ite Islamist movement that appears to have evolved from fully embracing Khomeini's goal of an Islamic state to becoming a pragmatic political movement that accepts and is willing to work within a society that includes not only Sunni Muslims but also a large Christian population. This transition is important not only in studying the evolution of Shi'ite religious organizations, but in the broader annals of Islamist movements.

Lebanon, of course, represents a special religious context. In Lebanon there is no state religion, but state and religion are not separated and cannot be separated. There are as many as 19 recognized and established confessions, and the sectarian system distributes power and political perquisites along the lines of these recognized religious communities. In this sense, we are not talking about a struggle between secular and Islamist forces as we do in many other Middle Eastern states, but of a balance of forces distributed throughout the system.

Of interest here is the apparent transition that Hizballah has made away from the goal of an Islamic state to acceptance of a multireligious state in which a conventional Islamic agenda would be out of keeping. How did such a transition come about in Hizballah and what are its broader implications?

When Hizballah was founded in the early 1980s it demonstrated an absolute commitment to the establishment of an Islamic state, led by clerical elements formerly part of Amal and others who rejected the secularization of that movement and followed more closely the ideology of Khomeini and Iranian directives. Like Amal, Hizballah was never a tight monolithic body but rather an umbrella for many like-minded groups who did not agree in all respects:

[Hizballah] brings together all of those fledgling groups that see Iran as their model and Khomeini as their leader. On the one hand, Hizballah is a palpable organization that receives orders and directions from Iran; yet, on the other, it is a fluid collection of groups over which Iran's real influence may be only nominal.[17]

Tehran's stamp upon Hizballah was quite explicit from the outset, in ideology and assistance. The clerics who founded the movement were close to the Islamic Republic and accepted the Islamist vision of the new Iran. This included acceptance of the notion of *wilayat al-faqih,* or clerical rule, in an avowedly Islamic state. The wide presence of the Ayatollah Khomeini's portrait in Shi'ite neighborhoods in Lebanon—often alongside portraits of Musa al-Sadr—demonstrate Hizballah's commitment to Khomeini's line of political thought, often referred to as the "Imam's Line" (Khatt al-Imam). Khomeini had a radical vision of the Iranian Islamic Republic, including its commitment to export of the revolution, the leading role of the clergy in directing state policies, and the eventual goal of working toward a pan-Islamic state, the "defining characteristic of [Hizballah's] relationship with Iran."[18] Hizballah's pan-Islamic vision was encapsulated in a four-stage strategy articulated in a 1985 manifesto: "armed confrontation with Israel; overthrow of the Lebanese regime; the liberation from any form of intervention by the Great Powers in Lebanon; and finally the establishment of Islamic rule in Lebanon which will be joined by other Muslims in the creation of a greater Islamic community."[19]

Throughout its first decade, Hizballah explicitly called for an Islamic state in Lebanon, declaring that, despite the multireligious, multisectarian character of Lebanese society, an Islamic state could be attained over time—not imposed by force, but through persuasion, education, and conversion. A key Hizballah proclamation to the "downtrodden of the world" on February 16, 1985, set forth Hizballah's broad policies, including the statement that

we do not hide our commitment to the rule of Islam and that we urge to choose the Islamic system that alone guarantees justice and dignity for all and prevents any new imperialist attempt to infiltrate our country. . . . We do not wish to impose Islam on anybody and we hate to see others impose on us their convictions and their systems. We do not want Islam to rule in Lebanon by force, as political Maronism is ruling at present. But we stress that we are convinced of Islam as a faith, system, thought, and rule and we urge all to recognize it and to resort to its law. We also urge them to adopt it and abide by its teachings at the individual, political, and social levels. If our people get the opportunity to choose Lebanon's system of government freely, they will favor no alternative to Islam.[20]

For all its emphasis on achieving an Islamic state, Hizballah has always contained considerable internal factionalism, usually reflecting ideological splits within Tehran itself. Much of this debate was over questions of tactics—especially the controversial hostage-taking—rather than about ideology itself. A debate over possible participation in Lebanese elections started within Hizballah in 1990 following the cease-fire brought by the Ta'if Accord.[21] The more radical faction represented by the then secretary general of the party, Subhi al-Tufayli, regarded the Lebanese state as illegitimate and therefore opposed endorsing it by participation in elections. The more pragmatic wing favored working within the political system by fielding candidates.

Hizballah's decision to enter parliamentary elections came despite its opposition in principle to political sectarianism within Lebanon—an objection it still maintains. Yet this objection need not be linked with Shi'ite theology or even Islam per se. A broad range of Lebanese thinkers—particularly secularists—have long opposed the country's system of political sectarianism that mandates rigid proportional representation at all levels of the national government. This philosophical opposition, primarily from elites, comes from liberals, leftists, and conservatives alike, but they have not been able to present their philosophical or practical objections to the system with sufficient persuasion to overcome both habit and the entrenched parochial interests of group benefits derived from the present system.

Hizballah apparently opted to forgo a revolutionary approach to gaining power in Lebanon and instead to work within the existing system. None of this signifies change in the party's long-range aspirations to eliminate sectarian politics, a goal shared by Amal, and indeed by many elements in other Lebanese sects as well—at least in principle. The critical question is what kind of system should replace the existing order, and how. Because any change of the present political system will obviously create winners and losers, not all groups, especially smaller ones, are willing to trade today's known benefits for tomorrow's uncertainties.

Hizballah's apparent acceptance of the present Lebanese political order is probably an encouraging indicator that it is evolving and no longer has a serious revolutionary agenda for the country. But of course there can be no guarantees. As long as Hizballah retains a formidable armed militia, the party still evokes nervousness among many other Lebanese as to whether it may simply be concealing a longer range radical agenda and a willingness at some point to employ violence if necessary. From the beginning, "Hizballah's pan-Islamic revolutionary struggle has been predicated on Islam's triumphs in adjacent territories, spearheaded by . . . Iran."[22] Such a vision, however, represents long-term ideal goals lacking much realism; its lack of realism 20 years after the Iranian revolution may therefore explain Hizballah's willingness over time to adopt more pragmatic policies in consonance with Lebanese conditions. The Sunnis themselves were not completely exempt from these same ideological goals: as the civil war began to intensify, the chief Sunni religious institution, Dar al-Fatwa, issued a fatwa stating, "The true Muslim in Lebanon could only be loyal to what Islam imposes on him, including the establishment of a Muslim state."[23]

Despite whatever pan-Islamist views Hizballah may have espoused in the 1980s, in 1997 Hizballah leader Shaykh Hasan Nasrallah stated, "Hizballah is a part or movement with Lebanese members and Lebanese leaders who take Lebanese decisions. It fights on Lebanese soil to liberate Lebanese territory for the sake of the honor and freedom of the Lebanese people and the entire nation. We reject this accusation [that Hizballah is "Iran's party"] and say that Hizballah is by any gauge a Lebanese Islamist movement."[24]

Hizballah, of course, represents the most radical wing of Lebanese Shi'ism, but it is not the only Shi'ite group with a religious focus. The supreme official body of all Lebanese Shi'a has an unambiguously religious designation—the Higher Islamic Shi'ite Council (*al-Majlis al-Islami al-Shi'i al-A'la*). In March 1997, Shaykh Muhammad Mahdi Shamseddin, the council's head and the de jure spokesman for the entire Shi'ite community,

> seemed to hint that he was opposed to the creation of a single Shi'ite political bloc in Lebanon and instead favored greater intercommunal cooperation to overcome the sectarian tensions inflamed by the 1975–1990 civil war. [The Council] was created not just to end political discrimination and socioeconomic disadvantage from which the Shi'ite community suffered, but also to uphold Lebanon's national unity which the confessional system had harmed. . . .
>
> On the first issue, the Council believes it has succeeded. There is no longer disadvantage [for the Shi'a] on the political front, in terms of participation in the regime and in government. There is no longer an inferior position. . . . It is now up to the Shi'ites themselves to shoulder their responsibilities sincerely, capably and responsibly, and to treat the state's program as their own. . . .
>
> Shamseddin said that while in principle he would like to see [the political sectarian system] ditched in favor of a purely meritocratic one, he realized this could not be done quickly. . . . "I believe that to proceed now with a formal, legal, constitutional decision to abolish political confessionalism would create new problems of acclimatization for us." . . . Instead Shamseddin said he preferred a two-track approach. Action to tackle "sectarianism in the mind" through education and intercommunal dialogue, coupled with the gradual introduction of laws designed to reduce the number of state jobs . . . that are allocated on a sectarian basis.
>
> Shamseddin added that he saw much scope for Moslems and Christians to work together as partners in faith on contemporary global issues, ranging from political questions with moral overtones such as nuclear arms proliferation, to the moral and spiritual problems posed by developments, such as genetic research and cloning.[25]

It is clear, therefore, that by overwhelming consensus, the Shi'ite community in Lebanon, including the two major Shi'ite parties, has come to a modus vivendi with the present Lebanese state specifically as constituted in the Ta'if Accord of 1989 that ended the Lebanese civil war.

For Amal, an acceptance of the new political order after Ta'if has not been difficult since Amal under Birri's leadership has long been non-ideological and has benefited immensely by working within the new system, and its ability to control much of the distribution of the largesse of the state. For Hizballah the Ta'if Accord presents less direct benefits. Hizballah believes, for example, that the Shi'a were shortchanged in Ta'if, given their numbers and their "sacrifices for the liberation of Lebanon."[26] But the fact of its co-operation is there. Non-Shi'ite observers, even Christian MPs, point out that Hizballah deputies work seriously and constructively in parliamentary working groups. They show up at all meetings, are well prepared, and are interested in reaching constructive conclusions. Hizballah is, in fact, now widely accepted by nearly all in Lebanon as a normal fact of political life, even where suspicions or fears about it may still reside.

Debate nonetheless remains about whether Hizballah is "sincere" in joining the political process or simply is playing along for a longer-term, more radical agenda. It could be argued that actions are usually more powerful than ideology as indicators of goals. Furthermore, political parties and movements that have had to adapt to certain political norms for tactical reasons frequently end up with a stake in those norms over time. In the end, the question of sincerity is less relevant than the actual conduct and performance of Hizballah within Lebanon's political system. Moreover, this question applies to political parties everywhere when there is a gap between party ideals and aspirations on the one hand and the forces of reality on the other. The democratic system is predicated on just such cooptation. Hizballah's accommodation is clearly demonstrated in its involvement in the workings of state politics. Doubts about the "real intentions" of any other of the Lebanese political parties can be raised as well, based on their past positions or aspirations—for example, hopes among some Maronites to eventually restore their previous long-term domination of the political order, or hopes among some Sunnis that future restoration of Sunni power in Syria could elevate the Lebanese Sunnis to the top of the Lebanese political order. It is perhaps Hizballah's exceptionally violent past and once intimate links with a foreign power that quite rightly perpetuate doubt about the party's commitment to a new, nonviolent, nonsectarian democratic order. Even today Hizballah says it hopes that one day an Islamic state will be recognized by all as an enlightened form of government for all of Lebanon. The party would still like to see the state agree to uphold religious values in general, as a broader goal of Islamists.

Any change of heart by Hizballah must be seen in the broader context of change within the region. Time and the harshness of the civil war may have softened its own revolutionary zeal, a softening evident even among many of its senior clerics such as Fadhlallah. Lebanon's civil war is over. Hizballah has had some success in the democratic political arena. The party is still able to pursue its quest for the armed liberation of Lebanon from Israeli occupation. Syria no longer tolerates armed political conflict within Lebanon with the securing of its Pax Syriana. And Iran has been moving toward considerably greater moderation of its own pan-Islamist ideology and toward practical foreign relations. Finally, a reality of Lebanon has always been its exposure to the West, its sophisticated and urban way of life, its multisectarian character that makes it different from many other states in the Muslim world. It is simply prudent—but not necessarily a foregone conclusion—that Hizballah should come to accept these realities. A new Lebanon presents the requirement to adapt to its realities.

In short, Hizballah seems to have moved toward acceptance of the existing multireligious political order and the new regional political realities. If Hizballah is in fact responding to changes on the ground, for whatever reasons, the mellowing of its revolutionary zeal represents an important milestone in the evolution of Shi'ite and Islamist political thinking and action in the late twentieth century.

Shi'ite Relations with Sunnis

The political system of Lebanon today is dominated by a three-way rivalry among the Shi'a, the Sunnis, and the Maronite Christians of Lebanon. From a Maronite Christian point of view the Shi'a and the Sunnis are both Muslim and hence equal rivals to Christian power in Lebanon. In the first decade of the rise of the Shi'a, the Maronites hoped that the Shi'a might be their allies against the Sunnis, who had traditionally been the chief challengers to the Maronites. Indeed, the Sunnis once were the sole sect strongly backed and empowered by the surrounding world of Arab Sunni governments and the forces of Arab nationalism outside the country, and potentially most able to overturn the Lebanese political order. Maronites and Shi'a, therefore, appeared to share minority status in the greater Arab Sunni world.

However, following the implementation of the Ta'if Accord and the full incorporation of Amal and Hizballah into the political system, Maronite sentiment may be changing. New Maronite (and Sunni) fears arise from the fact that the Shi'a are a plurality in Lebanon and from the sheer dynamism of Shi'ite empowerment. Syria is interested in maintaining a balance of forces in Lebanon and is not likely to grant any particular sect advantage over all the others except as a temporary phase in an ever-shifting balancing game. Nevertheless, Amal appears to have forged a close alliance with the Syrian regime for onward of a decade and does not exhibit the same resentment of Syrian influence in Lebanon expressed by many Maronites. Hizballah also enjoys restrained backing from Syria, and although Iranian support has waned, it is still evident. The Maronites, therefore, may be in the process of reassessing their attitudes toward the Shi'a in a more complex set of calculations than those that prevailed in the 1970s, when the Shi'a were a weaker presence. It is too early to tell whether the equilibrium that now exists (thanks in part to Syria) can be sustained: the Sunnis, Maronites, and Shi'a are in a continuous process of evaluation of their relative strength, and even minimal, temporary shifts in alliances are scrutinized for their implications.

Although Musa al-Sadr made every effort to forge good terms with the Sunni establishment in Lebanon, some sense of rivalry was present from the start. The Shi'a, after all, had been persecuted in Lebanon under Turkish rule during the Ottoman empire as heterodox Muslims—distinctly beneath even the legally protected status of Christians as recognized minorities within the empire. Al-Sadr was sympathetic to the Palestinian plight as the preeminent Muslim international cause, and he never preached an anti-Sunni message. But with the move of Palestinian guerrillas into southern Lebanon, the Shi'a were physically threatened and drawn inexorably into the Palestinian-Israeli battleground. At the same time, some Sunnis in Lebanon were drawn into Sunni Islamist movements that attempted to bolster their Islamist legitimacy through ideological attacks against the Shi'a as "not-quite Muslims." Indeed, one Sunni cleric declared it was licit to spill Shi'ite blood.[27]

Given Shi'ite hostility to the encroachments and the often high-handed behavior of the Palestinians in southern Lebanon, it was difficult for the Shi'a to avoid being cast in an anti-Sunni role. It was the Israeli invasion of 1982 that helped end this ambiguity, as the Shi'a themselves began to move heavily into the anti-Israeli resistance, thereby winning back to some degree their Islamic and Arab legitimacy. The later withdrawal in 1982 of the PLO from Lebanon under international aegis removed the proximate cause of Shi'ite-Sunni conflict. Since that time, Shi'ite-Sunni relations have improved greatly, particularly with Syria's blessing to both as key elements in the confrontation with Israel.

The Shi'a have a number of advantages over the Sunnis. They are more active in forming and working through religious institutions than are the Sunnis. Lebanese Shi'ite clerics are more highly regarded as thinkers on Islamic issues than are Lebanese Sunni clerics.[28] Whereas Shi'ite clerics are players in the political arena, Sunni clerics do not possess the same stature in Lebanon, or they prefer not to enter into Sunni politics to the same extent. Another critical factor favoring the Shi'a is the special political support they draw from Syria. Given the minoritarian character of the Syrian regime ('Alawi, or heterodox-Shi'ite), Syria has a strong interest in maintaining Shi'ite power in Lebanon while keeping Sunni power at bay, lest it make eventual cause with the Sunni majority in Syria in upsetting 'Alawi rule. Finally, the role of other Sunni Arab states such as Egypt, Libya, and Iraq has diminished in Lebanese politics, depriving the Sunnis of other sources of political support.

Even though most Sunnis in Lebanon acknowledge that they too have been among the major losers in the Shi'ite rise to power, the Shi'a have avoided casting their movement in any kind of anti-Sunni context. Indeed, the Shi'a are acutely conscious of the need to shore up the legitimacy of their credentials as orthodox Muslims—an almost obsessive anxiety among many Shi'a across the Muslim world. The name of the supreme representative body for all Lebanese Shi'a—the Higher Islamic Shi'ite Council—expresses this desire for broader legitimacy.

Since its establishment, the Higher Islamic Shi'ite Council under Shaykh Mahdi Shamseddin has worked assiduously to cooperate with the Sunni community. Some would say Shamseddin clearly acts as a Muslim spokesman, rather than strictly a Shi'ite spokesman. The Shi'ite Council cooperates with the Dar al-Fatwa, the Sunni clerical center in Lebanon. Shamseddin has also initiated a Summit of Islamic Leaders of Lebanon to institutionalize regular meetings between Shi'ite and Sunni clerics on national issues of concern. A key goal is to show the Shi'a as active participants within a broader Muslim context. In the eyes of Lebanese Sunnis, furthermore, Shaykh Shamseddin is the most "Arab" and Lebanese of Lebanon's Shi'ite clerics—unlike Shaykh Fadhlallah, who is now more intent on building major international stature as a Shi'ite thinker. Shamseddin was received at al-Azhar, the center of Sunni jurisprudence in Cairo. He also enjoys direct contact and influence with the Saudi government, which traditionally remains cool in cooperation with Shi'a of any kind. In the past, Shamseddin has also expressed interest in serving as an intermediary between the Bahraini Shi'ite community and the ruling al-Khalifa family in Bahrain.[29]

Present conditions in Lebanon have thus brought the Shi'a and the Sunnis closer together. But the newfound rapprochement may not yet be solidly based. Sunni-Shi'ite rivalry remains objectively grounded in Lebanese sectarian rivalry—the heart of the system. The situation could change markedly under new political conditions. If the Ta'if Accord breaks down, or if it is fundamentally challenged by any of the key sectarian players, conflict could reemerge in which the Shi'a might push for full reflection of their demographic plurality within the political order.

More serious, when eventual crisis occurs within the power base of the minoritarian 'Alawi regime in Syria, sectarian tensions between Shi'a and Sunnis in Lebanon will be directly and heavily affected as the Sunnis attempt to regain power in Syria. Under such circumstances, Lebanese Sunnis could seek to tip the balance against Shi'ite power in Lebanon. In effect, the presence of Syria, Iran, and Israel in Lebanon distorts the true political realities and balances of sectarian power within the state. These three countries have for all intents and purposes molded the political configuration of Lebanon in the past two decades. It is difficult to speculate how a Lebanon fully independent of these major intervening factors would sort out the sectarian issue.

In the meantime, however, Shi'a and Sunnis in Lebanon have reached a modus vivendi. Like so many other conflicts in Lebanon, one hopes that the lessons of the Lebanese civil war and the subsequent settlement have been taken to heart by all and that a true Shi'ite-Sunni coexistence has come into being. The sad reality is that, in daily practice, Lebanon is more deeply in the grip of political (and social) sectarianism today than at any time in the past. Sectarianism penetrates the school system, hospitals, TV channels, the court system, the bureaucracy, and almost every aspect of public life. Lebanese of different confessions acknowledge that sectarianism is more deeply entrenched now than prior to the civil war. Thus the question remains whether coexistence will be strengthened by sectarianism or by its elimination. Shi'ite-Sunni cooperation, especially at the clerical level and on national issues, has not been commonplace in the Muslim world and is an encouraging first step. Perhaps only in Kuwait has a similar beginning been made toward cooperation between the sects, especially in the context of a genuinely open parliament in which sectarianism is not practiced.

The Future of the Lebanese Shi'a

With the rise of Shi'ite power in Lebanon, Shaykh Muhammad Hussein Fadhlallah has emerged as the leading Arab Shi'ite cleric. After a decade of close adherence to the Iranian vision of the Islamic state, the rule of the clerics, and the "Imam's line," Fadhlallah has assumed a far more independent role. He is in the process of acquiring a position of religious authority in Lebanon and the broader Arab Shi'ite world that would rival the ayatollahs of Iran. His new vision of the role of the Shi'a in a multi-sectarian state departs from Iran's earlier views, as does his ruling on many other issues. Such issues include his official rejection of a time-honored Shi'ite belief that the Caliph 'Umar in the seventh century had mistreated the Prophet's daughter ('Umar being an object of traditional Shi'ite dislike). He has also addressed controversial contemporary issues on aspects of female sexuality. Fadhlallah is widely believed to be developing a following that would entitle him to the role of a marji'. There are few if any Arab marji'—not to mention Iranian marji'—who enjoy the political and intellectual freedom to speak out on politico-religious issues today in ways that challenge the dominant "Imam's line" in Iran. Fadhlallah's newly emerging authority and role will undoubtedly challenge Iran's desire to dominate Shi'ite discourse across the Arab world, and he has already drawn criticism from Iranian clerics.

The question is whether Iran will be able to monopolize all Shi'ite theological thinking indefinitely, as it has for decades with the suppression of Shi'ite clerics in Iraq and the decline of Najaf. The Lebanese Shi'a may have been quiescent and isolated in the Shi'ite world for centuries, but it is important to remember that they played a critical role in supplying eminent clerics and mujtahid to the newly founded Safavid dynasty in Iran in 1500, and helped bring Shi'ism to the broad body of the Iranian population, which knew little of Shi'ism and required religious instruction and new institutions. Will the Lebanese Shi'ite community, after centuries of isolation, come to represent a new international Shi'ite center in its own right, enriched by ideas of accommodation with the modern realities of democratic practice and multireligious society in a Westernized state?

The political contribution of the Shi'ite movements in Lebanon addresses secular rather than religious issues. Shi'ite members of parliament and the cabinet speak of economic and social policies, not the religious policies of the state. They are more interested in the configuration of power than in its religious content. Hizballah's concern with social issues may be driven by its effort to promote its religious ideology, but its arguments are rarely shaped in Islamist terms. Musa al-Sadr saw his mission in Lebanon largely in secular terms, as the quest for identity of the Shi'a and their mobilization for political, social, and economic gain. Indeed, the community had little expectation of finding leadership among a traditional and isolated clergy who enjoyed little respect among the community and whose scope of interest and competence was viewed as minimal.[30] While al-Sadr drew heavily upon Shi'ite symbolism and religious history, the message and the goals were primarily secular and integrative and became ever more worldly with time. The Higher Shi'ite Council as well was concerned with communal rather than religious issues. Amal as an organization came into existence as a militia, and by the time it moved into the political arena it had, under Nabih Birri, dropped nearly all ideological or theological aspects and avoided even significant orientation toward Iran.

When the bases of a movement are built upon a community defined strictly in religious terms it is difficult to separate the religious from the political impulse in general. This is part of the dilemma of Shi'ism: How Shi'ite can the movement be if it is based on secularism? If it is secular, then why is it limited to Shi'a? In the case of Hizballah, it is harder to separate the movement from religious concerns. But Hizballah's aims from the outset were also heavily oriented toward the political goals of liberating Lebanon from Israeli occupation and the U.S. political power that facilitated that occupation. Would these have been viable goals for the Shi'a had Iran not lent major support to Hizballah? It is debatable. Iran's ideological, material, and financial help to Hizballah was overwhelming, especially for the first five years of its guerrilla activities. But Hizballah's goals do not cease being Shi'ite goals simply because they coincide with the great-power interests of outside states, in this case both Iran and Syria. Amal, too, while battling all other sectarian militias in Lebanon, fought against Israel as a direct territorial threat to the Shi'ite areas of south Lebanon. The specific targeting of the American presence was probably strongly bolstered by Syrian and Iranian interests, but it also coincided with more radical or violent Islamist visions everywhere due to the perception of Washington's largely uncritical backing of Israel over decades.

Apart from ridding Lebanon of the Israeli and American presence, the main religious aspiration in Hizballah's program was, of course, the creation of an Islamic state in Lebanon—a long-range goal at best, as we have seen. Hizballah's religious interests may also be seen in its pan-Islamic rhetoric in its early years. (While these were ideological goals shared by Iran, they were not shared by Syria.) Apart from its foreign policies, Hizballah has also worked to promote Shi'ite customs, rituals, celebrations, and other features of Shi'ite life related to its sectarian and religious character.[31]

Hizballah clearly espouses a conservative Muslim lifestyle—beards for the men, scarves or head covering for women—as a major part of its social agenda. The moral regeneration of the Shi'ite community in Lebanon is an important goal of the movement. The party explicitly says that it believes there are ideals that are appropriate for Lebanon that are of Muslim origin but of "universal value."[32] Hizballah's differences with Iran today are more political than religious. And Hizballah's interests in parliament seem to be focused not so much on moral as on social and welfare issues. These issues, to be sure, are not outside the realm of religious concern, but they are also hardly unique to a religiously based party. In this sense, Hizballah reflects the preoccupations of a large number of Islamist movements for whom political and social issues come first.

Clerical leadership of Hizballah is obvious, as is the presence of clerics in the Higher Shi'ite Council that represents all Lebanese Shi'a, while Amal has an entirely secular leadership. Clerical involvement in Shi'ite political movements seems difficult to avoid historically, owing to the importance of the clerics as unofficial leaders of the community over the years. In this respect, which of these two movements will end up blending into the Lebanese political scene most smoothly over time: a driving and ambitious secular Shi'ite movement with little focus on moral issues such as Amal, or a movement with a more "universal" moral focus that seeks some common religious ground for broader cooperation such as Hizballah? The question has yet to be answered in Lebanon.

The Relevance of the Lebanese Shi'ite Experience

The experience of the Shi'a in Lebanon, while reflecting a number of uniquely Lebanese characteristics, has relevance for the broader Muslim world. Pertinent issues include:

- The phenomenon of the emergence of a social group out of backwardness and isolation into near dominance of a political order.

As we have tried to demonstrate, the emergence of the Shi'a in Lebanon resulted from the confluence of extraordinary conditions, not all of them desirable. Lebanon underwent a civil war while evolving to the present conditions. But was civil war the sole process by which these changes could come about? Clearly the Shi'a had already registered a great many gains by the time the civil war emerged and these gains were clearly not the cause of the civil war. The civil war in fact grew out of the massive destabilization visited upon Lebanon by the flight of Palestinian guerrillas into the country in their quest for a base of operations against Israel. Lebanon was turned into a proxy battleground between Israel and Syria in particular. In short, the changes in Lebanon were not only the product of communal rivalry, but of the violence that visited the country and turned political rivalry into armed conflict among militias. Lebanon's civil war and period of chaos certainly created the conditions under which political forces in the country were altered, including the strengthening of the Shi'a, but it was not a precondition for these changes. One hopes that there are some messages from the Lebanon experience, both positive and negative, that could benefit other states with sectarian rivalry.

- The potential role of political sectarianism as a possible formula for the solution of other bitter ethnic or religious sectarian issues in other states.

The breakdown of the system of proportional representation that operated in Lebanon prior to the civil war was one of several factors contributing to the breakdown of the Lebanese state as a whole. The system served Lebanon from 1943 until 1975, and indeed some form of proportional confessional representation existed prior to independence. It is worth examining whether a system based on confessional proportionality might serve as a kind of "halfway house" for the later development of broader nonsectarian democratic institutions.

There may be a sense in which political sectarianism—the creation of political and social organizations by various sects—presents a form of civil society operating independently of the state and hence, in this sense, a "progressive force" as opposed to the top-down power structure and forcefully imposed "national unity" that typify Syria or Iraq. Furthermore, political sectarianism is useful in providing minimum protection against the "tyranny of the majority" and in guaranteeing at least minimal representation for minorities who might otherwise remain voiceless.

But the Ta'if Accord in reality reaffirmed, and some say deepened, the sectarian nature of the Lebanese state, based since independence on confessional proportionality. What has occurred in Lebanon is the opposite of the integrative ideal proclaimed by Musa al-Sadr; the confessional social order now follows a "separate but equal" principle. The sects in Lebanon appear to lead parallel lives side by side, rather than together. Geographic enclaves in Beirut and its extended suburbs are virtually economically self-sufficient, providing residents with a full range of services. Each community has developed its own infrastructure of social services, its own radio stations and newspapers, its own schools and universities, and each sect pools around its own resources. These arrangements are neither exclusive to the Shi'a nor a consequence of their actions, but rather a result of 15 years of civil war and, equally important, of repeated Israeli attacks on Lebanon that have caused massive displacement of populations from the south into Beirut and from the capital to the foothills east and north of it.

In many respects the Lebanese system prior to the civil war had rested on a Maronite culture in which the Sunnis had a share. At Ta'if, the playing field was rearranged to accommodate the new balance of forces that emerged during the war, the various regional interests, and Lebanese demography. It is not surprising then that most people are unhappy about the Ta'if rearrangement. The Maronites chafe at the loss of their dominance, and the Sunnis no longer have the upper hand in the Muslim community. Both believe the power acquired by the Speaker gives the Shi'a a veto on the affairs of state. The Shi'a themselves feel that they have been short-changed, given the extent of their "sacrifices for the liberation of Lebanon." Many Lebanese object to the perpetuation of the sectarian system and call, with varying degrees of sincerity, for a nonconfessional system based on meritocracy. Not surprisingly, the strongest voices in favor of ending the system of confessional proportionality are the Shi'ite political leaders, who can expect a numerical expansion of Shi'ite participation in the institutions of the state, and, by extension, an increase in the power of Shi'ite leaders.

Indeed, political sectarianism, or any political system based on primordial identifications such as religion or ethnicity, is at best problematic, and at worst it poses serious dangers for a nation. The most obvious flaw is that it denies rights and opportunities to all citizens equally and recognizes the political rights of groups but not of individuals. The arcane electoral system in Lebanon is virtually insurmountable to individuals not sponsored by a confessional group. Further, the definition of political groups along sectarian lines, and the granting of political rights only on confessional grounds, stunts development of political parties and other forms of political association that might cut across sectarian divides, simply because such associations are redundant to the system and ineffectual as tools for expression. Sectarianism thwarts social integration and can deepen the existing cleavages in society, driving groups to turn inward and creating social, psychological, and political ghettos—as may be happening in Lebanon—that are antithetical to the growth of a national identity. Such formally stipulated "privileges" as each group may gain tend to be indefinitely perpetuated because they are not willingly given up by that same group in favor of some other system—unless that group perceives itself the clear winner in the new system.

Finally, in Lebanon the confessional proportionality that forms the basis of the political order ossified rapidly: it was determined in 1943, and to this day the Lebanese shy away from a census for fear of its destabilizing potential. It was the civil war followed by the Ta'if Accord, and not a national census, that modified the shares in the proportional representation system. This is the hazard of political sectarianism—that it is resistant to demographic evolution and calcifies the political framework even while society itself is changing. In Lebanon specifically, because no social group has an overwhelming majority and the economic and educational disparities are narrowing, a nonsectarian political system should be far easier to achieve than in other Arab countries.

• The adaptation of Islamist movements to multireligious societies.

Lebanon is unique among Arab countries in the absence of any single sectarian majority. Although Muslims together probably outnumber Christians, the Muslims are divided and the sects are fairly evenly distributed. This near-parity has placed constraints on the Islamist movements, principally Hizballah, in pursuing an Islamist Shi'ite agenda and on any realistic expectation of imposing religious Shi'ite rule in Lebanon. Musa al-Sadr was quick to understand this and went out of his way to reassure the other communities in Lebanon that he sought friendly coexistence. This part of his legacy, at least, continues in the agenda of the Amal movement, which, despite the early Shi'ite religious symbols and observances that served to rally the community, is increasingly secular in its outlook and its practices.

Hizballah's Islamic message was much clearer and its agenda was twofold. In the immediate term, it sought to increase the Islamization of society by encouraging religious adherence and invigoration of Shi'ite culture and education. Over the long term, Hizballah harbored hopes of creating an Islamic state in Lebanon through the peaceful transformation of society, as the text of the 1985 manifesto (quoted above) demonstrates. But the complexity of demographic distribution and entrenched social habits forced Hizballah to revise any timetable it may have had. The watershed was Hizballah's decision to participate in the national elections of 1992, which was an implicit acceptance of the multiconfessional system in Lebanon and an acknowledgment that Hizballah could only hope to influence its immediate vicinity and had limited ability to affect the wider, diversified Lebanese environment.

All other Arab countries have clear sectarian majorities, and therefore Islamist groups suffer fewer constraints. Nevertheless, the willingness of Hizballah to operate in a culturally diverse context sets a precedent for other Sunni and Shi'ite Islamist groups the effect of which is already visible in countries such as Kuwait. The precedent will be particularly important for Iraq, which has equal social and ideological diversity even though the Shi'a form a majority. Hizballah can also provide an example of operating methods in its willingness to form alliances with other groups on specific issues and its espousal of social welfare causes in parliament.

There is no guarantee that the delicate peace among Lebanese sectarian communities will hold, but it has lasted eight years and withstood a number of tests albeit with the stern control of Syria. All the communities, and particularly the Shi'a, have gained a degree of political maturity from Lebanon's agony that augurs well for the future of the country. The transition from guerrilla movements to political parties is well under way. Does this experience offer any hope for a similar evolutionary process in other countries where the state has used only repression in dealing with its internal opposition, and where violence has only escalated on both sides, as in Egypt, Iraq, Algeria, or Bahrain?

The evolution of Lebanese politics has hardly reached any stable end-state—nothing ever does, of course—and the Lebanese state is still far from equilibrium even if the violence may now be largely behind it. But the key question mark remains the impact of ultimate Syrian disengagement from intense involvement in Lebanese affairs based on Syrian national interest. This creates an abnormal state of affairs for Lebanon. When the Syrian presence ceases to be the dominant factor in Lebanese politics, and an Arab-Israeli peace settlement removes Lebanon from the heart of the conflict, how then will these sectarian relationships settle down? The role of the Shi'a will be central to that process.

In tracing this remarkable transition of the Lebanese Shi'a over the past three decades, we believe they have in fact passed beyond a long "period of struggle" as we have formulated it—although some Shi'a might contest this. If the Shi'a have now moved into a "period of consolidation," how might its characteristics be identified? The challenges are clearly different in this period and have more to do with the Shi'ite movement(s) becoming accountable to the Shi'ite community, the broader nation, and the state.

A second feature of this phase may be characterized by intra-Shi'ite rivalry, splintering, realignment—all of which may become standard for Shi'ite communities elsewhere in a consolidation period, and are already visible in Lebanon as well as in Kuwait and among the Iraqi Shi'ite diaspora. Under these conditions it is difficult to foresee whether the once-radical, religious formula of Hizballah or the secular approach of Nabih Birri will gain political strength and popular support over time. It is also unclear what the Shi'a who stand outside these two movements will do to regain some of the initiative they lost in the past two decades. Several counterpoints will distinguish the relative strengths of Hizballah and Amal. Hizballah's approach is to emphasize issues of social reform, social programs and social welfare, and the fight against widespread corruption and nepotism. These issues have some resonance among the public, and especially among the youth. Amal's strengths lie in the power and prominence of its leader, Nabih Birri, his close ties to Syria, Amal's position within the state, and its ability to deliver material benefits from the state as part of a patronage and spoils system. It has significant control over state contracts, especially the patronage benefits that flow from the Commission for the Reconstruction of the South. On the one hand, these material benefits from Amal—that is otherwise relatively devoid of ideology—are attractive to many. On the other hand Hizballah's ideals of reform, morality, national struggle, and its Shi'ite symbolism may in the end prove at least as powerful, especially to a younger generation. But should Hizballah lose the material wherewithal to maintain its own community programs and services in the future, and in the event of Israeli withdrawal from the south, its ideology will probably not suffice to sustain it as a major player within the Shi'ite community. However, if Lebanon should face further ideological crisis and deep popular dissatisfaction with the nature of the Lebanese system, Hizballah might stand to benefit more than Amal from that kind of environment.

As we have seen, the Lebanese state has undergone some extraordinary crises, transitions, and hardships over the past 30 years. The country's search for a viable political order is far from over and a truly stable equilibrium has not yet been attained. Indeed, it cannot be attained as long as the Israeli occupation continues, the broader outlines of an Arab-Israeli settlement have not been achieved, and, therefore, Syria is still able to maintain a critical hold over the Lebanese state. At such time as Lebanon can achieve a state of "normal" sovereignty, it will need to focus upon building a long-term national order—one that is based primarily upon domestic issues rather than external ones. In the meantime, the immense progress the Shi'a have made in establishing the dignity of their community within society and their power within the state should mean that the Shi'a need no longer represent an explosive factor in Lebanon's development in the way they have in the past.

CHAPTER TEN

The Shi'a
and the West

Our research shows that the views of Arab Shi'a toward the West vary considerably from country to country, movement to movement, and circumstance to circumstance. It may be no more meaningful to talk about Shi'ite views of the West than it is to talk of Sunni views of the West. These variations express in part the ambivalence of Shi'ite attitudes toward the very societies and states in which they live.

Sources of Shi'ite Moderation Toward the West

In some respects the Shi'a as a population are more inclined even than Sunnis moderation toward the West. First, all Arab Shi'a, regardless of whether they constitute the minority or majority in their societies, stand to be the primary beneficiaries of regime liberalization, democratization, and attention to human rights. In Iraq and Bahrain democratization will actually bring the Shi'a to power; in Saudi Arabia it will immediately ameliorate their situation and status—as it has already done in Kuwait. Since the West is perceived as the primary source of these values today, and the primary source of potential pressure upon authoritarian regimes, the Shi'a are in principle sympathetic to those forces that can improve their lot.

Second, the Western presence in the Middle East historically has focused on minorities—first and foremost as instruments to facilitate Western rule. Minorities were often used as the key cadres for colonial administration, such as the Maronites in Lebanon, the 'Alawi in Syria, the Berbers in Algeria, etc. Western imperial powers have also for centuries regularly exploited a selective concern for the welfare of certain minorities (almost always Christian) at certain times and places in the Middle East as a pretext for intervention. Minorities within these states typically looked favorably upon outside powers that could protect or improve their status.

In more recent times, the Western presence in Bahrain and Saudi Arabia directly benefited the status of the Shi'a. In Saudi Arabia it was the Arabian American Oil Company (ARAMCO) that was the chief employer of Shi'a in the Eastern Province; ARAMCO had a good record in bringing prosperity to the region and treating Shi'ite employees with equality. The major U.S. presence in the Eastern province probably also helped limit some of the more obvious Wahhabi abuse and oppression of the Shi'a and created a more Westernized atmosphere than would have been the case under pure Wahhabi rule. British colonial rule in Bahrain also protected the Shi'a to some extent from arbitrary treatment from the al-Khalifas. British and later American firms such as BAPCO and ALBA treated Bahraini workers, Shi'ite and Sunni, with an equality not present in daily Bahraini life. Additionally, many Shi'a have been educated in the West and appreciate Western values and norms— even if these norms are often disregarded by the West in their actual policies toward the regional states in the name of broader national interests.

Third, in cultural terms, the Shi'a have not been as closely linked to the Arab nationalist project and its strong antiimperial character as have the Sunnis—although the Shi'a were deeply involved in the anticolonial struggle in Iraq. This lesser Shi'ite involvement has probably been due to their general exclusion from the political process more than to any disagreement with the Sunni attitude per se. The Shi'a have traditionally been more distant—geographically, intellectually, and emotionally— from the Palestinian issue that has been a key source of anti-Western attitudes among Sunnis in the Arab and Muslim world. (It was only the Israeli invasion of southern Lebanon in 1981 that ended up transforming a formerly anti-Palestinian Shi'ite population into one strongly hostile to Israel.)

Fourth, the policies of Arab states toward the West have both a direct and an indirect impact upon the attitudes of the Shi'ite community—or even counter-impact. Saddam Hussein's strong anti-Western views and his harsh oppression of Iraqi Shi'a obviously led the Shi'a to conclude that the West can't be all bad. The Shi'a perceive that they share certain common goals with the West such as change of the Iraqi regime. Conversely, regimes that are strongly pro-American yet oppress their Shi'ite populations, as in Saudi Arabia, can have the opposite effect—the U.S. cannot be perceived positively by the Saudi or Bahraini Shi'a as long as Washington is seen to tacitly ignore the heavy-handed treatment by Riyadh and Manama of their Shi'ite minorities.

Overall, then, there are ample grounds for large numbers of Arab Shi'a to maintain positive views of the West. Increasing numbers of Shi'a have traveled to the West, do business with the West in some capacity, or have sent their children for education to the West. Certain cultural features of the West such as its technology and popular entertainment can often have broad appeal, though some of it can have quite a negative impact when Western media is seen to violate Islamic cultural norms.

Sources of Shi'ite Hostility to the West

Conversely, there are also numerous sources of potential Shi'ite antipathy against the West. Of all the Shi'ite communities in the Gulf and the Arab world, it is perhaps the Iranian and Lebanese Shi'a who have grounds for the greatest grievances toward the West. Iran has held direct anti-American grievances over the years, starting with the British/CIA overthrow of elected Iranian premier Mossadegh in favor of the Shah in the 1950s, continuing through American long-term support of the Shah despite his repressive domestic policies, and Iranian suffering under U.S. sanctions in the 1990s. As the largest and most important Shi'ite state in the world, Iran's attitudes—and the state of hostility between Iran and the West—clearly has a direct impact upon broader Shi'ite communities in the region.

The Lebanese Shi'a, too, have quite specific anti-U.S. grievances. They perceive themselves as among the primary victims of the Israeli invasion of Lebanon in 1982, of the continuing Israeli occupation of southern Lebanon through the 1990s, and of Israeli support of Christian forces in the south against the Shi'a. The U.S. diplomatic and military presence was therefore targeted directly in the early 1980s by Shi'ite guerrilla and terrorist forces—with clear encouragement from Iran and Syria. As the Shi'ite community in Lebanon asserts its newfound self-confidence and prominence, it will be influenced by the degree to which U.S. policies either benefit the Shi'a (as the largest single sect in the country) or support the community's rivals.

For other Shi'a of the Gulf, the grievances against the West and the United States are less direct, but they exist. First, the failure of the West, despite its rhetoric about human rights and political liberalization, to show any sympathy to the Shi'ite predicament can end up alienating them from the West In Bahrain, for example, though their secular goals in calling for restoration of Parliamentary rule in Bahrain are modest, and there has been a remarkably low level of lethal violence in their protests against the state over the years, the Shi'a seem to find little sympathy or response from Washington. Indeed, during a visit of an American Assistant Secretary of State Robert Pelletreau to Bahrain in the mid-1990s he publicly stated that the

United States stood beside the Bahraini regime in "its struggle against terror" which the Shi'a understood to be directed specifically against them.

The U.S. annual State Department Human Rights Report on Bahrain has been welcomed by Shi'a in Bahrain, as has lessening U.S. protection for Bahrain on U.N. Human Rights resolutions on the Bahrain situation. But to the extent that the United States is unwilling to take a firm public stance on shortsighted and repressive Bahraini government policies against the majority of the population, it runs the risk of being perceived by Shi'a no longer as part of the solution but as part of the problem. Eventual Shi'ite terrorism against the U.S. presence cannot then be too far behind.

In Iraq the British could be viewed as responsible for permitting the minority Sunnis to dominate the state during the days of the Mandate. In more recent times, the United States is perceived as having supported the regime of Saddam Hussein during the Iran-Iraq war and for having stood by after the end of the Gulf war in Kuwait and permitted Saddam's troops to brutally put down the Shi'ite uprising—an uprising called for by President Bush at the end of the war. There is much ambiguity in current U.S. policy toward Iraq as to whether it is comfortable with pushing for a democratic regime in Iraq, partly because it would involve the "unknowns" of permitting Shi'a the dominant voice in Iraq—including fear of how Iran might "use the Iraqi Shi'a" to dominate Iraq. U.S. policy is also influenced by Saudi and Kuwaiti preferences, which firmly oppose Shi'ite political dominance of Iraq, that is, a democratic outcome. It is hardly surprising then that politically active segments of the Arab Shi'a, especially Islamists, when placed under heavy pressure from the state, will have little choice but to gravitate toward Iran as the sole protector state by default.

Conversely, if the Shi'a can achieve better integration into the societies in which they live, the need for an external mentor and protector will fade. The Shi'a will then come to reflect the same spectrum of political attitudes as their Sunni fellow citizens, including attitudes toward the West. As we have seen in earlier chapters, when Arab Shi'a have been able to join broader Arab political movements in the past, they often gravitated to leftist movements that also happened to be quite anti-Western. But the attraction of these leftist movements was not so much their anti-Western attitudes, but that they provided a nonsectarian, antiregime forum open to Shi'a as well as Sunnis— a forum in which Shi'a could break free of customary anti-Shi'ite prejudices. In fact, secular Shi'a, who consciously opt out of the nearly compulsory religious identity that defines the Shi'a, may have few alternatives other than to turn to liberal-leftist circles; the left by definition is more nonsectarian than traditional nationalist groups that carry a "Sunni flavor." Finally, when Shi'a have an opportunity to become truly integrated into the societies in which they live, they will find the question of Shi'ite identity playing an ever smaller role in defining their lives. But prospects for integration depend more upon the state and society in which they live than it does upon the Shi'a themselves.

It is important to note that if the Shi'a are allowed to participate in building a *democratic* agenda, it will almost surely have to be a *secular* agenda. The Shi'ite community may have strong clerical representation, but its representatives in a democratic order cannot call for an Islamic state— that by definition would have to be Shi'ite—and against the wishes of a large segment of the population that is not Shi'ite. Thus the democratic process itself tends to diminish the zeal of the Shi'ite religious case and works toward a system in which all religious elements within society must accommodate each other.

How would the Arab Shi'a greet a significant rapprochement between the West and Iran? On one level, some might regret the disappearance of their external "champion" for Shi'ite rights in the Gulf in the absence of any others. The Shi'a would then be left to fight their own battles, perhaps even losing ones, against oppressive state regimes. Shi'ite hostility toward the United States could still be maintained if Washington were seen to be still unsympathetic to the human rights issue, in the name of broader U.S. state interests. Indeed, Saudi Arabia's striking gesture toward normalization with Iran in the summer of 1997—even in the face of strong public suspicion that Iran was the chief culprit behind the bombing of U.S. forces in Dhahran in 1996—suggests the importance Riyadh attributes to improved relations with Tehran as a key to modifying Saudi Shi'ite attitudes toward the Saudi regime. A less radical stance by the Iranian regime could cause all the Gulf states to treat their own Shi'a with less distrust. Change in Iranian policies, then, is another key determinant on the Shi'a's position in Sunni society, one that is largely beyond their control.

The absence of local Shi'ite maraji' is still one of the key factors that leads many Shi'a to look outside the country for spiritual guidance. While this factor need not be a source of international conflict—any more than international Catholic interest in the pronouncements of the Pope—in states where autocratic rule and bad governance predominates, the presence of external channels for pursuit of grievances is viewed with deep suspicion.

Indeed, some independent local maraji' are emerging in a number of states: Saudi Arabia (Hasan al-Saffar), Kuwait, and especially Lebanon (Shaykh Muhammad Fadhlallah.) The emergence of local maraji' is a positive development in that it diminishes the need for ties between either Qom or Najaf and their respective followers outside the country. It means that local Shi'a will have less interest in religious events in Iran and Iraq and will be able to look to local authority for guidance on key religious issues. The fact that Iran and Iraq are deeply problematic presences in the Gulf region today complicates even further the question of maraji' resident there. When politics are eventually "normalized" in Iran and Iraq, the issue of the role of their maraji' will lose some, but not all, importance.

Shi'ite unhappiness with the United States, then, is directly affected by U.S. policies toward the states in the region, which in turn impact upon the Shi'a who live there, whether intentionally or not. There are no inherent reasons for the Shi'a to be more anti-U.S. than the Sunni community over the longer run. Left unintegrated into their social and political surroundings, the Shi'a may well become anti-Western if they perceive no concern for their plight, or worse, hostility, from the West. If they turn to Iran for support they may also imbibe anti-U.S. views. But socially integrated Shi'a will demonstrate the same spectrum of beliefs toward politics and the West, in both positive and negative respects, as do Sunni Arabs.

Terrorism

U.S. policy, especially in public rhetoric, often fails to distinguish among a variety of forms of political violence, not all of which can be accurately described as "terrorism" in its more precise meaning. We do not propose to offer an exact definition of terrorism here but wish to point out that the word embraces a spectrum of acts, depending on the subjective views of the observer. There are very significant differences, for example, among:

- guerrilla attacks, including suicide operations, against foreign troops and installations in occupation of one's country or land, such as attacks upon Israeli troops in south Lebanon or the West Bank;
- sabotaging the property but not the personnel, of the state as part of an internal struggle against a regime (as the Shi'a have in Bahrain);
- guerrilla or suicide attacks upon the security, military, and police personnel of one's own regime as part of the same internal political struggle;
- the export of political violence overseas against foreign states or their foreign presence as a form of warfare;
- the indiscriminate killing of innocent civilians (whose presence at a site is purely fortuitous), such as on public transportation or in public places.

In ideal terms no one should condone the practice of any violence, but in the real-world Middle East there are important distinctions to be made in characterizing and combating these various forms of violence.

A classic definition of the state involves, among other things, a legitimate monopoly on the use of violence within society. In many cases in the Middle East, the question of the "legitimacy" of the state is a key issue. Is the state legitimate if it is nonrepresentative, nonelected, incompetent, oppressive, not answerable to the public, corrupt, employs arbitrary violence against its citizenry, and has as a major goal the perpetuation of the regime? Large numbers of regimes in the region fall into many of these categories. When the state itself denies channels of dissent and employs arbitrary and uncalibrated violence against political opposition, then it is not surprising that violence against the state—its institutions, personnel and even allies—should emerge. This argument is not meant to condone terrorism, including the "state terrorism" that we so often observe in many parts of today's world.

All states have a right, indeed an obligation, to defend themselves against attack. But a second reality in the Middle East is that the state actually often prefers to deal with terrorism than to deal with political opposition. "Combating terror" justifies the use of any kind of extreme measures to put it down, absolves leaders from inconvenient problems of human rights or political compromise, and provides decisive responses to any human rights inquiries from abroad. Therefore the state has an interest to paint its political opposition with a terrorist brush, sometimes even to goad political opposition into violent acts that then permit the state to curtail political discourse and turn to forceful repression. Most states in the Middle East today, including Israel's approach to the Palestinian problem under former Prime Minister Netanyahu, often prefer dealing with terrorism from the state's position of strength. And when "counterterrorism" becomes a key pillar of any state's policies, it transforms problems of political opposition and freedom of speech into security and police problems that are then handled accordingly by force.

Shi'ite terrorism has been driven by several motives, some with specific, and others with more general objectives:

- Terrorism has been used as a coercive tactic to achieve specific objectives, such as freeing prisoners or evicting foreign troops. Hizballah in Lebanon has used violence for such ends since the 1980s with devastating effectiveness. On the whole, they were highly successful in achieving the desired withdrawal of U.S. and Israeli troops, though at a high cost to Hizballah's domestic and international standing.
- Shi'ite groups have also employed violence to protest actions by their own governments—such as retaliation for what are considered outrageous acts by the government. The armed Shi'ite resistance in southern Iraq, both before and after the Gulf war, was driven by anger against Iraqi regime behavior, including the wanton executions and other extrajudicial killings of senior Shi'ite clerics and community leaders.
- Less specifically, terrorism has been used as a way to delegitimize and destabilize a regime—and the effects are cumulative. This tactic was most evident in attacks against several Gulf regimes at the outset of the

Iran-Iraq War; it primarily reflected deep Iranian concern for the solid Arab support for Saddam Hussein against Iran, rather than reflecting Shi'ite community grievances. Terrorism of this nature can warn and intimidate a foreign state in order to change its policies. It is unlikely to destabilize a government sufficiently to force its downfall or bring it to negotiation unless such a terrorist campaign is long, sustained and uncontrolled. Those Shi'ite terrorist attacks in the Gulf in the 1980s did not bring the desired results.

- Finally, terrorism is a way to attract world attention to the Shi'ite problem, and here it has proven its efficacy. The conditions of the Shi'a remained obscure and uninteresting to the world until Iranian actions directly affected Western interests, and they were followed by Hizballah's attacks against American and French Marines in Lebanon. Bahraini Shi'a, primarily employing peaceful or violent demonstrations, have also sought to publicize their case.

- When foreign governments (Iran) have been involved, they have primarily served as enablers, providing funds, arms, possible training, and logistical and moral support, rather than as actual participants in the operations. Foreign governments can rarely create these operations from whole cloth but can only build on existing grievances and ready cadres to perform operations, often with the tacit support of the larger population.

Most of these motives for terrorism are hardly confined to the Shi'a. It is the Sunnis in Saudi Arabia who have used violence with the goal of destabilizing government, protesting government policies, and driving American troops out of Saudi Arabia.

What are the factors that can increase or decrease the potential for violence in the future? An increase in violence is likely in countries such as Bahrain and Iraq, where the state has excluded the possibility of negotiation with the Shi'ite community and has increased the pressure on it (although Bahrain may have begun a modest shift in policy as of July 1999.) Absent any breakthroughs, larger segments of the Shi'ite communities in both countries will be radicalized against the state, and terrorism will become more acceptable and logistically easier to carry out. If the West shows no sympathy or acts to deter the possibility of Shi'a gaining political dominance within the state, Western institutions may well become targets of violence.

Policy Implications For The United States

- Strategically, the Shi'ite population of the Arab world is important to the West because it lies at the heart of the largest oil-producing area of the Middle East and along major oil transportation routes. Together with Iran, the Arab Shi'a could in theory come to have major control over the oil-producing regions of the Gulf, albeit from within different states.

- The nearly 13 million Arab Shi'a clustered around the Gulf, with an additional one million in Lebanon, have historically been ignored by Western policymakers. They were only put on the policy map after the Iranian revolution by Iran, who took advantage of major existing Shi'ite grievances to help spark the violence that ensued.

- The stigmatization (even tacitly) of the Shi'a and their stereotyping is unwarranted and counterproductive. The Shi'a are no more fanatical or prone to violence than Sunni Muslims—or Hindus, Jews, Catholics, or Protestants. But they do tend to be the object of systematic discrimination in the region. Instead of buying the stereotypes, the United States should recognize the diversity of the Shi'a and also be prepared to listen to their demands. It is time for the West in general to overcome a widespread "Shi'aphobia."

- There is a real danger that the Shi'a will be pushed into a corner in many states, with all exits cut off. This is currently happening in Bahrain and Iraq, and it can only create explosive situations. The United States can help, at least in Bahrain, by suggesting reconciliation strategies and pressing for their adoption by states and Shi'ite communities together.

- The United States should be wary of efforts by some regimes to cast the Shi'ite problem exclusively as a "terrorist" problem. Terrorism has been practiced in all of these countries, but it is a manifestation of a deeper and wider problem—the status of the Shi'a as inferior citizens in their own states. Unfortunately, most regimes would prefer to deal with a "terrorist" problem than with the necessity of opening dialog with political opposition—and would like to win Washington over to that same view.

- The potential for Shi'ite violence is thus directly affected by at least three factors: the pressure on the Shi'a by local regimes, the indifference of Western opinion; and by the availability of external support to the Shi'a. At least the first two of these conditions can be mitigated by U.S. policies.

- To lessen the potential for violence, the United States should advocate greater integration of the Shi'a into their societies rather than increasing their isolation or condoning discrimination or even state violence against the Shi'a.

- Failure to integrate the Shi'a also contributes to the growth of religious extremism, both Shi'ite and Sunni. Radical Islamist views are a natural product of Shi'ite resentments and often fuel Sunni radical Islamist views in opposition. Conversely, ongoing integration of the Shi'a in Kuwait and Lebanon has been part of a process in which these societies are now moving toward greater reform and stability.

- The integration of the Arab Shi'a into their respective societies in the Middle East is thus an integral part of the process of the maturation and stabilization of the region. As such it should receive serious policy attention.

- The Shi'ite problem in **Bahrain** is the single most burning case (while the situation in Iraq is a disaster for *all* parties) and more amenable to gradual pressure and solution. In the face of regime obduracy against opening up the political order and implementing the 1975 constitution, the situation has been steadily worsening, with negative implications for long-range U.S. interests there and in the region. The United States should therefore take a public stand on the importance of necessary reforms required for settlement of the problem. Washington should openly call for dialog between the regime and the Shi'ite community, and support those Sunni liberals who have long called for an open and representative order.

- In **Saudi Arabia**, if the negotiated agreement between the Saudi government and the Shi'a—limited though it is—holds and is implemented fairly, it will work in the interest of coexistence. There is no clear sign as yet that the regime does plan to implement it. One factor that can undermine the situation in both countries is the political rise of *salafis,* Wahhabi fundamentalists, with their intense ideological opposition to the Shi'a. Indeed, intercommunal violence could be triggered by the Wahhabi fundamentalists themselves. Certainly any spread of Sunni extremism will be seen by the Shi'a as threatening their very existence, and it will be countered by Shi'ite extremism.

- In Saudi Arabia, the United States should call for religious freedom for all, but it is the Saudi Shi'a—one of the oldest settled Muslim communities in the country—who are discriminated against most blatantly. The United States should call for an end to cultural discrimination against them, and urge the inclusion of the Shi'a as part of a move toward more representative government in Saudi Arabia. The future of the Saudi oil region is partly at stake.

- The trend toward democratization and participation in **Kuwait** so far has been the best example of integrating the Shi'a and marginalizing extremists. The United States should continue to closely follow and publicly applaud this progress as a major step toward long-term stability in the country and in the region.

- In **Lebanon** the situation is more complex because much of the violence has been directed against Israeli occupation and has the support of Iran and Syria in this regard. The new Israeli government under Prime Minister Ehud Barak has pledged to withdraw all Israeli troops by mid-2000; if he does so, the key justification for Hizballah to maintain an armed guerrilla capability will disappear, and sectarian tensions in Lebanon involving the Shi'a will sharply diminish. Much too, will depend on developments in the Middle East peace process and U.S. relations with both Iran and Syria. However, one type of emerging Shi'ite violence specific to Lebanon should be considered. The Shi'ite community, now free from the pressures of extreme discrimination and disenfranchisement, may itself tend to fragment along political and ideological lines; intra-Shi'ite rivalry may then emerge as a new and powerful source of potential violence. This could go beyond armed clashes between contending factions and spread to acts of terrorism against civilians and the economic sector. Western interests can be affected depending on whether Western involvement is perceived to influence the fortunes of one or another faction. In Lebanon the United States should now move to open dialogue with Hizballah and should cease opposing the integration of Hizballah into the political order—a development now accepted by all Lebanese due to Hizballah's constructive role in parliament. This entails an essentially positive development for the interests of all, as long as Hizballah shows its continued willingness to play by the rules of the system and abandons its armed guerrilla capability following an Israeli withdrawal.

- In **Iraq** the United States should make quite clear that it favors representational democracy in the country after the fall of Saddam Hussein as the only long-range solution to Iraq's severe sectarian and ethnic divisions. Washington should ensure close ties with Shi'ite forces—along with other forces—in the opposition, and work for the integration of the Shi'a into any future solution in the area. An Iraq that does not permit the Shi'a to play the role accorded to them by their demographic majority is doomed to failure, schism, and manipulation by outside forces, especially Iran. Saudi and Kuwaiti objections to the establishment of democratic processes in Iraq should be ignored.

- Finally, in a broader approach, the United States needs to more actively encourage democratization and respect for human rights in the Arab world, as the surest path to long-range stability in the region. The disenfranchisement of nearly 13 million Shi'a clustered around the Arabian Gulf is a constant threat to stability. It is easy, of course, to speak in the abstract of liberalization, democratization, and human rights, but it is admittedly difficult to place these items high on the agenda of senior policymakers in their formulation of bilateral relations with other states. Yet Washington is the ultimate loser in persistently focusing on short-term

goals in the Middle East that are sometimes contradictory to achievement of long-range goals that inevitably requires political change—in a
region in which democratization as a process is more retarded than in any
other region in the world. At least one of the factors contributing to this
situation are U.S. policies in the Middle East where the goal of liberalization and change simply ranks near the bottom of the list of priorities.

- An improved overall political relationship between the United States
  and Middle Eastern countries *and publics* will reduce the temptation
  for foreign interference and agitation that has lead to manipulation of
  the Shi'a or their exploitation by others for anti-American ends. While
  this sounds like a pious wish, we must observe that at this point U.S.
  relations with the broader public in the Middle East are tenser than in
  any other region of the world. The nature of U.S. relations with unrepresentative regimes will not be the main measure of the success of
  those policies in the eyes of its often muted citizenry.

CHAPTER ELEVEN

Conclusions

As a result of researching and writing this book, we have developed a number of general conclusions about the role and place of the Shi'a in the Arab world. Many of these points have emerged in specific chapters of the book, but we would like to draw them together in succinct form for this concluding chapter. Taken together they form a body of observations and hypotheses derived from our understanding of the overall issue. We hope it will elicit corroborative, or even alternative, assessments from other readers.

Diagnosis of the Problem

- Sunnis view the Shi'a as religious dissidents who over the centuries have frequently rejected Sunni authority. The Shi'a suffer from being seen by the Sunnis as "different" or "rejectionist," and they are an object of discrimination on this basis. Still, the problem of relations between the Shi'a and the Sunnis in the Arab world today is not fundamentally a religious problem. At heart Shi'ite-Sunni frictions involve the existence of two different social communities, mutual prejudices, and a deep imbalance of power relationships between them.
- The Shi'a, merely by proclaiming their distinct form of Islam—even by their existence—pose a "sensitive" problem that assails the core aspiration of Muslim unity and undermines the traditional historiography of the Muslim state, which presents Muslim history as a seamless and unified continuity.
- The essence of the Shi'ite grievance is that they now form a special breed that is recognized neither as a majority—in those countries where they constitute the majority—nor as a minority, where they should be

granted minority rights. Additionally, the Shi'a face a number of almost intractable dilemmas: the Shi'a are Arabs, yet treated in effect as non-Arabs; they are also Muslims, yet often treated as non-Muslims. If the Shi'a downplay their Shi'ite identity and try to assimilate into Sunni society they are often denied entry into society and politics because they are Shi'a. Yet if they insist on their Shi'ite identity they are called divisive and sectarian and are accused of seeking special privilege.

- The Shi'a are far from a homogeneous, monolithic community. They are divided horizontally by economic and social status, and vertically by political orientation and degree of religious commitment. Shi'ite communities additionally differ from country to country and with their attendant political cultures. It is therefore misleading to think of the Shi'a as an undifferentiated group.

- Many Shi'a who would otherwise identify themselves in nonsectarian terms understand that it is others who first classify them as Shi'a, regardless of their own self-definition. To the extent that this is a label imposed upon them by the outside world, they are powerless to change it. Shi'a complain that there is no escape from the label of Shi'ism, and that even if a Shi'i were to convert to Sunnism, he or she would forever remain a Shi'i in the eyes of Sunnis.

- The Shi'a share a common diagnostic consensus on their grievances as a community, but there is less agreement on remedies. Questions of solutions and strategies generally divide the Shi'a, nor is there any degree of cooperation or consultation among them at the international level as regards their local problems.

- While secularism need not, in principle, intrude upon the self-expression of Shi'ite culture, it is nonetheless religion itself that becomes the outward expression of community solidarity, becoming a force resembling ethnicity in its emotive power and centrality to community identity. Secularism must be understood and implemented in ways that do not damage community religious identity. A solution to the integration of the Shi'a into Arab society likewise involves processes comparable to resolution of internal ethnic conflicts. But the Arab Shi'a are just as "Arab" as the Sunni Arabs, speak the same language, and share most elements of a common culture. Shi'a acknowledge all the main features of Islamic theology. The Shi'a would deeply resent the idea that anyone might consider them or treat them as a different ethnic group.

- Because the Arab Shi'a share so many cultural features with other Arabs, in their own self-definition the Shi'ite element of their identity generally ranks below their identity as Arabs, as Muslims, and generally as citizens of the country in which they live. But the Shi'ite identity takes on special salience when it is the source of their persecution and discrimination, or when they are functionally denied the attributes of citizenship. The Shi'ite identity will remain particularly salient as long as they are under pressure as a community. But the force of this identity is not static and tends to recede with integration into society.

- To a considerable extent the problem today is a Sunni problem: a Sunni reluctance to grant the Shi'a full political and social equality. But the blame is not totally one-sided. At least historically, the Shi'a have often isolated themselves by remaining outside Sunni society, distrusting it, and criticizing its institutions of power. Today, however, given the general Shi'ite desire to integrate into their respective societies, the power to resolve the problem lies mostly with the Sunni community and the state.

- The problem faced by the Shi'a is both specific and general. Specifically, the Shi'a are out of the mainstream and have unequal status in their societies. But in broader political terms, the Shi'a face the more general failing of Arab states that limit or deny democracy, pluralism, and respect for human rights within the political order. This larger problem affects not only Shi'a but all Arabs, and all share equally in a solution.

- While the Sunni state may demand "loyalty" from the Shi'a, any issue of loyalty also raises serious questions about the relationship between the autocratic state and society in the Middle East: loyalty to whom or what? To regime, ruler, ruling family, state, country, or society? And with what justification is that loyalty demanded? This problem affects Sunnis as well as Shi'a, but it is the Shi'a whose loyalty is questioned first. For the Shi'a to remain loyal to a ruling family ironically tends to be viewed by Sunni reformers, liberals, and Islamists alike as nonpatriotic and self-serving.

Shi'ite Political Options

- The Shi'a have more incentive than almost any other group in the Arab world to press for greater democratization and human rights. They are probably the most immediate and direct beneficiaries of any movement toward democratization and human rights in the states in which they live, since, as a group, they are the primary victims of the absence of these freedoms. In countries where the Shi'a are a minority—Saudi Arabia and Kuwait—both Sunnis and Shi'a will benefit from democratization. In countries where the Shi'a are a majority or plurality— Iraq, Bahrain, Lebanon—everyone may gain from democratization, but the Shi'a will gain more than the Sunnis, and mostly at the expense of the Sunnis, as happened in Lebanon. Sunnis in these countries are sometimes inclined to describe democracy as "a Shi'ite agenda."

- The Shi'a confront a dilemma in attempting to develop secular leadership: by definition they are distinct only by virtue of their religion. Aspiring Shi'ite leaders risk cutting themselves off from the essence of community identity if they ignore the sectarian/religious aspect, at which point they become little distinguishable from non-Shi'ite leaders and must abandon the special problems of the Shi'ite community. The Shi'ite community may then be less inclined to support them. When aspiring leaders emphasize Shi'ite sectarian interests, the clerics then often have the advantage in seeking political leadership.

- Often denied avenues to political and social participation via mainstream political organizations or movements, the Shi'a are thus impelled to move toward the outer areas of the political spectrum: either toward sectarian Islamist movements—even extremist movements, if the level of persecution is high enough—or, toward radical left-wing movements, such as the Communist party, who welcomes all sects without any discrimination. Therefore it is hard for the Shi'a to avoid drifting toward polarization of political views.

- Nothing in Shi'ite belief itself predisposes them to radicalism or violence. However, since Shi'ism emerged from a movement of dissent, it tends toward criticism of traditional authority and establishment power that throughout history has been primarily Sunni. Additionally, the history of the Shi'ite experience predisposes them to expect further suffering, possibly facilitating an embrace of martyrdom as a last resort in an "historically determined" role for the beleaguered community.

- However violent its past, even radical groups such as Hizballah in Lebanon have begun the process of entering the political process and playing by the rules where permitted to do so. Similarly, Shi'ite clerics in Kuwait have entered parliamentary life successfully and are cooperating with other political elements in the parliament.

- Radical or violent action from the Shi'a, however, is more likely in those countries in which the Shi'a constitute the majority, where they have less to lose and everything to gain through change. Violence is also most likely where the state resists change by employing violence itself.

Shi'ism and Iran

- Iraq in almost every sense is the original center and heartland of Shi'ism, and especially of Arab Shi'ism. It is only in the sixteenth century that Shi'ism became the state religion of Iran. And it is only in the mid-twentieth century that Iran superseded Iraq as a center of Shi'ite religious study—mainly due to the severe persecution and execution of leading Shi'ite clerics in Iraq that drove most of them into Iran.

- In effect, the Arab world has ceded domination of Shi'ism to Iran. When the Shi'a of Iraq one day achieve political power commensurate with their majority status, Iraq will gradually regain its position as the center of Arab Shi'ism and—less likely shared with Qom—a center for all Shi'a in the Muslim world.

- Iranian political doctrine is not necessarily theologically binding on all Shi'a, although to firm adherents to the Khomeini doctrine of *velayat-e-faqih* (clerical rule), the Supreme Leader's political views in Iran have weight when pronounced as religious doctrine. Iranian radical religious ideas—not shared by all Shi'a even within Iran—may also have resonance for those who see themselves as oppressed and with little recourse except to external forces. And some Shi'a—and some Sunnis as well—may accept Iranian doctrine on the role of Islam in countering Western imperialism, but on a political and not a religious basis.

- The Arab Shi'a emphatically do not see themselves as an extension of Iran. In the 1980s both Iran and some Arab Shi'a attempted to use each other for their respective political goals. Apart from putting their cause on the world's political map, the Shi'a ultimately lost out from this association, except in Lebanon.

- So long as the Shi'a remain underdogs and perceive themselves as outcasts, they will again be vulnerable to manipulation by Iran or possibly Iraq in the future. In desperation they could even seek political backing from either of these countries again if their communities are sufficiently threatened.

- Today, most Arab Shi'a are at pains to distinguish themselves clearly from Iran and to assert their independence. They recognize that the policies of the Islamic Republic toward external Shi'a have been largely self-serving. If oppression should again force the Shi'a to turn in desperation to Iran they will probably do so with little ideological fervor and fewer illusions—it will be more of a pragmatic transaction. Such a cooling relationship may already be developing between the Lebanese Hizballah and Iran in recent years.

- Iran itself under President Khatami is less interested in supporting the external Shi'a and seeks to normalize relations with neighbors in order to lessen Iranian isolation.

The Shi'a in the Arab World

- Over the past two decades the Shi'a have made major strides toward greater equality of treatment in Lebanon and Kuwait. The Shi'ite Speaker of the Lebanese parliament (currently Nabih Birri) is the most powerful Shi'ite political figure in the Arab world today. Conditions for the Shi'a in Iraq, Bahrain, and Saudi Arabia remain abysmal. The issue will be explosive in all three countries in the future.

- To the discomfiture of Sunni elite in the Arab world, Iraqi Shi'a will challenge the fixed notion that all Arab governments must necessarily be Sunni and will break the custom of equating Arabism with Sunnism that has been implicit in the culture of the Arab world. More boldly, Iraqi Shi'a have the ability to "influence the past" as well: they can recast Arab historiography to incorporate Shi'ism as an essential component of that history.

- Because the Shi'a have already been radicalized by 30 years of repressive Ba'th rule and the particular brutality of the Saddam Hussein's regime against the Shi'a in March 1991, it is unlikely that the Shi'a will remain passive if a new, weaker regime attempts to preserve the discriminative status quo. The potential for violence in Iraq is likely to rise, pitting Shi'ite dissidents against the central government in escalating confrontations. In such a polarized climate, the clashing parties may all seek external support, and foreign interests will have ample windows for interference in Iraq's internal affairs.

- In Lebanon the collapse of the old inequitable state order via civil war seems almost to have been the necessary prerequisite to the later emergence of a more equitable state order. Does it take a cataclysm of this magnitude to create the conditions for moving toward democracy and greater equality among the citizenry? The democratizing process in Kuwait too has been the result of the trauma of Iraqi invasion and the Gulf war. It is disquieting to think that a similar violent state breakdown and extreme civil conflict in Iraq and Bahrain might have to be the prerequisite for change and liberalization to occur there. Yet no other options currently appear on the horizon for peaceful transition of power in these two Shi'ite-majority states.

- In every Arab country except Kuwait the Shi'a have been compelled to turn to external organizations and external media in exile in order to prosecute their case for equality of rights and greater democratization.

- If the Shi'a come to power by majoritarian vote in Iraq and Bahrain, Shi'ite clerics will play a definite role in the process. But most of these clerics do not support Iran's concept of clerical rule, and they have been cooperating over the years with secular Shi'a to attain community goals. There are few indications that most Shi'a in these countries favor an Islamic state; they recognize it as unrealistic and incompatible with conditions, and the Iranian model has not been attractive to any but a small handful.

The Shi'a and the West

- Shi'ism is in no way intrinsically hostile to the West. Shi'ite attitudes toward the West vary, but they are especially determined by (1) the political orientation of the individual, (2) Western attitudes toward the Shi'a, and (3) the degree of Western support for governments that repress the Shi'a. Additionally, the Shi'a are also influenced by factors that affect other Arabs and Muslims, including the Arab-Israeli problem and Western perceptions of Islam. In Kuwait, for example, Shi'a and Sunnis—even the Islamists—agree that the American military presence is a "necessary evil" for Kuwaiti security against Iraq.

- The Shi'a today in a few respects may have more grievances against the West than Sunnis have: in Bahrain due to strong Western support for minority Sunni regimes; in Iraq where the Shi'ite majority has caused the West and the Middle Eastern Sunnis to flinch before the implications of Shi'ite majorities coming to power; in Lebanon the West has supported the then politically dominant Maronites and Sunnis, and turned a blind eye to Israeli occupation of Shi'ite areas. In other words, the Shi'a probably feel that they have been specifically targeted for marginalization by the West. The West demonstrates a dangerous tendency to equate Sunnis with secularism and Shi'a with Islamist movements. Neither is accurate.

- Sunni Islamist radicalism is probably more of a threat to regional regimes than is Shi'ite Islamist radicalism. In both cases, they pose a challenge to their own governments first and foremost—unelected governments that are often despotic, repressive, corrupt, and incompetent. The Shi'a in some countries wish to change the status quo in order to gain more internal power via constitutional means. This in itself is not a threat to the West.

Shi'a and Solutions

- In all Arab states the breakdown of primordial allegiances within the political system and their replacement with issues-oriented politics will benefit the Shi'a—but not only the Shi'a—by blurring the sectarian lines and expanding the dialogue between Sunnis and Shi'a.

- The Shi'a have every incentive to push for greater democratic practice in the Arab world. For this reason, their declared (but untested) long-term commitment to a democratic agenda should reassure the West, where democratization is valued as a form of governance that leads to greater moderation and stability. Of course, no one can guarantee that the Shi'a, once in power, will be any more democratic than any other group or party has been in a region where democratic practice has never historically been strong. The way in which any group comes to power has a lot to do with its subsequent political liberalism. Coming to power under an oppressive situation via revolution is the least conducive setting for the inauguration of liberal governance.

- Once the Shi'a come to power as the majority force in Iraq and Bahrain, it is fallacious to think that they will represent a monolithic group. Shi'ite politics will always be divided by class, regional, ideological, clan, and personality differences. Even when possessing majoritarian power, differing Shi'ite groups are likely to form coalitions with like-minded non-Shi'ite groups in future democratic orders.

- As the Shi'a gain acceptance into society and the political order it will enter a new phase of politics characterized by intra-Shi'ite rivalries, splinterings, realignments, and coalitions with non-Shi'ite groups. This process is already visible in Kuwait and among the Iraqi Shi'ite diaspora.

- Overall, Iran's radical policies over the past two decades have served primarily to complicate the political existence of the Arab Shi'a. We believe it is in the interests of all Shi'a everywhere to develop local religious authority (*maraji' al-taqlid*) within each country in order to diminish the opportunities for any external Shi'ite religious authorities from having undue politico-religious influence over nonlocal Shi'a. Such a situation will serve to lessen Sunni Arab fears that the Shi'a bear allegiance to "outside forces," especially to non-Arab Iran.

- The two cases in which the Shi'a have been able to gain a major degree of equal rights within society have been in Kuwait and Lebanon. These gains came through the growth of democratic process. Both these political systems opened up in the end as the result of major cataclysm—Saddam Hussein's invasion of Kuwait, and the long Lebanese civil war among all sects. The Shi'a had little or nothing to do with the emergence of either of these events. These situations do suggest, however, that many political regimes in the Middle East may have to undergo some kind of cataclysm before democratization and fairer distribution of rights are achieved. Western policymakers may wish to consider whether they could avoid the more bruising transition by seeking early on to facilitate this inevitable transition to more democratic governance.

- A key problem is how to keep politics in the region from becoming "zero-sum" in nature between Sunnis and Shi'a. One means is to accept some form of proportional representation or political sectarianism such as in Lebanon. While U.S. political philosophy finds such political mechanisms unappealing, proportional representation and guarantees to each community of certain positions and powers may serve to reassure them in what will be particularly difficult transitional periods in Bahrain and Iraq. Proportional representation could also help provide the Shi'a with some protections in Saudi Arabia. Kuwait may no longer require such a system if the present political order there continues to function and evolve successfully. The danger, however, is that proportional representation also tends to concretize numerically-determined proportional relationships that are then hard to change, and it inherently discourages the development of political alignments that transcend ethnic or sectarian interests.

Appendix

Divisions within Shi'ism

Divisions within Shi'ism occurred as early as the eighth century and arose from disagreements over succession and rival claims to the Imamate by descendants of Imam 'Ali. Three principal branches of Shi'ism—Twelver, Isma'ili, and Zaydi—survived and are espoused by Arab Shi'a as well as Shi'a in other countries with Muslim populations. Twelver Shi'ism, which recognizes twelve Imams culminating in the occultation of Imam al-Mahdi al-Muntadhar (The Awaited), is by far the largest and most widespread of the three branches. The Isma'ili branch departed from Twelver Shi'ism when it proclaimed Isma'il Ibn Ja'far the next Imam after Ja'far al-Sadiq and terminated the Imamate with Isma'il's son. The Isma'ilis established the Fatimid Dynasty in Egypt, which played a large part in spreading Shi'ism and patronizing Shi'ite scholarship. Isma'ili Shi'ism leans toward an esoteric philosophy of religion that is accentuated in its small offshoots, the Druze and Nizari sects. Isma'ili Shi'ism and its offshoots have adherents in the Indian subcontinent, in Iraq, and in Lebanon. Zaydi Shi'ism regards Zayd al-Shahid as the legitimate fifth Imam and traces the Imamate through his descendants. Zaydi jurisprudence follows the Sunni Hanafi school, bringing Zaydis closer to Sunnis than other branches of Shi'ism. Zaydi Shi'ism is established in Yemen, where the Zaydi Imam Yahya founded the kingdom of Yemen in 1918. A fourth branch of Shi'ism, the 'Alawiyya or Nusariyya, is usually considered a branch of Twelver Shi'ism, and it counts millions of adherents in Syria and Turkey.

Twelver Shi'ism itself has two schools. The Usuli school is today the most prevalent, but it was closely rivaled by the Akhbari school until the seventeenth century. The Akhbaris emphasize reliance on the Traditions (akhbar) of the Prophet and the Imams rather than on interpretation of Principles (usul) known as ijtihad and practiced by the learned 'ulama, or mujtahids. It thus gave less prominence to the Shi'a mujtahids and was closer to Sunni Islam in matters of jurisprudence. The Akhbari school was fought and defeated by the mujtahids in the seventeenth century, but it continued as a minority school within Twelver Shi'ism. In the Arab world, Bahrain, Kuwait, and Basra in Iraq have sizable numbers of followers of the Akhbari school. A third, much smaller school of Twelver Shi'ism is the Shaykhi, which has adherents in the Gulf countries and in Basra.[1]

The Institution of the Marji'iyya

The marji'iyya is the institution of juridical referral on matters affecting religious practices, social relations, and theology. It is specific to Twelver Shi'ism, especially the dominant Usuli school, and closely connected to the principle of Imamate, or guidance of the Muslims.

The principle of imamate stems from the belief that God, who sent the Prophet Muhammad and the Qur'an to Muslims to enlighten, instruct, and lead them in the true Prophet's death. God's love for the umma, and His concern for the welfare of every Muslim in life and in the hereafter, dictates that in every age Muslims must have guides, Imams, to continue the essential function of instructing the umma in the path of righteousness

The associated principle behind the marji'iyya is the importance of 'ilm, or erudition, to deeply understand the holy texts of Islam in all their richness and complexity. An Imam must master the texts to interpret Islam to the mass of people who do not have the means to become learned in the holy texts that comprise the Qur'an and the Sunna.

> [A[cquiring detailed knowledge of the principles of the injunctions and laws of religion through use of the basic documents of the Book and the Sunna and technical reasoning based upon them is not possible for every Muslim. Only a few persons have the capacity for demonstrative jurisprudence, nor is such acquiring of detailed knowledge required of everyone.[2]

Instead, the umma must have guides who devote their lives to the study of the holy texts of Islam, the tradition of Islamic jurisprudence, and the principles upon which interpretation and jurisprudence are based. This expertise is *fiqh*, and is acquired by the *faqih*.

The exercise of interpreting the doctrines of Islam and validation *(tahlil)* of specific modes of conduct, whether in religious or social practice, is *ijtihad*, or interpretation. Ijtihad is particularly important in issues on which the holy texts are either silent or ambiguous, including situations arising from social, economic, political, or scientific change.

The Shi'a believe that shortly before his death, the Prophet designated his cousin and son-in-law, 'Ali, as his successor at a place outside Mecca called Ghadir Khum, saying: "He who accepts me as his lord *(mawla)* accepts 'Ali as his lord."[3] 'Ali therefore became the first Imam by prior designation from Muhammad. Altogether, there were twelve Imams, all descended from 'Ali, the last of whom went into occultation when still a child. The twelve Imams enjoyed attributes exclusive to them. They were divinely guided and *ma'sum,* sanctified from error by God's grace. They had perfect knowledge of the holy texts and the laws because this knowledge was inspired directly by God. During the life of the twelve Imams, the Shi'a and followers of Ahl al-Bayt (people of the house of the Prophet) referred their questions to the Imams and requested their judgements on points of Islamic law. The juridical opinions of the Imams were observed by their followers as the true expression of God's will.

The twelfth Imam went into occultation twice in what are called "the lesser occultation," when he communicated with only designated people, and "the greater occultation," when he ended communication. During the lesser occultation, four successive deputies, *nuwwab* (singular, *na'ib*), designated by the Imam, became his intermediaries with the Shi'ite community. When the period of the lesser occultation and the four nuwwab ended, the period of greater occultation began for the Shi'a. The greater occultation will end only when the twelfth Imam, al-Mahdi al-Muntadhar (The Awaited Guided One), reappears and establishes Islam and justice among the nations of the earth.

The Shi'a, however, continued to need legal and moral guidance during the greater occultation, and since there were no longer any deputies designated by the Imam, a period of general deputization, *niyaba 'amma* began, when multiple guides could emerge. Although none but the twelve Imams could have divine inspiration and *'isma* (sanctification from error), and despite the absence of designated deputies, others could achieve *'ilm* in the laws of Islam and purity in their personal lives. Devout and learned men, *fuqaha* (literally, experts in the principles of Islamic jurisprudence) would devote themselves to the study of the texts, of Shari'a, or Islamic law, and of the principles of Islamic jurisprudence upon which judgements may be made. The expert understanding acquired by the fuqaha would help them answer questions from ordinary Muslims for which there are no explicit directives in the Qur'an, the Sunna of the Prophet, or the traditions of the twelve Imams. This interpretation of texts and their application to questions of Islamic legality, what is allowed *(halal)* and what is forbidden *(haram),* constitutes the vast realm of ijtihad, the distinguishing feature of Twelver Shi'ism.

The final disappearance of the twelfth Imam was a great loss to the Shi'a that left a vacuum in doctrinal and moral leadership. Without specific pronouncements from the Imam, the gates of ijtihad were thrown wide open out of necessity. The class of mujtahids (those who practice ijtihad) proliferated within a brief period after the greater occultation. It was, in many ways, not only a practical need for the Shi'a, but also a spiritual need, as the mass of the Shi'ite community turned for religious mentorship to the mujtahids. The greatest mujtahids became *maraji'* (singular, *marji'*), that is, juridical consultants, and Muslims who sought their opinions were *muqallidun* (singular, *muqallid*), emulators. The practice of ijtihad and the development of marji'iyya were therefore a logical extension of the concept of imama and the belief that the umma needs temporal and spiritual guidance.

Using the term "institution" for marji'iyya is somewhat misleading and needs to be modified. Islam does not have a formal clerical hierarchy. Although they both have a class of clergy who have studied the different disciplines within Islam and usually serve as leaders in prayer and speakers in mosque, in both Shi'ism and Sunni Islam anyone that the community accepts can lead prayers. The status of marji' is not achieved through an academic degree or designation by a panel of higher maraji'. Although great learning, piety, and purity of life are prerequisites for a marji', an indispensable requirement is a following of muqallidun who seek and abide by his jurisdiction on questions they raise to him, and who contribute the *khums,* a set portion of their income, to him for charitable distribution. In a sense, the title of marji' is only a formal recognition of an existing reality: it is bestowed upon a learned mujtahid who has already amassed a large following of emulators, probably of several nationalities and in several countries, and receives substantial contributions of *khums.*

Until the eighteenth century, Twelver Shi'ism was more or less evenly divided between the two schools of Usulis and Akhbaris. Three major differences separate the two schools. Whereas the Usulis rely on the Qur'an, the Sunna, consensus, and reason to understand doctrine, Akhbaris only permit recourse to the Qur'an and the sunna; whereas the Usulis give broad latitude to ijtihad, the Akhbaris reject ijtihad; while Usulis distinguish between the category of mujtahid and muqallid, the Akhbaris believe that all people are muqallid of the Imam. These and other subtler differences allowed the Usuli school to rely heavily on 'ulama and mujtahids, who could use a range of tools and resources and had broad license to interpret and pronounce decision on virtually all aspects of life. In contrast, Akhbari 'ulama were far more restricted in their resources, tools, and interpretative authority. The Usuli school was therefore far more favorable to the mujtahids, and the marji'iyya system came into full flowering in the eighteenth century when the Usuli school won decisively in its rivalry with the Akhbari school. Currently, the majority of Twelver Shi'a belong to the Usuli school, but there are Akhbaris in Bahrain, in pockets on the eastern coast of the Arabian peninsula, and in Basra.

As the Usuli school flourished uncontested over the next two centuries, the jurisdiction of the maraji' expanded beyond explication of Shari'a laws to cover matters of financial transactions, family relations, social conduct, and, eventually, political affairs. By the late nineteenth century, the maraji' wielded enormous power and were able to influence affairs of state from positions outside of, and independent of, the state. Thus they helped overturn the tobacco concession offered by the Shah to British interests in Iran in 1892, they supported the constitutional movement in Iran in 1904, and they led the anti-British revolt in Iraq in 1920.

The power of the senior clerics derived from doctrinal authority, moral stature, and material resources. First, because Usuli Shi'ism divided the community into mujtahids and muqallids, all practicing Shi'a had to follow the directives of one or more mujtahids in almost every aspect of their lives. Mujtahids were venerated for their justice (*'adl*), the purity of their lives, and their personal piety, and they were exemplars for devout Shi'a. Financially, the highest class of mujtahids, the maraji', commanded considerable resources. A practicing Shi'ite is required to pay the *khums* as well as *zakat*, a charitable contribution, to the marji' for distribution to the needy. Many wealthy Shi'a also made endowments *(awqaf)*, usually in the form of income-producing property, which were administered by mujtahids or maraji'. These financial contributions in fact became a measure of the importance of a marji' and the size of his following. Although the contributions were not strictly given to the marji' for his personal use, they were placed at his disposal to apply as he saw fit. Thus many maraji' could establish seminaries and other schools, support students of theology and lesser clerics, build orphanages, and finance publications, as well as give alms to the poor and needy. The financial resources were not only a measure of the importance of a marji', they also helped to expand his influence.

Finally, as the representative or deputy of the Imam, the marji' also carried political weight, although the precise nature of his political role remained somewhat nebulous. The twelve Imams were regarded as the divinely ordained leaders of the umma in both the spiritual and temporal realms. The Muslim rulers who came after 'Ali were illegitimate because they had usurped the leadership of the umma from the Imams and governed in *dhulm*, injustice; these rulers can be tolerated or challenged, but they cannot become the ultimate authority over the conscience of the Shi'a. Thus the issue of who can have legitimate political authority over the Shi'a after the occultation of the twelfth Imam was left unsettled. The maraji', as representatives of the hidden Imam, and because of their expertise and justice, were most suited to rule the umma in the absence of the Imam. Thus in the early 1970s Ayatollah Khomeini published a landmark book that developed the concept of *wilayat al-faqih* (the governorship of the jurisconsult) to resolve the uncertainty, but the concept has not been universally accepted by the senior 'ulama of Shi'ism. Nevertheless, the maraji', as the highest authority over the Shi'ite community, have had considerable political sway even when they did not hold the reigns of power, and they were consulted by practicing Shi'a on political issues including opposition to the government, jihad, formation of political parties, and other purely political questions. The apogee of clerical political rule of course occurred in Iran after the revolution of 1979.

The maraji' therefore exercise authority over their followers and act as a binding force uniting their emulators and followers, who can be regarded as belonging to the same school and following the same mentor. However, this unity is somewhat diminished by the important fact of the multiplicity of maraji'. During the lesser occultation, the four nuwwab who represented the twelfth Imam were specified *(khass)* by him, and there was one representative at a time. After the great occultation, representation was general *('amm)*, meaning that no single representative was designated, and several could strive to achieve this status at the same time. In practice, there have always been several mujtahids in any given era, and only rarely was there a supreme marji' to whom all deferred.

In part this proliferation was necessitated by the wide geographic spread of Shi'ism and the difficulties of communication; when Shi'ite communities needed a local authority to respond to their pressing questions, and the multiplicity of mujtahids presented limited scope for friction. However, the concentration of mujtahids in cities such as Qom, Tehran, and Najaf, as well as vastly improved communications, does create occasions for conflict among mujtahids and, by extension, among the maraji' and can even choose a different marji' for different needs, although this rarely happens, for once a personal bond is established with a marji' loyalty usually stays firm. Because the maraji' occasionally disagree on both secondary and even major issues, their divisions are reflected in divisions within the Shi'ite community as a whole. One of the salient examples of such differences was the activist political role adopted by Khomeini in the 1970s and 1980s, as contrasted with the apolitical stance of several senior maraji', including Ayatollahs Khoei in Iraq and Rouhani in Qom. These senior clerics, who had a higher religious station, together commanded a far wider religious following than Khomeini.

Notes

Chapter One—The Shi'a Identity

1. A government official in a Gulf country expressed surprise that the authors should want to write on such a "sensitive" topic.
2. See discussion of "proto-shi'ism" in Moojan Momen, *An Introduction to Shi'i Islam,* (New Haven, CT: Yale University Press, 1986), esp. chapter 2, "The Question of Succession to Muhammad" and p. 20.
3. Ibid., p. 97, for origins of Shi'ite ulama in thirteenth and fourteenth centuries.
4. Ibid., pp. 98, 108.
5. Fuad Ajami, *The Vanished Imam,* (Ithaca, NY: Cornell University Press, 1986), p. 138.
6. See Ajami for an interesting exploration of this concept, op. cit., pp. 138–141.
7. Farhad Ibrahim, *Al-Ta'ifiyya wa'l-Siyasa fi'l 'Alam Al-'Arabi* (Sectarianism and Politics in the Arab World—the Model of the Shi'a in Iraq), (Cairo: Madbouli Bookshop, 1996), p. 85
8. Saudi Shi'a contend that Islam was carried to their regions on the eastern coast of the peninsula by the early *Sahaba,* companions of the Prophet, and that their Islam has retained its purity.
9. Although this term fell into disuse, it has been revived in Saudi Arabia, as evidenced in a paper entitled "Waqi' al-Rafidha fi Bilad at-Tawhid" (The Reality of the Rafidha in the Land of Unitarianism), presented to the Council of Higher Ulama in Saudi Arabia in 1993. The paper, written by a fundamentalist Wahhabi, is a dogmatic condemnation of the Shi'a (the Rafidha) in Saudi Arabia (Bilad al-Tawhid) and a call to impose further restrictions on their activities.
10. This duality is mirrored in Ayatollah Khomeini's use of *mustadh'afun* (the oppressed) and *mustakbirun* (the arrogant).

11. Hanna Batatu, *The Old Social Classes and the Revolutionary Movements of Iraq,* (Princeton, NJ: Princeton University Press, 1978), pp. 44–45.

12. See for example series of articles in the Iraqi official newspaper "*Al-Thawra*" in April 1991, entitled "What Happened at the End of 1990 and these Months of 1991, and Why Did it Happen?," reprinted in "Iraqi File," September 1993, published by the Centre for Iraqi Studies, Surrey, England.

13. See Sa'id al-Shihabi, *Al-Bahrain 1920–1971, Qira'a fi'l-Watha'iq al-Baritaniyya* (Bahrain 1920–1971, A Reading of British Documents [in Arabic]). (Dar al-Kunuz Al-Adabiya, Beirut, 1996).

14. Bernard Lewis, *The Political Language of Islam,* (University of Chicago Press, 1988), pp. 92–94; Sayyid Muhammad Husayn Fadhlallah, *al-Islam wa Mantiq al-Quwwa* (Islam and the Logic of Strength), (Beirut, 1985), pp. 49–62; Sayyid 'Abdullah al-Gharifi, *al-Tashayyu* (Shi'ism), (Beirut, 1990), pp. 335–346.

15. Muhammad Husayn Fadhlallah, *al- Islam wa Mantiq al- Quwwa. Quwwa* can mean strength, force or power.

16. According to Batatu and others. However, Da'wa members interviewed by the authors and Farhadi, op. cit., date the first formation of the party to 1958.

Chapter Two—The Arab Shi'a in the Sunni State

1. From Liora Lukitz, *Iraq: The Search for National Identity* (London: Frank Cass, 1995), p. 130.

2. The earliest example of a social and political contract in Islam is "The Constitution of Medina," a contract between the prophet Muhammad, Muslim tribes, and their followers from the city of Medina. Quoted in full in W. Montgomery Watt, *Islamic Political Thought* (Edinburgh University Press, 1968).

3. See Bernard Lewis, *The Political Language of Islam* (University of Chicago Press, 1988), pp. 58–59, for a discussion of the term.

4. Moojan Momen, *An Introduction to Shi'i Islam* (New Haven, CT: Yale University Press, 1985), p. 64, and W. M. Watt, op. cit. p. 83.

5. For a study of Shu'ubiya, see Abd-al 'Aziz al-Douri, *al-Judhur al-Ta'rikhiyya Li'l-Shu'ubiya* (The Historical Roots of Shu'ubiya) (Beirut, 1963).

6. Only the first four caliphs were selected through consensus. Once the 'Umayyad dynasty was established, the caliphate became hereditary under what had become essentially realpolitik secular power and the new caliph was designated by his successors or by struggle. The 'Umayyad caliphs were not descendants of the Prophet, and were not in the line of Imams.

7. Momin, p. 73.

8. W. Montgomery Watt, *Islamic Political Thought,* p. 45.

9. For a discussion of early Shi'ite dissent in Saudi Arabia, see Hamza al-Hasan, *History of the Shi'a in Saudi Arabia,* vol. 2.

10. Sa'id al-Shihabi, op. cit., pp. 20, 158–169.

11. Ibrahim, op. cit., pp. 122–123.

12. Joyce Wiley, *The Islamic Movement of the Iraqi Shi'a* (London: Lynne Rienner, 1992), especially chapter 3 on the formation of Da'wa; Farhadi, op. cit, pp. 245–246, on the influence of Muslim Brotherhood; interviews with party members.

13. Ranstorp, *Hizballah in Lebanon: the Politics of the Western Hostage Crisis* (New York: St. Martin's Press, 1997), p. 26.

Chapter Three—Shi'ite Demands and Strategies

1. See Ranstorp, op. cit., pp. 30–31, and Waddah Sharara, *Dawlat Hizballah: Lubnan Mujtama'an Islamiyan* (The Hizballah State: Lebanon as an Islamic Society) (Beirut: Dar An-Nahar, 1996), pp. 119, 202.

2. For an interesting discussion of relations between the Muslim Brotherhood and Iran, see Ahmed Yousef, "The Muslim Brotherhood and Iran," *Middle East Affairs Journal* (Summer/Fall 1998).

Chapter Four—The Iranian Connection

1. Moojan Momen, *An Introduction to Shi'i Islam* (New Haven, CT: Yale University Press, 1985), pp. 127, 130–131.

2. Talib M. Aziz, "Popular Sovereignty in Contemporary Shi'i Political Thought," pre-publication draft.

3. Based on authors' interviews with a leading Iraqi Shi'ite activist in exile, London, January 1997.

4. Sadegh Hedayat, "Seeking Absolution," in *Modern Persian Short Stories,* ed./tr. Minoo Southgate (Washington, D.C.: Three Continents Press, 1980), pp. 5–6.

5. Quoted in Robin Wright, *In the Name of God: The Khomeini Decade,* (New York: Simon and Schuster, 1989), p. 173; and in Chibli Mallat, "Iran, Shi'ism and the Arab Middle East," in *The Middle East into the 21st Century* (Syracuse, NY: Syracuse University Press, 1996).

6. Waddah Sharara, *Dawlat Hizballah* (Beirut: Dar al-Nahar, 1996), p. 198.

7. Indeed, the Iranian clergy had spoken out on the issue of Muslim peoples in the Russian Empire, many of whom had once been under Persian influence if not actual rule; the clerics in 1826 successfully demanded that Fath 'Ali Shah carry out a jihad, ultimately defeated, to liberate these Muslims in the Caucasus. Momen, op. cit., p. 138.

8. Reuters, January 4, 1994

9. *The Guardian,* May 13, 1996.

Chapter Five—The Shi'a of Iraq

1. Total population figure according to government census of 1997. There is no separate figure for the Shi'a.

2. Ghassan Atiyyah, *Al-Iraq: Nash'atu Dawla* (Iraq 1908–1921: The Emergence of a State) (London: Laam Ltd., 1988), p. 406.

3. Prince Faisal bin Hussein, son of the Sherif of Mecca, was crowned king of Iraq in August 1921. Iraq joined the League of Nations on October 3, 1932. See Stephen Hemsley Longrigg, *Iraq, 1900–1950: A Political, Social and Economic History* (London: Oxford University Press, 1956), p. 187.

4. Ibid., pp. 264, 331–333.

5. See Yitzhak Nakash, *The Shi'is of Iraq* (Princeton, NJ: Princeton University Press, 1994), pp. 25–42. Moojan Momen, however, states that in the tenth century southern Iraq, with the exception of Basra, was Shi'ite. See Moojan Momen, *An Introduction to Shi'i Islam* (New Haven, CT: Yale University Press, 1985), p. 83.

6. Momen, op. cit., p. 84.

7. Ali al-Wardi, *Lamahat Ijtima'iya Min Tarikh al-Iraq al-Hadith* (Social Aspects of Iraqi Modern History), (Baghdad, 1974), provides insight into the rural-urban dichotomy of Shi'ite life at the turn of the century.

8. Hanna Batatu, *The Old Social Classes and the Revolutionary Movements of Iraq* (Princeton, NJ: Princeton University Press, 1978), p. 49.

9. Majid Khadduri, *Republican Iraq* (Oxford: Oxford University Press, 1969), pp. 234–236.

10. The classic account of imperial struggle in Iraq is told in S. H. Longrigg's *Four Centuries of Modern Iraq* (Beirut: Librarie du Liban, 1968).

11. Atiyyah, op. cit., p. 355.

12. For a discussion of the role of the 'ulema in the 1920 revolt, see Nakash, op. cit., pp. 66–72.

13. Text of memorandum cited in Abdul Karim al-Uzri, "Mushkilat al-Hukm fil Iraq" (The Problem of Governance in Iraq), London 1991.

14. Batatu, op. cit., table 7–4.

15. Ibid., tables 55–1, 58–1, 58–2, and A-49. There are suggestions that the abrupt termination of the first Ba'th regime by the staunchly Sunni general Abdul Salam Arif was carried out from fear of Shi'ite dominance. However, the first Ba'th regime was both bloody and incompetent, and it departed unlamented.

16. Iraqi patriotic appeal, by contrast, was nurtured by invoking Iraq's ancient, pre-Islamic past, which was portrayed as the cultural heritage of all Arabs. See Amatzia Baram, *Culture, History and Ideology in the Formation of Ba'thist Iraq, 1968–1989* (New York: St. Martin's Press, 1991).

17. Muhamad Sa'id al-Sahhaf, Iraq's foreign minister, and Sa'dun Hammadi, Speaker of the National Assembly, are both Shi'ite. However, neither has any part in political decision-making or real authority.

18. Joyce Wiley, *The Islamic Movement of Iraqi Shi'as* (Boulder, CO: Lynne Rienner, 1992), Appendix 3.

19. Confirmed to the authors by a veteran of the party.

20. Wiley, op. cit., p. 46, and authors' interviews with Iraqi clerics in London.

21. Ibid., Appendix 3.

22. Wiley gives a figure of 16 killed and 2,000 arrested (p. 52). Many of those arrested would almost certainly have been executed or died under torture.

23. The position of Iraqis in Iran at the time was awkward, and they confined their efforts to propaganda against the regime. There were only individual defections from the Iraqi armed forces to Iran, and there are no reports of infiltration of Iraqis from Iran to Iraq to encourage rebellion among the armed forces.

24. UN Report on Human Rights in Iraq, UN document # E/CN.4/1995/58, February 25, 1994.

25. For an account of the first days of the uprising in the south, see Kanan Makiya, *Cruelty and Silence* (New York: W.W. Norton, 1993). The uprising is said to have been triggered by Shi'ite soldiers and junior officers returning defeated from Kuwait.

26. Hussein Kamil is reported to have rhetorically challenged Imam Husayn at his shrine in Kerbala by stating, "I am Husayn and you are Husayn. Let's see who is the stronger." Kamil defected to Jordan in 1995, returned to Iraq in 1996, and was killed by the regime upon his return. Information about the uprising was gathered by the authors from participants and eyewitnesses interviewed over a number of years.

27. Reported to the authors by a Kurdish leader who attended meetings with al-Majid in April 1991.

28. "Madha Hasal fi Awakhir 'Am 1990 wa Hadhihi 'l-Ashhyr min 'Am 1991" ("What Happened at the end of 1990 and these months of 1991?"), articles appearing in Iraqi *Al-Thawra* newspaper, April 1991, reprinted in *al-Malaff al-Iraqi,* (London, 1993).

29. Authors' interviews with participants. Cf. Also Akram al-Hakim, Al-Dictatoria wa'l Intifadha (Dictatorship and the Intifadha) (London: Al-Rafid, 1998).

30. The authors have witnessed bitter arguments over this issue among participants in the uprising.

31. Al-Hakim, op. cit., Appendix, p. 268.

32. Authors' translation of the Arabic text of statement issued on October 31, 1992.

33. The Iraqi communists agree with the Islamists in condemning the Ba'th party in Iraq. However, both have good relations with Syria, which has a Ba'thist regime. Syria has served as refuge to Iraqi nationalists, Ba'thists, communists as well as Islamists.

34. The al-Khoei Foundation's monthly magazine, *al-Nour,* is a valuable resource for students of these topics.

35. See relevant country chapters for Da'wa connections.

36. Interview by authors in London.

Chapter Six—The Shi'a of Bahrain

1. Isma'ili Shi'ism took over in Egypt under the Fatimids (909–1171); it also had a powerful presence independent of Egypt in the Gulf known as the

Carmathians (Qaramita). The Isma'ilis were distinguished by their belief that there are internal, esoteric, and secret interpretations behind all the apparent, external meanings of the Qur'an. A branch of this movement, the Assassins, also based itself in (then Sunni) Iran, and threatened and assassinated Sunni statesmen in the Muslim world for over a century.

2. Momen, op. cit., p. 90.

3. Momen, p. 120.

4. Mansoor Al-Jamri, "Prospect of a Moderate Islamic Discourse: the case of Bahrain," paper presented at the Middle East Studies Association 31st Annual Meeting, San Francisco, November 22, 1997, published in *BFM Bulletin,* January 2, 1998.

5. Momen, op. cit., p. 145.

6. Mansoor Al-Jamri, p. 145.

7. Interview with a long-term specialist on Bahrain.

8. The Usuli school predominates in Iran and gives wide latitude to ijtihad, or interpretation. Many younger Bahrainis are turning from the Akhbari school to the Usuli.

9. Based on interviews with Shi'a and Sunni leaders in Bahrain in June 1997. See also Joseph Kostiner, "Shi'I Unrest in the Gulf," in *Shi'ism, Resistance and Revolution,* ed. Martin Kramer (Boulder, CO: Westview Press, 1987), pp. 176–177.

10. Sa'id al-Shihabi, *Al-Bahrain 1920–1971, Qira'a fil Watha'iq al-Baritania* (An Examination of British Documents) (Beirut, 1966).

11. Interview with an economic specialist on Bahrain.

12. For an excellent description of the problem of deterioration of human rights and civil liberties in Bahrain, see *Routine Abuse, Routine Denial: Civil Rights and the Political Crisis in Bahrain* (Washington, D.C.: Human Rights Watch/Middle East, 1997).

13. Human Rights Watch, op. cit., p. 2.

14. Kostiner, op. cit., pp. 177–178, 180, and interviews with members of the petition movement in Bahrain, June 1997.

15. Interviews with Sunni and Shi'a members of the petition movement, Bahrain, June 1997.

16. On July 7, 1999, two months after Shaykh Hamad al-Khalifa succeeded his father as emir of Bahrain, al-Jamri, after a brief trial, was sentenced to 10 years in prison and fined 5.7 million dinars ($15 million). On the same day, al-Jamri was released under stern conditions. Reuters report, July 7, 1999, and *Middle East International,* July 1999.

17. One Shi'ite leader commented that "the BFM doesn't have enough arms even to take over a police station." It is difficult to reliably assess this issue between conflicting government and opposition sources, each of which casts major doubts on the veracity of the other's account.

18. This view was expressed to the authors by a Sunni political figure close to the regime.

19. Human Rights Watch, op. cit., pp. 1, 43.

20. Al-Jamri, op. cit.

21. The Human Rights Watch report of 1997, for example, states that "No known Bahraini opposition groups goes by the name of 'Hizb Allah' and no communications or publications have appeared under this name. It is a term used exclusively by the government to refer to the spectrum of Shi'a opposition forces and in particular the Bahrain Islamic Freedom Movement (BFM). [The government] claims that Shaykh al-Jamri and seven other Shi'ite community leaders detained 'are leading members of the terrorist group Hizballah-Bahrain, primarily responsible for the terrorist campaign of violence and destruction.' While the possible existence of a Bahraini group of this name cannot be excluded, the government's effort to attribute the past several years' political unrest to its machinations has no credibility." Human Rights Watch, op. cit., p. 41.

22. These graffiti were recorded by the authors during their visit to villages in June 1997, where they can be found on almost every wall. Their vividness and poetic concision are striking.

23. From a Sunni liberal.

24. Human Rights Watch, op. cit., p. 37.

25. Letters from the Centre for the Independence of Judges and Lawyers (Geneva), February 11, 1999, quoted by the *Voice of Bahrain,* February 12, 1999, and from the International Bar Association, quoted by the *Voice of Bahrain,* February 16, 1999.

26. See note 16 above.

Chapter Seven—The Shi'a of Kuwait

1. Reuters report, April 15, 1991.

2. For example, in the 1996 elections, Ali al-Baghli, a secular candidate, lost to Sayid Husayn al-Qallaf, a Shi'ite cleric.

3. Magnus Ranstorp, *Hizb'Allah in Lebanon* (New York: St. Martin's Press, 1997), pp. 25–30, 91–92.

4. Author's interviews with Iraqi Da'wa party members

5. *Los Angeles Times,* April 12, 1991.

6. Hujjat al-Islam 'Abbas Muhri, a Shi'ite cleric who represented Ayatollah Khomeini in Kuwait, was expelled as early as 1980. In a sign of changing attitudes in Kuwait, he was invited back in 1997. Most deportees were Iranian nationals.

7. Interviews in Kuwait and AFP report, November 10, 1996.

8. *Mideast Mirror,* October 15, 1996, quoting an article in al-Hayat newspaper of London.

9. According to a Shi'ite member of the National assembly interviewed by the authors. This was also confirmed by other Shi'a and Sunnis in Kuwait.

10. Women's suffrage was proposed by the Kuwaiti Emir in June 1999, while parliament was suspended pending elections on July 3, 1999. The new Assembly must ratify the Emiri decree. The Shi'a MPs have not opposed it, but most MPs object to the unconstitutional manner in which it was introduced.

Chapter Eight—The Shi'a of Saudi Arabia

1. *Saudi Arabia Handbook* (Washington, D.C.: Federal Research Division, Library of Congress, Internet Edition).

2. *Mideast Mirror,* August 27, 1996, p. 15, and author interviews with Saudi Shi'a.

3. Goldberg, Jacob, "The Shi'i Minority in Saudi Arabia," in *Shi'ism and Social Protest,* eds. Juan R. I. Cole and Nickie R. Keddie (New Haven, CT: Yale University Press, 1986), pp. 230–231.

4. Goldberg, pp. 231–232.

5. Goldberg, pp. 233–236.

6. Minnesota Lawyers International Human Rights Committee Report, Chapter IV, (1996), as reproduced by the Committee against Corruption in Saudi Arabia, Internet Website <http://www.miraserve.com>.

7. Ibid., chapter IV.

8. Saudi Shi'ite views of the Kingdom, its history and its failings are detailed in an anonymous exile work, *Al-Shi'a fi'l Mamlaka al-'Arabiyya al-Su'udiyya 'an al-Madhi al-Hadhir wa'l Mustaqbal* (The Shi'a in the Kingdom of Saudi Arabia: Past, Present and Future), presented to the Al-Kho'i Foundation, London, 1995.

9. Minnesota Lawyers International Human Rights Committee Report, op. cit.

10. Minnesota Lawyers International Human Rights Committee Report, op. cit.

11. Mamoun Fandy, *Saudi Arabia and the Politics of Dissent* (New York: St. Martin's Press, 1999), p. 5.

12. Nasir Bin Sulayman al-'Amr, *Al-Rafidha fi Bilad al-Tawhid* ("The Rejectionists [i.e., Shi'a] in the Land of Orthodox Faith").

13. Based on statements made to the authors by Saudi Shi'ite leaders in exile.

14. Textbook entitled "Al-Tawhid," (Ministry of Education, 1992), used as part of ninth grade curriculum.

15. "Saudi Shiites quadruple their share in expanded Shoura Council," *Mideast Mirror,* July 7, 1997.

16. Author interview with Saudi Shi'ite leader in exile, September 1997.

17. See *Mideast Mirror,* August 27, 1997, p. 15.

18. Fandy, op. cit., p. 6.

19. Minnesota Lawyers International Human Rights Committee Report, op. cit.

20. Fandy, p. 7.

21. For a detailed discussion of these events, see *Mideast Mirror,* August 27, 1996, p. 15, drawing on material by Riyadh Najib al-Rayyis in *al-Nahar,* March 1994, reprinted and reviewed in *Al-Quds al-'Arabi.*

22. Fandy, op. cit., p. 8.

23. Rayyis, op. cit., *Mideast Mirror,* August 27, 1996.

24. Rayyis, p. 17. This last item seems somewhat suspect, since it is hard to believe the regime agreed to grant Shi'ism recognized legal status when even other Sunni schools of jurisprudence have not received this dispensation.

25. *Mideast Mirror,* August 27, 1997, p. 15.

26. For information on Shirazi's harassment by security authorities in Iran, see Muslim Student Association News Website, November 2, 1997, carrying information from Shirazi's own headquarters in Canada, the World Council for Imamiah Affairs. <http://msanews.mynet.net>.

27. Interviews with Shi'a exiles in London.

28. Amnesty International, AI Index: MDE 23/10/96.

29. "No Foreign Role in Seen in Saudi Base Bombing," *New York Times,* May 22, 1998.

30. "Massa'ri [sic] Expounds His Plan of Sunnite-Shi'ite Saudi Opposition Front," in *Mideast Mirror,* November 13, 1996.

31 Hijaz is often used as a term even by Shi'a since it carries the weight of the religious centrality of the region to Islam, and is a venerable euphemism to avoid using the term "Saudi Arabia" which many Saudis find distasteful.

32. Emad S. Mekay, "Kingdom's Crackdown threatens Islamic Peace Deal," November 22, 1996, Gemini News Service, Internet.

33. Mas'ari, *Mideast Mirror,* op. cit., p. 15.

34. Fandy, op. cit., p. 9.

35. Fandy, p. 27.

36. *Mideast Mirror,* November 12, 1996.

37. "Massa'ri [sic] Expounds His Plan of Sunnite-Shiite Saudi Opposition Front," *Mideast Mirror,* November 13, 1996, p. 15.

38. Mamoun Fandy, "Muhammad al-Mas'ari," op. cit., p. 38.

39. Authors' personal interviews with Shi'a in exile.

40. Based on Interviews with Saudi Shi'ite dissidents abroad in 1997.

Chapter Nine—The Shi'a of Lebanon

1. Figures are unreliable and differ among Shi'a and non-Shi'a. There is no doubt, however, that the Shi'a represent the largest sectarian group in the country.

2. Augustus Richard Norton, *Amal and the Shi'a: Struggle for the Soul of Lebanon* (Austin: University of Texas Press, 1987), p. 35.

3. The two best sources are Fouad Ajami, *The Vanished Imam: Musa al-Sadr and the Shia of Lebanon* (Ithaca, NY: Cornell University Press, 1986), and Norton, op. cit.

4. This mission from Iran began under the Shah's blessing 20 years before the Islamic revolution—at a time when Iran was concerned with combating, in Lebanon and elsewhere, the rising force of revolutionary pan-Arabism under Egyptian direction. For further background information see in particular Abbas William Samii, "The Shah's Lebanon Policy: The Role of Savak," *Middle Eastern Studies,* January 1997.

5. For an excellent discussion and a sense of the character of this traditional Shi'ite feudal leadership, see Ajami, op. cit., chapter 2, and Norton, op. cit. p. 136.

6. Ajami, op. cit., pp. 97–99.

7. For the role of the Da'wa party in Lebanon, see Wadah Sharara, *Dawlat Hizballah: Lubnan Mujtama'an Islamiyan* (Beirut: Dar al-Nahar Li'l-Nashra, 1996), chapter six.

8. For kinship within the circles of ulema, see Sharara, op. cit. p. 109.

9. Bruce Hoffman, *Recent Trends and Future Prospects of Iranian Sponsored International Terrorism* (Santa Monica, CA: RAND, National Defense Research Institute, March, 1990), p. 11.

10. For an analysis of the May 17, 1983 agreement, see Norton, op. cit. pp. 97–99.

11. Hoffman, op. cit., p. 11.

12. Hoffman, op. cit., p. 10.

13. The West and the Soviet Union similarly elevated their political confrontations with heavy reference to abstract causes such as democracy or "the forces of history."

14. Magnus Ranstorp, *Hizb'allah in Lebanon: The Politics of the Western Hostage Crisis* (New York: St. Martin's Press, 1997), p. 32, p. 50.

15. Ranstorp, p. 58.

16. "A revolution of the hungry looms in Lebanon," *Mideast Mirror,* June 27, 1997.

17. Norton, op. cit., p. 101.

18. Ranstorp, op. cit., p. 49.

19. Martin Kramer, "Redeeming Jerusalem: the pan-Islamic Premise of Hizballah," in *The Iranian Revolution and the Muslim World,* ed. David Menashri (Boulder, CO: Westview Press, 1990), cited in Ranstorp, op. cit., p. 48.

20. From "An Open Letter Addressed by Hizballah to the Downtrodden in Lebanon and in the World," February 16, 1985, as quoted in Norton, op. cit., p 174–175.

21. From an interview with a Hizballah member of Parliament, November 1997.

22. Ranstorp, p. 56.

23. Ajami, op. cit., p. 165.

24. *Mideast Mirror,* March 17, 1997.

25. *Mideast Mirror,* March 17, 1997.

26. Authors' interview with leading Hizballah members, November 1997.

27. Norton, op. cit., p. 137.

28. Based on an interview with a Lebanese Sunni observer of Sunni religious institutions.

29. In an interview with a spokesman for the Bahrain Liberation Front.

30. Ajami, op. cit., pp. 104–105.

31. See Waddhah Sharara, *Dawlat Hizballah: Lubnan Mujtama'an Islamiyyan* (Beirut: Dar al-Nahar Li'l-Nashra, 1996), chapter twelve, for a good description of Hizballah's encouragement of Shi'ite practices.

32. Expression used by a Hizballah spokesmen in an interview with the authors, Beirut, November 1997.

Appendix

1. Allamah Sayyid Muhammad Husayn Tabatabai, *Shi'a*, tr. Sayyid Husayn Nasr (Qom, Iran, 1981), pp. 76–83; and Moojan Momen, *An Introduction to Shi'i Islam* (New Haven, CT: Yale University Press, 1985), pp. 35–40, 117–118, and 222.
2. Allamah Sayyid Muhammad Husayn Tabatabai, *Shi'a*, p. 103.
3. There are several variation of this hadith of the Prophet, with these words as their core. The hadith is very frequently cited in Shi'ite texts or books on Shi'ism. Cf. Sayed Abdullah al-Gharifi, *Al-Tashayyu'* (Shi'ism, Its Rise, Stages and Pillars) (Beirut, 1990), pp. 90–95.
4. Muhammad Bahr al-Ulum, *Al-Ijtihad: Usuluhu was Ahkamuhu* (Ijtihad: Its Principles and Laws), third ed., (Beirut, 1991), pp. 168–183; Moojan Momen, *An Introduction to Shi'i Islam* (New Haven, CT: Yale University Press, 1985), pp. 222–225.

Selected Bibliography

In addition to nearly 200 interviews, news reports, and articles, the following is a partial bibliography of books and papers consulted for this study. Many other books on various countries and topics were consulted for our general background, but not necessarily included here.

Ajami, Fuad. *The Vanished Imam: Musa Al-Sadr and the Shi'a of Lebanon.* Ithaca, NY: Cornell University Press, 1986.

Amnesty International, USA. Pamphlet on "Saudi Arabia," January 1990.

Al-Attiyyah, Ghassan. *al-'Iraq: Nash'atu Da'wa* (Iraq: Emergence of a State). London: LAAM Publishers, 1988.

Aziz, Talib M. "Popular Sovereignty in Contemporary Shi'i Political Thought." Prepublication draft.

Bahrul Ulum, Muhammad. *al-Ijtihad, Usuluhu wa Ahkamuhu* (Ijtihad, Its Principles and Rules), third edition. Beirut: Dar al-Zahra', 1991.

Bahry, Louay. "The Opposition in Bahrain: A Bellwether for the Gulf?" *Middle East Policy* (May 1997).

Baram, Amatzia. *Culture, History and Ideology in the formation of Ba'thist Iraq, 1968–1989.* New York: St. Martin's Press, 1991.

Batatu, Hanna. *The Old Social Classes and the Revolutionary Movements of Iraq.* Princeton, NJ: Princeton University Press, 1978.

———. "Iraq's Underground Shi'a Movements: Characteristics, Causes and Prospects." *Middle East Journal* (Summer 1981).

Cole, Juan R. I., and Nikki R. Keddie, eds. *Shi'ism and Social Protest.* New Haven, CT: Yale University Press, 1986.

Crystal, Jill. *Kuwait: the Transformation of an Oil State.* Boulder, CO: Westview Press, 1992.

Davis, Eric and Nicolas Gavrielides, eds. *Statecraft in the Middle East: Oil, Historical Memory and Popular Culture.* Miami: Florida International University Press, 1991.

al-Douri, 'Abd-al- 'Aziz. *al-Judhur al-Tarikhiyya Li'l Shu'ubiyya* (Historical Roots of Shu'ubism). Beirut: Dar At-Tali'a, 1986.

Fandy, Mamoun. *Saudi Arabia and the Politics of Dissent.* New York: St. Martin's Press, 1999.

Ghabra, Shafiq. "Kuwait and the Dynamics of Socio-Economic Change." *The Middle East Journal* (Summer 1997).

al-Gharifi, al-Sayyid 'Abdallah. *At-Tashayyu'* (Shi'ism). Beirut: Dar Al-Mawsem li'l-I'lam, 1990.

Goldberg, Jacob. "The Shi'i Minority in Saudi Arabia," in *Shi'ism and Social Protest,* eds. Juan R. I. Cole and Nickie R. Keddie. New Haven, CT: Yale University Press, 1986

Al-Haydari, Ibrahim. "*Trajidia Karbala': Sociologia al-Khitab al-Shi'i* (The Tragedy of Krabala: The Sociology of Shi'ite Rhetoric). London: Dar al Saqi, 1999.

Hedayat, Sadegh. "Seeking Absolution," in *Modern Persian Short Stories,* ed./tr. Minoo Southgate. Washington, D.C.: Three Continents Press, 1980.

Human Rights Watch. *Routine Abuse, Routine Denial: Civil Rights and the Political Crisis in Bahrain.* Washington, D.C.: Human Rights Watch/ Middle East, 1997.

Ibrahim, Farhad. *al-Ta'ifiya al-Siyasiyya fi'l 'Alam al-'Arabi: Numudhaj Al-Shi'a fi'l-'Iraq* (Political Sectarianism in the Arab World: the Model of the Shi'a in Iraq). Cairo: Maktabat Madbouli, 1996.

al-Jamri, Mansoor. "Prospect of a Moderate Islamic Discourse: the Case of Bahrain." Paper presented at the Middle East Studies Association 31st Annual Meeting. San Francisco, CA, November 22, 1998.

Khadduri, Majid. *Republican Iraq.* Oxford: Oxford University Press, 1969.

Kostiner, Joseph. "Shi'i Unrest in the Gulf," in *Shi'ism, Resistance and Revolution,* ed. Martin Kramer. Boulder, CO: Westview Press, 1987.

Kramer, Martin, ed. *Shi'ism, Resistance and Revolution.* Boulder, CO: Westview Press, 1987.

Lewis, Bernard. *The Political Language of Islam.* University of Chicago Press, 1988.

Longrigg, Stephen Hemsley. *Iraq, 1900 to 1950.* Oxford: Oxford University Press, 1956.

———. *Four Centuries of Modern Iraq.* Beirut: Librarie du Liban, 1968.

Lukitz, Liora. *Iraq: The Search for National Identity.* London: Frank Cass, 1995.

al-Malaff al-'Iraqi. London: LAAM, 1993. Reprint of series of seven articles in the Ba'th party newspaper, *al-Thawra,* April 1991:"Madha Hasal fi Awakhir 'Am 1990 wa Hadhihi 'l-'Ashhur min 'Am 1991? Wa li Madha Hasal Alladhi Hasal?" (What Happened at the End of 1990 and these Months of 1991, and Why Did It Happen?)

Mallat, Chibli. "Iran, Shi'ism and the Arab Middle East," in *The Middle East into the 21st Century.* Syracuse, NY: Syracuse University Press, 1996.

Menashri, David, ed. *The Iranian Revolution and the Muslim World.* Boulder, CO: Westview Press, 1990.

Minnesota Lawyers International Human Rights Committee Report, Chapter IV, 1996, as reproduced by the Committee against Corruption in Saudi Arabia, Internet Website.

Momen, Moojan. *An Introduction to Shi'i Islam*. New Haven, CT: Yale University Press, 1985.

Nakash, Yitzhak. *The Shi'is of Iraq*. Princeton, NJ: Princeton University Press, 1994.

Norton, Augustus Richard. *Amal and the Shi'a: Struggle for the Soul of Lebanon*. University of Texas Press, 1987.

al-Omar, Nasir Bin Sulayman, "Al-Rafidha fi Bilad al-Tawhid" (The Rejectionists in the Land of Unitarianism), unpublished letter and paper addressed to Shaykh 'Abdel 'Aziz Bin Baz and the Council of Ulema in Saudi Arabia, 1993. [Authors are in possession of a copy of the letter and the memorandum.]

Ramazani, R. K. *Revolutionary Iran: Challenge and Response in the Middle East*. Baltimore, MD: Johns Hopkins University Press, 1986.

Ranstorp, Magnus. *Hizb'Allah in Lebanon: The Politics of the Western Hostage Crisis*. New York: St. Martin's Press, 1997.

Richard, Yann. *Shi'ite Islam*, tr. Antonia Nevill. Cambridge: Blackwell Publishers, 1995.

Roy, Olivier. *The Failure of Political Islam*, tr. Carol Volk. Cambridge, MA: Harvard University Press, 1996.

Saudi Arabia Handbook. Washington, D.C.: Federal Research Division, Library of Congress, Internet Edition.

Sharara, Wadhah. *Dawlat Hizballah: Lubnan Mujtama'an Islamiyan* (The Hizballah State: Lebanon as an Islamic Society). Beirut: Dar An-Nahar, 1996.

"Al-Shi'a fil Mamlaka al-'Arabia Al-Su'udia: 'an al-Madhi, al-Hadhir wa'l Mustaqbal," (The Shi'a in the Kingdom of Saudi Arabia: the Past, the Present, and the Future). Unpublished paper submitted to the Khoei Foundation, London, 1995.

Al-Shihabi, Sa'id. *Al-Bahrain 1920–1971, Qira'a fi'l-Watha'iq al-Baritaniyya* (Bahrain 1920–1971: A Reading of British Documents [in Arabic]). Beirut: Dar al-Kunuz Al-Adabiya, 1996.

Tabatabai, Allamah Sayyid Muhammad Husayn. *Shi'a*, tr. Sayyid Husayn Nasr. Qom, 1981.

Voll, John. *Islam: Continuity and Change in the Muslim World*, 2nd edition. Syracuse, NY: Syracuse University Press, 1994.

Watt, W. Montgomery. *Islamic Political Thought*. Edinburgh University Press, 1968.

Wiley, Joyce N. *The Islamic Movements of Iraq*. Boulder, CO: Lynne Rienner, 1992.

Winder, R. Bayly. *Saudi Arabia in the Nineteenth Century*. New York: St. Martin's Press, 1965.

Wright, Robin. *In the Name of God: The Khomeini Decade*. New York: Simon and Schuster, 1989.

Index